Japan's Response to the Gorbachev Era,
1985–1991

Japan's Response to the Gorbachev Era, 1985–1991

A RISING SUPERPOWER
VIEWS A DECLINING ONE

Gilbert Rozman

PRINCETON UNIVERSITY PRESS
PRINCETON, NEW JERSEY

Copyright © 1992 by Princeton University Press
Published by Princeton University Press, 41 William Street,
Princeton, New Jersey 08540
In the United Kingdom: Princeton University Press, Oxford

Library of Congress Cataloging-in-Publication Data

Rozman, Gilbert
Japan's response to the Gorbachev era, 1985–1991 :
a rising superpower views a declining one / Gilbert Rozman.
    p.   cm.
Includes bibliographical references and index.
ISBN 0-691-03189-4 (CL)
1. Japan—Relations—Soviet Union. 2. Soviet Union—
Relations—Japan. 3. Japan—Foreign relations—1945– I. Title
DS849.S65R68   1991
327.52047—dc20   91–15307

This book has been composed in Adobe Sabon

Princeton University Press books are printed on
acid-free paper and meet the guidelines for permanence
and durability of the Committee on Production Guidelines
for Book Longevity of the Council on Library Resources

Printed in the United States of America

10 9 8 7 6 5 4 3 2 1

Contents

Preface

THE HISTORY of Soviet-Japanese bilateral relations has often been charted, but not the perceptions that lurk in the background, and especially not the Japanese images treated as secondary to superpower convictions. To understand changing perceptions, it is important to scrutinize the Japanese debates, identifying who the debaters are and when controversies are aired. By leaning heavily on the writings of Japanese scholars, journalists, and diplomats, one can reach beyond stereotypes, such as those that have plagued Soviet-Japanese relations in the postwar era, and bring to life the changing images of the Soviet Union that have suddenly burst forth in the Gorbachev era. As a small step toward immersion in Japanese thinking, Japanese names are given here with the surname first, and the Foreign Ministry is referred to by its Japanese title, Gaimushō.

Chapters 1–4 are selective in presenting some background on Japanese ways of thinking, in identifying personnel influential in decision making, in reviewing the political spectrum, and in classifying types of relevant information. Chapters 5–8 simplify years of publications into a sequence of burning issues that aroused public interest. Chapters 9–12 adopt a topical approach in trying to extract the essence of Japanese images on Russian history, the development of the Soviet economy, Soviet national character and society, and the prospects for the political system and Soviet international behavior. Finally, chapters 13–15 draw conclusions about how Japanese perceptions have been formed, what strategies are competing to guide policy toward Moscow, and what one can learn about the new Japanese superpower.

The project to study Japanese-Soviet mutual perceptions received generous support from many sources. Above all, I wish to thank Japanese specialists on the Soviet Union for graciously sharing their knowledge with me. Although I lack the space to acknowledge the many individuals who met with me and responded to my questions, I appreciate the cooperative attitude expressed by so many. Some were also helpful in supplying me with the latest Japanese publications on the Soviet Union. Of these, I owe the greatest debt to Iwaki Shigeyuki at the National Diet Library, whose trained eye consistently selected useful materials for me after my return to the United States. When I tried out my tentative ideas, I found Japanese scholars more than willing to help. Kimura Hiroshi and Hakamada Shigeki are two of the many experts who were generous in the time they gave to discuss my work. Of course, none of the commentators nor the organizations that provided financial support is responsible for my approach, my interpretations, or any of my specific observations.

The National Council on Soviet and East European Research funded the research from 1986 to 1988, including almost a year of work in Japan. The Social Science Research Council added an award to support me during a one-month return visit to Japan in the summer of 1989. Princeton University, its Center of International Studies (through a grant from the Johnson and Higgins Foundation), and Keio University also graciously facilitated this project.

In the first half of 1990 I benefited also from comments by Mayumi Itoh, who had just completed a Ph.D. dissertation on the perceptions of the Soviet Union among Japan's foreign policy elite. She prepared chapter 12 as her own contribution.

Speedy preparation of this manuscript would have been difficult without the conscientious assistance of Blanche Anderson and Donna De-Francisco on the word processor. Thanks to their good cheer, I could always count on economies of time.

Chronology

March 10–14, 1985	Chernenko dies; Gorbachev becomes Soviet leader; Nakasone meets him at Moscow funeral
January 15–19, 1986	Shevardnadze visits Tokyo—first visit of Soviet foreign minister in a decade
May 29–31, 1986	Abe visits Moscow—Japanese visits to Northern Territories graves resume
July 28, 1986	Gorbachev's Vladivostok speech announces new approach to Asia-Pacific region
January 1987	Central Committee plenum affirms need for genuine democracy
June 1987	Central Committee plenum calls for fundamental reform of economy
Summer 1987	Soviet-Japanese relations set back by Toshiba submarine technology loss and Soviet expulsion of Japanese
December 6–9, 1987	INF agreement between Soviet Union and United States, Gorbachev in Washington
May 30–June 2, 1988	Reagan holds summit in Moscow; new goals for international arms control
July 20–23, 1988	Nakasone visits Moscow, Gorbachev discusses Northern Territories
September 17, 1988	Gorbachev's Krasnoyarsk speech intensifies Soviet interest in East Asia
December 20–22, 1988	Shevardnadze visits Japan; the two sides establish a working group
March 1989	Soviet elections bring political pluralism
April 30–May 5, 1989	Uno in Moscow proposes "expanded equilibrium"; the two sides widen agenda
May–June 4, 1989	Gorbachev summit with Chinese leaders; Chinese student demonstrations and their suppression
July 1989	JSP electoral success for Upper House of Diet
October–December, 1989	Fall of East European Communist system along with Berlin Wall
November 12, 1989	Yakovlev in Japan calls for a "third way" to settle bilateral dispute

January 1990	Kaifu tours Eastern Europe and promises aid; Abe visits Soviet Union in search of informal diplomatic breakthrough
February 18, 1990	LDP electoral victory for Lower House of Diet; reaffirmation of strong mandate to negotiate with Moscow
March 1990	Soviet local elections bring an end to Communist Party monopoly and independence movements spread
September 4–7, 1990	Shevardnadze shows flexibility in Japan, working-level forum to treat regional security and confidence-building measures
December 1990	Shevardnadze resigns in protest; Gorbachev turns to the right
January 1991	Persian Gulf War frustrates Soviets and bypasses Japanese; Nakayama visits Moscow and returns discouraged
April 16–19, 1991	Gorbachev visits Japan
April 23, 1991	Gorbachev and Yeltsin agree on partial reform course
June 1991	Yeltsin popularly elected Russian president
July 1991	Democratic Reform Movement founded in Moscow; Gorbachev seeks massive foreign aid to boost reform at London seven-nation summit

The Contemporary Background

CHAPTER ONE

The Japanese Worldview

How DID Japanese perceptions of the Soviet Union change during the first six years of the Gorbachev era? How did the Japanese people—both the opinion shapers and the public—respond to the tumultuous developments unleashed by Mikhail Gorbachev's policies inside the Soviet Union and in international affairs? Through answers to these questions one can trace the evolution of Soviet-Japanese bilateral relations and, even more, can uncover clues about the incipient worldview of the new Japanese superpower. A confident Japan in the fluid international environment of the 1990s differs significantly from a cautious Japan in the polarized atmosphere of Soviet-American superpower rivalry prior to 1985. The transition in Japanese thinking unfolds through a succession of changing images of the domestic and international meaning of Soviet socialism.

Faced with the unfamiliar prospect of a globe no longer polarized by the cold war or by a clear-cut division into socialism and capitalism, Japanese groped for a new understanding of the world and their country's place in it. This was no ordinary rethinking; as the Japanese were reflecting about Soviet decline and the collapse of an era, they were simultaneously beginning to appreciate their own rise as a central agent shaping a new era. To understand this process of reconceptualization in international affairs, this book follows Japanese debates, step-by-step, and, in the process, identifies some central themes that link perceptions of the Soviet Union to general attitudes about the world.

This inquiry requires drawing on a diverse range of Japanese sources. The following chapters summarize, for the six-year period, views in the mass media, in partisan publications, in specialized scholarship, and in official policy statements. Reviewing the changing results of public opinion polls makes it possible to relate mass opinion to the analysis of experts and to the responses of the political system. Many streams of information flow together in revealing the formation of a new national outlook.

Most books on great-power relations are largely concerned with official policies and the direct handling of strategic issues in international affairs. This study differs by: (1) emphasizing the debates rather than the diplomacy; (2) concentrating on the opinion shapers, who often do not have a direct role in policy making, rather than on officials and negotiators, except to the extent that the latter are active in the debate; and (3) discussing varied issues associated with Soviet socialism without narrowly centering on foreign policy matters. In this way, I try to look beyond the facade of monolithic Japanese government policy into the crevices of public uncertainty and anticipation of what is to come.

Japanese leaders are careful to avoid the hubris of proclaiming that they have a fresh vision for a new superpower. There is no sign of a consciously constituted ideology, such as that created by Communist leaders. There are not even the personalized doctrines or slogans often favored by American presidents. It takes the uncertainty of a topsy-turvy world, producing startling headlines month after month, to elicit a groundswell of speculation and prediction. From this I hope to discern an important part of what is creeping upon us: the worldview of the next superpower.

The Significance of the Soviet Union to Japan

Russia and the Soviet Union are significant to the Japanese worldview for at least four reasons. First, despite striking contrasts in historical background, Japan's northern neighbor epitomizes some central problems in Japan's own modern history: a country struggling for identity between East and West, a society balancing its foundation for social order between communalism and emergent forms of individualism, and a culture in flux between retention of deep-seated native traditions and wholesale borrowing from Western models. Both Japan and Russia began modernization late through vigorous state direction from above, and they have faced some of the same dilemmas as outsiders trying to break into the Western pack in the lead. The language used in Japanese sources about enigmatic Russia caught between two worlds[1] is reminiscent of Western publications on the paradoxes of Japanese development.

Second, the Soviet deterioration in recent decades as a result of overcentralization, militarism, empire building, and ideological rigidity represents what might have happened to Japan had it not lost the war and been pushed into democratization, demilitarization, territorial self-reliance, and ideological flexibility. Japanese analysts sometimes draw an analogy between Mikhail Gorbachev's attempts to shift the Soviet Union onto a new track and the reforms initiated during the American occupation of Japan.[2] There but for the grace of defeat might have gone Japan.

Third, the Soviet Union can be compared to a cork, which has kept Japan's vintage champagne of recent years bottled with nowhere to go. The postwar era has relegated Japan to a self-effacing political role, increasingly inconsistent with its economic standing. Only by Moscow popping the cork of the cold war, which had narrowly defined international problems in terms of the conflict between two blocs and two military superpowers, could Japan emerge as a superpower in its own right. The foremost obstacle to Tokyo's emergence from the postwar era is at last being removed.

Fourth, Russia and the Soviet Union are also long-standing rivals to Japan. This rivalry climbed closer to the center stage in the 1980s as other international disputes were being resolved through negotiations. Tokyo's demand that Moscow return the four small islands known as the Northern Territories rose to the fore as perhaps the principal barrier to normalization in the Asia-Pacific region. Yet, even a settlement of this dispute would not guarantee that major differences will not persist. The way the rivalry is perceived, as well as the way it is handled, is helping to define Japan's evolving international role. The Soviet Union matters greatly for Japan's emerging outlook on the world, even if it often seems that Japanese dismiss their northern neighbor as irrelevant to the economic division of nations that counts most.

In short, for Japan the Soviet Union represents a historical parallel, a negative alternative course of contemporary development, a bottleneck to its own aspirations, and a rival second only to the United States but with a different impact on Japanese self-perceptions. Each step toward figuring out the meaning of Soviet development moves Japan closer to formulating an image of its own burst onto the world scene in a rapidly changing world.

Of course, from the time that Gorbachev's reforms were first blasted across the media, day after day, other nations also plunged into a debate about the Soviet Union and socialism. On the surface, many commonalities can be found in the responses of Japan and the United States. For example, both nations reaffirmed a longing for a more secure peace and for the wider dissemination of values of freedom and democracy. And both favored an orderly transition within the USSR. It is not necessary to dwell on such shared reactions.

What is more intriguing is to search for Japan's distinctive images and its most intense clashes of opinion. These images differentiate three sides in the character of another nation: (1) cultural heritage, linking long-term historical development, national character, and existing social organization; (2) management of the economy and polity, linking economic development and political leadership; and (3) foreign outlook, linking strategic policies, foreign trade, and assumptions about the nature of the world. As argued below, Japan's images of these three sides of the Soviet Union differ importantly from American images. While one must not cast doubt on the shared outlook that makes Japan a reliable partner, one also needs to appreciate how its superpower worldview will be different and will make future partnership a complicated process requiring understanding and compromise from all concerned.

David versus Goliath. Recalling world geography, many would be tempted to see the relationship between tiny Japan and the huge Soviet Union as roughly the equivalent of England versus all of Europe or perhaps, ignoring the island location, as California versus all of the United States and Canada. The David versus Goliath theme is unmistakable. To this can be added the discrepancy between the monstrous Soviet military machine, fueled in the 1980s by no less than 15–20 percent of the Soviet GNP, and the modest Japanese Self-Defense Forces, only recently breaking through the psychological barrier of 1 percent of Japan's GNP. The victorious, self-confident Soviet Union—a superpower since 1945—further contrasts with the defeated, humbled Japan rising from the war's ashes under foreign occupation. This apparently unequal match-up has somehow produced the new superpower rivalry of our era.

More than the rivalries between the United States and the Soviet Union or the United States and Japan, this third superpower rivalry is not easily conceptualized by the familiar categories usually applied to global conflicts. Many of the striking differences are readily traced to historical and sociological patterns of organization. Wasteful Soviet command methods over extensive resources contrast with intensive utilization of carefully nurtured human resources in Japan. This is, to no small degree, a clash between two types of traditions and two approaches to organizing a society. Eventually it became a rivalry between the forceful, pompous exporter of ideology and revolution and the deliberately unobtrusive, prudent exporter of industrial products and technology. As Moscow sheds its Communist messianism and Japan loses its inhibitions born of defeat, the character of the rivalry continues to evolve.

The Soviet-Japanese rivalry did not arise suddenly in the 1980s as overall Soviet power slackened and Japanese power grew. The rivalry was intensifying in the second half of the nineteenth century, erupted in war in 1904–1905, helped create the collision course that led to World War II, and resumed in the context of the cold war.[3] Increasingly it was clear that Japan and the Soviet Union were great powers whose adversarial relations were contributing to the general atmosphere of international tension. A long-standing rivalry, temporarily obscured by Japanese weakness after 1945, had by the late 1980s turned into one of the decisive international competitions. What remained unclear was how well this competition would be managed after the tables were abruptly (but not completely) turned in the capacity of the two countries to project their international influence.

A Rising Superpower Confronts a Declining One. The second half of the 1980s will be remembered for convulsive change that spelled the precipitous downfall of communism across the north of Eurasia. It will also be recalled as another giant step—in financial terms, a spectacular leap—in the rise of East Asian capitalism. Dramatic developments in a short time span changed the way people in many countries look at international affairs. Arguably the biggest winner in this turn of events is Japan, suddenly thrust onto the top of the world stage as a superpower. Japan was at last relieved of its political and psychological burden as a defeated power in the Second World War and as a secondary actor in the cold war standoff between the military superpowers. The biggest loser in world standing and public self-image is, no doubt, the Soviet Union, unable to hold onto its network of Communist satellites and exposed for its hopelessly moribund system of economic organization and social control.

The turnabout from the 1970s' atmosphere of overconfident Soviet superpower arrogance toward Japanese weakness[4] ("looking down on Japan from the heights of socialism") into the newly emerging 1990s' atmosphere of somewhat muted Japanese superpower arrogance toward Soviet weakness[5] occurred with remarkable suddenness in the years 1988 to 1990. As worldviews everywhere were changing, perhaps no change would be more significant in the long run than the evolving Japanese vision, beginning with Japan's outlook on the decline of the Soviet Union and of socialism. World attention has been riveted to "new thinking" in Moscow, born of desperation, without corresponding interest in the less conspicuous "new thinking" in Tokyo, born of confidence.

Normalization as a Spectacle. The postwar era has produced a series of great-power normalizations. In the mid- and late 1950s it was the United States and the Soviet Union groping to coexist as superpowers. In the early 1970s it was the United States and China casting aside their deep differences, with Japan and China quickly reaching a reconciliation in their wake. In the 1980s the Soviet Union and China at last overcame their intense schism. At the start of the 1990s the fourth great postwar normalization is in progress: Japan and the Soviet Union are struggling to establish a new relationship. One finds the same hoopla in anticipation of setting a date for a summit meeting, in appeals for discarding outdated stereotypes of the enemy, in negotiations toward resolving outstanding territorial disputes, and even in analyses exploring prospects for a new world order. Normalization offers one of the exhilarating spectacles for traditional foreign affairs analysts and researchers interested in exposing mutual misperceptions among the world's leading societies and finding ways to increase the flow and accuracy of information that could lead to improved understanding.

The culmination of that spectacle was the visit of Gorbachev to Japan in April 1991, treated in an epilogue. This study shows the steps leading to that event as they were reflected in Japanese thinking and ends with the impact of the event itself. For the Japanese public, the spectacle of normalization had reached a high pitch by 1989, which continued to build in 1990 and early 1991 while attention was broadening to multisided superpower linkages including the United States.

HISTORICAL INFLUENCES

The Confucian Worldview. The way Japanese think about the world is a product of many influences, some originating far in the past. Confucianism played a formative role as Japan became a unified state and developed a sustained vision of the world beyond its own borders. It conveyed a long-term historical consciousness that, arguably, endures despite the vicissitudes of recent international relations. Japanese still are unusual in their tendency to link the present with the remote past in relations between peoples. Interpreting contemporary Soviet-Japanese relations, they often recall the history of Japanese images of Russia dating from the eighteenth century.[6] They take for granted that the present cannot be understood apart from the past, even though both countries have witnessed enormous discontinuities. Similarly, criticisms of West European and American mercurial reactions to the latest twist of events in the USSR or the Gorbachev "charm" offensive[7] appear to be rooted in the confidence that Japanese are capable of keeping in mind the broader perspective—the deeper historical meaning of the country with which they are dealing.

Japanese Confucianism existed in the shadow of China just as postwar democratic values operate in the shadow of the United States. The former experience prepared the way for borrowing without feeling inescapably inferior, for championing imported values with the confidence that Japanese have made them work.

The term "Confucianism" may not be popular in regional or national self-identification, but as the East Asian voice in international affairs becomes louder, the assumptions of that tradition are likely to be present in proposals initiated from the region. They will help to shift attention from a bipolar world to a single integrated hierarchy, from the institutionalization of conflict to the procedures that enhance harmony, and from military and economic concerns to the social relations, rituals, and moral education conducive to a world community. Soviet might and Communist hostility to capitalism had divided the world; only their partial eclipse has freed Japanese to draw on the nation's own historical experience to begin to think about how to put the world together.

The Tokugawa Rank-Order Syndrome. Personal relations in Japanese history were shaped by a stronger ascriptive and hierarchical principle than in China, as birth weighed heavily in community ranking and access to office. Families, organizations, and official positions maintained established hierarchical relations independent of the current occupants; this logic was extended to relations among the domains in the Tokugawa era (1600–1868), which formed a quasi-interstate system.[8] Thus, the relative ranking of Japan and the Soviet Union in past encounters and the ways those encounters were handled remain relevant today. Propriety depends on rank, and the Soviets are judged to be in violation of it. The fact that, in all previous major treaties and negotiations with Russia and the USSR, relative power has affected the allocation of disputed territory and that the territorial issue is now central gives added force to Japan's traditional outlook, based especially on the Tokugawa political experience.

Interdomain relations became highly ritualized. Arrogance and rudeness were seen as serious violations of propriety. Confucianism as well as the reciprocity inherent in the etiquette of a feudal hierarchy stressed moral rather than formal legalistic criteria. Abstract principles figured less importantly in Japan than in China; military traditions had reinforced situational ethics and the importance of reciprocity. Japan was prepared for a tit-for-tat approach with a strong moral component. Moscow's brusque conduct, flexing its military muscle and claiming ideological superiority, offended these persistent sensitivities. Because the Tokugawa interdomain system preserved peace for more than two centuries to the benefit of all (to be sure, some more than others), it provides one of the few historical models of possible relevance to future international integration.

Geographical Isolation. In addition to the Confucian worldview and the Tokugawa "state" system, Japan's outlook on the world was shaped by geographical isolation. No other premodern country with considerable bureaucratic, urban, and educational development remained so removed from international contacts. Never in recorded history having been invaded or subjected to notable migration, Japanese felt themselves to be separate and distinctive. Through self-imposed isolation lasting over two centuries until 1853, a feeling of uniqueness was nurtured. Along with this sense of separateness came a concern about vulnerability—the Mongols had launched two invasion attempts from the east, the Portuguese and Spanish coming from the south had been exposed by their European rivals as plotting to carve up the world and had made use of less than a century of residence in Japan to proselytize with considerable success, and finally the Russians were approaching closer and closer from the north, obviously eager to open Japan to new contacts with the outside. Along with news from the Dutch enclave in Nagasaki of striking transformations in the world, the threat from the north intensified Japan's sense of vulnerability.[9] When Admiral Perry eventually opened Japan from the west, the Russians were close behind; concerns remained about the danger from the north.

Dependence on other countries for virtually all raw materials and fuel and on the United States for defense helps to revive this predisposition. Above all, perceptions of the "Soviet menace" in recent decades sustained a geographical image that seems scarcely compatible with Japan's role as world trader par excellence capable of benefiting most from an "internationalized" or open world. The changing image of the Soviet Union forces Japan to confront the true meaning of "internationalization" as a prospect that no longer can be postponed. The domestic skirmish in 1990–91 over the use of Japanese funds for the Persian Gulf War revealed sharp differences over what form the new international responsibility would assume.

Catch-up Mentality. With the arrival of American warships in 1853 and a rapid adjustment to the reality of Japan's international weakness, a fourth factor became paramount. Japanese transposed their well-calibrated awareness of hierarchical relations to the world arena and determined to climb the ladder and catch up. Ranking countries as world powers, they modeled themselves on those at the top. In this calculation, Russia was passed over as only a second-rank country, which Japan at the third rank or lower need not follow.[10] Catching up—analogous to a lord expanding his territorial holdings in the struggle for relative standing in the warring states era that preceded the Tokugawa, to domains improving their national economic position, which sustained their consumption in Edo (Tokyo) where their lords competed due to the alternate residence system from the 1640s to 1862, and to capturing a greater share in the world market over the past century—has been an overriding concern of the Japanese. Although the terms of the competitive arena differ for the two countries, Japan has been catching up to the Soviet Union in the overall ranking of postwar powers.

Catching up establishes a clear goal but leaves the end point in the process unclear. Economic growth in the prewar era became closely identified not only with market share, but also with imperialist expansion. Although Japan eliminated unequal treaties in the 1890s and won acceptance as a major power through its defeat of Russia in 1905, it aspired to more. Recovering from the postwar economic collapse, Japanese again set their sights on catching up. After some obvious targets had been achieved by the early 1970s when the country's GNP easily became third in the world, the momentum stayed in place to allow Japan to keep gaining on the United States and the Soviet Union. What constitutes catching up? What goal should replace it? What precedent can be found for a condition of international equality among leading countries, and for the responsibilities implied in shared superpower status?

Closing the economic gap in the postwar era is accompanied by a political dimension. Japan must contribute to the struggle for the victory of the democratic nations over the aggressive and totalitarian socialist bloc led by the Soviet Union. Although Article 9 of its constitution limits the reestablishment of armed forces, Japan's Self-Defense Forces are a potent regional factor. Within limitations that have kept the military budget well below what Japan can afford, the Japanese government has recently sought to do its share for safeguarding the "free world." As in the 1870s–1890s, Japan has been eager to show the leading countries that it deserves respect. Opposition to the Soviet Union was what the United States wanted most from Japan, beginning in the late 1940s and continuing until 1988 when confusing mixed signals from Washington noticeably increased. Japan must still catch up to its economic clout through "responsible" international behavior, but its options for demonstrating leadership have widened.

Victim Nations and Victimizers. It would be a mistake to overlook the emotional factor in the Japanese worldview. Sentimentality is rife in Japanese life, and this is extended into perceptions of other peoples. Japanese are fascinated with speculation about national character,[11] searching for the essence of another nation and how it is manifest in national policies. They have a strong curiosity about what others think of their country and let that affect their reverse attitudes. The perceived lack of respect from Soviet officials has riled Japanese sensitivity.[12] In various ways the Japanese consider their nation to have suffered from Soviet conduct.

In certain cases, a bilateral relationship is categorized starkly as leaving Japan as either the victimizer or the victim. Although blocking out many of the gruesome and incriminating details of their country's conduct in China in the 1930s and 1940s, Japanese have borne a deep feeling of guilt. When in the 1960s and 1970s the Sino-Soviet split made it necessary to take sides, that guilt sharply tilted the balance away from the Soviet Union.[13] In contrast, the selective memory of World War II has convinced many Japanese that they were among the major victims of external aggression. Moscow's reputation suffers badly from this image. The last-minute Soviet entry into the war, turning Japanese territory into Soviet lands and Japanese soldiers into convict labor, has become a national fixation.

Japanese have a tendency to apply a double standard to their in-group and to those left on the outside. The Soviet Union is clearly excluded. Soviets were seen not as ordinary people but as cogs in a totalitarian and military machine. Subjectivity guided popular perceptions. While in general the normative element figures heavily in Japanese views of another country, the tendency to downplay empirical evidence is especially pronounced in views of the Soviet Union. Criticized as a mercantile people that separate politics and economics and let nothing stand in the way of profits, the Japanese actually subscribe to a worldview deeply affected by feelings toward other nations. No wonder Japanese scholars report that "history is a deeper source of Japanese perceptions of the Soviet Union than ideology."[14]

Despite the tremendous success story of their economy, Japanese are burdened with the belief that they have not reached their goal. The postwar era has not yet normalized. The symbols of this unsatisfactory situation are the four small islands known as the Northern Territories occupied by Moscow and the absence of a peace treaty resolving the loose ends of Soviet-Japanese relations left from the war era. Excessive attention to the symbols obscures the real aspirations of the Japanese people, which they themselves have hesitated to articulate. As self-confidence has grown, so have Japanese expectations about a final accounting to close the door on World War II.

The Hiroshima Syndrome versus the Northern Territories Syndrome. With the return of four scarcely habitable northern islands, it can be assumed that Japanese expect historical justice, a new balance of power, and heightened independence. Japan's relationship will change not only with the Soviet Union, but also with the United States. While avoiding signing another "unequal treaty" in 1956 with Moscow, Tokyo signed the security treaty with the United States, which, however justified at the time, many Japanese perceived as preserving the inequality born of the American occupation. Even if active opposition soon diminished and appreciation rose for the importance of the United States as Japan's "nuclear umbrella," increased pressure from Washington and American public opinion leaves an uneasy feeling. When there are no more "unequal treaties," Japan can at last realize its late nineteenth-century goal of becoming an equal partner. Normalization with Moscow holds one key to completing the process of catching up.

Advocates of two syndromes linked to Japan's wartime defeat competed in the 1950s to fire the imagination of the Japanese people. The Hiroshima syndrome focused on an aversion to nuclear arms and on the establishment of a neutral and pacifistic Japan. Repeated Soviet attempts to capitalize on this nuclear aversion proved counterproductive when the peace movement became increasingly identified with a global strategy that would have the effect of increasing Japanese vulnerability. The syndrome soon slipped in popular thinking. But it is not dead, and some on the right worry about a revival, particularly when they observed the resurgence of pacifism at the time of the Persian Gulf War. It is no surprise that Japanese authorities reacted suspiciously in 1988 to Gorbachev's interest in associating his arms reductions crusade with Hiroshima, including a proposed visit there during his much anticipated summit in Japan.

In fact, at the low point of Soviet-American relations before Gorbachev's rise to power and later at the time of the signing of the Intermediate Nuclear Forces (INF) agreement in late 1987, Japanese had been less fearful of a nuclear war than the people of other major nations, including the

Soviet people.[15] This shows that the Northern Territories syndrome, based on the Soviet threat, prevailed over the Hiroshima syndrome. Japan would rely on alliance strength aimed at Soviet expansionism rather than on popular pacifism associated with neutrality or active leadership in disarmament. World War II lives on in Japan, but not as the Soviets or, for that matter, Japan's East Asian victims had hoped.

THE CORRELATION OF FORCES

Economic, military, diplomatic, and propaganda forces are, to a greater or lesser degree, shaping the balance of power among the countries of the world, according to Japanese sources. Of these, economic (and technological) forces are decisive except perhaps in the short run. They, in turn, are determined by social forces, especially the study and work habits of individuals, and their readiness to sacrifice for the organization. The Japanese worldview places its faith in traditional values and in the organizations deemed vital to their continuation.

The Soviet Union as a Mirror Image. Concerned about the erosion of traditional virtues in their youth, Japanese look primarily to the West but also to the Soviet Union for the dangers that may lie in wait. Explanations of Soviet spiritual emptiness tend to be historical.[16] Steps taken to replace established family and community values have proven counterproductive; deep-seated patterns, once lost, are difficult to recover. As confidence in capitalism mounted, Japanese largely agreed that it provides a more favorable environment for honored values of the past. Handled with care, capitalism will not inevitably destroy what is cherished from the past, whereas socialism leaves a country spiritually impoverished.

A voluminous literature known as *Nihonjinron* (the theory of the Japanese) explains what is distinctive about Japanese history and how it favors Japan in the contemporary era, despite adulteration by some aspects of modernization and the introduction of external values. Indeed, what is extolled is the very blend of Japan's native organizational traits and behavioral qualities combined with the required forms of modernization. Simultaneously, a mirror image of Soviets called Sorenkan (the view of the Soviet Union) has spread. The very character traits deemed critical to Japanese success are seen as absent among Russians. Destruction of past values together with the lesser adaptability of those values in the first instance leaves Russians ill-suited for modern organizations. Pessimism about the run-down foundation of the Soviet economy correlates closely with optimism about the basic, long-term strength of Japan's economy. Nihonjinron and Sorenkan are inextricably linked.

Technological Determinism. Continued economic success contributes to an optimistic mood in Japan about the advance of technology. The Japanese worldview is inbred with expectations of rapid change based on new technologies. Applying this outlook to the Soviet Union in the 1980s, Japanese became openly disdainful.[17] It is difficult to detect any optimism about Moscow's long-term prospects in a world of high technology and the emerging "information society."[18] More than any other factor, a belief in technological determinism (and social organization based on personal character as the main determinant of aptitude for technology) in a rapidly changing future leaves the Japanese looking beyond the Soviet eclipse to a world to be guided by the powers capable of mastering technology, one of them Japan.

The American concept of Strategic Defensive Initiative (SDI) ideally suited the growing Japanese self-confidence. A military future based on high technology has doomed the Soviet Union, with its outdated economy, to backwardness.[19] At the same time, Washington must depend heavily on Japan's new technologies. At one stroke and at relatively low cost in actual military expenses, Tokyo leaves Moscow behind and approaches its aspiration of becoming a full partner to Washington. Moscow failed to understand the forces of history. Military power relies on technology, which in turn depends on the economy, and that in the final analysis rests on the quality of the people. The implicit Japanese understanding of the forces of history stands in stark contrast to the long-time Marxist-Leninist assertions about class struggle and the actual Soviet reliance on brute military force. Through technological inferiority, Moscow will yield to Tokyo.

A Meritocracy without Growing Soft. While Japanese are normally reticent to speculate about their future as a superpower, some commentators have slipped into a Japanocentric worldview, for example, through one formulation in which the United States becomes a granary, Australia a mine, and Europe a boutique for the potent Japanese industrial machine (a factory) and perhaps its East Asian subcontractors (shops).[20] This assumes that not only the Soviet Union but also the United States and other European-based societies are growing soft and losing the social foundation for a competitive economy. Essential for Japan, many insist, is to maintain its own society of hard-working students, diligent workers, family solidarity, workplace community, and meritocratic state guidance of a relatively unified population.

Japan remains a productive factory only as long as its citizens are toughened for a competitive world. All units in the society must work together to produce the right mind-set. Among the essential ingredients are intensive family supervision, traditional moral education in the schools, and a demanding examination system. Such elements are obviously missing in the contemporary Soviet setting. If the above analogy were extended, the USSR might appear as a junkyard that has lost its social potential for substantial participation in the international division of labor. In contrast, views of the United States and Western Europe are balanced with appreciation for the vitality and creativity of democratic societies.

Uneasiness over "Japan Bashing" and "Smile Diplomacy." The image of Japan on one side and the United States and the Soviet Union on the other sometimes appears in a more worrisome form to Japan. Some Japanese wonder if Washington can be trusted to use good judgment in negotiations with Moscow. After all, a declining America plagued by problems of its own may see an advantage in cutting a deal, for example, to reduce its military costs even at the expense of the security of its allies.[21] Mostly this concern focuses not on treachery but on a president eager to make his mark in history or a population made gullible by its own shortcomings. Japanese also find evidence of American unreliability in their acute awareness of "Japan bashing," which includes racial prejudice, actual or imagined, and a lack of respect. The debate on the Soviet Union is fed by this uneasiness.

What the Soviets cannot win through a superior military or economy, they might gain through misguided Western diplomacy or clever Soviet propaganda. This is a worry often expressed in Japan. The Soviet threat has shifted to "smile diplomacy."[22] Officials are prone to draw an analogy with the détente of the early 1970s when the West let its guard down and allowed itself to fall behind militarily.[23] Even with superior technology it is possible to lack the foresight and the will to match the Soviet military buildup. The gravest danger comes from the transfer of technology to the Soviets and from hasty support for rebuilding the Soviet economy, which could then be redirected into a military confrontation.[24] By 1990, worry about Soviet revival had diminished, and the basis for a worst-case scenario had shifted from Soviet "smiles" for the Americans toward American "frowns" for Japan. It is the United States that may be motivated to seek outside support against the Japanese.

Economic Power Politics. If the Soviet Union should convert to a peaceful and market-based society, do Japanese hold out new visions of a world order integrating the two countries? With few exceptions, the answer is "no." Former Prime Minister Nakasone's future-oriented comments during his visit to Moscow in July 1988 offered vague hope that a future exists after the return of the four islands,[25] but Japanese authorities were slow to follow this up after Moscow proposed an agenda for talks on diverse forms of cooperation before the territorial question was resolved.[26] Anxious to apply maximum pressure for the return of the islands, officials insisted that this was the first item on the agenda. In 1990 there were signs of forward movement on both negotiations and internal debates, but they had not advanced far when pessimism reappeared in the winter of 1990–91.

Japan seems prepared, in some fashion, to accept the Soviet Union as a member in the Asia-Pacific region, but the terms remain imprecise. Obviously, the pressure on Moscow to reform would persist even after the territorial issue was settled. If military tensions are diffused, then economic clout becomes all the more decisive. The beginning of Japanese economic power politics can be seen.

INTERNATIONALIZATION

Japanese are not complacent in thinking that they already have the right combination to respond to the challenges of the future. It is widely assumed that their country requires substantial change to meet both the legitimate concerns of its trading partners and the imperatives of the next age of technological progress. The code word "internationalize" conveys this sentiment. Japan must not selfishly pursue narrow national interests. It should fulfill its responsibilities to others. Opening more markets and providing increased foreign aid are two long-acknowledged means to this end. On the level of the individual, the appeal to internationalize implies becoming more open in making foreign friends, learning about the world, buying foreign products, and so forth.[27] As stated earlier, it also has the more elusive meaning of increased understanding of others as human beings. On the level of the state, to internationalize often means to assume responsibilities commensurate with Japan's financial resources, and to do so by putting the interests of the world before those of Japan. This is the noble, but ambiguous, ideal that has entered into thinking about the future. Competing visions of "internationalizing" are joined in the debate over the Soviet Union.

Japanese concern for public relations before the tribunal of world opinion has a long history. In 1988 Arai Hirokazu reminded his readers that Count Witte won the public relations battle in 1906, leaving Japan isolated at Portsmouth as it was negotiating the conclusion to the Russo-Japanese War. Witte met with French, English, and Italian reporters on his way to the United States, pressing his case. Arai warns that Gorbachev employs the same methods in dealing with Western reporters.[28] World acceptance is one measure of "internationalizing," but it runs the risk of manipulation when the outside world cannot be trusted.

Japan's Location on the Globe. Through what has become commonplace geographical juggling, both the Japanese and the Soviets lay claim to being part of the West. Writing in the 1970s about China and Japan, the Soviets argued that each country lacked certain Western traditions and followed a distorted path of development. Although Soviet ambivalence about Japan's identity as a typical Eastern country extends even to the premodern era, the reluctance to associate its development with Western development refers to Japan's entire history. Japan's samurai past yielded to an incomplete bourgeois-democratic revolution, which permitted feudal elements to endure, and (even after World War II) to an abortive reform process, which left alive the imperial institution and other paternalistic or traditional elements.[29] While at the same time largely identifying Japanese development as just another example of the laws of capitalist development, Soviets found it convenient to set Japan apart from the West with regard to military traditions, group relations, and other themes. Yet, in the second half of the 1980s, this ideological effort to disparage Japan declined as greater respect was shown for Japan's uniqueness and for the successes common to capitalism.

When Japanese write about Soviet socialism, they place their own country in the West and the Soviet Union in the East.[30] They have simply restated the popular East-West distinction found in American and West European sources in dealing with Moscow, but without ambivalence about Japan's placement in the West. Both countries seem to have in mind a standard model of development associated with the West and of late, at least, with their own country's transformation, and they use this to judge the other country's "Eastern" deviations. The very fact that Japan places itself firmly in the West registers its close identification with democratic Western values, even if these are not always interpreted as in the United States.

At the risk of anticipating the conclusions from this study, three coexisting visions of an internationalized Japan can be differentiated. First, there is Japan of the West. A convert to Western values, it becomes the defender of their purity and couches its claims for international equity in its adherence to these values. Second, there is Japan of the East. A spokesman for newly industrialized economies and others with similar aspirations, Japan opposes the narrow protection of Western interests. Third, there is Japan of the world. Champion of a comprehensive world order, it leads in the pursuit of a higher order of international integration.

The presence of an enemy image of the Soviet Union has served to narrow the Japanese view of the future. To catch up economically, to counter the Soviet military threat, and finally to regain four islands have been successive preoccupations. Now that worldview must be enlarged and made more complex; what was evil no longer seems so bad or so overriding a concern. If the Soviet Union was characterized as the East and the world could be neatly divided into two camps, then the Japan of the West took precedence. Increasingly, all three Japans can be clearly discerned within a composite that reinforces the identity of each.

Four Determinants of Japanese Perceptions. In Japan one often hears that the "minus image" of the Soviet Union among the Japanese people operates as a constant in the history of relations between the two countries. Small, isolated Japan has continuously felt the hot breath of expansionist Russia in relentless pursuit of territory and regional power. In this view, the bilateral relationship, not overall Soviet international conduct or domestic conditions in either country, has been foremost in shaping Japanese perceptions. Above all, Japanese have seen themselves as unfortunately situated next to an unruly neighbor.

Actually, images have fluctuated intensely over the past century and among different sectors of the population, influenced by various factors. At times, such as in the 1920s, the Soviet domestic factor combined with the Japanese domestic factor have seemed to be ascendant. At other times, as at the height of the cold war, international relations beyond bilateral ties have pulled opinions in one direction or another. Since 1985, all four factors have operated simultaneously, although the review in chapters 6 to 8 of a succession of short-term preoccupations suggests a cyclical pattern. First international issues rise to the fore, then the Japanese domestic response draws introspective attention. This is followed by a peak of concern centering on bilateral matters, and next there is a new wave of interest in Soviet domestic change. Of these concerns, bilateral issues exert a surprisingly strong impact on Japanese perceptions. After specifying the cycles and sequences in part 2, I attempt to explain them in part 4.

Three Phases in the Response to Moscow. Altogether three phases of response to the Gorbachev era can be distinguished. The first can be referred to as Japan's awakening, when an orientation to a Soviet behemoth unable to break away from its past was being set aside. The awakening lasted for over two years, to the middle of 1987. Slowly the Japanese were aroused from their stupor in thinking about Moscow. They came to realize that the times were indeed changing. The second phase was punctuated by a jolt in the autumn of 1987, when Soviet-American relations abruptly improved. A new cycle had commenced, which I call Japan's uncertainty. It lasted more than one and one-half years, and it was characterized by rapidly changing concerns and many challenges to old ways of thinking. In the middle of 1989 the third cycle started with the Sino-Soviet summit and the Tiananmen brutality, followed by an accelerated downturn in the fortunes of international communism without any attempt at Soviet interference in other countries. Japanese became more assured in their views of Moscow's commitment to change and more interested in looking ahead. Thus began the phase of Japan's confidence and its new future orientation. In the winter of 1990–91 the newfound confidence was jolted by a world at war and a Soviet swing to the right; the remnants and former allies of the old superpower are not likely to make the rise of a new power very easy.

Coincidentally, the three phases correspond rather closely to administrative changes in Japan. The Nakasone era ended in November 1987, and the Takeshita era lasted until the beginning of June 1989. After a brief Uno stint in office, the third phase unfolded under Kaifu's helm. Japan's prime ministers are not central forces in changing perceptions; only as a convenience would I identify their names with these periods.

The three phases of awakening, uncertainty, and confidence within a six-year span suggest a rapid transformation in Japanese thinking. To 1985 the world order largely established in the second half of the 1940s seemed to be a given for the foreseeable future. Although first China's split with the Soviet Union and its normalization with the United States and Japan had reduced concern about regional isolation, and then Japan's "economic miracle" followed by the flourishing of other East Asian economies had raised national confidence, as late as 1985 Japanese had foreseen no alternative to the cold war and the predominance of military power in international affairs. Conditions were predictable, relegating Japan to a secondary status with little responsibility for the world as a whole. The postwar lethargy persisted, setting a path for a defeated country driven by a single-minded obsession with gaining economic power. The Gorbachev era produced the immediate impulse that awakened Japan from this lethargy.

After an interval of complex emotions toward a changing world that seemed to be leaving Soviet-Japanese relations untouched, a new era of confidence about Japan's international importance has dawned. It became clear that Moscow needs Japan and would likely, some day, pay the price in the negotiated return of the Northern Territories to release the Japanese from their last unsevered bonds to the Second World War. Psychologically, the signing of a peace treaty with Moscow would represent the end of a special dependency on Washington and the full restoration of sovereignty, which Japan had lost in 1945 for the first time in its history. Anticipating the lifting of this burden, some Japanese began to look ahead toward the future of the Japanese superpower. Others, foreseeing a delay in the resolution of Soviet-Japanese differences, calculated how a more assertive Tokyo would keep Moscow at a distance. In our increasingly integrated world, the fall of one superpower holds special meaning for the rise of another.

CHAPTER TWO

The Foreign Policy Establishment

THE ACTORS involved in foreign policy decision making in Japan are largely familiar, but their functions are not necessarily those assumed elsewhere. With a focus on Soviet policy in the Gorbachev era, one can identify the role of successive prime ministers, the interplay of factions in the ruling party, the competition within the bureaucracy, the influence of various types of Sovietologists and international relations experts serving in official positions or as advisers to the government, and the relevance of the opposition parties. Together these actors form the core of the foreign policy establishment in Japan.

The next two chapters look beyond the establishment to the wider community of Soviet and international affairs experts and to public opinion. By this means the establishment is placed within the context of the entire political spectrum, and its policy deliberations within the framework of the overall national debate. With respect to the Soviet Union, where the commercial ties are weak, the Gaimushō or Foreign Ministry is at the center of the establishment; through cohesion and careful leadership it plays a dominant role, despite increasing diversity of opinion. From within and without, the forces of change are visible, but it would be premature to claim that they are threatening the Gaimushō's leadership or even its style of managing the national response.

THE PRIME MINISTER AND THE LDP FACTIONS

The prime minister in Japan is a compromise candidate unable to choose many in his own cabinet and beholden to the leaders of the largest factions in the Liberal Democratic party (LDP). Normally Japan's leaders do not stay in office long, compounding the weakness inherent in the office. Rapid turnover at the top reached a peak after 1985. During Gorbachev's first five years, Japan had four prime ministers, recalling the instability of Soviet leadership in the first half of the 1980s.

Personalized Diplomacy. The role of the prime minister in policy toward the Soviet Union successively diminished over these five years. Nakasone Yasuhiro had sought to become a "presidential prime minister" and to leave his personal stamp on history. Over the course of his unusually long, five-year tenure in office to the fall of 1987 and a succeeding year in which he still wielded influence, Nakasone followed an approach independently devised but also parallel to that of Ronald Reagan: he first rallied Japan against the Soviet threat and sought to turn it into an "unsinkable aircraft carrier" and then, after he gained a favorable impression of Gorbachev at the time of his visit to Chernenko's funeral in Moscow, began to look for a way to achieve a breakthrough in relations—a step toward his long-time dream of leading Japan out of the postwar era. In each case he was out in front of Japanese opinion, raising eyebrows at the Gaimushō by his departure from precedent and his personalized approach.

In contrast, Takeshita Noboru had a domestic orientation. He entered office ceding the Foreign Ministry to Uno Sosuke of Nakasone's faction and reverted to "standard operating procedures." For him each issue had its own jurisdiction. Yet Takeshita was unwilling to cede completely the popular appeal of international statesmanship. In the spring and summer of 1988 signs of rivalry with former Prime Minister Nakasone appeared. First Takeshita made a series of major policy statements during foreign visits to gain, at last, some of the limelight. As seen by some informed observers, these were efforts to use the Gaimushō for personal ends; Takeshita took personal credit for proposing new ideas for expanded foreign aid and boosting the United Nations. Then, at the seven-nation summit in Toronto, Japan's new assertiveness, as described below, splashed across the headlines. Soon Nakasone also became more active. He visited Moscow in July, hoping to extend his record of personalized diplomacy. As expected, his freedom was constrained. This potentially dramatic visit with Gorbachev followed an agreement reached with the Gaimushō on the limits of the former leader's flexibility in Moscow. Personal diplomacy was tolerated only within preestablished limits. According to the critical *Asahi shimbun*, in office Nakasone had sought a "final solution" to postwar politics, and in retirement he cultivated secret contacts with the Soviets to pursue the same agenda.[1] Such suspicions of him were further grounds for outside restraint.

From the autumn of 1988 involvement at the top declined, corresponding to the rapid eclipse of Nakasone and the abrupt fall of Takeshita first in the polls and then from office, a result of the Recruit stock-trading scandal. Weakened by the scandal, Takeshita refrained in the second half of his twenty-month tenure from foreign initiatives. After a brief flurry of activity culminating with the summer 1988 Toronto summit, where Japan pressed its allies to accept a negative view of the Soviet position in the Asia-Pacific region,[2] central leadership was muffled into 1991. This left the Gaimushō to revert to a more self-initiated approach. As negotiations with Moscow accelerated, interest intensified in how the Gaimushō was explaining events and what its expectations were about their outcome. The role of the prime minister scarcely drew any attention.

Never having been seriously threatened, the autonomy of the Gaimushō had apparently been fully restored despite backstage jostling by LDP potentates aimed at personal diplomacy.

Uno Sōsuke and Kaifu Toshiki each came to the prime minister's office in 1989 bearing a reputation as an interim leader to tide the LDP through a period of low popularity. Neither was expected to take major initiatives. Although Kaifu remained in office longer, he lacked prior experience in foreign affairs and then was weakened by ineffectual handling of Japan's contributions to the Persian Gulf War. A dearth of Japanese leadership made the Soviets hesitant for a time to launch initiatives, while leaving Japanese opinion rudderless to drift without a clear sense of Japan's response to changes in the Soviet international posture. Yet, accustomed to cautious Gaimushō guidance and bland direction at the top, most Japanese did not seem to notice the difference. Impatient to build a new relationship, Gorbachev was soon imparting new momentum to bilateral relations. The Kremlin's initiatives offered a temptation for behind-the-scenes diplomacy difficult for political leaders to resist. With the blessing of the Gaimushō, some contacts were pursued. There was even speculation in January 1991 that Kaifu might grasp for progress with Moscow to rescue himself from almost complete loss of power.[3] Nonetheless, as occurred in December 1990 when Kaifu appeared to be ready to help Moscow to overcome its food crisis, the Gaimushō insisted on caution.[4] When Soviet-American relations deteriorated later that winter as the Persian Gulf War came to an end, Tokyo's room to maneuver also decreased.

Factional Leaders. Factional divisions have encouraged LDP leaders other than the current prime minister to play a role in foreign policy. In 1987 Abe Shintarō apparently cut a deal with Takeshita for the two to serve successive terms as prime minister. At the same time, Nakasone left office, but with conditions that ensured his continued importance in foreign policy. Three of the largest factions in the LDP now shared an interest in influencing Japan's foreign relations. As prime minister, Takeshita sought some of the credit for new initiatives; jockeying within the Gaimushō helped to determine whether he or Uno would make major announcements and how Nakasone's continued personal involvement would be resolved. This competition in 1988 set the stage for revived activism in the second half of 1989.

After Nakasone and Takeshita lost influence, the foreign policy aspirations of the Abe faction benefited, even though Abe himself had also been muddied by the repeated revelations of the Recruit scandal. When Kaifu of the small Komoto faction assumed office in August 1989, Nakayama Tarō of the Abe faction became foreign minister. Abe himself had served in that post in the first Gorbachev years at a time when bilateral relations took a turn for the better. During the Takeshita era he had sustained his interest in Soviet affairs, on at least one occasion summoning Soviet experts for advice. With Nakasone apparently counted out, Abe became a more substantial party force behind foreign relations. Illness limited his activity in 1989, but Abe's trip to Moscow early in 1990 gave him new exposure.[5] Even from his hospital bed in the fall of 1990, unable to lead a delegation to Moscow, Abe became the center of a controversy over a Soviet proposal to return two islands passed to the delegation in a secret meeting with Abe's "man."[6]

As the heir apparent on the eve of the February 1990 elections, which were expected to bring, without much delay, the end of Kaifu's interim leadership, Abe offered the hope that he would be Gorbachev's host in Tokyo in 1991 and would restore at least a touch of personal diplomacy to Japan's highest office. Like Nakasone, he was a foreign affairs veteran and an ambitious leader appreciative of the glamor of regaining the islands for Japan. It was Kaifu, however, who led the LDP to an unexpectedly solid triumph.[7] Although the "old guard" of Nakasone and Abe could claim that their own personal election to the Diet meant that the voters had cleansed them of the stain of scandal, they needed to proceed cautiously before using their powerful factions to oust a newly vigorous Kaifu. Eager to maintain the cooperation of the large Takeshita faction, Kaifu leaned on seasoned politicians and bureaucrats for advice. Through his continued tenure, Kaifu helped Kanemaru Shin and others to strengthen their own position as power brokers. Kanemaru was not loathe to intercede in foreign policy. Not only did he arouse controversy in 1990 through concessions in visits to North Korea and China, he also floated a trial balloon suggesting that Moscow could return two islands in 1991 as part of a two-stage solution—an idea hastily rejected by the Gaimushō.[8]

The impact of factionalism on the conduct of foreign policy varies. As in other policy arenas, factionalism means that on controversial matters the minister's personal authority must be vetted by rival factions as well as by different ministries before it can be translated into government policy. Where a cordial atmosphere exists between the faction leader and the ministry, and the faction is recognized by the prime minister and others as having some kind of mandate in this area, there is a greater possibility of consensus. Abe's good relations with the Gaimushō and the expectation that he was due the prime ministership heightened the prospects for consensus. The fact that the Policy Affairs Research Council of the LDP, where interfactional divisions must be resolved, was also under an Abe man, Mitsuzuka Hiroshi, further enhanced the newly won edge of this faction in 1989. By the end of 1990 Abe's illness and Kaifu's failure to win Diet support for sending noncombatant Self-Defense Forces to join

Americans in the Persian Gulf left a vacuum in personal diplomacy at the top.

"Bandwagoning" for Soviet diplomacy reflects factional interests in the LDP. If somehow a leader could play a role in what would be a dramatic diplomatic breakthrough in dialogues with Moscow, he could markedly improve his personal image. Former Prime Minister Nakasone was a successor of Kōno Ichirō, a minister of agriculture, forestry, and fisheries, who, as a close aide to Prime Minister Hatoyama Ichirō in the mid-1950s, represented the soft line toward Moscow and was accused of having sold the Northern Territories for fish. The Nakasone group is especially interested in the Soviet Union. Its prewar nationalist roots make it somewhat critical of the pro-American mainstream and eager to end the cold war, as Nakasone tried to accomplish. Although Nakasone temporarily resigned from the LDP to deflect criticism for the Recruit scandal, he was still identified with his former faction.

The Gaimushō has been distrustful of many whom it sees as intruders in diplomatic dealings with the Soviets. It has regarded the newspapers as too far to the left, although over the years they scarcely waivered in supporting the return of all four islands. It is suspicious of the personal diplomacy of politicians. Nakasone, Abe, and Kanemaru all aroused concern for being too eager to strike a deal with Gorbachev. In the Gaimushō there remains the memory of Kōno Ichirō, who excluded Ambassador Niizeki from his meeting with Khrushchev and thus left the experts entirely out of critical negotiations when diplomatic relations were being restored.

Spurred by the upcoming Tokyo summit, some Japanese insiders in late 1990 were saying that it was time for high-level shuttle diplomacy. When Nakasone went to Iraq to gain the release of hostages from Sadam Hussein at the start of November, some people hoped that his rehabilitation would be complete and that he could not only rejoin the LDP but also begin "personal diplomacy" under close Gaimushō supervision in search of a breakthrough with Moscow.

In contrast to the Nakasone group, the once mainstream conservative faction, now headed by Miyazawa Kiichi, is heir to the long dominant hard line of Prime Minister Yoshida Shigeru. The Miyazawa faction was the only one of the three factions (the Takeshita and Abe factions were the others) vying for the prime minister's post in the fall of 1987 that placed Japanese-Soviet relations on its election program. Not in power of late, it has more freedom to discuss Soviet matters. Yet there has been no discernible impact. For all the competitiveness of LDP faction leaders, neither their speeches nor their maneuvering identify genuine policy differences toward Moscow.

When Eduard Shevardnadze visited Japan in December 1988, he met with Uno, Takeshita, Nakasone, Abe, and Doi Takako. According to Suzuki Yoshikatsu's analysis shortly afterward, the real target was Abe; arrangements for Nakasone's visit the previous July had simply been a ritual out of politeness. Nakasone is not seen as returning to the mainstream of LDP leadership, whereas Abe was a real power who was likely to become the next party leader. The invitation to Kanemaru to visit the Soviet Union from Gorbachev's close aide Evgenyi Primakov shows that the Soviet approach has shifted from the fringes of Japanese politics to the conservative mainstream—to Takeshita, Abe, and Kanemaru, among others. Moscow is taking a long-term view of Japan's economic power. Suzuki's partisan analysis adds that Abe too is able to look ten years ahead to see the three sides of relations: the bilateral side, centered on territory; the Asia-Pacific region side, centered on economics; and the East-West side, centered on the military.[9] Statesmanship requires seeing the larger picture.

Leadership confusion at the top complicated the search for statesmanship. In October 1990 a sick Abe, the beneficiary of a confidential Soviet message, and a wounded Kanemaru, whose recent North Korean verbal concessions had aroused a furor at home, were clashing. The press reported that friction existed between the two largest LDP factions over the conduct of Soviet policy.[10] Moscow's decision in September to bypass the Takeshita faction for Abe's man helped to spark the open conflict. The factional conflict continued in early 1991 as Kaifu barely held onto his office and Gorbachev, siding with Soviet conservatives, was losing flexibility toward Japan.

In early 1991 Kaifu was resigned to following the Gaimushō script closely, while other politicians still hoped to play an independent role. A debate was underway about who should visit Moscow and how much Tokyo should encourage concessions through economic assistance. Among the LDP politicians who were positively inclined were Abe, still entitled to the next shot at the prime ministership until on May 15 his illness ended in death, and Ozawa Ichirō, with high hopes for the future. After Nakayama's return from Moscow in late January, discussions persisted about how to accelerate preparations for the summit, but hopes were slipping.

In January 1991 Tokyo's reticence to take a strong position against Gorbachev's crackdown in the Baltic was reminiscent of its caution toward Deng Xiaoping's June 1989 suppression in Beijing. Human rights concerns do not play a central role in Japanese diplomacy. Moreover, endangering bilateral ties in order to appeal to public opinion or to stand with allies is a lesser concern in Tokyo. Worried that the momentum for the April summit was already slowed by personnel and policy shifts in Moscow, Japanese authorities hoped to stay as much on course as possible.

THE BUREAUCRACY

Japan is known for the independent power of its bureaucracy. The ministries, especially the Ministry of International Trade and Industry (MITI) and the Ministry of Finance, are credited with engineering the "economic miracle." Discussions of Japanese deliberations over opening markets to American and West European exports focus on interministerial struggles, often between the Ministry of Finance and the Gaimushō. More than the LDP factions, the bureaucratic ministries appear to be the battleground for policy disputes.

In studies of decision making related to the Soviet Union there are a number of ministries and agencies to consider, but only one to take very seriously. The Gaimushō is in charge, with slight and only intermittent involvement of MITI, the Japanese Defense Agency (JDA), the Ministry of Finance, and the Ministry of Agriculture, Forestry, and Fisheries. Over time, the tendency to view the USSR through the nets of fishing interests has declined, while the role of the JDA has risen, even if it remains decidedly secondary. MITI's interests have also lessened, first with the shift away from energy-intensive industries after the oil shock of 1973, then with the sanctions after the dispatch of Soviet troops into Afghanistan in 1979, and perhaps for a third time in 1987 after the Toshiba affair when COCOM trade restrictions were tightened to prevent a recurrence of the shipment of militarily sensitive technology to the Soviet Union. Japanese business realizes that it has more to lose from retaliation for violations by American import restrictions than it has to gain from selling high technology to Moscow, especially at a time when Soviets are hard-pressed financially and cannot satisfy even a small part of the huge appetite they have developed through window shopping.

In 1989 MITI began to show new interest in the Soviet Union. It set up a subdepartment on Soviet-type economies. SOTOBO, loosely affiliated with MITI and concerned with trade in the Soviet Union and Eastern Europe, began to be strengthened. Often in tension with the Gaimushō on other matters, MITI was not yet ready to assert its own position on the Soviet Union. The Ministry of Finance was even less active, but in January 1990 when Kaifu announced an aid package for Eastern Europe worth two billion dollars, the ministry was known to have cautioned against hopes for easy repayment. MITI and the Ministry of Finance play an enormous role in Asian policy, in sharp contrast to their still weak involvement in Soviet matters. This is beginning to change, even as the Gaimushō continues to invoke the territorial dispute to insist on its jurisdiction.

In the late fall of 1990, apparently over the objections of the Gaimushō, the Japanese leadership agreed to offer some "know-how" aid and a one hundred million dollar export credit to help combat Soviet food shortages. In January 1991 when Gorbachev's Baltic crackdown threatened to freeze Western aid, it was recognized that Tokyo was reluctant to reverse course while still clinging to some hope for progress at the April summit.[11] Disputes over money give additional ministries a say in Soviet policy.

By early 1991 there were reports that MITI was beginning to advocate closer economic ties in response to calculations by its research group about long-run Soviet potential. A few researchers from the Finance Ministry were being sent to Moscow or to the IIGP in Tokyo. Sakhalin natural gas was becoming a prime objective.

The Gaimushō and the JDA. Among the bureaucratic forces, the Gaimushō reigns supreme in Soviet affairs. Backed by the JDA, it insists on linkage between economics and politics to pressure Moscow to return the islands. There does not seem to be any major policy difference between the Gaimushō and the JDA, although the latter's lower status sometimes leads to dissatisfaction. The JDA is seen as an advocate of a military build-up to meet the Soviet threat, and the Gaimushō is seen as having a more comprehensive outlook, emphasizing close cooperation with the United States (leading some to make accusations of "dependent diplomacy"). After the INF agreement in December 1987, the impression developed that the JDA was less enthusiastic for the new détente, even though within the Gaimushō divisions could also be detected. With Gorbachev pressing for a rethinking of security in the Asia-Pacific region in 1991, JDA concerns are coming into the forefront. Yet, because in the postwar setting the JDA has not found as firm a niche as the lofty Gaimushō's, it will need strong backing within the Gaimushō itself and within the LDP to prevail.

Of course, by now vested interests have developed around Japan's Self-Defense Forces (SDF). They are not accustomed to much intrabureaucratic clout in the face of powerful ministries, but they made appreciable gains in the 1980s. In the aftermath of the INF agreement, the land Self-Defense Forces fear that they may face the budget ax. More than the sea or air forces, they are vulnerable because they would only be needed if the Soviets attacked Japan. Some analysts suspect that the sensational literature on the coming invasion of Hokkaidō that still was appearing as late as 1987 was really sponsored in some manner by the hawkish element in the Self-Defense Forces. In their view, the army is not likely to respond enthusiastically to a new Soviet relationship.

Professional officers are not allowed to write about security matters. Nakagawa Yatsuhiro, one of the most visible and extreme figures in the right wing's anti-Soviet campaign, may serve their purposes. Indeed, when a *Shokun* article in October 1988 fired a diatribe at Nakasone for plotting to betray Japan's national interests through concessions to Moscow,[12] one hypothesis suggested that Nakagawa and his friends in the land forces were behind it.

Hopes in the military had risen as the symbolic 1 percent of the GNP level for the official armed forces budget was passed in the mid-1980s. Yet public support for a substantial increase for defense has slipped from its zenith at the start of the decade when the Soviet invasion of Afghanistan, the Sino-Vietnam war, and the accelerated Soviet military build-up created a climate of anxiety. A consensus exists that the forces of the United States and its allies are superior in the Pacific, and that Soviet military expansion in the 1970s was directed more against China than Japan. Even if that changed over the following decade, Japanese alarm has receded. For a time, Moscow's promise to shift to a defensive strategy was less impressive than the continued impact of Soviet military modernization and the redeployment of naval forces to the Northwest Pacific where they save money by staying closer to home. Nonetheless, in 1990 the debate over the diminished Soviet threat was heating up, and it centered on the military budget hearings.[13] It also came into view as a result of differing perceptions of the Soviet threat in white papers issued by the SDF and the Gaimushō. Apparently diplomats and world affairs experts alike found the SDF assessment unresponsive to new world circumstances. There was talk of the need for new thinking in Japan, too. In contrast, the *Diplomacy White Paper* offered a genuine change from the previous year after consultation with academic advisers in the Soviet field. The clash was resolved on September 18, 1990, when Prime Minister Kaifu told the SDF to remove the assertion that Soviet forces pose a military threat to Japan.[14] Not long thereafter, SDF funding was slipping back to the 1 percent level.

The public mood in the fall of 1990 resisted the dispatch of SDF forces as noncombatants to the Persian Gulf. The first test of the post–cold war era found both public opinion and politicians hesitant to alter the military status quo. Yet, both the SDF and the Gaimushō were awaiting Soviet security proposals for Northeast Asia with lingering concern.

Leadership in the Gaimushō. Leadership within the Gaimushō is in the hands of career foreign service officers who have risen through the ranks in a seniority-based system. The few who reach the pinnacle of power as vice-minister or one of two deputy foreign ministers can make a difference. In 1988–89 appointments were fortuitous for a moderation of thinking on Soviet policy. Murata Ryōhei became vice-minister in 1988 after following Soviet affairs while ambassador in Vienna and serving as deputy foreign minister in charge of political affairs. He has a reputation for keeping the broader picture in mind, important after years of narrow focus on the return of the Northern Territories.

It may be happenstance that in the summer of 1988, at a critical juncture in relations, the cycle of promotions and reassignments produced an unprecedented constellation of moderate Soviet specialists also in the next highest positions within the Gaimushō. Experts cycle in and out of Soviet-related posts, largely in accord with seniority although performance is considered. In 1988 two leading hardliners, as seen by many in and out of the Gaimushō, were placed at arm's length from Soviet-related decision making. Arai Hirokazu became ambassador to East Germany, where he may have spent as much as half his time monitoring Soviet matters, though with little policy input in Tokyo. Tamba Minoru, who earlier as Soviet desk director had made a difference in solidifying a negative atmosphere, entered the Treaty Department. Two others seen as relatively hard line were also on the sidelines. Hyodo Nagao wound up in administration, and Shigeta Hiroshi found himself in the Economic Cooperation Bureau, where he took a leading role in the new foreign aid program for Eastern Europe. An apparent historical accident provided the first opportunity in decades for a relatively reform-minded group to predominate. In the next turn of the cycle in mid-1990, however, it was Hyodo who became the head of the important Eurasian Department.

With Hyodo's accession and the appointment of the not very reform-minded Liudvig Chizhov as Soviet ambassador to Japan, doubts intensified in the second half of 1990 that the diplomatic establishments would play a leading role in setting bilateral relations on a new track. The Japanese and the Soviets were both waiting for Gorbachev. At the same time, the debates in both countries became livelier. The two cautious Foreign Ministries were now slipping from the limelight as traditional diplomacy yielded to private and public probing through influential voices. Perhaps never before has a diplomatic breakthrough of this magnitude seemed to depend so much on academics and others operating on the fringes of diplomacy. Only when Shevardnadze and Yakovlev dropped out of the picture did it again become clear in early 1991 that the unofficial shadow boxing would be for naught if the more cautious establishment in each country, especially the Soviet military, holds a different outlook.

After Kaifu took office as prime minister, Murata left to become ambassador to the United States, while Deputy Foreign Minister Kuriyama Tokakazu, who had headed the new working group with the Soviet Union, advanced to vice-minister. Although formally in charge, along with Soviet Deputy Foreign Minister Igor Rogachev, of the new joint working group with Moscow during his term as deputy foreign minister, Kuriyama is an expert on the United States and had to give priority to the serious conflicts faced in Japanese-American relations. In his place, the succeeding deputy foreign minister for political affairs, Owada Hisashi, emerged as a strong leader on Soviet affairs. Stationed twice in Moscow, able to read Russian, and well enough versed in international law to have taught the subject at Harvard Law School, he is regarded as a formidable negotiator. Owada's personal knowledge of the Soviet scene may have reduced the impact of Soviet specialists. While this kept the conservatives at a distance, the shift out of key posts of Murata and Togō Takehiro (discussed below) also may have diminished somewhat the momentum of the moderates, which had been advancing over the previous year.

Owada served as special assistant to Fukuda Takeo and remains closely identified with the Fukuda faction, now headed by Abe. He was not the only Foreign Ministry official to be linked with a top politician. Previously in the post of director general of the Eurasian Department and then of the Asian Department, Hasegawa Kazutoshi was no less closely identified with Nakasone and his faction. He had a role in boosting Nakasone's personal diplomacy toward Moscow. Nakasone and Fukuda were bitter rivals from the same district of Japan. Even in the rather insular Gaimushō, factional LDP ties have some meaning.

The team in charge of Gaimushō Soviet policy as Gorbachev's visit drew near was Kuriyama, Owada, and Hyodo, all experienced in negotiations with the Soviets and informed by contingency plans drawn up over a number of years by the Eurasian Department. The three were guided by the theory that flexibility would easily follow once Moscow agreed to return the four islands, but their strategy for securing that agreement reached an impasse in the early months of 1991 before it could unfold.

The Soviet Desk. The Soviet desk (Sorenka) has primary responsibility for Japanese policy recommendations and day-to-day conduct of relations. It is the unquestioned conductor in orchestrating policy and, some Japanese add, perceptions toward Moscow. Five officials on the Soviet desk, including the director, form a decision-making group. Successive directors of the division, specialists on the Soviet Union about age forty-five with over twenty years' experience in Soviet watching, wield the most visible influence in day-to-day matters. Most entered the foreign service as elite products of the Law Department of Tokyo University, chose the Soviet area less out of prior familiarity or fascination with Soviet society than out of a sense of duty to preserve Japan's national security, were sent to Harvard or London for initial training in Soviet studies, and passed through a succession of lower posts including periods of service in Moscow. In this process, the traditions of the Soviet desk were deeply stamped into their consciousness, according to many informants. Throughout the postwar era, notably under the leadership of Hōgen Shinsaku and Sono Akira, the Soviet desk has stood as the fortress for opposing Soviet designs on Japan. An intensely adversarial relationship has prevailed, often justified by the Kremlin's policies in the cold war and its brusque behavior toward Japan and its diplomats.

Recently, as a successor generation has been entering this division, there have been signs of moderation. Those stationed in Moscow in the Gorbachev era are succeeding in breaking out of the customary isolation of their service and are responding to change by advocating a more open-minded approach. One of these is already at a high rank. After serving as Soviet desk director and eventually as the number two officer in Moscow under Ambassador Katori Yasue, Tōgō Takehiro emerged as the Eurasian Department director general (*Oakyokuchō*). The new post placed Tōgō Takehiro above the Soviet desk director (in 1988–90 Tōgō Kazuhiko) and in a powerful position to draft policy, drawing on his personal familiarity with the Gorbachev scene. Tōgō Takehiro's reputation for moderation and thoughtfulness cast a new glow on Gaimushō Soviet deliberations. Tōgō Kazuhiko also made a favorable impression. Given the expected delicate state of negotiations in mid-1990 when he was due for reassignment, his service as Soviet desk director was extended for another year, leading to Gorbachev's visit.

The Murata-Tōgō combination at the top gave a strong boost to realism toward Moscow. The old-boy network extending back to Hōgen and Sono, which had left some hardliners in the ministry, was now becoming a force of the past. Yet conscious efforts to balance "hard" and "soft" guarantee a mixture of views.

This was the case in November 1990 when the Moscow embassy staff was fortified through the addition of the cautious Shigeta Hiroshi in the number two post below the ambassador and the bolder Kawato Akio as the diplomat in charge of cultural matters and public relations. According to one source, the goal was to spot the contents of Gorbachev's briefcase prior to his arrival.[15]

One article in April 1990 presented the argument that the foreign ministries of the Soviet Union and Japan, continuing endlessly to stand on high-sounding principles and floating along completely out of touch with public opinion, were incapable of reaching a breakthrough. At a time when there seems to be a large shake-up of Soviet diplomats in the Japan field, the Soviet desk of the Gaimushō also needs to sweep out its conservative mainstream, insisted the article, warning that the Soviet side is strengthening ties to the LDP as well as seeking to influence Japanese public opinion.[16] The more common view, however, was that with the LDP faction rivals vying for diplomatic breakthroughs on many fronts and Kaifu weakly holding onto power, Japan was in danger not of inaction, but of slipping into two-dimensional diplomacy. This too would open the door to the Soviet policy aimed at splitting public opinion.[17]

Divisions in the Gaimushō. One analyst of the Gaimushō privately divides it into three schools: the European, relatively sympathetic to the Soviet Union and represented by Murata before his posting to Washington; the American, among whom is former Washington ambassador Ōkawara Yoshio, who played an active role in the joint U.S.-Japanese study group on the Soviet Union that functioned from 1987 to 1989; and the Soviet, known for its hostility to the Soviet Union. Through the intermediate role of the American school, the gap between the other schools was narrowing. From the second half of 1988 the European school appeared to gain influence. As the Gaimushō became more moderate, outside criticisms of inaction declined. The critical voice of the left-of-center, which had suddenly revived in the Japanese media in the first half of 1988, quieted somewhat in reaction to more encouraging views on Soviet relations from the top. Gaimushō leadership, even if not quite as unified as before, exerts an important influence on public debates.

Early in 1989 the new Gaimushō journal, *Gaikō forumu*, printed an article by Miyauchi Kuniko favorable to Gorbachev's reforms.[18] The choice of a former *Chūō kōron* editor to run the journal gave it some independence. Even if not all diplomats welcomed this new tolerance of diversity, it was a sign of a more open relationship between the bureaucrats and the public.

Former Ambassadors. Both Soviet experts and the more numerous Gaimushō generalists sometimes assume an advisory role. Niizeki Kinya, who became chairman of the Japanese Institute of International Affairs (JIIA), an international relations research institute directly under the Gaimushō, works with academics on Soviet-related projects and cooperates with foreigners in arranging conferences and in hosting lectures. His institute publishes *Soren kenkyū* (Soviet studies), Japan's principal journal on contemporary Soviet events, and relies heavily on the leadership of Kimura Hiroshi for involving the academic community. In the fall of 1988, the Gaimushō sent a director to work with Niizeki to bolster the research capacity of the JIIA, and it plans to second Soviet specialists there for a research stint as well as to send JIIA staff to the Moscow embassy. In contrast to Hōgen and Sono, Niizeki supports a range of scholarship, even if some critics complain that the JIIA is too close to the Gaimushō to encourage the airing of truly dissenting views.

When the Gaimushō itself was hesitant openly to criticize Shevardnadze's diplomacy, Niizeki presented what appeared to be an authoritative commentary in September 1990. He said that while Andrei Gromyko's "nyet" diplomacy familiar to him was a thing of the past, Shevardnadze's September visit showed that the fundamental Soviet attitude had not changed. Calling on the Soviets to recognize the wrongs committed at the end of World War II and in the forced labor in Siberia, as they had acknowledged the Katyn Forest murders of Polish officers and the Baltic annexation, he said that the Japanese people have the impression that the Soviet Union has not yet changed.[19]

Former ambassador Nakagawa Tōru maintains a concern with historical and legal details in the bilateral relationship. He has remained a temperate spokesman for the Japanese position. Katori Yasue, who is not a Soviet specialist, returned in the fall of 1987 from the ambassadorship in Moscow (and prior to that the ambassadorship in China) to become president of the Japan Foundation, which supports the study of Japan around the world. Katori quickly became an active spokesman on Soviet policy, presenting a relatively moderate position in an important period of transition just after his service in Moscow. When Ambassador Mutō Toshiaki returned from Moscow in May 1990, he told a distinguished audience of businessmen that there would be no Soviet retreat from the marathon of reform and no second Tiananmen incident in Red Square.[20] Within the Gaimushō, some circles have been wary that the Soviet desk is inflexible; the presence of senior figures who are not Soviet hands but have had personal experience helps to provide balance and a broader perspective.

Political Advisers. The advisory system outside the Gaimushō was broadened by Prime Minister Nakasone. Through the use of "brains" reporting directly to his office or perhaps to the foreign minister, he somewhat shifted the power center from the LDP Policy Research Council. In security matters, members of the Research Institute for Peace and Security (RIPS) gained influence. Inoki Masamichi, its head and also chairman of the Study Group on the International Situation for the Cabinet Research Office, frequently discussed Soviet affairs with the Gaimushō and top leaders. Kosaka Masataka, a professor at Kyōto University and affiliated with the International Institute for Strategic Studies (IISS) in London, chaired the Study Group on Peace to advise Nakasone on defense. Satō Seizaburō, a professor at Tōkyō University and Nakasone's choice to guide the new International Institute for Global Peace (IIGP), which Nakasone established in retirement, was influential in developing a comprehensive view of the world. Satō is known as an advocate of close relations with Washington and of caution in improving Soviet ties. Along with Kumon Shumpei, who once studied Soviet affairs but primarily advises on domestic matters, Satō works closely at the side of Nakasone. He may wield more influence at the top of the LDP than any other academic. Taking a global strategic approach, he has recently sought to improve Soviet ties on terms consistent with Japan's strong position.

The IIGP has not received the financial support anticipated in an ambitious original plan and has suffered with the decline of Nakasone's influence, yet it benefits from the seconding of personnel from the Gaimushō and other agencies, large corporations, and think tanks, especially the

Nomura Research Institute from which its director comes. Compared to the JIIA, the IIGP has a narrower focus. For instance, it was initially studying the Northern Territories issue rather than Soviet security policy or foreign bilateral relations more generally. Yet the special reports it issued in 1989–90 revealed a wide-ranging concern for the transformation of socialism and of the Asia-Pacific region.

The Nakasone group, despite some high-quality, up-to-date analyses of the political developments marking communism's collapse, was too closely associated with the fortunes of a former leader whose status had fallen to achieve its original goals. The Niizeki group produced the most substantial list of coordinated publications, such as on the history of Sino-Soviet relations, but remained too much a creation of the Gaimushō to develop an independent outlook regularly identifying alternatives. There was also a National Institute for Research Advancement (NIRA) group, which kept true to its roots in the business world, concentrating on the economics of the Soviet Union at a time when Japanese were slow to uncover any economic promise in that country. Clearly most effective in influencing policy makers was the Suetsugu group, described below, which eschewed the spotlight in favor of unpublicized meetings with Soviet scholars and reports distributed across Japanese official circles. Its secrecy, aimed at encouraging frank exchanges with the Soviets, was usually observed, although at a Leningrad joint symposium in October 1990 the Soviet Japanologist Aleksei Zagorsky made public his bold call for the return of all four islands to Japan and drew attention to the meeting. The Suetsugu group cultivated ties with the Soviets and concentrated its energies on the immediate problem of the Northern Territories and on the Soviet role in the Asia-Pacific region. A few Sovietologists actively contributed to the projects of two or three of these groups. Most notable was Kimura Hiroshi, who worked closely with Satō Seizaburō at the IIGP, with the JIIA, and with Suetsugu. Through the Suetsugu group Japanese cultivated close contacts with the Soviet Institute of the World Economy and International Relations (IMEMO), which was no less eager for direct access to the latest thinking in Japan's decision-making circles.

Suetsugu Ichirō leads the most influential group on Soviet matters, the Council on National Security Problems. He organized this group first to arrange for the reversion of Okinawa from the United States and then, after that was achieved, to press for the reversion of the Northern Territories. Suetsugu cultivated personal ties with high-ranking Soviet academics, including the successive directors of IMEMO Aleksandr Yakovlev and Evgenyi Primakov, who emerged at the end of the decade next to Gorbachev at the top of the Soviet decision making concerning Japan. Personal diplomacy outside of the foreign ministries became an important feature when ties were deadlocked over the Afghanistan situation in the early 1980s, and especially in the later effort to mend Soviet-Japanese relations.[21] Suetsugu regularly visited Moscow and facilitated meetings between Soviets and high LDP leaders such as Kanemaru Shin. Through 1988 Primakov often came to Tokyo. Yakovlev made two visits in 1984 and 1989. Informal ideas about how to break the impasse in relations were flowing back and forth. When other advisory groups withered after Nakasone's departure, Suetsugu's group was an exception. Although others, including power brokers on the right of the political spectrum, have tried their hand at personal diplomacy, Suetsugu stands alone for his behind-the-scenes influence on Soviet matters.

Suetsugu's ties extended to Sakurauchi Yoshio, the speaker of the Lower House who met with him prior to traveling to Moscow, and Owada Hisashi, the Gaimushō official leading the negotiations with Moscow. His research group on security matters had operated continuously from the late 1960s. Members with long service, such as Inoki Masamichi, were already in their seventies. Recent additions represented the generation in their forties, bolstering Soviet-watching and security analyses. Many from the group accompanied Suetsugu in regular conferences with IMEMO in Moscow. His trips were not confined to conferences; by 1990 he was traveling every one or two months to Moscow, often meeting with Yakovlev. From these sessions and the regular gatherings of the study group in Tokyo, reports were circulated to the Gaimushō. In effect, a "think tank" was operating in Japan, with one thought foremost—the return of the Northern Territories.

Foreign affairs experts describe Suetsugu's personal role as a throwback to the prewar era when influential figures operated from the shadows. Called a *kuromaki*, a dark figure pulling the strings in Noh drama, or a *ronin*, a masterless samurai not directly under any political leader, Suetsugu has spent many years cultivating ties with LDP politicians. He is praised for his efforts in the late 1940s on behalf of prisoners of war returning from the Soviet Union, for his spadework in the 1960s to secure the return of Okinawa, for his connections with Soviet officials including to Yakovlev even before the latter became Gorbachev's Politburo associate, and for his persistent activities to promote delicate bilateral communications in the years leading to Gorbachev's visit to Japan. The Gaimushō cooperated with him, considering him helpful. Top LDP leaders, including prime ministers, worked with him in the hope that they would gain credit for the breakthrough all were anticipating. Trained in the wartime Nakano spy school and secure in his ties to the right through his National Assembly for Youth Development and his nationwide organization to return the Northern Territories, Suetsugu promised secrecy. No wonder he is also described as the "gray eminence" for prime ministers, including Nakasone and those who followed in the top post.

Behind-the-Scenes Diplomacy. Frustrated by a hardline Soviet desk at the Gaimushō, Moscow leaders welcomed access to the power centers of the LDP. What they were getting was not necessarily a more compromising approach, but a commitment to working hard to find a solution.

The Suetsugu study group comprises mostly persons on the right of center and the far right, with a few Soviet specialists close to the Gaimushō and JDA, international relations experts, and familiar names from other advisory groups. Their recommendations would not likely be conciliatory and could be further toughened by Suetsugu's own long-standing leanings and strong association with the most ardent forces campaigning for the Northern Territories. The Northern Territories movement sought to maintain a high emotional pitch. By the end of 1990 over 52,500,000 signatures filled petitions to return the islands. At Nemuro, overlooking some of the islands, an observation tower built by the Sasakawa family, described below, stood as a symbol of the movement. One of its exhibits targeted the easy-going generation of youth who would come to regret in their old age not having struggled hard for the return of the islands. The call for commitment and determination for a cause echoed other appeals to young people by the older generation, including those eager to restore Japanese nationalism as a source of patriotic pride. Since the Northern Territories issue is the one that has most galvanized the extreme right, leading to harassment of the Soviet Embassy in Tokyo and to blaring loudspeakers cruising the streets of the city, it is not a promising base for compromise. Yet, for a Japan virtually united behind the return of four islands and a Soviet leadership in a rush to rejoin the global community, the involvement of ardent nationalists in the preparations for negotiations can be a wise step. This is especially so because most nationalists are less interested in riding anticommunism to a new place in power and more preoccupied with the immediate goal of regaining territory.

In 1990–91 a second "pipe" was operating. It was Sasakawa Yoi of the Sasakawa Peace Foundation. Having met with Gorbachev in Moscow and encouraged Soviets to expect assistance from the foundation (an early gift was a baseball field for Moscow State University), he was welcomed by influential circles. This was the sort of contact that raised Soviet hopes for close ties with East Asian business establishments. An ambitious foundation was seeking a new role, while Suetsugu's work represented the culmination of seventeen years of government and academic cooperation with frequent briefings. For example, after Owada returned from accompanying Foreign Minister Nakayama to Moscow on January 24, 1991, one of the first meetings on his busy schedule (he also had responsibility for the war arena in the Persian Gulf) was a meeting with Suetsugu's security group.

On occasion, when the Gorbachev leadership sought to ameliorate the climate of negotiations in a step-by-step fashion, rumors circulated that it was Suetsugu who impatiently pressed Japan's leaders to seek an immediate, complete Soviet capitulation, for example, warning Nakasone that the attitude of begging Gorbachev to visit Japan would repeat Prime Minister Hatoyama's fiasco of 1955–56 when no peace treaty was reached. Yet Suetsugu benefited from the fact that the Gorbachev leadership was also impatient and was eager to use him as an expediter to speed informal soundings. He skillfully filled a need for an informal channel with extraordinary access in each country.

An Unofficial National Security Council. The Council on National Security Problems (Anzen Hoshō Mondai Kenkyūkai) began in 1968 as a group to speed the reversion of Okinawa. It changed course in 1970 after an agreement was reached on that issue. Since 1973 it has promoted Soviet-Japanese contacts. By 1989 eleven "Peace in Asia" binational conferences had been held at roughly eighteen-month intervals, assuring continuity of the principal participants and a private atmosphere. From the Soviet side, leading foreign policy experts and advisers to the party secretary have served as the principal figures. On the Japanese side, Suetsugu is the founder and moving force, while Saeki Kiichi, Inoki Masamichi, Kamiya Fuji, Kanamori Hisao, Kimura Hiroshi, Sase Masamori, Miyoshi Osamu, Nagata Minoru, and Hakamada Shigeki are members (about half the total membership) who write prominently about the Soviet Union. The ongoing contacts provide a vehicle for mutual understanding and semiformal exchanges of ideas that might lead to new approaches in bilateral relations.

A "Pipe." Along with the regularly scheduled conferences, additional contacts among participants from both sides sometimes occur. Suetsugu has taken his mission for the islands to the Soviet Union over thirty times. His high-level contacts help him to gain access in Moscow, and he can offer similar access in Tokyo because of close ties to LDP leaders and to Gaimushō officials. Known in Moscow as Mr. Northern Territories, Suetsugu is regarded in both countries as a "pipe."[22] In addition to the formal Foreign Ministry contacts of the two governments and to the study trips increasingly taken by specialists who meet their counterparts, the informal pipeline of influential political advisers is valued by both sides. In this way, they can keep relatively up-to-date on developments in the other country and identify negotiating opportunities. Even during the years of diminished contacts in the first half of the 1980s, the pipeline kept going. Unlike the far right's most extreme voices, Suetsugu pays attention to differences of opinion in Moscow and recognizes changes that are occurring. Yet, unlike many in the center and even some to the right of center, his level of trust is rather low. He becomes involved in discussions of the Soviet desk at the Gaimushō, seeking positions that might spur negotiations but adamantly keeping the pressure on Moscow to return all the islands. As the chances for the return of all four islands were rising, Suetsugu gained credit for his single-minded determination.

Personal diplomacy is also tried by politicians who are not well connected at the top. In the words of Gaimushō officials, "they are driven by their personal interests and flirt with the Soviet Union." The Hatoyama dream of the mid-1950s has not died, some suggest.

There is diversity in the perceptions of the Soviet Union within the LDP, which is dominated less by ideology than by a compromise agreement among diverse interest groups. On the left is Utsunomiya Tokuma, who has his own research institute on disarmament. Also active is Sakurauchi Yoshio, former foreign minister and president of the Japan-Soviet Parliamentary Friendship Association, and Hatoyama Ichirō, vice-president of this group and president of the Japan-Soviet Friendship Society, which draws most of its support from parties on the left. Hatoyama, following the family tradition, regards himself as a "bridge" between Japan and the Soviet Union. Formerly Ishida Hirohide was active on an individual basis, but he was ousted from the Diet as "pro-Soviet." On the other side can be found numerous LDP Diet representatives who capitalize at home on their prominence in supporting the return of the Northern Territories and thus have an interest in Soviet policy, without looking for common ground with the Soviets.

Sometimes what appears to be personal diplomacy is less than meets the eye. The LDP is open to the operation of associations oriented toward diverse countries, even North Korea. These associations are monitored and even used when informal contacts are sought. In turn, the Gaimushō is well aware of the contacts and may even be shaping them. Over the long run there may have been a gradual shift of power from the bureaucracy to the LDP, but politicians actually take few initiatives. When they do so, as in the case of Nakasone, they prepare through careful consultations. The bureaucracy is still unquestionably in charge, without denying maneuverability to ambitious politicians.

THE OPPOSITION

Some opposition dietmen have developed their own associations and personal connections with Moscow. A former Japan Socialist party (JSP) dietman, Matsumae Shigeyoshi, founded the Japanese Cultural Association to promote academic exchanges and uses his financial resources and connections to influence the government. The Japan-Soviet Society associated with the Japan Communist party (JCP) has local branches in each prefecture and, after declining for two decades when interparty ties with the Communist party of the Soviet Union were often tense, launched a new journal and new institute in the late 1980s.[23] Doi Takako, the leader of the JSP whose popularity helped bring defeat to the LDP in the July 1989 elections to the Upper House, took an interest in alternative thinking about the Gorbachev era prior to meeting the Soviet leader in Moscow in May 1988.[24] Gradually but cautiously, the JSP was beginning to associate itself with the emerging left-of-center vision of Moscow described in this book rather than with a staunch territorial stance typical of the right and an embrace of socialism still suggestive of the far left. This was not easy because Doi's factional opponents included old-line socialists, long known for firm opposition to the U.S.-Japan security pact and to criticisms of socialist theory. In chapter 14 I return to the opposition's approach to dealing with Moscow. The JSP was the only party that could hope to play an influential role within the establishment from the time of its electoral success in mid-1989. It was too divided and too vulnerable, however, to capitalize on the opportunity, leaving guidance over national thinking still in the hands of the well-entrenched decision-making forces.

Occasionally out of personal conviction or grandstanding ambitions, a lone politician becomes involved in the search for a Soviet-Japanese breakthrough. In July 1989, Inoki Antonio won election to the House of Councilors (Upper House) on a nonparty, sports peace platform. Perhaps recalling ping-pong diplomacy between the United States and China, this wrestler-turned-politician aims to break the psychological barriers that cause Japanese to see Soviets as "gloomy characters." He finds the LDP worn out in its thinking and would use personal diplomacy to energize Japanese relations first with the Soviet Union and then with other nations.[25]

INFLUENTIAL FIGURES WITH ACCESS TO POWER

Consultations in Japan, as elsewhere, involve retired officials, international affairs experts, area specialists, and business leaders. The Gaimushō and occasionally LDP leaders seek the advice of individuals whose views are usually close to those of the people in power. Yet they also prefer informed assessments. As opportunities to travel to the USSR have expanded and conditions there have changed abruptly, the voice of the area specialists has grown louder, while retired officials appear increasingly out of touch with Soviet reality.

The Old-Boy Network. Retired Soviet desk officials from the Gaimushō have played a prominent role on the right of the Japanese spectrum. In the first half of the 1980s they were active in warning their nation about the Soviet threat and the prospects for Soviet reform and a renewal of détente. As Soviet-American relations thawed in 1987–88, they urged continued vigilance and remained doubtful about prospects for further

Soviet-American arms agreements. Some vocally opposed the Moscow summit. Hōgen Shinsaku and Sono Akira best typify the strident wing of former Soviet desk officials.[26] Itō Kenichi, who retired at a younger age in an unsuccessful attempt to win election to parliament and has established stronger claims as a Soviet specialist, also expressed indignation at suggestions of compromise on the Northern Territories issue and then became more flexible as currents were changing in 1989–90.[27]

The old government perception that academics could not normally be trusted for ideological reasons has acquired a new twist among some to the right of center. In their view, specialists are too close to their subject and thus tend to see the trees instead of the forest. They meet Soviet intellectuals who are in the forefront of glasnost. They read in search of new ideas, which appear in rapid succession. Long bored by stagnation of Soviet thinking, many academics understandably overreact to the new era. Their assessments tend to be one-sided, based on what intellectuals say rather than on how society as a whole is actually transformed. This is the skeptical reaction of the right to much of academia. The old-boy network plays the leading role in opposing what is regarded as the "academic lobby."

Experts with Access to Power. Kimura Hiroshi and Sase Masamori are two of the most prominent academics whose views are respected in the inner circles of power. Kimura has a Ph.D. degree from Columbia University and has earned his reputation by virtue of numerous publications and energetic leadership of Soviet studies. The fact that his views have generally been close to those of the Gaimushō makes his council all the more welcome. More than other Japanese, Kimura led in the cycle of confidence from 1989 to 1990 in floating ideas widely seen as trial balloons indicative of the growing flexibility of the Gaimushō.

Sase does not have the credentials of a Soviet expert but has long written on Soviet and international affairs while teaching at the Defense Institute of the JDA. In 1987–88 while Kimura was becoming cautiously hopeful about Soviet willingness to negotiate seriously on the return of the four islands and on ending the cold war on terms satisfactory to Japan and the United States, Sase was casting doubt on the desirability of the INF agreement signed in Washington and on long-range Soviet intentions.[28] He and Kimura represented the two major poles firmly inside the establishment. By early 1990 Sase had also become more positive. His views were welcomed in the Soviet press, and he now wanted perestroika to succeed.

Government officials could obtain a range of opinions from the academics they favored, but some Japanese on the left and center worried that the advice being heard was disproportionately from the right of center and the far right. Long-standing concern that the establishment is too narrowly conceived continues to leave academics uneasy, but the breakup of the coalition between the far right and the right of center since 1987 has diminished this concern.

Polarization among analysts was diminishing. Satō Tsuneaki, an influential specialist on the Soviet economy, continued to advise the JSP but also was sought by conservative academic groups and gatherings of specialists for his realistic assessments. Shimotomai Nobuo earned wide respect for his coverage of politics even though he was seen as well to the left of center and, after Gorbachev swung to the right, appeared to have been too optimistic.

The Business Community. Opposition to the Japanese government's tough line with Moscow could be detected among small-business circles at various times, even in the years of greatest unanimity in public opinion against the Soviet threat. Yokokawa Shōichi, who had served in the Diet to 1974 and then headed the Japan-Soviet Trade Association, wrote in a 1984 book that while Americans and West Germans were active in trade with the Soviets, Japanese were not. He complained that a tenacious anti-Soviet campaign, fueled by alarmist accounts of Soviet spies, had taught Japanese to hate the reds. In his view, the campaign was based on three elements from 1945: the Northern Territories issue, the memories of Japan's Siberian POWs, and the Soviet violation of the neutrality treaty. Yokokawa then argued with each of these reasons, saying that Japan had agreed to abandon the islands in the San Francisco Treaty in 1951, that Japan's cruelty to POWs in World War II means that the Soviets alone should not be criticized, and that the Soviets were more victimized by the war than was Japan, and, in any case, their government repudiated the neutrality treaty four months before attacking Japan and left Japan time to evacuate civilians or to take other action. Yokokawa blamed the anti-Soviet mood on American pressure beginning in the 1950s and on the Japanese right. He called Japan a faithful vassal of the United States.[29]

Most of the business community shows little concern over the low level of economic ties to the Soviet Union. Although in the 1960s and 1970s there were active and important business lobbies for government support in Soviet economic relations, these lost influence. Profits in the Soviet trade became minuscule in comparison to those elsewhere in the world. The main line of reasoning in the 1980s among critics of the government was that Japan was being unfairly treated by its allies; sanctions and restrictions on high technology disproportionately penalized Japanese firms. Yet these frustrations were not sufficient incentive to take a strong stance.

Business interests are well organized and can exert great influence on both the LDP and the principal ministries concerned with economic issues. They have chosen to stay on the sidelines. Soviets long worked through a small set of firms and secondary associations, already engaged in their market, to entice greater interest. In 1988–90, they were trying to cast their pitch more widely for a new era of joint ventures and a single integrated world economy.

Some research centers under private firms such as Nomura Securities or under economic associations play a role in evaluating the Soviet economy and influencing business prospects. They were becoming more active in 1989–90 as attention shifted from isolated joint-venture investments to large-scale aid along with the West to bolster perestroika or to smooth the way for Soviet concessions on the islands. Morimoto Tadao of the Torei Center became a popular commentator, combining sober criticism of the dreadful state of the Soviet economy with advice to Japanese business to provide help. His advice soon appeared in Moscow as well as Tokyo.

The Limits of the Establishment. The chapters that follow look especially at the views of three types of Japanese Soviet-watchers. The first type are the leading authorities—those whose publications are the best informed or the most analytical. Examples include Kimura Hiroshi on Japanese-Soviet relations, Shimotomai Nobuo on the Soviet political system, Hakamada Shigeki on the attitudes of the Soviet people, Wada Haruki on the reexamination of Soviet history, Akino Yukata on new Soviet thinking about international relations, and Hasegawa Tsuyoshi on Soviet-American relations and the Soviet military. In each case, these are world-class experts who follow their chosen topics with dedication and professionalism. Some are advisers with direct input into the establishment. Others are better known as critics, whose writings call for policy changes. All are prominently featured in the media and the leading journals, both popular and scholarly.

The second type are the commentators who are most outspoken for particular viewpoints. The extreme right of the political spectrum is well represented in the media and has access to the establishment. The far left speaks through its own journals and through occasional books, which lack the sensational titles and popular appeal of books from the other side.

The third type are those currently in government office and closest to official thinking, mainly Soviet experts at the Gaimushō such as Tōgō Kazuhiko, the head of the Soviet desk from July 1988. In a few cases, they write under a pseudonym (Saga Tōru). Mostly, however, they present their views under their own name in both government publications and the media. While not exposing to public view internal debates over policy, they often reveal individual approaches to Soviet or international issues not directly contradictory to established policy.

As seen above, politicians hungered to play a personal role in Japan's most significant international breakthrough of the postwar era (with the possible exception of the renewal of ties with China in the 1970s, but that occurred in the shadow of Kissinger's secret diplomacy), while diplomats cautiously steered the formal side of relations, and academics and journalists struggled in their writings to shape the response of the public below and the decision makers above. It is primarily through these writings that one can detect the changing tone of relations.

The Japanese debate on the Soviet Union signifies a democracy at work. A smorgasboard of ideas is set before the public. When these are uncomfortable for the establishment, as epitomized by the Soviet desk, its primary recourse is to respond, directly or indirectly, with ideas of its own. A dialogue unfolds between state and society, changing rapidly as new developments occur around the world. Over the six-year period, the establishment has not dictated the terms of debate or the pace of change in perceptions. It has not been monolithic, although on the central question of the Northern Territories it has acted with sufficient unity and consistency to deliver an unmistakable message to the Soviet people. Support among the Japanese public has wavered to some degree on various issues related to the Soviet Union, yet the state has kept adequately in touch with popular thinking to maintain a broad consensus on the policies that matter most. Above all, the powerful symbol of unjust Soviet occupation of Japanese territory has eased the job of managing Soviet policy in a time of flux. The establishment emerges from six years of intensified debate with no serious challenge to its authority.

CHAPTER THREE

The Spectrum of Political Debate

IN THE FIRST decades of the postwar era it was customary to divide Japanese into two sharply opposed forces on the left and the right. In views of the Soviet Union and socialism, polarization was pronounced for more than a decade and only gradually receded through the 1960s and 1970s. Many gradations along a continuum are now needed to appreciate Japan's diversity, and even these need to be reconsidered as the end of the cold war is playing havoc with traditional distinctions.

The right is now divided among those who continue to see the Soviet Union as the principal enemy, those who think more about ending dependence on the United States, and those who want to reassert Japanese regional leadership and pride in prewar traditions in the face of opposition from China. The left has been split into diehard supporters of communism now angry at Gorbachev, loose advocates of remnants of socialism eager for successful Soviet reform, pacifist isolationists disinterested in the Soviets, pacifist internationalists eager to help the Soviets, and an idealistic new left ready for a Japanese role in international peacekeeping, including cooperation with Moscow. Differences on pacifism, internationalism, identification of a principal threat, and other global issues are becoming muddled across the middle of the spectrum as well.

A CONTINUUM FROM RIGHT TO LEFT

At one end of the spectrum is a far-right group, whose most vocal elements were disappointed by the Washington and Moscow summits of December 1987 and May 1988, were negative on Soviet-American arms agreements, and stand in favor of vastly increased military expenses for Japan. The far right refuses to trust the Soviets. This group is well represented among such commentators on the Soviet Union as Nakagawa Yatsuhiro, who finds only lies in Gorbachev's statements,[1] Uchimura Gōsuke, a Japanese POW long incarcerated in Siberia and later influential as an author and critic at the intersection of literature and politics; and Nasu Kiyoshi, a publicist who suddenly in 1990 appeared correct for having insisted for years that the Soviet Union, which is immoral and not God-fearing, is doomed to collapse soon.[2] Less extreme is Teratani Hiromi, whose television commentaries and books on Soviet life feed Japanese prejudices about the negative Soviet national character and about the unlikelihood that Moscow will follow through on promises to let Eastern European countries find their own way.[3] The far right was a highly visible force in the Soviet field, but has been losing ground.

Interestingly, at least up to 1989 the extreme right was best identified as a supporter rather than an opponent of state policies. Apart from a small fringe group that favored freezing ties with the USSR and harassing Soviet diplomats, the prevailing response was to modify rather than replace the existing framework of great-power relations. This can be accomplished not through isolationism or abrupt military build-up, but through combining close cooperation with the United States with greater Japanese independence in certain areas of foreign policy.[4] Confidence in Japanese cultural superiority is not allowed to displace identification with the values of the "free world." Most in this group favor acceleration in the Japanese military build-up and, if necessary, constitutional revision to legitimate it, but, after all, this is what Washington has been pressing Tokyo to do, and it is consistent with a more active leadership role in the alliance. To be sure, a minority in this category carry their doubts about the United States further, insisting that Japan cannot rely on the United States and should reject the postwar order. Central to this option is the need for Japan's own nuclear weapons and the ability to confront the Soviet Union.

The far right worries that the Japanese public will not remain steadfast in the face of propaganda. It is concerned with the battle over information and public opinion. Long-standing complaints that the national newspapers are too soft on socialism resurface in objections to coverage of Gorbachev.[5] Some also seem to reason that it is traitorous for a Japanese to propose a compromise on the Northern Territories issue, which might weaken national resolve and diminish Soviet awareness of the need to meet Japan's demands. Responding to the spreading debate over the Soviet Union, forces at the right end of the spectrum are trying to hold together the coalition on the right and to keep the entire left isolated on the fringe. To make their case the far right often warned of new outbreaks of Soviet aggression. For instance, in the 1980s Niwa Haruki forecast that later in the decade there would be further aggression. The inaccuracy of his forecast was viewed as a sign of the failure of the right.

By 1990, the collapse of socialism was far enough along to cause some on the right to look beyond the agenda of common cause with Washington against Moscow. They were now wondering how to diminish dependence on the United States while filling the vacuum left by Moscow's retreat. In the Persian Gulf War the right was thrown on the defensive by the groundswell of resistance to any semblance of Japanese military assistance, although there was also a large faction on the right lukewarm to such aid because it might alienate the Arab world, where Japanese interests are considerable.

The Right of Center. The right of center differs from the right wing in its greater support for the status quo, especially a steady but not provocative increase in military expenses, and in its limited ambivalence about the May 1988 Moscow summit. Although still pessimistic in late 1987 and 1988 about the prospects for Soviet-American disarmament, the right of center favored cautious exploration of new opportunities and considered it possible for gains to be achieved.

As I indicate in the breakdown into periods in chapters 6–8, some figures in the right-of-center category could scarcely be differentiated from the less extreme right wing in 1986 when Gorbachev's reforms were still at an early stage, while by the second half of 1988, in the face of new evidence of Soviet flexibility, some figures from the right wing were shifting to the right of center, and some pessimists originally to the right of center were finding new hope and shifting to the center. Mood shifts continued as short-term tendencies came to the fore, but more and more people began to expect international breakthroughs toward arms reduction and a favorable fallout for Japan from Gorbachev's reforms. A focus on mid-1988 captures the midpoint in the three-phase transformation (awakening, uncertainty, confidence), when the right of center was still quite pessimistic but willing to go forward. Kimura Hiroshi is perhaps the best-known scholar in this category, and it was soon after the Nakasone visit to Moscow in July 1988 and his own followup visit in September that he turned cautiously optimistic.

The right of center supports Japan's gradual assertion of a more prominent world leadership role. It firmly sides with the West for reasons of morality as well as power politics, although doubts about Western society and its political process leave room for uncertainty about a long-term convergence of interests. There is no sign that persons in this category want to stir up Japanese nationalism. They favor using Japan's economic strength to pressure Moscow into change and, if Moscow does not yield, to persuade Washington to proceed slowly with negotiations so that the pressure becomes more intense. Confident that time is on Japan's side, they are more patient and cautious than Japanese further to the right in handling Moscow and more hesitant to arouse the distrust of Washington. Their scholarship also is more balanced, weighing options rather than resorting to unflinching advocacy.

The mainstream on the right of center is shifting from a status quo orientation to an active approach to managing a new Soviet relationship in the context of a changing world. It was not well prepared for this transition and was, at first, slow to contemplate the ramifications, however compelling the force of events. The preference is for an orderly, managed approach to the Soviet Union, relying on the establishment to lead, but not excluding a diversity of opinions for popular reflection.

The Center. At the center of Japan's political spectrum are individuals who welcomed the Moscow summit of May 1988 and were optimistic about arms reduction prospects. Representative of this outlook among Soviet commentators include persons in the Gaimushō who had learned from experience of the inflexibility of the Soviet desk in their ministry and were seeking a more open-minded response. Academics with unusual career experiences also stand out among the centrists. Hasegawa Tsuyoshi, who spent about a decade teaching Russian history in the United States before returning to Japan to become an active contributor to debates about the contemporary Soviet Union,[6] is a good example. Hakamada Shigeki, who completed the course of studies at Moscow State University after graduating from Tōkyō University, is another.[7] Overwhelmingly "home-grown" products cannot be completely excluded. Uda Fumio, who once taught the NHK television Russian-language program, is noted for his fair-minded coverage of Soviet society.[8] It is not that these centrists fail to take a strong stand, for they often do. What distinguishes them is their openness to new developments in the Gorbachev era, their sympathetic but also critical outlook on Soviet history and contemporary life, and their obvious concern for objectivity without a consistently formulated conclusion. Some of the students, such as Shiokawa Nobuaki, who had been active on the left in the 1960s, had shifted by the Gorbachev era to the center or perhaps slightly to the left of center.

There has been no burst of optimism from the center about the prospects for perestroika's success. Long hopeful about Gorbachev's commitment to push ahead, scholars at the center were often among the most pessimistic about short-term improvements in the Soviet economy. They have no overt political agenda for Japan, even if one can surmise that many are ardent advocates of internationalization and thus are more eager to see change in the establishment and openness in policy debates, perhaps comparable to that in the United States.

The Left of Center. The left of center, along with the right wing, is the most vocal advocate in debates over the Soviet Union. It is firmly rooted in academia, including a veteran group known for their praise in the 1960s of some major aspects of Soviet history and a younger generation trained at that time by the veterans. The list includes Wada Haruki, a historian at Tōkyō University who has led in popularizing the thought of current Soviet reformers;[9] Satō Tsuneaki, who often contributes articles on the Soviet economy to the Japanese media;[10] Shimotomai Nobuo, who is active in developing a discipline of political science in Soviet studies;[11] and Kikuchi Masanori, typical of the intellectuals who once sympathized with the Soviet revolutionary tradition, then showed a preference for the purer revolutionary course of China's Cultural Revolution, and finally turned negative toward socialism in general, even including rejection of Gorbachev as too socialist.

Academic activists to the left of center embrace the cause of transforming Japanese policy, scholarship, and opinions on the Soviet Union. If they support the Japan Socialist Party, they do not do so as utopian progressives typical of the 1950s and 1960s but as spokesmen for a revamped foreign policy line based on adherence to pragmatism as well as alertness to changing opportunities. Unlike some timid progressives of the past concerned about offending Moscow and some apolitical business interests ready to make a yen for themselves and their merchant nation from any direction, they have been formulating a principled position in favor of measured responses to Soviet reforms. In the opinion of these academics and journalists with similar views, Japan could avoid isolation from the West, as it became cozier with Gorbachev, by taking initiatives of its own and, through its leadership, can encourage reform forces in the Soviet Union.

Scholars to the left of center cannot be easily equated with either American democratic liberals or Japanese politicians of any party. Some have their roots in the old JSP, once sympathetic to the theories of Marxism and to the student movements opposed to American militarism, including the Vietnam War. They may have entered Soviet studies to satisfy their political ambitions, studying the Russian Revolution, Marxist theory, or early Soviet history to extract the purest features of socialism. By the second half of the 1980s these scholars had lost much of their naiveté, but they often remained idealist about achieving a new world order, about finding an alternative to the rightist control of the LDP, and about distancing Japan from American right-wing pressure. Essentially they spoke as individuals, not as part of any organized revival of a leftist alternative to the establishment. In fact, they fell between the two stools of the old socialist left, no longer capable of inspiration, and the cautious LDP, too long secure in power to excite idealists. Through the force of new information about a changing world, these individuals hoped to inspire their fellow citizens. When Moscow lurched to the right early in 1991, these Japanese felt let down.

The Far Left. At the extreme is the old left, which retained its fascination with socialism through the difficult years in the second half of the 1970s and the first half of the 1980s and, despite, in most cases, agreeing that Moscow should abandon its hold on the Northern Territories, opposed Japanese policies toward Moscow. Emeritus professors figure prominently in this camp. Taniuchi Yuzuru, earlier of Tōkyō University, trained many who are now on the left of center and, through detailed scholarship on the 1920s, led in the effort to separate good socialism from the bad wrought by the Stalinist deviations.[12] Acting as an individual rather than as part of an organization, he rarely published in the mass media or journals. Usami Shoichirō, earlier of Hokkaidō University, became very active in the Japan-Soviet Society (NisSo Kyōkai), which worked to promote friendship and dissemination of the Soviet viewpoint after its formation in 1957. Close to the Japan Communist Party in its outlook, this association continued to stress the achievements of the Russian Revolution in contrast to the serious problems that plague capitalist countries.[13] Some current university professors such as Mochizuki Kiichi, a specialist at Hokkaidō University on the theory of the Soviet economy,[14] can also be counted in the relatively small far-left camp.

Some Japanese may discern in these true believers in a type of socialism little more than pitiable relics of an age that has passed. Nothing they had to say seemed any longer of interest to the public. Whereas during the early 1980s' revival of cold war tensions, a feeling of heroism for a worthy minority cause that was consistent with the mood of postwar pacifism may have sustained some on the left, this was not easy to reproduce in the Gorbachev era as international socialism came crashing down. Even the claim to be the prime bulwark in favor of the postwar democracy and against a resurgent Japanese militarism has little credibility left. Yet recent signs of a rise in Japanese superpower mentality and intense debates over Japan's response to the Persian Gulf War are already prompting a new identification with international ideals of peace that bear some resemblance to the opposition currents in the old left.

A *Shifting Continuum.* This five-step continuum can be seen on three levels: public opinion, publications, and the foreign policy elite. The level of public opinion is most variable; there has been a gradual convergence on the middle range, with a decline in extreme positions. Part II considers the year-by-year changes in the polls, and chapter 13 reviews the sources of these changes. At the level of publications, the extreme right was disproportionately represented but receding, the extreme left was struggling to remain visible, the left of center and center were gaining ground but still a minority, while the right of center retained the leading position. Scholarship on the contemporary Soviet Union gained, reducing the role of sensational, extreme writings. The right of center was most strongly represented in the foreign policy elite, while the groups on the left remained weakest at this level.

Ultimately the quarrel among these groups over the Soviet Union is a dispute over Japan's future. The right is worried about a population growing soft, susceptible to Gorbachev's "peace attack" and to defeatism. The new youth *shinjinrui*, popularized by the media, are a growing concern to the older generation because of a decline in the work ethic, a rise in consumption-oriented priorities, and gradually spreading social pathologies such as crime and divorce. The "Western disease" is infecting Japan to the alarm of some who associate it with softness toward the Soviet Union.[15] The left worries about the incomplete state of postwar reforms, leaving believers in renewed militarism, narrowly conceived moral education, and bureaucratic intolerance well-positioned to reimpose their values. If Japan remains spiritually mobilized to face Moscow, according to the left, its democratic character may be threatened. Unlike the 1950s, the threat of the spread of Soviet values among the Japanese is not now in question, except to a tiny minority at the extreme right. The struggle unfolds between competing visions of the prewar past and of a possible convergence in the future with the West.

Faith in communications separates the left of center from the right of the political spectrum. On the one side, after Shevardnadze's 1990 visit Shimotomai Nobuo argued that at this critical time, through hard work to change mutual images, new Soviet-Japanese relations can be created. A psychological confrontation must be overcome. Despite an improved image of the Soviets in Japan, it does not yet function when actual problems arise. To solve the territorial question not just government efforts are needed. Shimotomai stresses the role of parliament and autonomous citizens' exchanges. He claims that improved relations are a test for all Japanese.[16] On the other side, Sono Akira bemoaned the outpouring of sweet talk in the mass media during the Shevardnadze visit, which has been aimed at breaking the mood of resignation among the Japanese people through "friendship" propaganda. In his view, the people cannot be trusted. Concessions by leaders can confuse the people, who might not only trash Japan's territory but even throw capital into the bottomless pit of a flawed system—in both ways making Japan the laughing stock of the world.[17] By 1990 the scholar Shimotomai was being taken more seriously than Sono, a voice of the past. But in early 1991 Shimotomai seemed excessively optimistic as skepticism was again on the rise.

The dialogue between opposing views has now widened. Polarization typical of the 1950s no longer poses a problem. The far left shows no signs of resuscitation. The far right declined with the intensification of Gorbachev's reforms and with increased Soviet flexibility toward Tokyo. Instead of polarization or a wide-ranging spectrum, one can discern two fluctuating modes of thought not very far from the center of the spectrum and uncertain prospects for a possible third mode further to the right. For clues about a new Japanese worldview one should look closely to the emergent conservative views on the right of center, which are likely to remain dominant, and to the potentially liberal left of center, which may continue to be weak and divided. Yet it is also useful to keep the extremes in mind, particularly the far right, because their views may be incorporated into a changing amalgam, if either Japanese-American or Japanese-Soviet relations turn sour. Also one needs to remember that there is no political party that clearly represents the liberal segment, nor is liberalism yet well rooted in the society. There is still a strong linkage between pacifism and the left. A middle-class society is changing the political debate, but that does not exclude a distinctive Japanese cast to perceptions of the Soviet Union.

ACADEMIC FISSURES

In comparison to the vast reach and diversity of English-language writings on Japan or Russia, the literature in both Japanese and Russian is, to a great extent, self-contained. Writers are keenly aware of what has been published previously. They have been firmly grounded in the existing terms of debate. However strong lines of division between rival academic centers and orientations may be, there is an awareness of community that fosters communication centering on a well-delineated set of themes. In Japan this common tradition can be clearly seen in the study of Russian and Soviet history. There is an association that has met annually since 1956 and also provides for regular seminars, in some years as frequently as once a month. The annual meetings focus on several topics at the forefront of research; the organizers have been deeply involved in association activities since its inception or since their own student days, and each year's themes are chosen in awareness of the past history of topics. The journal *Roshiashi kenkyū* (Studies in Russian history) offers a collective memory because it not only presents separate articles, but also—especially in the years of major anniversaries such as 1986 when the association celebrated its thirtieth—reflects on the state of the field. Every year the journal *Shigaku zasshi* (Historical studies) presents detailed reviews of the past year's publications in medieval, modern, and contemporary Russian and Soviet history, as well as reviews for every other region in the world. There is a keen consciousness of the collective history of Japanese scholarship.

At the same time, there is also a rapid "internationalization" of scholarship. In the 1980s interactions with Soviet specialists in the West increased dramatically. Cross-publications, visiting researchers, joint projects, and a sense of involvement in an international division of labor became commonplace. Even in their specialty of Soviet-Japanese relations, Japanese scholars closely followed foreign publications.[18]

Despite many commonalities in a homogeneous society with a shared core of information, the community of Soviet-watchers has remained deeply segmented. Mistrust and lack of communications persist as the legacy of the polarization after World War II. The fissures are not simply the left versus the right. The intellectuals and the masses, the academics and the journalists, the academics and the business community, the academics and the diplomats, and the separate associations of academics working among themselves have established boundaries that have not been easy to cross. Wherever one looks in the world of academia, signs of fragmentation abound. As Kojima Shūichi observes, bitter ideological disputes among Japanese intellectuals have exerted a strong influence on Soviet studies.[19]

The Division of Labor. Japanese Soviet-watchers have established an unusually sharp division of labor. Scholars concentrate on highly specialized fields, leaning toward theory and history.[20] In this way, they realize some success in avoiding ideological conflicts within their own field or association and remaining within their own like-minded circle. Other groups fill in some of the gaps. With the historians preoccupied with the abortive possibilities of Russia's revolutionary tradition and the origins of Stalinism, journalists were left with the task of explaining contemporary politics. Coverage of the interval between the mid-1930s and the 1970s remained skimpy. Without a movement to link diverse disciplines to area studies, sociology, anthropology, and other fields were largely ignored by academia; again journalists and also travelers with personal experiences to recount filled the void. Vast areas of Soviet life were omitted; systematic methods were nowhere in sight.

Since the formal study of the Soviet economy was made into abstruse theoretical discussions about socialist concepts, the business community keeps its own close watch over trade figures and economic projections. This left the structure of the Soviet economy and the prior history of reform attempts understudied. Lacking a developed field of expertise on bilateral relations, the academics yielded to closed-door deliberations of the diplomatic community, but not without misgivings. Meanwhile, the popular critics (*hyōronka*), with national reputations earned through wide-ranging writing for a mass audience, held tightly to a virtual monopoly on discussions of the global issues related to Soviet power. Their standards for evaluation of internal Soviet debates were often not very high.

One by one the artificial boundaries have been falling since 1985. Scholars have seized the abundant opportunities of the Gorbachev era. High-quality Soviet studies are bursting forth. As Shiokawa Nobuaki writes, Sovietology, which long was inclined toward historical research, under the influence of perestroika has directed its energy to the study of the contemporary era.[21] Japanese debates on recent Soviet developments have reached a high standard even if there remain glaring omissions. In a span of five years it is not possible to fill all of the gaps and transform all of the traditions in the field.

University Structure. The organization of Japanese universities works against the application of area competencies to contemporary social science problems. Studies in the humanities and social sciences at universities are divided into three macro departments: Law, Economics, and Literature. The Law faculty is also the home to political scientists and sociologists. The Economics faculty is where one teaches economic history, a wide-ranging field that includes much institutional history. The Literature faculty is the center for research on historical thought and the study of revolution. Area competency is well-developed in the Literature faculty, but those who have it are often obliged to spend much of their energy on language instruction.

In the other two departments generalists are frequently given precedence. The area experts who are present often teach general courses with little opportunity to teach about their region. This is one reason why their scholarship is likely to stick close to the path forged in graduate studies. The vacuum they leave is filled by non–area specialists, who base their claim to expertise on a general background in their disciplines. This is fertile soil for popularizers who lack in-depth knowledge and find it advantageous to cater to the public mood. Good scholars exist, but the academic environment is not conducive to their development as specialists and members of a regional program. Combined with the popular preoccupation with the "Soviet threat," this atmosphere drove scholars into a closed world of historical studies for other specialists.

Academics have less power to make decisions about hiring, course offerings, and reorganization of the program structure than is common in major American universities. University life is relatively bureaucratized. At the same time, in response to rising demand for international relations courses on the Soviet Union, former correspondents and, occasionally, former bureaucrats are recruited to teach at private universities, where a concern over the leftist leanings of established academics can often be detected.

A Groundswell in Soviet Studies. There has been a recent groundswell in the Soviet studies' community to take control over the destiny of their field. To overcome fragmentation and poor research conditions, meetings have been held, petitions signed, reports issued, and comparisons published with the state of Slavic studies elsewhere.[22] In the late 1980s Soviet specialists felt a sense of frustration and urgency, but had yet to find satisfaction for their demands. Having emerged in the confrontational atmosphere of the 1950s and 1960s, Soviet studies have never been fully institutionalized. As Kojima remarks, there are only seven Japanese universities with a department of Russian studies and language, and only one interdisciplinary institution of Soviet studies attached to a university, namely, the Slavic Research Center at Hokkaidō University.[23] Students also must contend with the "minus image" of suspicion by business firms that they have been tainted "red" by their studies; the major firms continue the practice (common in the era of the student movement in the 1960s) of weeding out political activists, new religious movement devotees, and others who cannot be trusted to accept the paternalistic community of the firm.

For much of the academic community, the prime concern was not how to influence the political debate on the Soviet question, but how to develop a democratic and scholarly communications flow appropriate to an "internationalized" society—to a new Japan that is a superpower, a leading country in the world of scholarship, and a product of the emerging "information society." They sought to open up the foreign policy establishment at the top, making its deliberations more public and accountable and expanding the foreign policy elites that have an input. In addition to concern with the information flow connecting to the top, they sought to improve the flow downward for an informed populace. The Gorbachev era gave reason for hope, above all, because Japanese opinion shapers were overcoming their own squabbles. After 1985 there was an explosion of information about the Soviet Union. Simplistic images of the enemy gradually yielded to better-informed views. Gaps in available information were, in many cases, covered. One milestone was reached in late 1989 when *A Dictionary to Know Russia and the Soviet Union* appeared; it covered 1,500 items, with well-coordinated, up-to-date articles by specialists.[24]

Eliminating the Scholarly Gap. Who is to blame for the universally acknowledged weakness of Japanese academic studies of the Soviet Union? Even if one recognizes that the field has improved considerably since the 1960s and particularly in the 1980s, the question cannot be put aside because the consciousness among specialists has now focused on the target of narrowing the gap with the highest world standards, as befits a country with Japan's emerging international responsibilities and bilateral problems with the Soviet Union. Some officials in the Gaimushō lay part of the blame on the Ministry of Education (Mombushō), which has direct responsibility. Through much of the postwar era this ministry, in its battle with the teachers' union and its attempts to revise textbooks on World War II, has symbolized the conservative thrust in the government. Most recently, hopes for educational reform, discussed for three years by a commission formed by Nakasone, were frustrated by this ministry.

Others appear to be at fault too. Academics assert that by preferring to train its Soviet specialists at Harvard and in England only after they have joined the government fresh out of university with no area specialization, the Gaimushō is bypassing its own country's programs and has no stake in improving them. In negotiations with Moscow, it has dragged its feet in expanding scholarly exchanges (finally there was some expansion in

1989) and in other measures to boost Japanese Soviet-watching outside of its own Soviet desk.[25] Having more experience living in Moscow and a monopoly on access to classified information, the Soviet desk can then display "information arrogance" in dismissing the competence of academics. Only in the last few years of frenetic changes that seem to render last year's knowledge quickly obsolete have the "old Soviet hands" trained by the government been losing the rationale for their special claim to authority.

The Mombushō has followed a traditional course of focusing studies on the models that Japan has chosen to pursue. Single-minded catching up narrows Japan's vision. Unlike the United States, Japan does not have a tradition of studying its enemies; for example, studies of the United States were not developed in World War II.[26] Since that time, area studies of China (drawing on a strong prewar tradition) and Europe and America—Japan's traditional models—have been most advanced. Despite the fact that Russian studies began in Japan in the eighteenth century, before studies of the West, the field had a low priority. Now that Japan is becoming a superpower, critics contend, this state of affairs is intolerable.

In the finely stratified hierarchy of Japanese society, Soviet desk officials, who, as a rule, have passed the entrance examination of the Law Department at Tōkyō University and then met the tough requirements and further examination standards of the Gaimushō, are close to the pinnacle. They have the credentials for expertise. It is not easy from the outside to assess the quality of their deliberations, but if the speeches and interviews of recent officials are placed alongside the writings of veterans, the critics appear to be right in their doubts. Privately they contend that the diplomats do not visit the Soviet Union early enough, when they are most impressionable, and fail to develop close Soviet contacts through long stays and informal interactions. The lack of first-hand knowledge applies to the whole country of Japan; with few exchange programs, most academics have had slight contact. In 1980 when four million Japanese tourists were beginning the tourist boom to many spots around the world, only thirty thousand went to Japan's nearest and largest neighbor.

Consistency or Rigidity? The Japanese bureaucracy lauds itself on its three consistencies, while its critics find fault with what they see as three rigidities. The Gaimushō is proud of: (1) its continuity in personnel; (2) its consistent image of the Soviet Union; and (3) its unwavering negotiating stance. In other words, a select group of Soviet specialists has retained its influential position in the Japanese government, remaining firm against recurrent Soviet propaganda to create a more favorable image, and insisting on Soviet concessions on the Northern Territories. When "Gorbachev fever" struck the American populace at the time of the Washington summit of December 1987, these officials could scarcely suppress their exasperation that the Americans were once again succumbing to the roller coaster of political gullibility. Although, as indicated below, some showed concern about the Japanese public's vulnerability, most took satisfaction from the fact that Japanese opinion was more steadfast in adhering to the distrustful mood of the first half of the 1980s.

Critics charge the Soviet section in the bureaucracy with stubborn indifference to changing circumstances. Continuity in personnel and consistency in viewpoint are taken as evidence of a closed clique. Inflexibility toward Soviet negotiators and disregard for contrasting evaluations from the scholarly community are treated as symptoms of arrogance. Critics complain about the rigidities of: (1) a closed circle of foreign service officers who cut themselves off from the scholarly community; (2) a closed mind-set not based on careful attention to the shifting tides of Soviet thinking; and (3) a lack of debate about alternative approaches to better relations. In turn, the Soviet affairs "clique" centered in the Gaimushō does not recognize the academic specialists as genuine experts on contemporary issues relevant to bilateral relations, nor does it look favorably on publications that suggest divisions inside Japan on the major topics under contention, especially how to approach the Northern Territories issue. The core of the establishment has often dismissed the critics as themselves lacking real knowledge of Soviet conditions and as living in an imaginary world of theories without a deep understanding of international politics.

Whether it was the Gaimushō or the Mombushō, or a combination of both, that lacked the vision to support strong centers of Soviet studies and diversification to meet vital needs in social science research on the contemporary period, the academic community showed its resilience in the late 1980s. The popular thirst for information has enticed many Soviet experts to fill unmet needs. Even without guidance, the market succeeds, to a degree, where democratic institutions such as freedom of the press are working well. Yet the task of establishing scholarly programs worthy of a superpower, for training and research as well as international collaboration, is still far from complete.

CHAPTER FOUR

The Information Society

THERE ARE three recognized major national newspapers in Japan: the *Asahi shimbun*, the *Yomiuri shimbun*, and the *Mainichi shimbun*. Large numbers of high school as well as university graduates read them, and in a society with an extraordinary level of mass educational achievement this provides for a remarkably homogeneous distribution of information on politics. The fact that all of the papers have a national constituency (five to ten million readers), that they are similar in format and intellectual level, that they have evening as well as morning editions, and that many intellectuals read two or three of them daily,[1] adds to the homogeneity.

There is a second group of national papers, which also figure importantly in this coverage, with some scoops on the Soviet Union. The *Nihon keizai shimbum* emphasizes economic news, including stories about Soviet perestroika. The *Sankei shimbun* offers extensive coverage of individual political opinions, especially in its "Seiron" column, which is carried also in the monthly journal with that name. Known for views on the right, this paper's many interpretive columns by outside and in-house authors (once read to learn a viewpoint and now among the best sources of information, as indicated by the award of the Japan Newspaper Guild's prize for news reporting in 1990 to its reporter Saito Tsutomu) add significantly to the political dialogue on socialism.

Regional papers also need to be consulted. The *Hokkaidō shimbun* follows Soviet issues, especially the neighboring Soviet Far East. The *Tōkyō shimbun* occasionally learns of new Soviet thinking from interviews with Moscow academics.[2] Papers from the southwestern regions of Japan tend to be less oriented toward Japan's northern neighbor.

The minor papers of *Sekai Nipo* on the far right and the declining *Akahata* (Red flag) on the far left air Japan's most extreme thinking. They are tangential to the popular debate yet help to sustain a wider spectrum of thinking. For Japanese who follow international affairs closely, it is not unusual to read, at least occasionally, all three of the major papers, one of the second group of national papers, and one of the regional papers. The two minor papers cater almost exclusively to believers in their partisan views.

Relying heavily on the press, Japanese are well-informed about the ongoing developments in the Soviet Union. When a major event occurs, one or another of the national papers as well as some journals will gather together two or three academics or "critics" for what is termed a *zadankai* (round-table discussion)—a media seminar to air what are often contrasting impressions. Editorials on the Soviet Union have appeared frequently in recent years. Although they do not usually convey a clear alternative to existing policy, they reveal noticeable differences among the papers. Through the press, citizens can receive direct guidance on how to interpret the Gorbachev era.

Analysts and polemicists alike argue that the newspapers do influence thinking. Indeed, although there is a high rate of television viewing in Japan, and news summaries appear in both the early morning and the evening, there is little discussion about the impact of the visual medium. The reports tend to be brief and noncontroversial, and the more audacious critics (*hyōronka*) usually appear at odd hours, such as Sunday morning, when viewers are few. They are more visible on the occasion of Gorbachev's summits with American presidents, but this is not enough to alter the reality of a population that digests its news largely through reading.

Reciprocal Impact of News on the Soviet Union and the United States. Kobayashi Yoshiaki presented an analysis in 1988 of mass media news and party support, studying coverage of the Soviet Union and the United States from 1973 to 1980 in the *Asahi shimbun* and *Yomiuri shimbun*.[3] He drew on enumerations of media articles for their frequency, their length, and whether they are pro or con for each country; monthly surveys of the population's views of each superpower; and monthly surveys of party support. The analysis revealed a causal relationship, affecting party support, and a reciprocal relationship whereby negative information on the United States (especially during the Vietnam War) was accompanied by an increase in the positive response to the Soviet Union. Kobayashi also found that negative articles have a greater impact than positive ones, with some effect of negative articles on the USSR in increasing dislike for that country, although the effect was muted by the fact that Japanese were used to such articles.

After 1973–74 Japanese views of the Soviet Union grew increasingly negative. Employees and university graduates responded to criticisms of that country by becoming more negative about it and turning more positive about the United States, which led them to shift their political support from the JSP to the LDP or to nonsupport for any party. Although JSP support was more anti-American than pro-Soviet, it was not aloof to the deterioration of the Soviet image. Kobayashi found, too, a correlation between increasing worker dislike for the Soviet Union and support for the LDP. Managers and the self-employed did not seem to be affected, while service workers responded primarily to unfavorable newspaper coverage on the United States. Rural residents became more negative about the Soviet Union as articles grew more critical, but this did not affect their political support. As expected, on a month-by-month basis, attitudes toward the United States fluctuated more than those toward the Soviet Union, indicating that both those against and those in favor of Moscow had become relatively fixed in their thinking. Obviously, much more is involved in choosing one's political allegiance than information from the two major dailies (and presumably evidence of the changing reality of Soviet policies). Nonetheless, given Japanese reading habits, it is likely that no other sources of information mattered as much. Kobayashi concludes that personal communications play a more limited role in politics in Japan than in the United States; correspondingly, the media has a bigger effect.

THE DEBATE ABOUT THE PRESS

Press Responsibility for the "Hate Rate." At the start of the Gorbachev era, attention to newspaper coverage of the Soviet Union was growing. The initial impetus came from the left, disturbed that public opinion polls revealed a phenomenally high "hate rate" toward the Soviet Union, with just about 5 percent of Japanese indicating that they like the Soviet Union while 60 or even, at times, up to 80 percent expressing a dislike.[4] After remaining virtually silent during the previous five to ten years of increased antipathy, critics on the left began to speak out as the Gorbachev era commenced. One of them, Nakamura Kenichi, writes that the Soviet Union has a scary and distorted image with little to counter it available to the Japanese people.[5] Japanese know the country only through the dimension of power. It has become a "one-dimensional" country. Nakamura suggests that Soviet children's movies be aired and portraits of Soviet people be presented to give Japanese a taste of Soviet life and mass culture. He further claims that in addition to Soviet government actions that damaged the country's reputation, the dislike and fear have been artificially fanned, with consequences for Japan's role in the world, not just bilateral relations. The successful campaign to blacken the Soviet image serves political interests in Japan and creates a closed consciousness, even a narcissism, contributing to the notion that the outside world is stagnant and disorderly and the Soviet Union is violent, while Japanese are civilized.

In the press itself, there is a critical spirit about one-sided and misinformed images of Soviet socialism that long prevailed in Japan and a call for a firm foundation for informed judgment.[6] The criticisms may be directed at the theorists on the left as much as at the nationalists on the right.

A Perception Gap. The theme that Japanese newspapers were failing to balance their critical coverage of Soviet foreign policy and politics with material to humanize or provide a long-term view of the Soviet people was repeated elsewhere, leading to concern about a perception gap. Eventually there were Soviet efforts to exploit this concern, such as by *Pravda* correspondent Yuri Vdovin writing in a Japanese publication.[7] Yet as Soviet reforms accelerated, criticisms of Japanese papers from outside and from the Japanese left declined.

While academic specialists continued to bemoan the hysterical "anti-Soviet" attitudes of the Japanese people, they tended to blame the mass-oriented popular literature rather than the newspapers. At about the time Prime Minister Nakasone visited Moscow for Chernenko's funeral and returned impressed with the new Soviet leader, Gorbachev, and eager to continue in personal correspondence with him, the *Yomiuri shimbun*, closely identified with Nakasone, apparently shifted its coverage. In any case, the daily news from Moscow became forward looking in ways that soon drew the attention of the Japanese people. The *Asahi shimbun*, traditionally more favorably inclined to Moscow, attentively followed Gorbachev's reform initiatives, and, in the keenly competitive world of Japanese journalism, the other leading papers refused to be left behind.

Charges of Soviet Disinformation. Soon it was the far right of the political spectrum that took exception to the press coverage. This raised the spectrum of Soviet disinformation—an old theme dating from the early postwar era when starkly contrasting images of Soviet socialism had been projected to the Japanese people. In 1983 Sono Akira, the veteran Soviet desk diplomat and ambassador to West Germany and other countries, complained that the left-leaning mass media had not reformed. For that reason Japanese people were signing antinuclear petitions by the tens of millions and in many cases were deceived into hoping for improved relations with Moscow on terms that followed Moscow's notion of friendship. Sono objected to positive coverage of Yuri Andropov and, in general, to receptivity to an intensified Soviet public relations strategy, as reported by a KGB defector. Cooperation also affected the television network NHK, which agreed to cover a trip on the Siberian railroad even though it was not allowed to film rundown places. Sono foresaw a strong psychological impact on the Japanese people from such propaganda.[8]

In 1988 Sono carried this argument further in an article explaining why he does not believe the newspapers.[9] He proposed that since World War II the growing information society has created a second, cheaper means of defeating the enemy in addition to military weapons. It is wrong to concentrate only on the military threat because the information bullet, however difficult it may be to see, can also destroy Japan's prosperity. The Communists wield an advantage in psychological warfare because they do not have free papers. They have used the nuclear danger to frighten the world, at times arousing excessive anxiety in Western Europe and Japan and leading especially the intellectuals, badly wounded by the bullets, to seek the goodwill of the Communists through defeatism and unilateral disarmament. Through the hegemony of leftist education and the free publicity in left-wing papers (the major dailies apparently included), Japanese are ignorant of the real Soviet Union. Now the psychological pressure has been renewed in the media's response to the INF agreement suggesting that a new détente exists. Sono emphasizes that the Japanese people are victims of the media and of international specialists who are merely echoing Gorbachev.

Another harsh rebuke to the press appeared in early 1987. Sakurai Yoshiko begins by asserting that, in the new circumstances of the Gorbachev era, more accurate information on the Soviet Union is needed. But this cannot be expected, since Japan's Moscow correspondents cherish sweet illusions about socialism. Based on articles in the three major newspapers in the spring of 1986, she finds little coverage by the correspondents of the Soviet military, frequent repetition of Moscow's criticisms of the United States, and little on dissidents and other subjects sensitive to Moscow. She explains that the reporters have secret understandings with their hosts that lead to taboos as well as to failure to fill in gaps in their reporting. They slant their coverage to stay in Moscow, which, as Soviet specialists, is the only place they can use their skills. Moreover, they are sympathetic to communism. Finally, if they did fail to heed Soviet warnings, they would lose privileges and access to interviews, and face isolation, without the benefit of support from the Tokyo office—a matter of protection of freedom of the press that other foreign papers would routinely provide.[10] Sakurai's accusations appear more plausible in the light of the self-censorship of the Japanese press in covering the Chinese Cultural Revolution and later developments in that country and also of the story of how *Asahi shimbun* failed to support its Moscow correspondent, Kimura Akio, during the Brezhnev era. Yet given the barrage of Soviet self-criticisms in the Gorbachev era, this article serves primarily to convey the frustration on the right that the Soviet Union no longer generates much news to sustain the theory of an "evil empire."

From the right one could hear that the *Asahi* is Japan's *Pravda*.[11] This paper, the *Mainichi*, and the *Hokkaidō shimbun* were accused of being uncritical of the Soviet Union. From the left one could hear that *Sankei, Sekai Nipo*, and several leading monthlies such as *Shokun, Bungei shunju*, and *Seiron* are old-style nationalistic publications, "anti-Soviet" in their approach. Such labeling preceded the Gorbachev era and has diminished with the new complexities of the post–cold war era. Yet, in 1992, when the *Asahi shimbun* called for "realism" through progress in stages and the *Tōkyō shimbun* editorialized in favor of a "cool head," looking to bilateral relations in the next century, the newspapers continued to press the government and to draw criticism.[12]

The journal *Sekai* devoted its February 1991 issue to the question, "have newspapers declined?" In recent coverage of the Middle East crisis, the UN response, and Japan's imperial succession, it noticed a failure to raise difficult questions. Authors blamed the Gaimushō for calling for press restraint at a time Japanese hostages were being held in Iraq. They also blamed Japanese sentimentalism for making the thoughts of the Arab side the foremost issue and mainstream conformity for quickly identifying a central issue that squeezes out other themes. Instead of leading public opinion into new lines of thinking, the papers trailed it and failed to set an agenda.[13] *Sekai*'s contributors charged that the papers are too much a part of the establishment and too little conscious of minority views, and, perhaps even more seriously, they fail to identify main points clearly.

Declining Interest in Bias. In contrast to the views expressed at the extremes, the middle ranges of the political spectrum appear to be little concerned with unduly biased press coverage. Japanese public views are shifting gradually, but not stampeding into Gorbachev's arms. Officials generally seem to have retained confidence that support for national policies will remain firm. The mainstream press is cautious in editorializing or straying much beyond the national consensus.

Increasingly, Soviets were meeting with Japanese reporters and stating their views in Japanese journals and newspapers. On the whole, the Soviet establishment sought to raise Japanese hopes. Representative of this approach was *Pravda* editor Ivan Frolov's interview on September 3, 1990, promising that Gorbachev would bring with him to Tokyo "something historic," followed by Japanese officials seeking to quiet any expectations with comments that there is little indication that the Soviets are inclined to return the islands.[14]

While on Soviet issues the differences among papers were not pronounced at the end of the 1980s, they widened again in early 1991. At the same time as sharp disagreements separated the relatively pacifist *Asahi shimbun* from the *Yomiuri shimbun*, which joined the LDP mainstream in supporting the United States in the Persian Gulf war, the question arose of how to handle the backsliding in Soviet reform and in prospects for concessions when Gorbachev visited. *Asahi* stood for keeping ties with Moscow moving forward without applying pressure. In contrast, *Yomiuri* and, even more, *Sankei shimbun* were quick to recognize the setbacks and to approve of not making premature concessions before Moscow had the resolve to deliver on the islands.

Television can also be used to arouse interest in improved relations. After all, in Japan as elsewhere, an increasing number of people are turning to television rather than to newspapers for interpreting the news. According to a 1990 NHK survey, whereas five years earlier newspapers were in the lead, television was now ahead 52 to 37 percent.[15] Eager to attract Japanese capital to underdeveloped areas, the Soviets have permitted filming through a wide region in the Soviet north. NHK produced a "superspecial" documentary called the "Hokkyokken" (North Pole ring), which was shown once a month over a year in 1989 and 1990. Three quarters of the broadcasts centered on the Soviet Union, including the development of Siberia in the days of imperial Russia. A series of books also appeared in conjunction with the widely advertised television programs. Such shows soon lost their novelty as political statements. By 1989 the controversies over media bias had receded.

A question of principle remained. Scholars warn that correspondents do not state their views candidly, since they worry that they might lose access by undercutting relations with Soviet officials and would not receive support from their editors. Rather than meeting Soviet intellectuals as friends who share a common interest in world culture, they tend to exchange presents for information and remain quite aloof from the intellectual community itself.

Competition in coverage of Soviet events intensified over the second half of the 1980s. To gain an edge, the major dailies: (1) vied to present and even to generate the latest public opinion poll; (2) carried and often organized international symposia to anticipate new developments; (3) rewarded Soviet reformers for giving them the scoop on the newest advance in Soviet thinking, especially related to bilateral issues; and (4) gained access to the islands, photographs of former Japanese POWs, and so forth. Vigorous reporting, even to the point of generating news, but not concocting it, made the newspapers the medium of greatest significance. After the announcement of a date for Gorbachev's visit, the competition became more heated. Even while carrying Soviet initiatives, the papers often worried about Soviet propaganda. For instance, on the front page of the *Yomiuri shimbun* next to the lead article on the release of four hundred POW photographs appeared an article on the Soviet aim to soften Japanese public opinion.[16] The lead article also editorialized in its final sentence by reminding readers that for Moscow to dissolve Japan's negative legacy, it must make public all documents and acknowledge its complete responsibility.[17]

THE GENERAL-INTEREST JOURNALS

In the postwar era the major debates about emotionally charged political issues have been played out in monthly general-interest journals (*sōgō zasshi*). They enjoy a sizable readership (circulation from about 100,000 to as many as 700,000 copies), including large newsstand sales (increased by their prominent display at a vast number of kiosks and bookstores and by ads on the first pages of the daily papers detailing their lead articles). These are not weekly news magazines that regurgitate the main stories covered in the press with some added color. Japan has those in abundance, and they too take on some of the atmosphere of the general-interest monthlies because their readers are already sufficiently familiar with the basic news that further commentary is essential. Editors target the general monthlies at arousing or heightening debates.

The monthly medium must entice the readers with a provocative viewpoint—catchy and even sensational titles on articles are not unusual. The articles do not, as a rule, constitute full-fledged scholarship. The aim is to air opinions that will attract the general intellectual community, not only specialists with a commitment to one field of inquiry or one world region. A survey in the late 1970s found that about 30 percent of Japanese intellectuals read three or more monthly journals, while almost an equal percentage read one or two.[18] Each month a floating community of at least a few million potential readers scrutinizes the titles of the latest think-pieces for general consumption and makes its choices. Since the Meiji era the general-interest journals have taken the lead in shaping the opinion of Japanese intellectuals.

Intermittently since World War II the Soviet Union has been a favorite subject of the general-interest journals. To no one's surprise, the Gorbachev era has brought it to the forefront again. Soviet specialists as well as the ubiquitous critics on international relations fine tune their arguments for easy digestion. Forty or fifty names—those of professors, journalists, former Gaimushō officials, think-tank analysts, and free-lance writers known simply as critics—recur in the tables of contents of these journals, and these same authors carry forward their analyses on the Soviet Union in the weekly magazines, in other monthlies that offer secondary exposure, and occasionally in the roundtable discussions of the daily press.

In fact, a full appraisal of Japanese coverage compared to that in other countries might well show many areas of superiority: in speed of publication of monographs on recent developments, in timely encyclopedic reference publications, in reporting on bilateral and multilateral public opinion polls, and in expert commentary available in newspapers and weekly and monthly journals. A bibliography of publications in 1989 identified 108 monographs plus 40 book-length translations and close to 2,000 articles. The leading commentators, such as Hakamada Shigeki (17 articles) and Shimotomai Nobuo (16), as well as many authors with 5 to 10 articles each, followed a similar pattern. They wrote a monograph at least once every two or three years, several articles each year in serious academic journals (usually quarterlies) and edited volumes, several articles in popular monthly journals, several in weekly news journals, and also timely contributions to the daily newspapers.[19] The popular or general-interest monthlies served as the linchpin in the development of this rich flow of information.

While the monthly journals are still lively, their role has declined from their heyday in the 1950s and 1960s. Especially the journals on the left have lost popularity, leaving the generation of ANPO (*anzen hoshō*, the movement against the security treaty with the United States that peaked in 1960) as their readership. Youth prefer television and other easy sources of information. American-style weekly magazines, such as *Japan Newsweek*, have filled a part of the void.

Rival Journals with Distinct Audiences. Kojima Shūichi published an academic article in 1988 devoted to the coverage of the Soviet Union in the general-interest magazines in the postwar era through 1983. He reviewed four journals: *Sekai*, critical of the LDP and sometimes sympathetic with socialism while targeted at university teachers and students; *Chūō kōron*, diverse in its contributors and in its audience of business leaders; *Bungei shunju*, with by far the largest circulation and a decidedly conservative posture attractive to much of the business community; and the now defunct *Tenbo*, which rarely covered the Soviet Union. Kojima found consistent differences in viewpoint among the journals and major turning points in Japanese perceptions over about three decades, which I will discuss in chapter 5.

He asserted that changes in the Soviet Union, rather than the traditional image of Russia and the USSR or changes in Japan, are most significant in inducing new attitudes among Japanese intellectuals.[20] When the number of articles peaked in 1956 and 1968, new thinking collided with the old. Views that had been shaped with little knowledge of actual Soviet conditions succumbed to expanded information and to disturbing new Soviet behavior. In his conclusion Kojima also redirected attention to postwar Japanese intellectual history, asserting that "the most important single fact . . . is that the shift of the Japanese approach to the Soviet Union was related to the changing modes of thought in postwar Japan."[21] Even if Japanese were responding to real changes in the USSR, what mattered most were the intellectual currents in Japan. The general-interest journals provide an ideal venue for following these changes.

The world of general-interest journals is subject to frequent changes. On the whole, journals on the right have fared better than those on the left. *Bungei shunju* has cleverly broadened its readership by printing centrist authors and some who, on particular issues, venture well to the left, such as Nakajima Mineo, who published a provocative compromise solution for the Northern Territories problem. This journal has also spawned an offshoot in *Shokun* with a more trenchant rightist outlook. Of the newspapers that have entered the market of monthlies, *Sankei*'s *Seiron* is well established with frequent political commentary on the Soviet Union. *Asahi shimbun* has begun its own journal, *Asahi*, which should add a voice on the left of center. *Chūō kōron* shifted somewhat to the right after a new editor took charge. On the left only *Sekai* still plays an important role. In Brezhnev's time the journal had almost fallen silent in covering the Soviet Union since there was little to praise; to join in the criticism would only please the right. Some Japanese say that Gorbachev is a god-send for *Sekai*, helping it reach beyond the students of ANPO who, as school teachers and in other "intellectual" positions, form a steadily aging core of readers. Whereas Kimura Hiroshi from the right of center often appears in *Seiron*, Shimotomai Nobuo, to the left of center, is a frequent contributor to *Sekai*.

Burning Issues to Excite the Reader. Through the monthlies one can trace a succession of burning issues dating from the start of the Gor-bachev era. At first there was the usual interest in who is the new leader and what are the problems he faces. Behind this inquiry rested the doubt that the new leader could make any real difference in the Soviet Union. With the announcement of Foreign Minister Shevardnadze's visit in Janu-ary 1986, a debate arose about Soviet-Japanese relations. How does Mos-cow treat the Japanese? Will it change its approach? Are the Japanese prepared for a new era? Curiosity about developments inside the Soviet Union became more intense late in 1986 and in the first half of 1987 when articles explored what is perestroika and can it succeed. By late 1987 excitement swirled about the INF treaty and the new debate in Soviet-American relations. In the second half of 1988 attention reverted to Soviet-Japanese relations. In mid-1989 it had somewhat shifted to Sino-Soviet comparisons and the Soviet role in the Asia-Pacific region. Speculation swirled through the journals. Is Gorbachev a hoax to trick the world? Is there a danger of a Moscow-Washington conspiracy? Should Japan settle for two islands? Are Japanese immersed in mispercep-tions of the Soviet Union? Is communism dead? Hardly a month passes without efforts to arouse new excitement. Part 2 of this book draws on these monthlies and other publications, from newspapers to books, to review the chronology of changing images.

Mass-oriented Books

The battle between right-wing exposés and left-leaning sympathetic treat-ments has also been starkly visible on the shelves of Japan's bookstores. In the first half of the 1980s the far right and right of center had the politics and foreign policy displays almost to themselves, along with foreign translations. One sensational paperback after another left a depressing account of Russian life, not only rightfully decrying the harsh conditions of daily existence but also one-sidedly overlooking the persistence and spiritual strength of those struggling for something better. In the aftermath of the dispatch of Soviet troops to Afghanistan, writers could find no bounds to future expansionism and treachery—books about the forthcoming invasion of Hokkaidō and even a Soviet nuclear attack on Japan[22] carried this penchant to an extreme. Although more sober-minded writers showed mundane aspects of daily life and possible limitations on aggression, there was little direct refutation of the hysterical literature.

By the second year of the Gorbachev era the battle had been joined. Soviet specialists, many long disturbed by the tone of the popular literature, tried their hand at writing for the masses. Their goal was to narrow what had been an enormous gap between the outlook of the Russian and area studies experts in the academic community and the population at large. Given the expanding market, editors, eager to satisfy curiosity about unexpected Soviet developments, pressed scholars to reach out to a wider audience. It was often historians and others not previously noted for their studies of current events who accepted the challenge. They did not altogether forsake their historical interests since they were able to show the enduring significance of historical issues in the Gorbachev era.[23]

Reviews faulted historians for failing to connect prerevolutionary and postrevolutionary history, for eschewing theory based on empirical findings, and for overlooking overviews of recent history. Yet even in these critical state-of-the-field articles, there was often mention that the field had advanced a long way since its takeoff in 1956.[24]

Academic paperbacks over a period of roughly two years put the Japanese intelligentsia through a crash course in the basics of the contemporary Soviet Union while, in one way or another, addressing the question of what is perestroika. Shimotomai Nobuo contributed a substantial review of political science theories previously in vogue in the Soviet field and of the character of the Soviet political system,[25] Wada Haruki surveyed Soviet intellectual life and the cast of reformers in the academic and literary fields,[26] Hakamada Shigeki probed the social psychology of the Soviet people and social class differences,[27] and Kimura Hiroshi continued his active role as a commentator on Soviet leadership prospects and foreign policy.[28] A foundation of basic knowledge now was in place for upgrading the debate over new Soviet developments.

By the summer of 1988 the press was reporting on a boom in Soviet publications. In a ten-month period as many as fifty books appeared on the Soviet state and system or on Secretary Gorbachev, said one report. The Japanese edition of Gorbachev's own book had sold 150,000 copies in eight months. "Anti-Soviet books" were also selling well, the article added.[29]

In late 1990 the newspapers were still reviewing the latest state of Soviet studies in Japan. One article explained that, according to Uda Fumio, they still were inferior to those in the United States, but recently the level had risen.[30] Glasnost had made much accurate data available, translations were more numerous, and lately a "publishing rush" had shed light on the crisis of reform.

SPECIALIZED SCHOLARSHIP

A 1988 analysis by Matsuda Jun takes a close look at the personnel in Soviet studies, beginning with a list of over 1,200 names.[31] Not surprisingly, it finds a predominance of males (89 percent) at the university level and in research. (The figure drops to 83 percent if junior colleges are included.) Persons in their fifties are most numerous. Before 1945, the field scarcely existed; thus, few are much older than sixty today. The lack of job openings and declining interest among youths, however, means low numbers in their twenties. A successor problem exists. Politics and international relations are poorly represented in comparison to history, economics, and language and literature. But this problem is not unique to Soviet studies among area studies since enrollments in the literature department (*bungakubu*, including most history) are high in general.

In Chinese there are twenty or more journals on the Soviet Union or comparative socialism.[32] In Japanese there are only a handful. The major journal for historians, *Roshiashi kenkyū* (Research in Russian history), is nearly three decades old. Yet the new contemporary-oriented journal, *Soren kenkyū* (Soviet studies), is a product of the Gorbachev era. In the absence of many specialized outlets, articles are scattered among dozens of university bulletins and disciplinary journals. The lack of appropriate journals hinders the sustained advance of cumulative research.

Soviet experts in Japan are becoming more involved in international exchanges. Translations from foreign languages have increased. When articles cause a sensation in the West, reverberations quickly spread through Japanese publications. Nonetheless, the internal Japanese debate remains distinctive. If less self-contained than earlier, it still has its own traditions and outlook. These concerns include comparisons with Japanese history, interest in the historical roots of Soviet behavior, fascination toward Soviet involvement in the Asia-Pacific region and especially long-term Soviet-Japanese relations, and an orientation toward the implications of recent changes for Japan. Internationalization is coming.

For many from the left of center to the right of center, one way to resolve problems in Japanese perceptions and relations with the Soviets is to increase the flow of information—to scrutinize and debate the reality of that country. As Shiokawa Nobuaki asserted, one hundred flowers are blooming in Japan, leaving unresolved what standards should be used by each person.[33] Some turn optimistic, others turn pessimistic. Old political divisions often do not hold. The information era has arrived.

A genuine national debate is in progress. Intellectuals from many circles—bureaucrats, politicians, academics, and many others distant from foreign policy concerns—are well-informed about the progress of the debate. They follow the central papers in which most of the arguments first appear. The wider community knows the cast of active discussants, their latest viewpoints, and even how others received them. In comparison to the sporadic debates in the United States centering on a president's policies and perhaps the views of a few other officials or former officials, the Japanese cast of debaters, numbering in the dozens or, by some calculations, even over one hundred, operates on a national stage before an avid audience and it sustains a lively and sustained discussion.

PART TWO

A Chronology of Changing Perceptions

CHAPTER FIVE

The Historical Background

RUSSIAN-JAPANESE contacts can be traced back almost three hundred years. The Gorbachev era marks one of the infrequent periods of intense activity and reexamination that punctuate the long periods of resistance by one side to the other and of little momentum in bilateral relations. Japanese have not welcomed Russia as a neighbor, have avoided normal neighborly contacts, and have expressed suspicions about Russia's intentions. Even when Russia has inspired the Japanese people as a world center, this has not led to good-neighbor feelings. In reacting to the new developments of the Gorbachev era, the Japanese are influenced by this long history of mixed but, on the whole, suspicious feelings.

The End of the World. Russia's relentless march eastward reached the Pacific in 1639 at about the same time as Japan's determined turn inward culminated in the policy of *sakoku* to close the country except for a tiny island in Nagasaki harbor open only to the Dutch. The most irrepressible territorial advance in world history coincided with the most secluded self-imposed isolation of a major country. The Russian advance continued to the northeast into the Kamchatka peninsula at the end of the century and down into the Kurile Islands in 1711. Discovering a shipwrecked Japanese on Kamchatka, Russians took him back to the new capital at St. Petersburg and, with Tsar Peter's personal support, opened a Japanese language school in 1705. In contrast to Japan's policy of seclusion, Russia's eagerness for contact could be easily detected.

Russia and Japan first met in perhaps the most remote, sparsely settled frontier in the world, except for Antarctica. Their proximity in Kamchatka and the Kuriles might be called a meeting at the end of the world. Neither country initially placed a high priority on the region. While its existence made the two nations close neighbors, it did not give them a sense of shared interests or (for the Japanese) of advantageous border trade. Perhaps no boundary in the world dividing major countries has been so little crossed for so much of the history of neighboring settlements. End-of-the-world neighborliness produces a spirit different from other frontiers.

The Russian "Complex." The Mongols briefly frightened Japan in the late thirteenth century with two invasion attempts, the Spanish and Portuguese raised alarm in the late sixteenth and early seventeenth centuries with plans to carve up the world, and next it was Russia early in the nineteenth century that caused officials to reflect on national defense. This was the beginning of the Russian challenge or, as one writer puts it, the "Russian complex."[1]

THE LEGACY OF PREWAR PERCEPTIONS

In the early eighteenth century the Japanese discovered that they had neighbors to the north, apart from the Ainu and other tribal peoples. Already familiar with the European seafaring nations and their unreciprocated enthusiasm for expanded contacts with Japan, the Japanese authorities could not have been altogether surprised that Russia also sought ties with them. Yet there was no immediate alarm about the proximity and seriousness of the new threat.

Japanese indifference did not give way to concern until the 1770s. A Polish baron fleeing Kamchatka in 1771 falsely warned the Japanese that Russia was preparing an attack. By this time Russians had occupied some of the Kurile Islands, but their interest in Japan centered on trade. Whatever the intent, their mere presence stimulated rumors, which provoked a Japanese literature on the "northern problem." Should Japan build its defenses in the north and prepare to resist? Should it sell rice and meet other economic demands because it is too weak to refuse? Who are the Russians and what are their real intentions? The questions of the 1780s about those called the "Red Barbarians" were remarkably similar to those raised two centuries later. Catherine the Great sent Lieutenant Adam Laxman in 1792 as her official envoy to return additional castaways and seek commercial ties.[2] Yet, for political not economic reasons, the bakufu refused. To maintain the political order and stability as it was, Japan rejected the Russian overtures.

Typhoon relations made it possible for Japanese to learn about the Russians, as they had assisted Peter the Great and other Russians in learning about the Japanese. Occasionally Japanese swept far off course by typhoon winds were found by Russians, and more than once sent across the vast reaches of Siberia, given access to intellectual life in St. Petersburg, and then either remained as language teachers or returned to Japan. After returning with Laxman, Captain Kodayu became a Russian expert whose knowledge soon produced a book for the Tokugawa era audience. Other books quickly followed, drawing on Dutch and even Chinese sources. Unlike Dutch studies, which was the name given to Japanese writings on the West that mainly focused on the sciences, Russian (or Ezo) studies centered on geography, history, and the military.[3] They marked the beginning of area studies in Japan.

To date, more than half of the two and one-half centuries of Japanese perceptions of Russia comes from the vantage point of Tokugawa self-imposed seclusion. Except for a tiny number of shipwrecked Japanese fishermen and a few Russian adventurers who tested the waters before being warned or driven away, images were not based on actual interactions. From the outset, Japanese saw Russians through the eyes of their Western, more developed competitors. Translations of Dutch books provided a filter for vivid impressions that the Russians were coming and a rather unflattering image of their backward state. A long-term history of oppression, geographical expansion, military expeditions, and stereotypically brutish national character filled the pages of such accounts.

On a map, the huge mass of Russia, reaching down close to Japan's shores, towers over the small slivers of islands that comprise Japan. An alarmist literature such as Hayashi Shihei's *Discourse on Defense of a Sea Nation* appeared as early as 1792. With virtually no direct or even indirect recent experience with the outside world, Japanese were understandably apprehensive.

In 1804 Nikolai Rezanov, another Russian, arrived with a new group of shipwrecked Japanese. When Japanese refused his plan for trading relations, he raided northern settlements to frighten them. In retaliation, the Japanese captured Captain Golovnin and held him for two years before a prisoner exchange was arranged. Using his presence on Hokkaidō, officials began to train Russian experts and to expand their area studies materials.[4] Although a lull in relations of half a century followed, a "Russian complex" in the Japanese people had been born.

Russia as One of Many Teachers. For the sixty-odd years from the Treaty of Shimoda signed in 1855 to the Treaty of Portsmouth of 1906, the two Northeast Asian countries grew to know each other increasingly well. Vice-Admiral Putiatin followed in the wake of Admiral Perry; in 1855 Russia had its own treaty opening Japan. In the early 1860s Japanese began to travel to Russia, and Russians grew active in sponsoring studies of their country in Japan. Father Nikolai, who arrived in 1872, had an influential role in educating Japan's Russia specialists, a small Japanese colony in St. Petersburg from the mid-1870s provided travel accounts and other information, and Japanese government schools soon graduated an impressive cast of experts.[5]

Seen through the eyes of modernizers eager to reform conditions then considered to be backward, neither country made a big impression on the other. Russians continued to look to the West, where development was most advanced, while Japanese decided after scouring the globe for appropriate models, that the Russian way would not do for any of its planned new institutions—administrative, financial, military, educational, etc. In the main burst of wholesale borrowing, Russia did not play a central role as a teacher to Japan. A government journal in 1865 classified Russia with Portugal and the United States in the second level of enlightened countries (*kaika no kuni*), between the enlightened countries (*bunmei no kuni*) in most of the West and the semi-enlightened countries (*hankai no kuni*) such as China, India, and the northern African states.[6] As far as the Japanese state was concerned, Russia was an inappropriate model for its march toward civilization. Yet, Wada Haruki suggests, this was not always the case. In the Tokugawa era Japanese had discovered from Dutch sources about Russian history a single message of immense significance: the model of modernizing reforms to catch up to the West.[7] In 1838 Sakuma Shōzan suggested that Peter the Great had Westernized Russia in a single generation, a prospect soon to appeal to Japan's leaders.[8]

Increasingly, the Japanese people also saw Russia through the eyes of the individual looking for an understanding of the world and through the eyes of the artist seeking models for literature and drama. Already in the late 1880s and 1890s, translations of Pushkin, Tolstoy, and Turgenev were gaining a large following.[9] With qualified translators from Russian in short supply, Japanese turned to English, German, and French translations of the originals. The still fledgling Meiji literary culture was deeply affected. There was a close spiritual affinity. Russia finally became one of Japan's teachers.

Two directions of interest developed simultaneously. Led by Hasegawa Tatsunosute (Futabatei Shimei), who in 1888 translated Turgenev into colloquial Japanese and followed with as many as thirty more translations of Russian works, the literary school gained enormous popularity. Indeed, Peter Berton and his coauthors suggest that although Russia lost the war in 1905, it soon conquered Japan through its literature.[10] With the interest in literature, especially in Tolstoy, who became the most popular of all, arose a fascination with the Russian outlook on social problems and its philosophy of life. In the years before the Russian Revolution, there was much interest in pacifism, anarchism, and social movements in general. From this foundation a favorable outlook on socialism emerged among the new Japanese intelligentsia.

Russia as Adversary. Xenophobia reached panic proportions in the 1850s and 1860s. Even in the 1870s, fear of an invasion and colonization was not inconsequential. Former ambassador Niizeki Kinya recently described England, France, and Russia in the 1870s as tigers ready to pounce if Japan should fall into disorder.[11] Such prominent Meiji figures as Mori Arinori and Fukuzawa Yukichi were among the earliest visitors to Russia who succumbed to Russophobia.[12]

After Russia joined with Germany and France in the triple intervention to deny Japan some of its expected fruits from the Sino-Japanese War of 1894–95, a second tendency in Russian studies along with interest in literature and social thought also became pronounced. Closely associated with applied governmental interests and often with the special needs of army intelligence, this tradition may have been second only to Chinese studies in the Japanese list of area study priorities. Both long predate substantial area study programs in the West. In the late 1890s, the Amur Black Dragon Society sponsored this Japanese interest in Russia. When Japanese took over the Manchurian port of Dalian in 1905, they gained a good base for Russia watching, from a city supplying library resources, Russian speakers, and a strong Russian identity. The South Manchuria Railroad Company led by Gotō Shimpei developed rapidly after 1917. Under its auspices, the Harbin Institute became an extraordinary area studies training center, which graduated six hundred Russia specialists between 1922 and 1937.[13] Just as Western Soviet studies eventually drew on émigré knowledge, the Japanese utilized the émigré resources of Harbin.

Indeed, in 1986 a Soviet specialist, Nonomura Kazuo, wrote a book reflecting on the experience of the Manchuria Railroad research bureau and exploring the need for the creation of a similar large-scale research unit today.[14] This is a subject of no small interest in the current era of no substantial research centers in Japan for Soviet studies.

For many decades Japanese officials perceived the Russian military as Japan's chief rival for influence and direct control on the Asian mainland. After a second treaty clarified the boundary between the two countries in 1875, competition for power in Korea and Manchuria rapidly accelerated. When Russia began construction of the Trans-Siberian Railroad in 1891, Russophobia developed rapidly in Japan. That same year the "Otsu incident" in which a Japanese policeman injured the visiting Russian heir apparent, the future Tsar Nicholas II, indicated the depth of antipathy.[15] One after another disputes flared as the two countries competed for imperialist goals—spheres of influence, ports, railroad construction, and direct control or colonization. Japan won, but without a sense of genuine satisfaction; its citizens felt frustrated in both 1895 and 1906 that Western powers were siding with Russia in denying Tokyo some of the spoils of its wars. Russia was an adversary whose motives were much disparaged by the Japanese, claiming to act in defense of their brethren in East Asia.

Russia as a Special Teacher. Nakamura Yoshikazu and his coauthors are among a growing number of Japanese who regard the study of the history of Russian/Soviet relations with Japan as one of their specialties. In their writings one can find an unusually positive image of past perceptions and relations. For instance, the 1987 volume *Japan and Russia* fits into this mold. The first article in the volume, by Akitsuki Toshiyuki, challenges the impression that Japanese have traditionally felt only threatened by Russia. She traces back to the Tokugawa era the expression of feelings of friendship toward Russia as a country that could be trusted.

At roughly the same time as a Dutch man spread the erroneous story that Russia planned to invade, a returned shipwrecked Japanese reported that Russia was not using military means to expand its territory and that Catherine II should be understood as a tsar who could achieve this through benevolence and concern for nomadic peoples. At that time there was only faint consciousness of the lands in question being Japanese, and few people expressed the view that military defense against advancing Russians was needed. According to this argument, not worry about Russians but economic aims primarily led Japan to take initiatives in the north. The origins of pro-Russian views in the 1850s and 1860s can be seen in this division of thinking about whether Russia's earlier intentions were aggressive.[16] Other articles in the 1987 volume point to favorable Russian images of Japan. Sasaki Teruhiro describes the view of a member of the Narodniki movement that Japan could have its own movement of this type and could use its own traditions to modernize, if it were to turn away from excessive respect for superiors and a lack of individual personality.[17]

Nakamura may have in mind the possibility of a second dramatic upturn in the years just ahead when he writes about the first decade of this century as the time of the sharpest turnabout in the views of Russia held by Japanese. From 1900 to 1905 feelings of antagonism toward tsarist Russia dominated in Japan. Then, following the peace agreement that ended the 1904–1905 war, attitudes began to improve. Nakamura recounts that even in the war years, interest in humanistic Russian literature did not slacken much. After the war the progressive part of Japan's intelligentsia inclined to socialism and anarchism considered Russian revolutionaries who were struggling bravely against autocracy to be their teachers. While in the atmosphere of hysterical anti-Russian agitation that gripped Japan from 1900 to 1905 there were many books arousing Japanese against Russia, a more "objective" opinion could be found among others, such as those who understood the significance of Russia as a state that could shed itself of tsarism and establish socialism.[18]

The decade before the Bolshevik Revolution stands as an interlude in Russo-Japanese relations. The rivalry between intersecting imperialists in Northeast Asia faded before a mood of alliance and mutual sympathy oriented toward worldwide and social concerns. Many Japanese grew to admire the creativity of Russian intellectuals, and not a few also sympathized with the struggles of the Russian people for a new social order. Taishō democracy lifted individual Japanese fascination with the very things the Russian people symbolized: the articulation of generational differences (*Fathers and Sons*) about confronting the sharp contradictions between old and new ways, sentimentality in values about preserving nature (*The Cherry Orchard*), the elusive search for a macrohistorical view to make sense of human drama on a world stage (*War and Peace*), the introspective problems of man's uncertainty about his purpose in life (*The Brothers Karamazov*), efforts to right injustices associated with official red tape (*Dead Souls*), and so forth. The Japanese realized their affinity for the worldview conveyed in Russian literature more than for any other foreign outlook.

Russia as an Ally. From the conclusion of the Russo-Japanese Treaty in 1907, Japanese diplomacy relied heavily on the new friendship, which in 1916 became a close wartime alliance. For a decade this relationship became the centerpiece of Japan's international relations. Friendship organizations met, and for the only time in history close neighborly ties linked Vladivostok and Sapporo as well as other, more distant cities.

Even after the Russian Revolution and the Siberian Intervention by Japan, which had brought the two countries into direct conflict for a second time, a faction in Tokyo sought to revive the pro-Russian policy as an alternative to the Washington system negotiated in 1922, which excluded the Soviets from the planned world military order. In the mid-1920s Moscow hinted at a Russo-Sino-Japanese alliance to exclude the West. Common interests in Manchuria, access by Japan to oil concessions in North Sakhalin, and the Japanese navy's perceptions of the United States as the primary potential enemy all made Moscow appealing to some Japanese. Although they were in a decided minority, their arguments helped to develop a pragmatic course for a time. When the Soviet-Japanese Basic Treaty of 1925 restored relations, Foreign Minister Shidehara rejected a confrontational approach to Russia and resisted countermeasures against the Comintern in China. For about five years stable relations followed, although both governments were increasingly turning toward militarism.

Russia as Target of Aggression. As Japanese policy toward North Manchuria became more aggressive, Sakai Tetsuya finds, the army pressed for a tougher stand towards Moscow. The demarcation between the two countries' spheres of influence in China, as agreed in 1907, was no longer acceptable to Japan. The Japanese intervention in China soon provoked a deterioration in relations. At first Moscow was conciliatory, but after Moscow resumed relations with Washington and won a measure of cooperation in the Pacific while rapidly building its own defenses, it could afford to be more resistant. At the same time Tokyo perceived that the USSR was again a formidable foe. Another period of internal debate ensued before the army pushed Japan into an "anti-Comintern" policy, straining Soviet relations.[19]

The "Red Scare." After the revolutionary change of November 1917 and the dispatch barely a year later of Japanese troops as an expeditionary force to Russia's Far East maritime zone, the lines were drawn for a direct clash between two images of Japan's northern neighbor. On the one hand, an increasingly militaristic Japan revived the image of rivalry and threat, conjuring up the "red scare," which had some basis in the reality of messianic communism organizing a local party in Japan and fanning the fires of revolution in China. Censorship tightened in the 1930s to control information about the Soviet Union. As Japan's war machine marched deeper into Asia, it squared off against Soviet troops and, with the specter of a northern war not far in the background, fought a large battle at Nomonhan in 1939. This battle should be seen as a major factor affecting the course of World War II.[20] Soundly defeated by Soviet troops, Japan was encouraged to turn its aggression to the south. The Hitler-Stalin pact of 1939 also played a role. Japanese ambitions for a greater East-Asian Co-Prosperity Sphere had threatened to unleash war against the Russians; now Moscow was spared the disastrous prospects of a war launched from both ends of the country. For four years from early 1941 a neutrality pact operated between Moscow and Tokyo, without much affecting the negative, anti-Communist image held by most Japanese.

The Red Hope. While official relations were tense and suspicious, the frustrated aspirations of Taishō democracy were becoming identified with the radical ideology of worker and peasant opposition to capitalism. Intellectuals, in substantial numbers, turned to Marxism for a worldview to overcome oppression at home and expansionism abroad. Two types of romanticism fused; the literary and revolutionary aura of Russia combined to achieve wide authority. The harsh realities of Stalinism were not yet well known or easily believed when they filtered through the often inaccurate lens of domestic censorship.

During the early 1920s, the return of veterans of the Siberian expeditionary force gave Japan its early news of the new Soviet state. In the still open conditions of Taishō democracy much excitement could be aroused. Young intellectuals turned to the study of the social sciences and Marxism. The Communist movement as well as various proletarian parties gained an important following. After 1930 many of their journals were closed—even reading the writings of Lenin or Stalin might be risky—yet many in the intellectual community retained a deep commitment to the Marxist worldview.[21]

Among some Japanese, as among intellectuals in the West, there arose a fascination with Soviet industrialization in the 1930s. In the midst of a negative or "despising" tendency among many other Japanese and the mutual tensions associated with Japan's advance into Manchuria, the excitement of state mobilization in the name of the entire people appealed to Japanese who found their own state's claims of this sort to be hollow. Disillusionment with Western individualism and Japanese militarism drove many idealists to look wistfully at Soviet socialism.

The threat of socialism has assumed diverse forms in the minds of Japanese authorities and conservative groups. Prior to 1917 socialism was but one of the various systems of thought that opposed the existing political order in Japan. Relying on censorship and repressive measures against organized opposition, the Japanese government succeeded in keeping the socialist movement small and excluded from parliamentary politics. It saw socialism as a threat to the centralized and well-ordered society that had developed in Japan, and it watched as the socialist movement splintered and anarchist tendencies came to the fore.

Three factors combined to intensify the perceived threat of socialism in the 1920s. First the victory of the Bolshevik Revolution gave socialism a home, both as a model to emulate and as an agent to support Communist party members in other countries. Although initial reactions to the events in Russia were confused, the Soviet state became a rallying point by 1922 when the Japanese Communist Party was founded. Second, the deterioration of the Japanese economy, after a period of rapid expansion to fill foreign markets left without European suppliers during the war years, brought riots and protest movements to Japan on an unprecedented scale. Uneven economic performance led to agitation by workers and by tenants' unions, which took illegal forms due to the government's continued hostility to a participatory democracy. Again in the Great Depression from 1929 a mood of economic crisis and severe social problems spread among some groups in Japan's population. Finally the era of Taishō democracy and the early Shōwa years as well gave people experience with more representative institutions, but at the same time clearly revealed how far Japan remained from genuine participation of the masses. In the eyes of many, bourgeois democracy was discredited—because it failed in Japan to realize its own principles and because its individualism and conflict orientation were at variance with Japanese social relations.

The prewar Japanese state suppressed the organizations supported by the Communist party, including labor unions, tenant farmers' associations, and other mass political movements. As many intellectuals were attracted to the Marxist critique of the empty shell of bourgeois democracy in Japan, the Japanese right became convinced of the need for harsher methods. The government imprisoned many activists. Nonetheless, in the decade 1927–37 the Japanese state did not exercise the vice-like grip on publications and education that increasingly could be found in the Soviet Union. Marxism was hotly debated and gained a strong foothold among intellectuals, particularly in university departments in the social sciences and humanities. As Germaine A. Hoston writes, it was an "appealing intellectual system and political program."[22] The facade of Japanese democracy, the ready degeneration into militarism, the lack of redress for economic grievances through legal organizations, and the continued moral concern for the development of Japanese society without egoism and individualism all undermined belief in reformism and in capitalism. The intense prewar debate established the background for a revived pro-Marxist movement after August 1945. Marxism represented not so much an organization that mobilized the masses as a way of looking at the world that claimed to explain the causes of domestic and international problems.

THE FIRST POSTWAR DECADE: 1945–55

For the first forty-five years of this century, Japan's focus centered on East Asia and the fruits to be gained by military strength applied there. Russia and the Soviet Union figured as the chief rival just beyond the region but claiming a stake in it. For the past forty-five years Japan's worldview has focused on the West and the fruits to be gained by economic strength applied there. The Soviet Union again entered the picture as the chief enemy, an outsider prepared to disrupt the West's and Japan's plans. Moscow was ready to export revolution to a vulnerable Japan shaken by defeat, it was eager to keep a reemergent Japan a regional outcast by making the Asian mainland north of Hong Kong uniformly Communist-controlled, and it was prepared to flex its growing military superiority to pressure a now economically strong Japan. No wonder the enemy image carried forward from the prewar to the postwar era.

Stalin's Gloating. Stalin gloated in September 1945 at Japan's expense. He claimed that the Soviets had defeated Japan after waiting forty years for revenge; they had erased the humiliation of 1905.[23] The events of 1945 became an integral part of a long history of bilateral relations—a stain that it was now Japan's turn to remove.

The summer of 1945 and the decade that followed gave substance to the new image of the Soviet Union. In desperation in the waning weeks of the war after Germany had been defeated, Tokyo sought Moscow's intervention to bring an end to the war short of unconditional surrender. Instead, as promised earlier, Moscow agreed to Washington's entreaty to break its neutrality pact with Tokyo and enter the Pacific War. Lingering Japanese anger was aroused by a combination of six factors: (1) the violation of a treaty, (2) the late declaration of war on August 9 seen as a way to be "in on the kill," (3) the venality of Soviet troops in encounters with Japanese civilians and soldiers in Manchuria, (4) the prolongation of the Soviet advance into September even though Emperor Hirohito declared Japan's complete surrender on August 15, (5) the seizure of territory that was unmistakably part of Japan and had never been in contention before, and (6) the harsh detention and forced labor of about 575,000 Japanese prisoners of war for years, and in some cases for over a decade.

Selective Memory. All combatants have many unpleasant memories of the behavior of their opponents in the war. The Soviet attack was a brief episode producing relatively few casualties and only slight loss of territory within Japan's nineteenth-century boundaries. In comparison to the tens of millions who died as a result of the war, the great massacres of civilians, some of which were committed by the Japanese, the perfidy of other surprise attacks such as at Pearl Harbor, and the loss through defeat of enormous and highly valuable territories on the Asian mainland, one might expect that the psychological scar in Japan left by the Soviet war behavior would be minor. On the contrary, this memory is the only one that has left a peace treaty between combatants unsigned until the final decade of the century and has continued to produce a huge literature by a defeated power about how it was wronged. Hitler's ability to capitalize on the alleged injustices of the Versailles Treaty shows how potent a force feelings of victimization in defeat can become. In the thinking of some Japanese, including Itō Kenichi writing in 1988, all differences between the two countries are rooted here.[24] Moscow must understand the pain inflicted on the Japanese people.

The Memory of the POWs. The writings of former Japanese prison inmates recall the Soviet Union at its worst—in the abject poverty of the postwar years, with millions performing forced labor in Stalin's camps. Whereas a similar perspective through memoirs and fiction reached a high pitch in the West in the 1960s, it reached Japan in large volume and a closely identifiable form earlier and continued through the 1980s. The Japanese people themselves appeared as the victims. Yet many who returned had been intensively indoctrinated; they arrived back on Japanese soil mouthing pro-Soviet slogans. This may have added to the emotional element in the struggle against Soviet injustice.

At the same time, the returnees helped to arouse interest in Russian music and other forms of culture, which appealed especially to students of the 1950s. The POW effect was mixed at first, but it turned increasingly more negative as the pain lingered while the "brainwashing" wore off.

One of the most famous of the former POWs is Uno Sōsuke, who served as foreign minister and then briefly as prime minister in 1989. Uno's first book, *Home to Tokyo*, described his two years in a Siberian internment camp. In Uno's words, the book "was made into a film and even had a major impact on the government of the day. It was this experience of the power of public opinion that led me to enter politics."[25] Public opinion concerning the Soviet Union has remained a powerful force for Japanese politicians.

The POW question has been kept alive. In March 1989, the *Asahi shimbun* noted that the number of books on Siberian POWs is reaching two thousand.[26] Many are reports of personal experiences. The article reported one opinion that the treatment of Japanese was really not so bad since conditions for the Soviet people were no better. In fact, Soviet children and women ate crumbs fallen from the plates of the prisoners. Another writer's view was that the work of felling timber was naturally hard for inexperienced Japanese; the severe weather plus bad food only took their expected toll. In other words, Japanese did not suffer unduly, he suggested, offering decidedly a minority opinion.

Despite the vast outpouring of prison camp memoirs, the 1989 article in the *Asahi shimbun* called the story of the 575,000 Japanese who were scattered across 1,700 places in the Soviet Union an empty page in Shōwa history. Trying to fill in the gap in information, the article explained that the primary aim in holding them was to rebuild the Soviet economy in conditions of labor shortage. Perhaps 70,000 Japanese died, suffering from the "three pains"—cold, hard work, and hunger. Not excusing Soviet behavior, the article put it into a not altogether critical context, even suggesting that the old military organization of Japan created a latent desire for liberation that fueled the democratic movement among the prisoners.[27]

The Soviet propaganda about democracy and imperialism was effective, in part, because old hierarchical relations among the Japanese had been severe, and in the first one and one-half years of imprisonment envy was aroused toward officers who enjoyed superior rations. Moscow had merely turned to a tested method from its old revolutionary history of propaganda among soldiers. While the Soviet Union cannot be excused for preventing correspondence with home for one to two years, refusing to report numbers captured and understating numbers who died, Japan also is at fault. Japan had not taught its soldiers how to behave as POWs and showed in its own cruelty to POWs that it did not respect rights based on international law. Both countries were fanatical, disdaining their soldiers who fell into enemy hands. In other words, the Soviet Union does not bear a special onus for brainwashing or violence, the *Asahi shimbun* article implied.

Of the various Japanese commenting for the article, Wada Haruki was most forgiving, asking Japanese to understand that the allies brought the Soviet Union into the war and, at last, to let the past die in order to achieve understanding today. Another commentator disagreed, stressing that the harsh reality is that the Soviets violated the neutrality pact, and youth today should know that.

Items on the POWs continue to appear. The emotional appeal is strong. In August 1989 the *Yomiuri shimbum* carried an article entitled "Forty-four Years" by a woman whose father had been led away by Soviet troops in 1945.[28] After years of waiting for his return, she and her mother cannot yet put the matter behind them. All they know is that he disappeared in the Soviet Union. A nation that practices a kind of ancestor worship and annually sends hundreds, when permitted, to visit the graves on the Northern Territories will not let such memories die easily. No wonder much interest has centered on Moscow providing a full tally of prisoners and burial sites.

In 1989–91 the light of glasnost finally fell on the Siberian POWs. Aleksei Kirichenko led in the Soviet effort to assuage Japanese feelings, promising a symposium on the long-hidden subject, then archival information on the Japanese prisoners, and finally the first list of names. At last, the Japanese were at least receiving the details they had long awaited. The records showed 639,635 prisoners, of whom more than 64,000 died.[29] The *Asahi shimbun* started to publish prior to Gorbachev's arrival three volumes of materials drawn from the Kharbarovsk newspaper of the POWs.[30] While the Gaimushō seemed less than enthusiastic about the spotlight thrown on this peripheral issue, popular interest was considerable in the Soviet records about Japanese in captivity.

In 1988 William F. Nimmo published a book on the Japanese who were held in Soviet custody after the war. It is the first substantial English-language study of the POWs and offers a broader treatment than can be found in Japanese memoirs. Nimmo examines the phases of the experience from internment to repatriation. He concludes that the gains of billions of manhours of economic reconstruction and more than 100,000 active collaborators were offset by the hostile aftermath of Japanese anti-Soviet thinking.[31]

Pro-Soviet Sentiments. In the immediate postwar period, every Japanese citizen had to rethink a worldview that had rained disaster on the country. Two contrasting trains of thought attracted the greatest following. Those who saw the causes as external to Japan or present mainly in the political, legal, and educational systems of the country agreed that a reform course should be pursued. Those who identified the causes as inherent in the international system of competition among states to which Japan had contributed or internal to Japan's system of social classes favored a more radical course. The United States and the leading capitalist countries were clearly attractive to the former side; the Soviet Union became the model for the other side. After all, since 1917 Japanese had been conscious of the Soviet Union as the alternative social system, Communists had gained credibility by opposing the policies that had brought disaster on their country, and now the world was divided into two camps with the Soviet Union the obvious alternative to the emerging reform program under American sponsorship. American compromises with the established order, compounded from 1949 by what is known as the "reverse course" when reforms were softened and many who had held high posts in the old order returned to office, left the believers in radical change dissatisfied. Among intellectuals, the trauma of defeat had produced many such believers. Knowing little about Soviet reality, they grasped at the Soviet model for a path to move forward.

For a second time Japanese views of their northern neighbor formed in conditions of isolation from the other country. Unlike the long period of Tokugawa seclusion when there were no positive attractions, this time Russia's appeal was considerable. One factor in the Soviet favor was deep-seated Japanese guilt toward China, which was now joining the Soviet side with florid propaganda about a glorious future. Another was opposition to the loss of reform momentum in Japan; only socialist and Communist parties seemed to offer a clear choice. Finally, the Soviet model itself appealed to a populace feeling impoverished both spiritually and materially in the aftermath of defeat.

Japanese images of the Soviet Union have often been influenced by negative images of Soviet opponents. Negative images of those who are seen as anti-Communists, as in the early postwar years, rebound in a positive image of what they oppose. Intellectuals idolized Soviet socialism in reaction to prewar Japanese anti-communism and its perceived continuation. Through the rebound effect, they scarcely had to look directly at the Soviet system.

In the 1950s and early 1960s, rather than appearing as an aggressor, the Soviet Union was often presented as a victim. Often invaded in history and its cities burned, its people had developed a will to defend themselves. Even in difficult circumstances, they believed that they would not lose. The Russian people built their economy and culture to help stop the invaders. Drawing on European culture, they reached a high level of development. Rather than seeing Russia as the successor to hunters, nomads, or Mongols, some sympathetic observers of this early era when the "democratic intelligentsia" held sway even glorified Russia as a unification of Europe and Asia into one culture.[32]

By establishing ties with Moscow, Japanese on the left hoped to sign a comprehensive treaty to put the war behind them and lead to a world no longer threatened by war. They sought independence, which would restore national dignity on a new foundation. At home they envisioned a compact between intellectuals and the masses of workers and farmers to overturn bureaucratic power and the privileges of the old elite in favor of a new social order. Associations for research on the Soviet Union were established as early as late 1945; yet the priorities of bilateral friendship and advocacy of a new relationship took precedence over research. A decade later the Japanese left knew little more about Soviet reality than it had at the start of the postwar era.

In 1990 Shiokawa Nobuaki described the second half of the 1940s and all the 1950s as the time of the greatest authority of Marxism and the strongest sympathy for the Soviet Union by the Japanese intelligentsia. Indicative of the support for the cult of personality and deformations connected to it was the popularity of the translation of the *History of the Communist Party: Short Course* among the stratum of intelligentsia, not to mention the specialist Sovietologists, who researched the history of the USSR through excerpts from it.[33]

Images of Soviet socialism became a pawn in a bitter domestic confrontation captured on the pages of Japanese journals. "Remarkably contrasting views of this country" appeared in the general-interest magazines.[34] As Kojima Shūichi reports, *Sekai* praised great developments in Soviet science, a reorganization of collective farms that would bring rapid growth to agriculture, magnanimous efforts at equalization by helping less advanced nationalities, national planning that forestalls the economic crises of capitalism, and in general a process of catching up to American economic power. In the 1950s attention shifted to the problem of restoring relations and signing a peace treaty. Many on the left accepted Soviet propaganda about support for peaceful coexistence and argued that if Japan could escape from American designs to become a force in the containment against Moscow it could, as a neutral country and with Moscow's cooperation, become a leader in establishing a peaceful world.[35]

In comparison to the prewar and wartime years, the fulcrum of Soviet studies had shifted from the government to academia, from extreme anticommunism to the ideology of the left, and, within academia, from the safe areas of language and literature to the fields identified as the social sciences. The left latched onto Soviet studies (mostly theoretical rather than empirical), using organs within and outside of universities to transmit its worldview. A huge gulf opened between academia and the government. Images of the Soviet Union became polarized; the country was often depicted as godlike or the devil incarnate.[36]

Continuities in Images to the 1980s. Clear lines of continuity can be traced from the early postwar state of Soviet studies to the present. By the mid-1950s, the following groups were active:

1. The Gaimushō Soviet desk already had a strong hostility to Moscow, for some, retained from the 1930s, and for most, formed in the context of Soviet behavior in 1945 and the following years. Sono Akira served five years beginning in the Occupation as head of the Soviet section. Hōgen Shinsaku became head in 1955. Niizeki Kinya, of the Riga group trained at the end of the 1930s, played a significant role in negotiations with the Kremlin in 1955–56 before becoming ambassador in the early 1970s. These men retained some of their authority in retirement from diplomatic service, while still active as writers through the 1980s. Although their views were far from monolithic, they could write with the authority of their prestigious service. Hōgen and Sono led in the harsh

criticism of the Soviets. The traditions of the Soviet desk endured. They helped to fend off the capitulationist views on the left, but they may also have delayed awareness of the opportunities in the Gorbachev era.

2. Kiga Kenza of Keio University, a leader in conservative economic analysis of the Soviet Union, along with associates sharing his views, remained steadfast in their criticism. The organization of Soviet experts Kiga later headed remained active through the end of the 1980s. This was the critical academic right, smaller and less vocal than the following groups.

3. Nonomura Kazuo at Hitotsubashi University was a prominent Marxist economist. His approach, emphasizing socialist theory, was still identified three decades later with the Hitotsubashi school and an enduring association of Japanese specialists on socialist economies. Here was the sympathetic academic left, as also found in the next two groups.

4. Eguchi Bokuro at Tōkyō University (Tōdai) took a strong and sympathetic interest in the Russian Revolution. The study of Russian history in the 1910s and 1920s, with sympathy for some of the ideals of socialism, remained the trademark of Tōdai training—the primary graduate program for academic specialists.

5. The Waseda University tradition of training Russian and Soviet literature specialists also deserves mention. Writing in 1956, Peter Berton et al. called Waseda the "world's largest center for the study of Russian literature outside the Soviet orbit."[37] For a time, this group also tended to be sympathetic to the Soviets.

While all of these groups persisted, the balance among them changed, as described in the following sections. From the 1950s to the 1980s the academy lost ground to the government and to ex-government sources, the ideological left in economics declined, the study of Russian literature plummeted from its postwar heights, the Tōdai ideological left shifted toward a nonideological, left-of-center approach to Soviet history, and the Sapporo Slavic Studies Center, once known for research on literature and theory, became a diverse center with a major political science orientation. The forces of the early postwar years continued to operate, but in a different context.

The image of a dictatorial and threatening Communist state gained credence with the unleashing of the Korean War at close proximity to Japan and the almost simultaneous switch of the Japanese Communist party to underground and violent revolutionary tactics. For many Japanese, Moscow was threatening their country from both without and within. Traditions of negative Western publications on Soviet history and current affairs were already in the early 1950s accepted by officials and a portion of the intelligentsia, while perhaps the largest and certainly the most vocal part of the intelligentsia dismissed such materials as propaganda. They preferred theoretical writings on Marxism-Leninism and translations of Soviet materials. Stalin's death did not immediately lead to a decline in this polarized atmosphere. The stalemate continued at full force. On the one side was the outspoken intellectual community—academics, teachers, artists, critics—insistent that a red herring had been thrust before them by American McCarthyism and its willing accomplice, Prime Minister Yoshida Shigeru, and on the other side was the newly formed LDP and the bureaucratic leadership accusing their opponents of being duped by Soviet propaganda.

THE DECADE OF REBUILDING RELATIONS: 1955–65

Events in 1956 sharply shifted the terms of the debate. It might not be an exaggeration to say that this was the year that Japan discovered the Soviet Union as it really was. Travel suddenly became easier; first-hand accounts were soon available. Some were positive, confirming that the worst warnings from the right were exaggerated. On the whole, Soviet reality in the 1950s did not have as sobering an effect as it would later. Japan had still barely recovered from its economic collapse at the end of the war, and Soviet spokespersons could present a united front to foreigners with limited access to reality.

One early visitor to the Soviet Union published a travel report, commenting that at last the illusions born of the lost spiritual equilibrium after the war were dissipating. To be sure, he found an unexpectedly poor population, much restricted, and not very happy in appearance. Responding to the polarized images of the preceding era, he observed that Russia was neither heaven nor hell.[38]

The restoration of relations in 1956 after difficult negotiations from early 1955 seems to have changed few minds on the left; Moscow's willingness at that time to relinquish two of four islands indicated some flexibility. Feelings about the territorial question were not yet at a high pitch. While some circles preferred a breakdown in negotiations if all of the islands were not returned, the general-interest journals indicate greater support for an early agreement that would enhance peaceful coexistence, along with postponement of the recovery of territory until international relations had improved.

Divergence of the Intellectuals and the General Public. De-Stalinization came as an unexpected blow to many on the left, raising doubts about the gap between reality and the theories on which Japanese had relied. In later years it would be cited as the beginning of the decline in Soviet popularity. Yet the journal articles in 1956 show widespread sympathy with the new-found Soviet flexibility and pragmatism, suggesting that the gains achieved under Stalin could be consolidated in a new stage.

A second blow hit when Soviet troops repressed the revolt of the Hungarian people. Although a defense for the Soviet intervention appeared in general-interest journals, critical responses predominated in Japan. Soon, however, the Khrushchev thaw, the launching of Sputnik, and the politicized domestic atmosphere at the time of the agreement on a revised security treaty with the United States all reaffirmed leftist sympathy for the Soviet Union. Mass opinion in the tumult of the 1960 ANPO demonstrations was as negative toward the Soviet Union as it would be until the second half of the 1970s,[39] while the intelligentsia in many fields was still enamored with socialism and the Soviet Union.

Russian literature and Soviet socialism reinforced each other in arousing Japanese sympathy for the Soviet people. Russians were the suffering heroes of epic writings, they were the brave fighters for a new social order, and now they had become the "new Soviet man," building a glorious future. The implied contrast was between the revolutionaries who struggled from the nineteenth century and won in Russia and the Japanese people's movements, which were suppressed, leading to the ignominy of 1945. Russia exerted a profound impact on the social thought of Japanese intellectuals.

In the 1950s academics studied the courage of Russia's prerevolutionary Narodniki as the symbols of populists battling an unjust state. The public was moved by the arrival of the Bolshoi Ballet, the heir to Russia's grand culture. The image of rigorous math training in Soviet schools readying the Sputnik scientists appealed to the education-minded Japanese.[40] The appeal of Soviet culture and literature became so pervasive that it was widely assumed that one's consciousness was not high if one was bored by them.[41]

After the events of 1956 the next turning point in perceptions occurred in the early 1960s when the Sino-Soviet split splashed across the newspapers. Chinese accusations damaged Moscow's populist image and undermined its theoretical claims. What Japanese had most admired in the theory and purity of socialist populism was attacked by a source with tremendous authority of its own within leftist circles. From three sides Japanese were bombarded with negative impressions: from the West with its improving scholarship on the reality of the Soviet Union, from China with its ideological rhetoric against "revisionist" deviations, and from the Soviet Union itself with its measured de-Stalinization in justification of reforms. Intellectual support for Moscow gradually declined.

Among the wider public, an opposite trend could be detected. As Moscow shed its revolutionary image, some people came to regard it as a state converging with the West. Visitors remarked on the rapid improvement in the standard of living and the similarity of the people's aspirations with those of people elsewhere. Japanese discovered that Soviets are not very different from other people. As economic ties between the two countries rapidly expanded, predictions of convergence overtook those of confrontation. The principle of separation between politics and economics then in operation gave Japan reason to look ahead to a surge in trade between the growing Soviet economy rich in raw materials and the booming Japanese economy with its huge appetite for them. Public opinion toward Moscow slowly became more tolerant, if not actually favorable.

THE DECADE OF IMPROVED RELATIONS: 1965–75

While fairly widespread Japanese doubts about or opposition to the Vietnam War in the second half of the 1960s had the inverse effect of boosting the Soviet Union, Moscow lost its advantage and more through the Czechoslovakian invasion in 1968. It would not be an exaggeration to conclude that at this time the intellectual left abandoned its twenty-odd years fascination with the Soviet Union. Moscow lost whatever lingering reputation it had as a peace-loving country. This opened the way to a fixation on the Northern Territories—Japan's earlier and most symbolic Soviet evidence of expansionism and military buildup. When Washington soon returned Okinawa, extricated itself from Vietnam, and resumed relations with China, the entire Japanese political spectrum united against Soviet foreign policy.

In the 1950s and most of the 1960s an active left pressed the Japanese government to demand the return of Okinawa more than the Northern Territories and to oppose American imperialist expansion more than Soviet expansion.[42] Moscow appeared to be the lesser villain. In the 1970s after Okinawa was returned and the United States had disengaged from Vietnam, many on the left chose sides against Moscow. As anti-Americanism subsided, the lesser of two evils argument also was abandoned.

The Good Russian and the Bad Soviet or the Bad Russian Who Lives On. Among informed Japanese, the Soviet image also slipped as a result of Brezhnev's domestic policies. As in the West, hope for convergence faded. Attention to dissident literature and its harsh suppression had the effect of severing the connection between the earlier Russian literary tradition and the existing Soviet system. Two alternative outlooks on the Soviet people became widespread: (1) some popular accounts contrasted the good Russian seen through literature and the bad Soviet seen through politics;[43] and (2) others took an avid interest in tracing negative national character traits back through both Soviet and Russian history.[44]

Sympathy at Its Peak. In the early 1970s an atmosphere of détente prevailed. Soviet-Japanese economic ties also were expanding; Tokyo was already Moscow's foremost capitalist trading partner, and the possibilities seemed almost limitless as ambitious megaprojects for the joint development of Soviet Far Eastern resources came under active consideration. Following Japan's sudden opening of relations with China, Prime Minister Tanaka went to Moscow amid new hopes that the territorial dispute would be settled and full normalization could be achieved. Japanese public opinion toward the Soviet Union continued to improve gradually, reaching a peak in 1974.[45] Favorable attitudes were no longer enthusiastic approval by a minority in search of a model; they signified cautious optimism, and they bode well for future relations because they came from the mainstream of an increasingly middle-class society. Unlike the next wave of hope fifteen years later, Japanese were not yet anticipating an end to the divisions between capitalism and socialism or the cold war, and they were not anticipating their own rise to the center stage as a superpower.

THE DECADE OF TENSER RELATIONS: 1975–85

Rodger Swearingen estimates that in the late 1940s "perhaps 40 percent of all university students in Japan supported the party's program." The Soviets and the JCP were successful also in appealing to business hopes for trade with the continent. Yet self-destructive radicalization of policy first by the Kremlin's militant line in 1947 and then by the JCP itself undermined their support. Swearingen pinpoints the mid-1970s as the time when Japanese public opinion and the press shifted from mildly hopeful views of the Soviet Union to preoccupation with coping with the Soviet threat. He attributes this to such factors as traditional distrust from the eighteenth century, Comintern policies both prewar and postwar, Soviet behavior in 1945, and Soviet interference with Japanese fishing boats.[46] Robert Scalapino offers more evidence on how the JCP isolated itself, stressing the Sino-Soviet dispute as the decisive blow.[47]

Soviet Arrogance. The conduct of Soviet foreign policy was the primary force in the deterioration of Japanese goodwill toward the Soviet Union. As early as 1960, in response to the revision and renewal of the Japan-U.S. Security Treaty, the Soviet leadership angered many Japanese by informing Prime Minister Ikeda that the clause in the Japan-Soviet Joint Declaration of 1956 in which Moscow indicated its intent to return two islands was no longer applicable. In 1973 an apparent verbal acknowledgment by Brezhnev to Tanaka that the territorial issue remained unresolved was soon denied, with the explanation that Brezhnev had been coughing rather than acquiescing with the words "da, da."

This kind of unreliable and insensitive conduct was becoming less acceptable to a newly confident Japan. Soviet arrogance, fueled by increased military might, clashed with Japanese pride, reinforced by economic successes. The Soviet effort to pressure Tokyo away from an "antihegemony" clause in the Sino-Japanese treaty signed in 1978 proved counterproductive. The crude handling of a proposal for a Japan-Soviet Good-Neighborliness and Cooperation Treaty as an alternative to a peace treaty, first in 1975 and then in 1978, again left Japan's foreign policy elite indignant.

Soviet Power Politics at Fault. Soviet power politics intended to bring Tokyo to its senses in its dealings with a superpower produced negative psychological repercussions. On the sensitive subject of fishing rights, Moscow took unilateral steps such as extending territorial waters in the second half of the 1970s that damaged Japanese interests. Moreover, in 1976 Moscow reversed a decade-long practice of permitting Japanese using only identification cards to visit ancestral graves on the Northern Territories around the time of the Obon holiday in August. Japanese understood that just as Moscow had broken the promise to return the two islands as a reprisal for the revision of the Japan-U.S. Security Treaty, it was banning the grave visits in retaliation against the Sino-Japanese rapprochement. They calculated that these two Soviet actions originated from the same "root." Stationing a division of Soviet troops and advanced fighter planes on the islands made a deep impression. In addition to the other signs of military buildup and expansion that angered Japan's partners in the West, Moscow aroused a deeper kind of Russophobia in Japan through such direct provocations.

The Soviet invasion of Afghanistan is widely acknowledged to be another turning point for Japanese perceptions. Joining in the economic sanctions against Moscow in 1980 as well as in the boycott of the Summer Olympics, Japan unmistakably departed from its usual practice of separating economics from politics. (Some observers argue that the departure actually began around 1976–77). This left a legacy of linkage that Moscow has had difficulty reversing.

Later incidents kept Japanese apprehensions alive. Following the defection of KGB agent Stanislav Levchenko in Tokyo, the disclosure of his testimony by the CIA in 1982 revealed disinformation operations and "active measures" (primarily to obtain secret technology) on a scale startling to the Japanese.[48] When the Soviet Union shot down a Korean airliner in September 1983, killing 269 persons including 27 Japanese, Moscow's secrecy and lies in handling the matter left an especially unpleasant aftertaste in the Japanese. Before Gorbachev came to power, the shadow over bilateral ties cast by a succession of such headline-grabbing events had scarcely begun to lift.

In 1982 Itō Kenichi set forth a scenario for a Soviet blitzkrieg of Japan, overrunning the country in days much as the Germans had overrun parts of Europe in 1939. If the Japanese-American alliance were severed, if public opinion inside Japan failed to be unified, Moscow, which believes only in the logic of force, might take the offensive. Weakness, by which Itō means not only neutrality but also a nonnuclear capability, invites the enemy. He appealed to the Japanese to understand the Soviet Union as an enemy, to strengthen the American lifeline, and to build a stronger military capability for Japan.[49]

Shimizu Hayao developed the same line of reasoning. He explained that it is difficult for the United States to control the Soviet Union by itself. Moscow is turning to foreign adventures in order to avoid internal problems. If the West is moderate in its response, this only encourages Soviet expansionism. Japan is in danger of falling into a state of unarmed neutrality. Having lost its will after the defeat of 1945, it has not recovered its old "Russia complex." The "sophisticated" leftist intelligentsia still influences the media. Japan, Shimizu concludes, should be guided by a strong sense of alarm about the Soviet threat and should overcome its powerlessness before the Soviets.[50]

At about the same time Sono Akira, who had served in Moscow for two years in 1941 and risen to become ambassador to three countries before retiring from diplomatic service in 1975, bemoaned the weak spirit of the Japanese people. He saw evidence of a Soviet Communist party "war against Japan, using its embassy as a strategic base and sowing illusions of 'friendship.'" The battle is none other than the Soviet offensive to undermine Japan's readiness to defend itself.[51]

After the "oil shock" of 1973, Japanese industrial restructuring proceeded rapidly. Industry succeeded in conserving resources at the same time as international sources for them became more diversified. The need for Soviet raw materials diminished. Confidence in Japan's economic success rose rapidly as huge trade surpluses began to accumulate. In contrast, the Soviet economic growth rate plummeted. The reality of late Brezhnev era "stagnation" was soon registered in international consciousness. This disabused Japanese of the feeling that they needed the Soviets economically or even that they could deal with them profitably on a large scale. No longer was there anything left about the Soviet Union or its image to impress the Japanese. Soviet popularity plunged lower and lower. As 1985 began, the Soviet popularity rating with all segments of the Japanese population could hardly have sunk lower.[52]

Reasons for Anti-Soviet Feelings. Writing in 1988, Kimura Hiroshi suggested three reasons why Japanese had become "anti-Soviet": (1) the illegal occupation of the Northern Territories; (2) Soviet militarization of this land; and (3) Soviet high-pressure behavior, looking down on the Japanese. He traced the last of these to unnecessary bluster, as in the 1976

Mig-25 defection incident when Moscow roughly demanded the return of the plane and pilot and the 1983 Korean Airlines incident.[53] The Japanese public even became self-conscious about its antipathy toward Moscow, questioning in writing why the nation hated the Soviets.[54]

OVERVIEW OF PRE-GORBACHEV PERCEPTIONS

The current rivalry between Japan and Russia contains elements of four eras. From the premodern era can be found the threat to Japan of an intruding neighbor. From the age of imperialism survives the competition for hegemony in East Asia—the threat of a regional rival. From the decades of cold war remains the clash of East versus West or, more precisely, of a Communist superpower endangering the free world and capitalism in various spots around the world. Increasingly there is also the emergent factor of a rivalry between two superpowers in a more complex post–cold war environment. For the Japanese the overlay of past and present complicates the resolution of bilateral problems.

Periods of warm relations and substantial mutual benefit have been no more than relatively brief interruptions of the long-term, deeply felt antagonisms or the times of virtual disregard of the Soviets. Japanese and Soviets have trouble seeing each other accurately. Yokote Shinji writes of the problem Japanese have in imagining the vastness of the Soviet Union and the problem Soviets have in appreciating the compactness of Japan. They have both suffered from one-sided and simplistic information about the other. To overcome stereotypes, he urges both nations to view in relative terms their image of the other over a long history and to deepen cultural exchanges.[55] Along with many Soviets, Yokote and like-minded Japanese believe that a history of negative stereotypes should be overcome as an essential step in setting relations on a positive course.

A Healthy Sense of Threat. The opposite conclusion is drawn by other Japanese. For example, Shimizu Hayao described Japan's "Russian complex" dating from early in the nineteenth century as a valuable asset. Deepened in the early 1980s by Soviet actions, the Japanese sense of threat is a "healthy" force for the country. Shimizu warns in 1984 that a part of the mass media, especially the *Asahi shimbun*, is responding differently. The leftist intelligentsia claims to be too "sophisticated" for the traditional "Russian complex." If their view prevails, the Japanese people may lose their will and become defenseless without this needed complex.[56]

A minority view from far on the left could still be faintly detected in the first half of the 1980s. Societies for promoting friendship, trade, and contacts with the Soviets continued to operate, although with a whimper rather than a cry. Former Diet members who had committed themselves in the halcyon days of the early 1970s were left to champion an unpopular cause. One of them, Yokokawa Shōichi, director of the Japan-Soviet Trade Association, published a book in 1984 setting forth his views.[57] He complained that Americans, West Germans, and others were again energetic in trade with the Soviets, but Japanese were not. The lag, he added, is because of anti-Soviet feeling. Japanese are educated to hate the "reds," and a tenacious anti-Soviet campaign fills the general-interest journals.

Yokokawa, whose views were discussed in Chapter 2, finds the mood in his country one-sided. It is a Japanese vice, he asserts, to perceive their country as the victim, when, in the history of the two nations, Japan has also victimized Russia, both in the war of 1904–5 and in the Siberian Expedition after the Communists took power. Yokokawa blames American direct and indirect pressure in 1956, 1973, and at other times for driving a wedge between Tokyo and Moscow, for making Tokyo a faithful vassal of Washington. He also blames the rising tide of right-wing nationalism, aroused by the hawks in the LDP who use the ruse of an anti-Soviet campaign to stay in office. They have enjoyed so much success in their theories of the Soviet threat and the Northern Territories that in the most recent 1983 elections, according to Yokokawa, there was a kind of taboo among the left against mentioning the Soviet Union.

Yokokawa was virtually a lone voice in the resistance against the stampede to oppose a widely perceived Soviet threat. The left had lost its credibility. The right could make dire predictions with nary a peep to the contradictory. Many intellectuals, especially those with a postwar left-leaning education, quietly objected to this one-sidedness of coverage on the Soviet Union. At the same time, they found Soviet behavior sufficiently reprehensible to discourage them from swimming against the tide. The result was a lull in the debate, opening the way to increased attentiveness to Western polemics on the subject. Japanese diversity of thinking no longer seemed to be of consequence.

False Starts toward Better Relations. False starts have plagued improving Japanese images of Russia and the Soviet Union. As many as seven turns for the worst in this century should be noted. In each case a war or revolution played a pivotal role. After almost two decades of growing interest in Russian literature, the Russo-Japanese War of 1904–5 caused a setback to perceptions. Following a quick recovery and a newfound spirit of political cooperation as well as literary fascination, the Bolshevik Revolution in 1917 produced a turnabout in thinking. Over the next ten to fifteen years interest rose in Marxist-Leninist thought, but censorship, which intensified from Japan's 1931 entry into China and its first steps toward the Pacific War, drove such ideas underground. Moscow's declaration of war against Japan and seizure of soldiers and land in August

1945 somewhat reduced the rising backlash in favor of Communists who had bravely opposed Japan's militarism. The postwar excitement with the Soviet model ran into the unexpected reef of de-Stalinization and the Hungarian invasion in 1956. Nonetheless, the attitude that Moscow was interested in peace endured and gained new support during the Vietnam War, only to be contradicted by the invasion of Czechoslovakia. Then the spirit of détente and improved economic cooperation declined abruptly with Moscow's dispatch of troops to Afghanistan. A cycle of disappointment (eleven-and-one-half year intervals, from August 1945 to October 1956 to May 1968 to December 1979) has operated. Seven times hopes had been aroused; seven times a sudden shower of bullets had doused them. The Gorbachev era, highlighted by his visit to Japan eleven and one-half years after the Afghan invasion, may be seen as Japan's eighth opportunity for a favorable image of Russia in this century.

CHAPTER SIX

The First Cycle, 1985–1987

Question 1: Does the World Have Reason to Anticipate Gorbachev
            Favorably?
Question 2: Why Do the Japanese Hate the Soviets?

IN 1983 a flurry of international speculation that Yuri Andropov was a
new-style leader and perhaps even a reformer left some Japanese wondering what all the fuss was about. When Gorbachev came to office, the
same question reappeared with greater intensity. First Japanese responded by looking at the world reaction, then they looked inward to try
to understand their own sentiments. While during Andropov's brief tenure and, even in foreign policy, during the Chernenko year in office, tiny
boomlets arose from time to time among Western Soviet-watchers, nothing of the sort occurred in Japan. On the one side, hope springs eternal;
on the other, there was only an uninterrupted stupor. Gorbachev's start
in office produced the biggest boomlet yet; Westerners threw themselves
into anxious speculation about this man and his first promising speeches.
Immediately Japanese began to react to the Western excitement, perhaps
more than to the Soviet developments.

The Washington-Moscow Connection. From the moment of Gorbachev's ascent to the Soviet leadership, scarcely a day passed without a
new headline suggesting a warming in American-Soviet relations: "America Hopes for an Era of New Dialogue," "The Soviet Union Is Enthusiastic for Disarmament Negotiations," "The Path to an American-Soviet
Summit Meeting." The papers rang out with the words "détente,"
"change," "turning point." The imagery of summitry long preceded the
real thing. The world seemed to revolve around the Washington-Moscow
axis, and the young, confident Mikhail Gorbachev engaging the hopeful
Ronald Reagan made the biggest splash in the Japanese press.

Japanese sensitivity to Soviet-American negotiations shows a lack of
trust. On the one hand, there was little hope that Moscow would genu-
inely change its spots, indicating that nothing good could come of cooper-
ating with it. On the other hand, there was some concern (although only
among a minority) that Washington might not act with Japan's best interests in mind. No doubt, the huge gap between Japan's economic power
and its political power created fertile soil for suspicions. In the background was the reality that Japanese increasingly felt that the postwar
political era was unsuitable to their country's needs.

Japan's Distorted Response. In the April 1985 issue of *Sekai,* articles by Nakamura Kenichi and Shindo Eiichi addressed popular theories of the Soviet threat and Soviet expansionism. Their focus was more on Japanese images than on Soviet realities. Nakamura contrasts the one-dimensional image in Japan with the more variegated American image. He complains of one-sided news, failing to portray the Soviet people as anything but scary. He then recounts the "hate rate" (*kirai*) statistics, which had continued to rise through 1982–84, reaching 60 percent from a low of 24 percent in 1974. Describing the intensified views, Nakamura notes three changes: (1) the penetration into mass thinking of fear and antagonism; (2) the politicization of the theory of the Soviet threat into a factor in the political decision-making process; and (3) the adoption of policies based on Japanese power politics as part of an alliance facing Moscow.[1] It has become popular to describe how the Soviets would invade Hokkaidō, he bemoans. Even in the context of the heightened vigilance characteristic of the Western alliance led by Ronald Reagan, these are extreme reactions of national concern, exclaims Nakamura.

Nakamura's observations are characteristic of long-standing concerns on the left. In addition to the substantial effects of Soviet military actions, Soviet internal controls, and information restrictions, Japanese attitudes were seen as artificially stimulated by two domestic factors. The first is traditional nationalism. While Japan's role in the world is rising, its public consciousness remains closed. Nakamura calls this narcissistic. Japanese looked down on the world as stagnant, poor, and disorderly, and, with added contempt, on the Soviet people, through what was described as a distorted sense of their low living standards and cultural level. Nakamura also decries the one-sided memories of World War II, in which the horrors of the Nazi treatment of Soviets and of Japan's occupation of China and Korea are forgotten while the Soviet conduct toward Japan is remembered. He accuses his fellow Japanese of applying a double standard.

The second domestic explanation for a distorted response to Moscow is the strategy of the ruling circles within Japan to "normalize" the country's military. The struggle against postwar pacifism is a long one in which American complicity became a factor as early as 1951. Washington urged Tokyo to insist on the return of the Northern Territories, and in 1956 John Foster Dulles even went so far as to threaten not to return Okinawa if Tokyo relinquished its demands on Moscow, effectively ruining negotiations on the peace treaty.[2] According to critics, increasingly it was Japanese authorities who were pressing for an expanded military budget, manipulating the Soviet image to suit their ends. The Northern Territories issue was artificially fanned in the interest of rallying the Japanese people around the need for normal national security.

Nakamura and Shindo both recommend a more relaxed view of the

Soviet Union. Shindo argues that if the doves in the West gain ground, the Kremlin will become more conciliatory.[3] Nakamura recalls that Japanese images changed abruptly toward America in 1945 and toward China in 1972.[4] They can change toward the USSR, too.

Scholars seized the opportunity created by rising interest in Gorbachev to seek a new approach to Soviet studies in Japan. They expressed alarm that Soviet-watching was inadequate. For many the issue was not that a conspiracy on the right was distorting reality, but that there were many holes in the picture of the Soviet Union that had formed, resulting in only a sketchy understanding of new developments.[5]

Clinging to the "Evil Empire" Image. The Japanese right stood constantly ready to pounce on any sign of "new thinking" about Moscow. This was already apparent at the end of 1983 in Hōgen Shinsaku's book, *For Japanese the Soviet Union Is a Dangerous State.* Chapter 1, entitled "Aren't There Mistakes in the Soviet Vision of the Japanese?" notes the Soviet effort to capitalize on Andropov's new leadership by fostering an image of cooperation, peaceful intent, and reform. The book objects to the "neutrality" of Japanese papers that fail to cover the Soviet military buildup accurately. Andropov, Hōgen reminds the reader, is no Deng Xiao-ping.[6] The Soviets are not going to change, and they cannot be trusted.

In 1984 Tamba Minoru took a similar position in his book, *A Country that Seeks a 200% Security Guarantee.* Neither under Andropov nor under Chernenko is Moscow changing, he insisted. Of first importance is the need for understanding and support from the Japanese people for diplomacy to make Moscow take Japan seriously.[7] As Hōgen, Tamba drew on his credentials as an experienced former head of the Soviet desk to warn Japanese against being deceived by misinformation about a new Soviet outlook. Unlike Hōgen, Tamba was still in the Gaimushō, in fact, serving in Moscow at this time. That this concern with the Japanese people being duped remained strong and even intensified after Gorbachev took power can be seen in Sase Masamori's 1986 article harshly reviewing the *Asahi* newspaper's 1985 coverage of security issues.[8]

In 1985 the clash between right and left remained largely at the level of a debate over information. The left insisted that ignorance prevailed, warning that Japanese lagged behind Americans and others in their understanding of Soviet society. As a result, Tokyo's policies would remain rigid and unresponsive to new opportunities. With this argument, they hoped to find common ground with the scholarly community on the center and the right of center. The right warned that Soviet propaganda could undermine Japanese unity. A monolithic image stressing the negative character of the country did not need to be challenged by new information. To rush to impressions of change would only confuse the Japanese public. Europeans and even Americans may be vulnerable; Japan's superiority could be demonstrated by consistency of thinking and reliance on bureaucratic experience for guidance on how to respond. The right sought to make a negative image of Moscow a patriotic duty and to isolate the left as an extreme element driven by ulterior motives to find something new where it does not, in fact, exist.

Having argued a similar case against so-called Soviet sympathizers with convincing results over the past decade, the right continued to prevail. Bookstores were still filled with an alarmist literature,[9] the debate in the general-interest journals remained low-key, and public opinion barely registered the arrival of the Gorbachev era. At the same time, without necessarily changing their conclusions about the Soviet Union, many Japanese became aware of the excessive character of Japan's "Soviet complex."[10]

Question 3: Is Moscow Serious about Japan?

The first stages of Japan's response to Gorbachev were enlivened when Foreign Minister Shevardnadze's forthcoming January visit to Tokyo was announced in the fall of 1985. Was the bilateral relationship at last breaking out of a deep freeze? Through the middle of 1986, articles explored Soviet intentions toward Japan. They also self-consciously examined the Japanese response. Bilateral relations took the spotlight, the glow from which soon spread to Soviet international relations in general.

Pessimism about Gorbachev. A December 1985 poll of Hokkaidō residents' view of the Soviet Union (*Sorenkan*) provides a starting point for tracing changes in attitudes on this island closest to the USSR. Among the population, 80 percent felt threatened by the Soviet military build-up, fewer than 20 percent felt friendly to the Soviet Union, and fewer than 30 percent entertained the possibility that Moscow would return the Northern Territories. About 48 percent expressed a certain degree of interest in the Soviet Union because it is a neighbor or a superpower, 22 percent more even had a strong interest, while another 28 percent had little or no interest because of the difference in the Soviet system or its dark, cold image. Under 30 percent of the respondents held high hopes for a positive evaluation of Gorbachev. Nonetheless, the analysts of the poll were struck by how large this figure was. It was largely males who expressed a strong interest (31 percent versus 13 percent for females), a friendly attitude, and a "plus evaluation" of Gorbachev. The specific interest of Hokkaidō residents can be detected from the choice of fishing diplomacy as the first item Japan should pursue in the forthcoming diplomatic talks.[11]

Is Gorbachev Coming? As the first Soviet foreign minister in a decade to visit Japan, Shevardnadze raised some hopes. Only four months later Japan's Foreign Minister Abe Shintarō reciprocated with a visit to Moscow. The agreements that were signed regularized communications disrupted since the mid-1970s, for example, resuming meetings of the Japan-Soviet Science and Technology Committee and visits to graves on the Northern Territories, but the principal effect was to arouse speculation that Gorbachev would visit Japan, as Prime Minister Nakasone had invited him to do. This prospect and the fanfare accompanying Shevardnadze's visit were met with suspicion from Japan's right, who discerned a ploy to divide public opinion, to obtain Japanese technology, to block involvement in SDI, or even to stir opposition to the LDP. Many extrapolated Gromyko's methods to the new Soviet leadership. The shift from Gromyko's "nyet diplomacy" to Shevardnadze's "smile diplomacy" only exacerbated their apprehensions.

By the second half of the year the Japanese decided that Moscow was not serious about a new bilateral relationship. There was no progress on the territorial issue. Despite a false rumor in July that the much reviled, long-standing adviser on Japanese policy in the Central Committee, Ivan Kovalenko, was now ousted, Japanese could observe little fresh thinking on the Soviet side.[12] At the same time, N. Solovyev, Gorbachev's new ambassador, impressed some as a genuine Japan expert who respects their country. A growing group urged patience since Gorbachev faced tremendous problems that could not all be addressed at once; they were encouraged because unexpected flexibility could be detected on other fronts.[13]

Summing up official and mainstream Japanese thinking in early 1987, Kimura Hiroshi explained the state of bilateral relations. The Soviet Union had isolated itself from East Asia by its military policies. Gorbachev's Vladivostok speech of July 28, 1986, offered little that was new, although there were positive themes that had needed reaffirmation. Moscow has not yet changed its bipolar approach. Moscow underestimated Japan in 1986 and still is not prepared to pay the price of returning the four islands, although it now clearly realizes its need for Japanese technology and economic cooperation. Despite his pessimism, Kimura found it significant that Gorbachev had become the first Soviet leader to express a desire to visit Japan. Kimura was confident that Japanese are not susceptible to Gorbachev's diplomatic offensive; their interest in him will cool down as fast as they warm up to the visit. In any case, he and others decided by 1987 that a visit was unlikely because U.S.-Soviet relations stumbled at the Reyjkavik summit in October 1986, because Nakasone had become a lame duck prime minister, and because Soviet realists were aware that if no "souvenir" was brought for the Japanese people, the visit would only disappoint them.[14]

The Taboo. While the official view insisted that nothing had changed on the Japanese side, a quarrel in the general-interest journals over the suggestion that Japan consider accepting two islands marked the opening skirmish in a substantive debate over the new era. The Gaimushō sought unanimity, tenacity, and repetition for the Japanese demand to return all islands as the starting point (the "entry" approach) for better relations, but a few academics braved its rancor and that of the Japanese right by violating the unwritten taboo against suggesting compromise positions. A modest debate over the acceptability of the Soviet return of two islands or over abandoning the "entry" approach was kindled by Shevardnadze's first visit in January 1986 and then grew more visible, reaching a peak in early 1987 and persisting into 1988. Along with Wada Haruki, Nakajima Mineo took the lead in late 1986 in breaking with the "taboo" on support for some sort of two-island proposal.[15] Warning that just as the United States shocked an unsuspecting Japan in the early 1970s with its opening to China, "Japan is again left dangling in the wind," Nakajima called for action before it is too late.[16] He argued that Japan's national interests would be served by improved relations with the Soviet Union, that only diplomatic means are available, that the hysterical anti-Soviet debate will do no good, and that Japan can exert pressure to affect the outcome of change in the Soviet Union. He accused Itō Kenichi and others of being imprisoned in the theory that no matter who leads the country, the Soviet Union does not change, and of failing to notice that at Vladivostok Gorbachev accepted the existence of the Japan-U.S. security treaty. Now that the "red Kennedy" is in charge, Japan needs a new consciousness. This requires thinking openly about the territorial question. Recognizing that there are Japanese who react hysterically to his views on Moscow, Nakajima insistently defended a compromise and associated it with the new era of Japan's internationalization. On the other side were some who draped themselves in the flag. Itō Kenichi wrote of hallowed land inherited from ancestors and referred to Wada Haruki, the historian at Tōdai who raised the two-island idea, as having the face of a Japanese, but the heart of a Soviet.[17] Also critical of what they called the "exit" approach—of improving relations first and creating an environment for the Kremlin to cede territory—were the majority, who were confident that the balance of overall power between the two countries had shifted, putting the pressure on Moscow to meet Tokyo's demands. The harsh response to the lonely trial balloons intended to inspire a debate and the near unanimity in support of the return of all four islands in public opinion polls only strengthened the confidence of the Gaimushō.

Sase Masamori was one of many who took exception to Nakajima's arguments.[18] He refuted Nakajima's claim that the Soviet Union is now nonideological because Marxist-Leninist books are ignored while Japanese authors sell out fast, responding that the Soviet interest in books printed in editions of only tens of thousands is insufficient to be a fad and, in any case, long predates Gorbachev. Soviet eagerness for Japan's high technology also is "old stuff." Likewise, Sase accused Nakajima of exaggerating the need for mutual dependency and its impact on Soviet thinking; prospects for some agreements based on mutual interest would not change the spirit of relations. Sase concluded that Moscow would not become economically dependent and Tokyo would not gain the leverage expected by Nakajima. Concessions to regain two islands would be made in vain.

Of even more concern to the political right was an article by Miyoshi Osamu, writing in what was considered to be an organ of the LDP at almost the same time as Wada's and Nakajima's articles. Miyoshi called on Gorbachev to come to Japan bearing an unconditional present of two islands. Some interpreted this suggestion to be Nakasone's personal wish and a sign that he would settle for the two-island alternative. Soon sources on the right, including *Sekai Nipo*, launched an attack that induced Miyoshi to make a repentent call for all four islands. This came at a time when a Gorbachev visit at an early date still seemed a possibility.

A Lost Year. At the end of 1986 hopes dimmed that Gorbachev would visit in January 1987 or even at some unspecified date in the near future. Observers noticed that Moscow was throwing its energies into relations with Washington, leaving no room for Tokyo. Tokyo too seemed to be in no hurry, figuring that the ball was on Moscow's side to play next. While hopes had diminished, probably few foresaw that it would take well over a year for the next significant move toward improved relations. In 1987 relations actually deteriorated. After the Toshiba affair in the spring when a Japanese firm was caught selling important submarine technology to Moscow, Tokyo was embarrassed into tightening export controls under COCOM restrictions, and Moscow accused Japan of engaging in an anti-Soviet campaign. In August Moscow expelled a Japanese citizen. The two sides exchanged accusations. Although the atmosphere began to improve in the fall, for all intents and purposes 1987 was a lost year in bilateral relations.

The changes in Japanese perceptions from 1984 to 1987 were positive if not spectacular. The *Yomiuri shimbun* conducted a poll in October 1987 and found 17 percent of Japanese friendly (0.8 percent very friendly) to the Soviet Union in comparison to 7.6 percent in 1984 when the prime minister's office had asked a similar question. In the Hokkaidō and Tōhoku regions closest to Soviet territory, the figure reached 24 percent, but in Kyūshū in the southwest it was just 11 percent. On the left of the political spectrum, JCP and JSP supporters registered 33 and 27 percent respectively. Again, females were less informed. Some 27 percent, as opposed to 9 percent of males, could not answer any factual questions, such as that the name of the Soviet capital is Moscow (39 percent of all respondents missed this one) or that Gorbachev is the Soviet leader (48 percent failed on this one). The Soviet people as well as the Soviet government fare badly. Japanese thought of them as collectivist and proud, but rarely as honest, trustworthy, or well-mannered.[19]

Question 4: What is Perestroika, or Is the Soviet Union Changing?

The final stage in the first cycle of Japan's response to the Gorbachev era came when Japanese at last got around to taking a close look at what was happening inside the Soviet Union. To be fair, it was not until January 1987 that the rhetoric of perestroika became compelling. Yet the process over almost two years had been cumulative, and many observers in the West were following it with rapt attention. In recognition of this gap, in 1987 it was not uncommon for Japanese to complain that their country was slow to appreciate what was happening in Moscow.[20]

At last the Soviet Union aroused a substantial debate, which for the first time made Japanese reexamine the character of Soviet society. In place of the critics, specialists now took a leading role. In the spring issues of the general-purpose journals, they vied to explain what is perestroika. Shimotomai Nobuo in *Sekai* presented a relatively hopeful account, stressing how much is changing inside the Soviet Union.[21] Kimura Hiroshi in *Shokun* was more cautious in evaluating glasnost, identifying limitations in its reach.[22] Less committal on this point was Hakamada Shigeki in *Chūō kōron*, explaining eighteen angles of Japanese misunderstanding.[23]

Motives for Perestroika. Two contrasting views on the motives for perestroika were expressed in the 1987 debate. Critics on the right looked from the top down and saw a desperate Communist leadership frantic to preserve its domestic power and its military might, tampering with a system they really did not believe in changing fundamentally. Noticing that one of the first priorities of perestroika was to rebuild the machine industry, they saw the stress on a more efficient economy as little more than a means to make Moscow competitive in high-technology weapons. Later, as it became clearer that some military cutbacks were planned, the critics still discerned a motivation to rebuild an obsolescent economy for the old purposes of expansionism and party control. On the other side, those who took Gorbachev most seriously in 1987 argued that the impetus for reform came from a changing Soviet society. The reforms could not be merely cosmetic because the society requires a fundamentally new approach. Although particular policies may fail, the momentum exists to push the reforms in an increasingly radical direction in response to social needs. The deeper the motives from within the society, the greater are the prospects for full-scale transformation of the Soviet system. Observers on the left expected Gorbachev to push further and further, as he has done, while critics on the right always seemed to trail one step behind the next stage of reform on the assumption that he is not serious about taking the process further.

The Right versus the Left. The far right redoubled its criticisms in the midst of the new uncertainty. Having been reduced to endless repetition in the period of unmitigated condemnation to 1984, it seized the opportunity to reappear in print. Nasu Kiyoshi published one book called *The Collapse of the Soviet Union* in 1986 and then responded to the acceleration of Gorbachev's reforms with a second book in 1987, *The Collapse of the Soviet Union Is Drawing Nearer.* The only hope, as he sees it in his first book, is access to advanced technology from the United States or Japan. Soviet bureaucrats turned to Gorbachev out of desperation. Yet he cannot expunge such enormous problems as bribery, alcohol, and the burden of expansionism that are destroying the system. Nasu adds that when Moscow tries to avert collapse by turning to Tokyo, it naturally will find that the return of the Northern Territories is a precondition for aid. In the second book Nasu adds that the Soviets are making many changes because they foresee the approaching collapse. Yet, there is no hope domestically; so the real intent is, as Lenin puts it, to induce the capitalists to supply the rope to hang themselves. If foreign countries remain firm, the only question is which scenario of collapse will be followed. Nasu raises the possibility that the Soviet Union will take the Chinese reform path, then dismisses it with the argument that the Cultural Revolution had already undermined China while the Soviet Communist system is too solid to be reformed.[24]

Although there were others who, without examining them closely, dismissed Gorbachev's policies as a trick or a hopeless venture, for the first time a degree of dialogue developed between positions that were less extreme. In this debate the right of center and far right were beginning to lose their shared framework of recent years. To the right of center were pessimists such as Kimura Hiroshi prepared to take a close look at domestic reforms and to discuss their prospects with those who were more optimistic about the advance of reforms. A left-of-center or center position became prominent; those who had bothered to study Soviet life closely and could be counted on to give an informed judgment about aspects of the new reforms, based on contacts with Soviet reformers, anticipated a sustained momentum that would carry change forward. In 1987 it became customary for a journal to reach out for diversity in a roundtable discussion or through paired articles. A genuine debate ensued.

Japanese now keenly sought information about actual Soviet conditions. The Gaimushō turned to its own Institute of International Affairs to start a new journal called *Soren kenkyū* (Soviet research). The *Asahi shimbun* greeted the opening issue warmly, then added the chilling warning that the number of Japanese researchers on the Soviet Union was absolutely inadequate. Those who did visit the Soviet Union were largely in fields such as literature, the arts, and history. It is hard to find jobs in Soviet studies, the article also noted.[25] Even if the field of Soviet studies was not well prepared for the new challenges of Soviet watching, a small number of researchers (some of whom shifted their focus from historical topics) had become active by the middle of 1987 in reporting on each major turn in Soviet policy. The groundwork was laid for a more intense debate in a population slowly awakening to dramatic changes initiated from Moscow.

CHAPTER SEVEN

The Second Cycle, 1987–1989

Question 5: What Does the INF Agreement Mean, or, Are East-West Relations Changing?

IN THE FALL of 1987 Japanese-Soviet relations were at a standstill, while the debate on perestroika limped along with neither side able to prove its point convincingly. Because Gorbachev's approach kept growing bolder, the left of center felt that its view that the leadership was determined to achieve genuine reforms was more correct, while the worsening state of the Soviet economy reaffirmed the pessimism of the right that nothing substantial would come from the reforms. After a short lull in the debate, a second cycle of discussion commenced. Again international events roused the Japanese to reexamine their thinking. The INF agreement of December 1987 stood as the centerpiece in this reappraisal.

Already at the time of Gorbachev's Vladivostok speech in July 1986, a few voices to the left of center had found evidence of a new Soviet outlook on the world.[1] On the whole, however, the speech did not produce many ripples in the sea of Japanese doubters. This frustrated Soviet hopes to move quickly from the first cycle of awakening in response to Shevard-nadze's visit in January to a second cycle of serious Japanese doubts about the continuation of past ways of thinking and eventually a sharp split in public opinion. Nor did indications through the first half of 1987 of gradual improvements in relations with the United States, China, and Western European countries register strongly on the Japanese. Yet, as the year progressed, there were signs of uneasiness that Soviet-American relations and Soviet-Japanese relations were out of sync.

After a relatively hopeful year in 1986, 1987 was a bad year for relations between Tokyo and Moscow. To some degree Washington was blamed. It was suggested that Washington had a double standard—cautioning against Tokyo moving out in front toward Shevardnadze in 1986 while itself pushing rapidly ahead in 1987; responding to the Toshiba affair with tough demands for controls on Japan's industrial exports, while eagerly selling its own grain;[2] and later discouraging easy Japanese bank credits for the Soviet economy, while itself basking in the friendship of summit meetings. A lack of confidence in Washington—even accusations that it was playing a double game of a soft approach to Moscow and a hard approach to Tokyo—set the stage for a divergent response to the news of a breakthrough in Soviet-American relations.

Distrust for the INF. Japanese opinion was not well prepared for the INF agreement and the new spirit of superpower cordiality at the Washington summit where it was signed. One of the first questions that Japanese tried to answer was what were the motives of the Soviet Union. For years Japanese had been searching for the underlying motivation for Soviet conduct. Although during the period of détente in the 1970s some argued that Moscow was behaving as just another big power, and earlier in the postwar era the left had been enamored of the idea that a socialist country was inherently peace-loving, in the first half of the 1980s only two viewpoints were common: either the USSR was driven by its ideology or national character to seek world domination, or it was immutably opportunistic and could not be trusted to forgo any advantage it could seize except in the face of the superior strength of its opposition. These differences in assessing Soviet motives resurfaced in late 1987.

Many commentators reiterated the theory that Moscow is driven by the goal of world hegemony. Temporary retreat is merely a tactic toward its latent enemies. A few went so far as to brand the INF a KGB trick aimed at smashing SDI development or obtaining American or Japanese technology. Détente in its new garb was nothing more than a hidden military confrontation to be followed soon by a repeat of Moscow's contempt for treaties, as seen in 1945. Now the battlefield will be public opinion in Japan, the United States, and Western Europe. A psychological attack will leave citizens fearful of war and of nuclear weapons and eventually defenseless before the Soviets.[3]

Moscow's Opportunism. More common were criticisms that Soviet opportunism would continue. From the Gaimushō as late as the early summer of 1988, and from the critics favored by the general-interest journals for much longer, could be heard the warning that Soviet objectives had not changed.[4] Gorbachev had merely proven himself more astute than his predecessors in recognizing that with all of its conventional might, Moscow has sound military reasons for agreeing to the INF treaty, which, after all, only will eliminate 4 percent of nuclear weapons. Furthermore, his real worry is SDI, which he hopes to forestall by paying a small price. The INF does not represent a breakthrough. It is a tactical step that does not alter the overall Soviet strategy, while Moscow uses the time it has bought to restructure its machine-building industry and to obtain high technology from the capitalist countries intended for its weapons industry.

The Japanese right warned that history is repeating itself. The "new détente" would be similar to the 1970s: the West would drop its guard, and Moscow would consolidate it power after, in this case, removing unnecessary appendages to which it had unwisely overcommitted itself. To compromise with Moscow is only to encourage it to become aggressive again.[5]

On the right of center there was also an intermediate position that did not reject the INF agreement but also did not credit it with bringing significant change. It was a reserved judgment on Soviet motives. Kimura Hiroshi expressed this position.[6] Was the messianic drive of a country driven to world conquest now over? He answered that we must wait to see whether Moscow continues to export revolution—not as extreme a position as that of those who argued that until the pullback from Afghanistan, Cuba, Nicaragua, and so forth is complete, there is no reason to conclude that motives have changed. Is Moscow still opportunistically on the offensive? Yes, he said, it still seeks "amoeba-like growth where the chances of success are good." Yet he recognized that there are both opportunistic and defensive elements in its behavior, indicating that he accepted a portion of the argument that Moscow is simply behaving like a great power. Acknowledging that Moscow urgently needs the INF to stabilize its foreign environment, to respond to a sense of crisis over its economic difficulties, and to forestall the increasing superiority in American missiles based on high technology, Kimura cautiously supported the reasoning that this gives the West and Japan an opportunity to negotiate. He also made it very clear that he disagrees with those who say that Japan "should take an independent initiative toward disarmament and improving relations with the Soviet Union." He asserted that Moscow "respects countries with real power," Japan supported the United States and succeeded in getting the removal of SS-20s from Asia, and Japan has no alternative but to coordinate again with the United States.[7]

Moscow's Sincerity. While the message from many on the right was that the INF agreement and later the pullout from Afghanistan buys time for Moscow and improves its propaganda image, the message from the left and center was that a fundamental change had occurred. A genuine opportunity now existed because of new thinking in the Kremlin. This was not a repeat of the first détente.[8] As an ordinary great power, Moscow understood the futility of its past policies and the ill will they had engendered. It realized that its national interests can be best pursued by a different strategy of development and foreign relations. The old days are gone.

Morimoto Yoshio likened Moscow's dilemma to Tokyo's in the early 1940s.[9] It had followed a self-destructive course of combative relations on three fronts. Its motivation in doing so was largely that of a normal great power, for example, shock over the loss of China or over the encircling alliance of the United States, Japan, and China. Yet now the Kremlin is interested in a reduction of fronts and in a period of quiet in order to address domestic problems. Given these motives, Gorbachev cannot turn back. He is a realist, not an ideologue or opportunist. Akino Yutaka carried the argument further, predicting that Soviet dependence on the West will grow.[10] The new détente serves reform; internal motives are the driving force.

Within the Gaimushō were officials who had made a similar assessment. They had closely followed the spring 1986 Moscow conference on foreign policy, where Gorbachev had presented a new doctrine. They reported that the new approach to defense called only for sufficiency; economic diplomacy was gaining precedence over military diplomacy. While in the past diplomats returning from Moscow tended to heighten concerns about Soviet intentions, Ambassador Katori's return in the fall of 1987 and the supporting evidence from the younger individuals on the Soviet desk both in and outside Moscow strengthened the pro-INF group. The Gaimushō was divided: some inside it and some retirees with Soviet expertise were vocally skeptical of the INF, an influential group firmly supported it, and the mainstream handling Soviet matters took a middle position of expressing cautious acceptance while warning of potential dangers.

Implications for Japan. Japanese analysts also asked what the INF signifies for Japan and for American-Japanese relations. Some on the right concluded that there was now less reason to be confident of Washington.[11] Either its motives for cutting the INF deal were less than pure—Reagan's personal ambition to extricate himself from a decline in domestic support or to achieve a glorious place in history and a Republican victory in the fall, American eagerness to stop its slide as a declining power, or even American apprehensions about the economic threat from Japan—or it was gullible. Having forsaken his view of the "evil empire," Reagan had demonstrated that he did not understand Leninism.

Reliant on this sort of ally holding a nuclear umbrella needed for the protection of Japan, Tokyo presumably must now act. Yet critics of the INF could not agree on what response to take except to remain firm against Moscow and to redouble efforts to unite the Japanese people in their resolve. The implication that Tokyo must pursue a more independent policy led to occasional proposals of substantially more military spending or even a Japanese nuclear deterrent, but these ideas came from earlier advocates of the same unpopular positions. Whatever the recommendation for Japan's proper response, critics on the right expressed concern that Washington and Tokyo differed in their appraisal. Inoki Masamichi likened the current situation to 1940–42, threatening to erupt into a dangerous crisis in Japanese-American relations.[12] At the same time, there was growing concern that Washington was picking on Tokyo, although violators of export restrictions were known to exist in Europe too.

The other side in the Japanese debate over the INF argued not only that the agreement would promote world peace, but also that conditions were now favorable for Japanese-Soviet relations. These observers concluded that while some in Moscow in the first half of 1986 may have overestimated Japan's eagerness to normalize relations (even to the point of regarding Tokyo as more eager than Moscow), the Gorbachev leadership was increasingly realistic. It was signaling that Japan matters to Moscow a great deal. Should Tokyo not provide some encouragement, after hesitating so long to respond to the Vladivostok speech and other overtures? Why should Japan remain a bystander? If American-Japanese relations are experiencing some turbulence, then would it not be helpful to remind Washington that Tokyo has its own voice, just as Western European capitals do? How much further must Soviet-American and Soviet-Chinese relations improve before Japan does something to redress Japanese-Soviet relations?[13] These were some of the impatient questions being asked by a minority located to the left of center along Japan's political spectrum.

Japan's Fresh Diplomacy. In the spring of 1988 Japanese policy-making circles took a fresh look at bilateral relations with Moscow. They were motivated both by slight signs of an opportunity for a breakthrough, encouraged through signals from Moscow, and by growing frustration that their diplomacy seemed to be at a standstill and world opinion might become suspicious of Tokyo's motives. They adopted a two-pronged approach, largely in accord with moderate thinking and discarding the views of the extreme right. On the one hand, they chose the course that led to the Toronto summit tough line on Moscow. Moscow's thinking, they insisted, did not extend to the Asia-Pacific region, and the Soviets were still building up their military power in this area. Tokyo's allies must firmly support it in demanding the complete return of the Northern Territories and in separately assessing the European and East Asian fronts, with acknowledgment of Japan's special position on the latter. Japan would remain firm by restating its position and demonstrating its tenacity.[14] The allies obliged Tokyo in this strategy.

On the other hand, the Gaimushō moderate faction prepared to test Moscow's flexibility. They agreed to a visit by former Prime Minister Nakasone to Moscow if conditions were met for him to discuss the territorial question with Gorbachev and freely to address the Soviet people. The moderates reasoned that Gorbachev is indeed serious in his intentions toward Japan. His domestic economic situation is close to desperate, and he is eager for further diplomatic breakthroughs. Moreover, he is a strong and consistent leader with whom Tokyo can deal.

Why Tokyo Changed Course. Moderates could detect a calculated order in Soviet initiatives—domestic reform induced INF discussions, which were followed by withdrawal from Afghanistan and flexibility on Cambodia, leading to Sino-Soviet normalization, and finally to a willingness to take a new approach to Japan. Although not an immediate priority, Japan matters a great deal to a country whose central concern is to rebuild a shattered economy with foreign assistance.[15] These calculations by experienced diplomats—not a major swing in Japanese public opinion, a resurgence of the Japanese left, or pressure from Washington—shifted Tokyo onto a new course. The long-standing coalition between the far right and the right of center was broken. Nonetheless, the break was not sufficiently sharp to worry many on the right of center, who were persuaded that there was little to lose, or to upset delicate behind-the-scenes politics, including the balance between the cautious Takeshita and the bolder Nakasone.

Question 6: Is Japanese Public Opinion Vulnerable?

With Japanese in early 1988 wondering why their nation was not caught up in the excitement buzzing through other world capitals, the mood turned introspective. Many Japanese wondered if their fellow citizens were also beginning to change their thinking. From March to June, polls on the public's image of the Soviet Union and the new international security situation catered to this mounting curiosity.

Single-mindedness. Varied motivation existed for self-consciousness about the Soviet Union. The far right worried about dangerous illusions from the "Gorbachev fever" or the "Russia boom." They took for granted the existence of a Soviet plot to infiltrate the minds of the citizens in the West and to achieve Soviet objectives through an end-run around the existing political leadership. In a tone of alarm or, at least, concern, spokesmen on the right recognized the existence of easily coopted groups, individuals prone to misunderstand, and those harboring political ambitions who consciously or unconsciously become susceptible to giving the Soviets an easy propaganda victory. Their advice to their fellow Japanese was to keep soberly in mind the immediate objective of regaining the entire Northern Territories. This end justifies self-restraint in interpreting Soviet developments and even retention of the enemy image.[16] Idealism about a new era, if eventually justified, could be postponed until Moscow had met Tokyo's one fundamental demand. In short, the right preferred single-minded to open-minded responses to the new circumstances.

Diverse Advocates for Change. On the other side of the issue stood a varied, less vocal group, interested, first of all, in waging a national debate. They were not afraid of losing diplomatic leverage. Some sought an informed citizenry that could play a role in developing national policy—a challenge to the prevailing expectation of administrative guidance from above. Some were disturbed by the effects of misinformation, fearing that Japan's policies would be premised on old stereotypes, on a perception gap. A rather small group of Japanese had already developed a sympathy for Gorbachev and Soviet reformers and sought to achieve a broader reflection of their views in the Japanese population. Unlike 1985–86, they were no longer asking pessimistically, "Why do the Japanese hate the Soviets?" but a little bit hopefully, "How realistically are the Japanese responding to a new-style Soviet Union and to its changing international relations?"

Factors Affecting Images. From 1960 to 1974 the Soviet image in Japan had improved through four principal factors.[17] Moscow projected a forward-looking image of reform. It showed an interest in peaceful coexistence and détente. Its expanding trade with Japan, coupled with the immediate aftershocks of the oil crisis in 1973, convinced Japanese that they benefited from these contacts. Finally, a declining image of the United States affected by the Vietnam War inversely boosted the Soviet image. Some of these factors again came into play in the Gorbachev era. From 1985 the first two factors were renewed, but the third factor was absent. Moscow met with little success in persuading the Japanese of any tangible benefits from improved relations. The bilateral bottleneck meant that economic self-interest played little role in the open debate. Also, despite some increase in Japanese-American tensions, the inverse effect that had earlier operated as the fourth factor largely disappeared. The impression of increasing Soviet-American cooperation made it difficult to decouple the strategic changes in the two countries, and, in any case, Tokyo's quarrel with Washington was economic, which brought no payoff to Moscow.

Comparison through the Polls. At the end of December 1987 the *Asahi shimbun* published the results of a multinational poll on whether East-West relations will ease.[18] The English were optimistic, with 66 percent of respondents saying "yes." The Americans were cautious; 51 percent answered in the affirmative. The Japanese were pessimistic; only 35 percent expected an easing of relations. Responses to a question about whether we can trust the Soviets were similar. The West Germans reported a high of 73 percent; the English stood at 65 percent; the Americans, following Gorbachev's successful summit in Washington, recorded 55 percent—almost the same as the French at 54 percent; and the Japanese trailed sharply in their level of trust at only 34 percent. Their inquisitiveness piqued by quantitative and qualitative indications of greater Japanese skepticism, pollsters soon decided to take a closer look.

On February 20–22, 1988, Kyodo News Service and Tass conducted a joint poll of the Japanese and Soviet populations. An enormous gap in thinking could be detected. The headline in one Japanese paper expressed it as follows: "A Gap in the Mutual Sympathy Rate: Toward the Soviet Union 17%, toward Japan 88%."[19] The antipathy rate comparison was even more lopsided: 47.4 percent of Japanese negative toward the Soviet

Union in contrast to 2.4 percent of Soviets negative to Japan. Of the Japanese who expressed either sympathetic or antipathetic feelings, three-fourths did not consider the Soviet Union to be peace-loving (Soviets were evenly split in their responses on peace-loving Japan); three-fifths did not consider the Soviet Union to be economically developed (99 percent of Soviets thought Japan was); and six-sevenths did not consider the Soviet Union to be democratic (a majority of Soviets also did not consider Japan to be democratic).

Also striking was the gap in what was desired of the other country. Of Japanese volunteering a clear response, more than one-quarter did not consider the development of trade and economic relations useful as opposed to 1 percent of Soviets; over 90 percent of Japanese said the current boundary between the two countries is unjust, while 97 percent of Soviets called it just; and 10 percent of Japanese did not desire improved relations as opposed to less than 1 percent of Soviets. While the Japanese press also highlighted the positive result that there is overwhelming support for better relations in both countries, the deepest impression left by the poll was the tenacity of Japan's "minus image."[20]

The *Yomiuri shimbun* joined Moscow's Institute of Sociology in a March survey that probed more intensively into mutual perceptions.[21] Again a huge gap was revealed. While 3.8 percent of Soviets considered current Soviet-Japanese relations bad and another 0.1 percent chose very bad, 37.3 and 3.0 percent of Japanese respectively selected these answers. Consciousness of the Soviet problems ran high. Although most Japanese joined the Soviets in expressing a desire for improved relations, they were less enthusiastic (27.8 percent vs. 56.7 percent considering it a must) and there were more dissenters (9.7 vs. 1.3 percent not considering it desirable). For the Soviets, trade and economic cooperation (82 percent), scientific and technological exchange (52 percent), and, to a lesser degree, cultural and human exchanges (34 percent) were a priority. For the Japanese, only the return of the Northern Territories (60 percent) and developing fishing (49 percent) were checked by more than 27 percent of respondents, each of whom could indicate up to two choices. Of those answering yes or no, 37 percent of Japanese (as opposed to 12 percent of Soviets) did not think that perestroika or glasnost would be useful in the development of friendly bilateral relations.

A Friendship Gap. Other questions in the joint survey examined attitudes toward the other country and information about it. As in the earlier survey, this poll revealed a gigantic friendship gap. Nine times as many Soviets felt a strong friendship (13.6 vs. 1.5 percent), and almost three times as many felt some friendship (63.2 vs. 23.4 percent). Given more choices than in the Tass-Kyodo News Service poll, Japanese preferred to say they are not very friendly (60.2 vs. 9.1 percent) rather than that they feel antipathy (7.0 percent vs. 0.4 percent). Describing the Soviet people, Japanese volunteered such labels as closed, dark, cold (each 8 percent), self-centered (7 percent), and stoical (5 percent), with no more than 3 percent of respondents agreeing on any positive images such as big-hearted. In contrast, there was considerable Soviet consensus on industrious and serious (together 41 percent) to describe Japanese.

Japanese disinterest could be seen in the fact that when asked to choose up to three things they would like to know about the Soviet Union, 23.7 percent answered there was nothing in particular (an answer not selected by the Soviets). Also, while 74.7 percent of Japanese said they receive news on Soviet-Japanese relations from the newspapers and 80.9 percent from television, the figures for magazines (15.7 percent vs. 28.5 percent of Soviets), books (4.7 percent vs. 16.4 percent), movies (2.4 percent vs 17.4 percent), acquaintances and relatives (1.5 percent vs. 3.6 percent), and nothing in particular (6.9 percent vs. 1.3 percent) suggest a state of indifference contrasting with Soviet interest in Japan.[22] Japanese regarded Soviet-Japanese relations as less important for reducing world tensions and were less concerned about the possibility of nuclear war. The polls showed a mixture of antipathy and apathy in the Japanese response.

Improving Images in 1988. Other polls in the first half of 1988 drew further attention to the relatively negative Japanese attitudes. When asked for their response to the May summit in Moscow between Gorbachev and Reagan, 3 percent were strongly against, another 17 percent were also negative, 46 percent were positive, and 22 percent were very positive—results very similar to those after the Washington summit in December, although the very positive category had dropped from 26 to 22 percent and the negative category had risen by 1 percent. When asked at the same time whether they expected progress in disarmament, 12 percent who were positive about the summit joined the negative side. Only 5 percent were very positive on both the summit and disarmament.[23] Skepticism prevailed on the eve of former Prime Minister Nakasone's visit to Moscow.

The annual prime minister's office survey of views on the Soviet Union appeared in October. This time 3.1 percent of Japanese felt friendly (*shitashimi o kanjiru*), up from 2.1 in October 1987, 1.9 a year earlier, 1.5 in June of the year Gorbachev took office, and an all-time low of 1.2 percent in June 1984. The figures for somewhat friendly were also creeping upward from a 1984 recent low of 6.4 percent (in 1980 and 1981 the nadir of 6.0 and 5.9 percent had been reached) to 7.1 and 7.0 percent in 1985 and 1986, 7.7 percent in 1987, and 11.0 percent in 1988. Correspondingly, those who felt unfriendly slipped from 48.4 percent in 1984 (50.1 percent in 1981 was the only figure to top that) to a plateau of 43.2, 44.0, and 43.2 percent in 1985, 1986, and 1987 respectively, and finally down to 36.9 percent in the fall of 1988. The accompanying analysis rather hopefully noted that in comparison to survey results over the past eleven years, even if many still disliked the Soviet Union, the friendliness rate was the highest yet.[24] From just before the INF agreement through the national debate following the Nakasone meeting with Gorbachev, Moscow had made its most substantial dent in the "hate rate" in any single year. The ascendance of Gorbachev had made a small impact in 1985, but the period from 1986 to 1987 had scarcely left any impression on Japanese sentiment. Only in 1988 did friendliness notably improve.

The prime minister's office offered a breakdown of the fall 1988 data, which again showed that men are friendlier (4.4 vs. 1.7 percent, and, for somewhat friendly, 13.0 vs. 9.0 percent for women).[25] Individuals in their fifties registered the highest combined rate for the two friendly categories (3.2 and 14.3 percent), while those in their sixties (educated in the wartime years) were the least friendly (1.7 and 7.8 percent) and most decidedly placing themselves unequivocally in the unfriendly category (46.8 percent vs. 33–38 percent for all other age groups). At the other end of the age spectrum, there was no sign that Moscow could count on youth to improve its image.

On a separate question, Japanese were continuing a pattern evident since 1984 of gradually seeing the state of Soviet-Japanese relations in a more favorable light. The number who did not see relations as good had fallen almost by half in four years (37.0 to 19.4 percent), while the number who considered them quite good had tripled from 7.1 to 22.2 percent. Still, there was little change in the popular "not very good" category, hovering around 40–44 percent.

In late November there was also a poll by the *Hokkaidō shimbum*.[26] It found that Hokkaidō residents were more interested in nature, culture, and social conditions in the Soviet Union than in any other of the seven regions of the world listed (the top choice of 14.9 percent exceeded North America at 14.5 percent). Here, close to the Northern Territories, the rate of friendliness was 20.1 percent as opposed to 75.0 percent who did not feel that way. The highest level of outright unfriendliness appeared at the two age extremes—of those in their sixties (37.7 percent) and in their twenties (33.3 percent). Women were both more negative and less informed (20.3 percent could not say whether relations are good or bad as opposed to 9.5 percent of men).

In late 1988 the doubtful atmosphere remained widespread, but there were many with some hope. Of respondents, 51.4 percent did not expect much from perestroika for Japanese-Soviet relations, while 4.2 percent (males had a slight edge over females) had high expectations. Idealism was lacking among youth; those in their twenties had the lowest expectations. Private businessmen had the highest expectations, forming the only group in which as many as half expressed some degree of optimism, and were least apt to answer that the Soviet military poses a big threat to Japan (16.7 vs. an average of 26.4 percent). At least in Hokkaidō some economic interests operated in favor of improved relations.

Gaimushō Confidence and the Soviet Strategy. The Gaimushō remained confident of support from the Japanese people although recognizing that in the first half of 1988 Gorbachev's book sold more than 100,000 copies and the Soviet peace offensive retained its momentum in the United States and Western Europe. The polls produced some minor changes of concern, but no reason for alarm.

At the same time, Japanese organizations friendly to Moscow could at least take satisfaction from the new-found interest of a minority of Japanese in the Soviet Union. *Izvestia* reported in May that the Japan-Soviet Society had set a new line in March to acquaint the Japanese public with the life of the Soviet people and Soviet policies through meetings, demonstrations, exhibitions, propaganda, and tourism.[27] Although the article complained that Soviet service does not always correspond to world standards, and indifferently dictates to the client what he or she will drink and in what buses he or she will move, it added that there is now great interest among Japanese in seeing the Bolshoi Theater and the Kremlin. The current figure of twenty thousand tourists a year could at least be doubled without special effort. These modest hopes scarcely offered grounds for a peace offensive. Obviously such paltry efforts could not transform the Soviet image in Japan and, indeed, taking into account the warnings about quality of service, might prove counterproductive. Aware of the dark image of their country in Japan, Soviet strategists adopted a new and different kind of bilateral strategy in the summer of 1988, highlighted by the visit of former Prime Minister Nakasone.

Question 7: Is Moscow Serious about Discussing Territorial Concessions, or, Has Soviet Policy toward Japan Really Changed?

Since 1956 Japanese had been awaiting the second stage of peace treaty negotiations after stopping with an agreement limited to restoring diplomatic relations. Since 1960 they had waited for Moscow to reverse itself and at least repeat its offer to return two islands earlier withdrawn in response to the new U.S.-Japanese security pact. Since 1973 Japanese had hoped that another Soviet leader would dare to state that a territorial problem exists, after Brezhnev had apparently let slip his assent to this reference in a summit with Tanaka only to have Soviet authorities retract it soon afterward. Yet, what hope could there be for Japan when the military balance so decidedly favored the Soviet side? The Japanese internal campaign for the return of the islands intensified in the 1980s, but debate about how it might happen seemed futile. When Gorbachev came to office, faint hopes slowly began to gain some substance.

The Nakasone Visit. In 1986 the two countries failed to make progress on the territorial question. Japanese expectations had been low, although Nakasone had vainly sought to extend his career in office and to reach a long-standing goal through securing Soviet concessions. It can be assumed that among Nakasone's hopes, in the fall of 1987, in arranging for Uno Sōsuke of his faction to carry on as foreign minister and in founding a new International Institute for Global Peace (IIGP), which formally opened in June 1988, was to play a personal role in the eventual breakthrough with the Kremlin. The announcement in the early summer of 1988 that he would soon meet Gorbachev in Moscow revived excitement in bilateral relations after a two-year interruption.

The Gaimushō approved Nakasone's visit despite misgivings that it would send the wrong signal to Gorbachev about Tokyo's eagerness or that the ex–prime minister's personal (some Japanese would add bold and potentially irresponsible) diplomacy might reach beyond the bounds of the cautious approach favored by the diplomats. While some may have hoped that this step could have the potential of starting Japan's transition into a political superpower, the reality was a modest exploration to break a stalemate, to try to catch Gorbachev's attention, and to act in concert with allied support. Yet the Gaimushō remained pessimistic that much would be accomplished. After the meeting with Gorbachev the stenographic record was examined closely. Apparently the Gaimushō was, on the whole, satisfied that Nakasone had not strayed.

Moscow tried hard to impress the Japanese public with its flexibility. A barrage of background remarks at conferences and in interviews coincided with the Nakasone visit. Soviets would now discuss the POW issue.[28] They would invite joint ventures on the islands.[29] Hints appeared about Soviet willingness to return two islands.[30] In addition, Nakasone was granted a meeting for nearly three hours with Gorbachev, who for the first time personally referred to the previous Soviet offer to return two islands. Japanese commentaries did not fail to note hopeful signs in the calm bilateral discussion between the two "lawyers"—one from the Tōdai Law Department and the other from the Moscow State University Law Department. The Soviets promised to send Shevardnadze to Tokyo before the end of the year, and Gorbachev himself pledged his best efforts to come at the earliest possible date.

Substantively, Japan had apparently not gained anything concrete from the Gorbachev-Nakasone meeting. As one paper phrased the outcome, "Gorbachev spurns Nakasone on matter of northern islands."[31] The Japanese visitor's own reaction was different. It was summed up as, "Nakasone lauds Soviet words, urges to take initiative further."[32] Upon returning to Tokyo, he wrote a series of four articles for the *Yomiuri shimbun*.[33] First he explained that he had presented the Japanese case for all the islands, reviewing the historical record. Never before had Japan succeeded in doing that in the presence of the top Soviet leader. This sincere talk between the two countries represents a big advance, not one hundred meters but perhaps ten to fifteen meters, as Nakasone put it. Second, Nakasone took credit for gathering together Soviet opinion leaders on international strategy and diplomacy to clarify for them Japanese philosophy and strategy. To the Japanese people attentive to international problems in correctly understanding their country, such communications carry symbolic value. Third, in accordance with his strong wish, Nakasone was permitted to speak directly to the Soviet people with no cuts. With this visit, the way the Soviets and Japanese interact diplomatically has changed; Japanese will now appreciate that the age of glasnost has arrived.

Had the Soviet position toward Japan changed? Nakasone wrote of the need to pursue very delicate nuances in Soviet responses through diplomatic channels. He said that this visit should not be assessed at once. Yet he also acknowledged that Gorbachev had insisted that the two countries must start from postwar realities, and that the Soviet Union can develop its Far Eastern and Siberian regions without assistance from Japan. Nakasone reminded the Japanese people that the Soviet Union is an Asia-Pacific country and that it is wrong to ignore Soviet existence or to say Soviet cooperation is unnecessary. Although there are numerous unresolved questions related to regional concerns, Gorbachev enthusiastically affirmed that no matter what the difficulties in achieving joint steps forward, the Soviets want to proceed. The *Yomiuri shimbun* also reminded its readers that without the Nakasone-Gorbachev talks there would be no progress; the atmosphere had improved.[34] With this start, both sides now needed to prepare the environment for negotiations when Shevardnadze would next be coming to Japan.

The Public Reaction. One train of thought that developed in the wake of the July visit sympathetically centered on Gorbachev's plight. Nakasone laid the blame for the territorial problem and a breakdown in trust between East and West on Stalin's mistakes, implying that Gorbachev might find a way to rethink bilateral relations in the context of accelerating criticisms of Stalin. In his articles the former Japanese leader called expectantly not only for new thinking, but also for a Copernicus-like change from the legacy of expansionism and containment.[35] Optimism in Japan might derive from expectations that Soviet leaders, opinion shapers, and the public can be educated on the history of bilateral relations even if a sudden policy change would not easily win support. The soil for a new approach now exists. Time will tell what will flower.

A mixture of cautious optimism and uncertain skepticism greeted Nakasone's remarks. Follow-up contacts were quickly planned. In September Sase Masamori, Kimura Hiroshi, and others formed a six-person delegation to visit Moscow. In October an international forum followed in Vladivostok, then dietmen participated in a roundtable in Moscow; and finally Evgenyi M. Primakov and Giorgyi Kunadze of Moscow's Institute of World Economy and International Relations, who were working together to shape a new Soviet-Japan policy, returned to Tokyo. The wheels of informal diplomacy were grinding as Japanese analysts continued to reflect on the new developments.

Matching Moscow's Flexibility. One could detect a wide spectrum of responses. From the left of center came a revival of ideas for seizing a propitious opportunity and meeting Moscow's flexibility part way. Wada Haruki asserted that at last the deadend is being broken. Now both sides need to reflect and compromise. Since the Soviets won the war, it is natural that Japan compromise more, taking as its starting point the San Francisco Treaty of 1951, which saw Japan abandon its rights to the Kurile Islands with the reservation that two islands belong to Hokkaidō rather than to the northern chain above it. Wada recounted the recent Soviet reexamination of stereotypes toward Japan which are intended to break the deadlock. He suggested that by a detailed review of the postwar Japanese process leading to San Francisco, when under U.S. pressure Prime Minister Yoshida rejected a flexible Gaimushō position, Japanese awareness will be altered and a historical basis for compromise found. Wada's plan is for the return of two islands with demilitarized and joint development on them, and free movement on the others, even though they would remain Soviet territory.[36] This is the "exit" approach, much dreaded by the Gaimushō.

Fujimura Shin (Kumata Tōru is the real name of this Paris reporter) also urged compromise. He said a terrific opportunity exists to resolve a relic of the past that keeps Japan a dwarf on the political stage even when it has become an economic giant. If Japan could play the Soviet card, it would achieve an independent position in international diplomacy and at the same time widen its worldview. Now the world is in the midst of enormous change. As seen from Europe, the Northern Territories are a mystery. Why should Tokyo be deepening instability in the Far East and losing the Soviet market and raw materials over this minor item? After all, Dulles created this deadend. Now Moscow has swept away its old generation of leaders and is moving toward an objective approach. Gorbachev's September 16 speech at Krasnoyarsk further indicates his effort to reduce tensions in the Far East. It is time, Fujimura urged, for objective thinking in Japan too, including glasnost about the documents that led Japan to follow the United States into the cold war. Japan should agree to take two islands back and put the other two under UN management as Soviet trust territories while further talks are held. Tokyo should understand Soviet unease about Japanese militarization of the area. Fujimura made this appeal in the name of the internationalization of Japan—to develop an autonomous, independent consciousness of its international responsibilities and to step out of the shadow of the big American tree.[37]

Remaining Firm. Such calls for Japan to change were in a small minority. More typical was the response of Hasegawa Keitarō, who insisted that it is Moscow, not Tokyo, that must solve the Northern Territories obstacle to good economic relations. Japan lacks national resources but is confident of access to them in a buyers' market. The Soviet Union only has raw materials, not technology or capital. The seller must sell following the free-market mechanism, or drop out of the market—a situation unlikely to change until the middle of the twenty-first century. The Soviets are alone in not even having a branch bank in Tokyo. Clearly, the power balance is on the side of Japan. This is the reality.[38] The Japanese public was not alone in paying heed to this message. Hasegawa's article appeared in *Izvestia* on November 17 before its publication in Japan.

A Turn toward Optimism. From the center and even from some to the right of center on the Japanese political spectrum came a subdued version of the same message coupled with a degree of optimism that Moscow was now listening. For instance, Kimura Hiroshi welcomed subtle changes in the Soviet position. Along with some in the Gaimushō, Kimura had become noticeably more hopeful about bilateral relations.[39] In comparison to previous periods, with the slight exception of the first half of 1986, an optimistic mood was building and would continue until the start of 1991, despite some setbacks in 1989. Yet opinions on the far right and even from others on the right of center remained decidedly doubtful. In their view, nothing had occurred to indicate a genuine departure from the old Soviet policy.

New articles by Wada Haruki, updating his earlier advocacy of a compromise on the islands, drew harsh replies from the right as nothing more than the two-island Soviet trick. Wada garnered a more respectful commentary from *Nihon keizai shimbun*, although the latter faulted him for not incorporating Washington's attitude into the analysis.[40] On the eve of the much anticipated Shevardnadze visit, the discussion was heating up.

A Warning against Nakasone. While many considered the Nakasone visit to be an information breakthrough, causing Soviets to understand Japanese views better and Japanese at last to realize that Soviet attitudes are changing, a curious article in the October issue of *Shokun* judged the visit a failure.[41] Speculation was rife that the article represented a stab in Nakasone's back by the envious Takeshita faction. There were rumors that Takeshita had not been pleased with the idea of the Nakasone "elder statesman" (*genrō*) diplomacy in the first place. Then Nakasone's *Yomiuri* articles may have seemed to exploit the success for his own purposes. Other Japanese analysts traced the article to the disgruntled right in the ruling party and the bureaucracy, who feared that the remilitarization of Japan would be thrown off course by a rapprochement with Moscow. For the first time in decades, divisions within the LDP on the Soviet issue were rising to the forefront in Japanese diplomacy.

The *Shokun* article by Kishida Kazuhiro speculates about a complex plot between (1) the crafty efforts of Gorbachev's "brains" to arrange for Japanese economic and technical cooperation for Soviet Far Eastern development (without which perestroika would fail) by constructing a "pipe" to the powers of Japan's ruling party; and (2) the behind-the-scenes views of a regretful Nakasone, who left office before having completed his biggest life work and having brought postwar politics to a full resolution by eliminating the thorn of the Northern Territories question. The article asserts that in the past Nakasone had flustered the Gaimushō once while in office by suggesting at a news conference at the fortieth anniversary of the United Nations that he and Foreign Minister Abe may visit Moscow after Shevardnadze's January 1986 visit to Tokyo, but Moscow scotched the idea by pointing out that already a Japanese leader had gone to Moscow four times, so it would be appropriate this time for the Soviet leader to go to Tokyo. Nevertheless, Nakasone pressed forward through Hasegawa Kazutoshi, a high Gaimushō official labeled the "Japanese Kissinger," through N. N. Solovyev, the Soviet ambassador, and through other contacts. In May 1988 a member of Nakasone's faction met Shevardnadze, as secret plans developed, while in Japan a week later, Primakov held an unannounced meeting with the powerful LDP boss Kanemaru Shin, through the go-between Suetsugu Ichirō, whose role in the return of Okinawa is recalled in the article. Kanemaru's approval of a Nakasone visit now cleared the way. Throughout this lengthy account tracing the route of preliminary contacts, Kishida gives the impression of something not quite proper taking place.

Kishida's critical account suggests that Nakasone's talk of a breakthrough represents his own personal desire. Kishida contrasts the former leader's wide-ranging Moscow talks for advancing bilateral relations with the Gaimushō's careful approach of addressing the Northern Territories first (the "entry" approach) and limiting economic exchanges until later (i.e., making politics and economics inseparable). Since it is in Moscow's interest to follow the former strategy and to have a "pipe" to the LDP for negotiations, Nakasone is, the article implies, doing Moscow's bidding.

In Kishida's opinion, Moscow had tried before to bypass the Gaimushō through a "second diplomacy," even approaching the number two LDP leader Nikaido before the Gaimushō quashed the idea. A pro-Soviet clique of dietmen has also been used. After the Kanemaru-Primakov meeting the Gaimushō again became alarmed. According to Kishida, there then occurred a sudden shakeup in the Gaimushō as Hasegawa Kazutoshi was shifted, long before the end of a normal tenure, from head of the Eurasian Department to the head of the Asian Department—the first time in recollection that one person had served as head of two regional departments in the Gaimushō. This could only be explained as an effort to move a pro-Nakasone man out, Kishida adds. The Gaimushō placed conditions on the Nakasone visit, but Nakasone saw the visit as a way to regain his power in the foreign field while leaving domestic matters to Takeshita. The media splash he made boosted his confidence beyond what was justified from the results of his talks. The Gaimushō had to remind him that Gorbachev's oblique reference to the subject of returning two islands actually only repeated what had occurred in the Soviet leader's meeting two months earlier with the JSP leader Doi Takako, although the media had mostly overlooked that occasion.

Kishida concludes that Moscow miscalculated in assuming that Nakasone enjoyed real power in the Takeshita regime and at the Gaimushō. Hasegawa wrongly believed that Nakasone could copy former Prime Minister Tanaka as a kingmaker and could control Takeshita, hoping in this way that Nakasone might win the Nobel Prize or become prime minister again. Meanwhile, Moscow pursued a multi-angled approach to Japan's conservative mainstream, for instance, arranging a secret late July meeting with Abe in a Tokyo hotel. The immediate Soviet aim was entry into the Asia-Pacific economic sphere. To achieve this, Kishida authoritatively asserts, its real negotiating partner could not be Nakasone.

Itō Kenichi's criticism of Nakasone's enthusiasm was more muted.[42] He called the meeting with Gorbachev 99 percent successful, only faulting a failure to respond to Gorbachev's mention of the twenty million Soviet victims in World War II. Itō argued that the proper response should have been that the Soviet attack on Japan in 1945 was separate from the world war. Acknowledging that Moscow has finally noticed the ineffectiveness of its "threat diplomacy," Itō contended that this signifies only a change in tactics, not in strategy. He further warned that Japanese responses to the July meeting reveal the danger of Soviet orchestration to divide Japanese opinion. The formal Soviet side plays hard, while the informal, nonofficial Soviet side plays soft. Under a single conductor, the Communist party, the percussions and the strings play different parts to confuse the Japanese. Itō asserted confidently that Moscow's real intent (honne) is not to return more than two islands.

Sase Masamori made the same case, but he added that the informal side sometimes exceeds its limits; earlier, when a Soviet spokesmen was carried away with his remarks, there was unease back in Moscow. Sase pointed directly at the Japanese vice of blowing up Soviet trial balloons, which in turn originate as floating ideas from Japanese such as Wada. Moscow realizes that they can be used to suggest a catchy tune to the Japanese public, as long as it is sufficiently elusive so as not to disconcert the Soviet conductors.[43]

Long a critic of Nakasone, the *Asahi shimbun* had been one of the first sources to cast aspersions on his purported "comeback plot." It suggested in late August that there had been no letup in his diplomatic fever and that his clique (*batsu*) was now meeting in Karuizawa to pursue this goal while Nakasone was preparing further trips to world centers.[44] The weekly *Shūkan shinchō* also stressed Nakasone's ambition in flying over the Gaimushō in search of glory.[45]

The Shevardnadze Visit. By the time Shevardnadze arrived in December, the Japanese internal debate had become rather heated. Kimura Hiroshi was now somewhat optimistic, leaving behind Sase and other unimpressed colleagues on the right.[46] Some observers on the left were raising expectations, talking of a possible breakthrough and of Japan now even becoming the Soviet diplomatic focus.[47] If late July produced the first peak in optimism that Moscow at last recognizes the territorial problem, December represented the second and higher peak suggesting that a solution to the problem is at last possible.

The December foreign ministers' meeting proved to be a little disappointing. In the final communiqué there was no mention of the territorial problem. Kimura still found evidence of a slight advance in the lively discussion that occurred and in the Soviet television coverage that he watched on his satellite receiver.[48] Lauding the working group that was newly established to discuss a peace treaty, Kimura suggested that the Soviets are preparing domestic opinion for a compromise on the territorial issue. Because forward movement still seemed possible through the newly established channel, disappointment at year's end did not lead many to reassess their expectations.

A Newspaper Angers the Gaimushō. In January 1989 the *Hokkaidō shimbun* published its poll from late November mentioned previously. The forward to its booklet (released after Emperor Hirohito's death) begins with the statement that now we are greeting the first year of the Heisei era, and we have come to expect that Soviet-Japanese negotiations addressing the Northern Territories problem will advance steadily.[49] In the December meeting the two countries decided to establish a working group to conclude a peace treaty, and the Soviet side displayed an attitude of formally discussing the Northern Territories question. The working group meets in March, Foreign Minister Uno goes to Moscow in May, and preparations will be made for Secretary Gorbachev to come to Japan.

His coming within the year is seen as almost certain, and if summit talks are held, a lot of work will be accomplished toward a breakthrough on the territorial question.

With this optimistic outlook, the paper reported the poll results on the problem of the islands. Asked if the Soviets would return the Northern Territories, 37.4 percent answered "yes" and 53.4 percent "no." Among persons in their fifties, a slight majority said "yes," while the youngest respondents in their twenties were so pessimistic that the negative side prevailed by a ratio of 5:2. Optimism rose with age until the expected drop for the prewar educated group in their sixties (4:3 negative), which in its response resembled persons in their forties but with many more not answering either way. When asked what is the territory sought from the Soviets, only 50.6 percent (58.2 of males and 43.3 percent of females) of respondents answered four islands. As many as 30.9 percent said the entire Kurile chain, and 10.5 percent said only the two nearest islands of Habomai and Shikitan.

For the first time a Japanese poll also asked what would be the response if the Soviet Union offered to return two islands. As many as 48 percent of the Hokkaidō residents said that Japan would have to take them and leave open the path for the return of the two more distant islands of Kunashiri and Etorofu later. Just 26 percent insisted on no concessions from the "entry" approach of four islands returned in one batch, while 10 percent said that Japan would have to give up the other two islands, and 6 percent insisted on demanding the entire Kurile chain. Women were less tenacious than men, while, when offered this variety of choices, younger respondents proved to be especially flexible (only 18 percent of those in their twenties insisted on four islands at once, and almost 13 percent would settle for two without seeking a later deal).

The *Hokkaidō shimbun* editorialized about the survey.[50] It said that the people were long accustomed to a hard Soviet diplomatic posture and were slow to alter their consciousness and expectations toward more optimism. Reading the survey results, analysts wondered instead about the large percentage of respondents prepared to accept only two islands. Was this a peculiarly Hokkaidō complex among Soviet neighbors both attached to nearby territory and eager for good ties with the Soviet Union? The Gaimushō was not pleased with this sign of division and flexibility toward Moscow at a crucial time in negotiations. According to rumors, foreign service officers were told not to grant interviews to *Hokkaidō shimbun* reporters.

The Paris Setback. In January 1989 Foreign Minister Uno met again with Shevardnadze—this time in Paris. A still powerful right-wing lobby urged him to take a tough stance on the assumption that Moscow is anxious for a breakthrough and will best appreciate the inevitability of re-

turning four islands to achieve that if Tokyo takes a hard line. Shevardnadze, meanwhile, was promoting the idea that mutual compromise is
necessary. Now that Moscow has met Japanese demands part way by
recognizing the existence of the territorial problem and other steps, it is
time for Tokyo to propose something new, he apparently reasoned. The
Kremlin also may have objected to the way the Gaimushō formulated its
position on the territorial problem in December, accusing the Soviets of
behaving in August 1945 like a robber at the scene of a fire (*kajiba
dorobo*) and of taking advantage of Japanese distress by plundering.[51]
Whatever the provocation, the tone of the dialogue, including Soviet journal articles, degenerated in the winter of 1989.

Dampening Expectations. Some Japanese articles sought to dampen
the still high public expectations. In February Hakamada Shigeki reminded readers that although the atmosphere now was completely different from that of Shevardnadze's 1986 visit when Japanese were not expecting progress on the territorial problem, the official Soviet essence
(*honne*) was to return two islands and to pigeonhole with continued discussion the return of the other two in return for economic and scientific
and technical cooperation.[52] Moscow fears stirring territorial demands
elsewhere and even unwinding the Yalta system and the Helsinki accord
of 1975 that ratified it. Despite such cautionary statements, expectations
remained rather high. On February 7, which in the 1980s became the day
of remembrance for the Northern Territories, the usually hostile annual
atmosphere was broken by an NHK television call to a Soviet journalist
on the island of Kunashiri, who spoke of his government's willingness to
talk about the territorial issue.

A Rekindling of Interest. Direct communications with the islands
sparked further interest. An April 1989 booklet by the *Hokkaidō shimbun* staff, which was permitted to visit Kunashiri, colorfully portrayed
life on the islands.[53] Soviets continued to float proposals for joint use of
the islands, which had first surfaced the previous July as soft background
music for the Nakasone visit. When it had appeared late in the summer of
1988 that members of the Ainu minority with historical ties to the area
might take the Soviet bait, the head of the Soviet desk in Tokyo had
rushed to Hokkaidō and managed to persuade them to wait for a territorial settlement.[54]

Deputy Foreign Minister Kuriyama Takakazu, who headed the Japanese side in the peace treaty negotiations working group established in
December 1988, asserted skeptically that there is still no fundamental
change in bilateral relations and restated Tokyo's December position on
the history of the territories. His Soviet counterpart, Igor Rogachev, responded in kind. Although the atmosphere in the Gaimushō and its new
journal, which covered perestroika favorably in a special February issue,

was, on the whole, flexible, the tone of discourse remained strained for a time.

The Soviet side was initially very disappointed and said that if Japan concentrates all problems into the territorial question, Gorbachev might be better off not going there. Then Soviet commentaries became severe, retreating from December's gains. The Soviet disappointment in January 1989 was eventually interpreted by Tōgō Takehiro as only a misunderstanding.[55] Without admitting that the Japanese side had earlier intentionally toughened its stance or exploring why that happened, Tōgō touched on a sensitive phase in the negotiating process. The Japanese side, he noted, had tried to explain that if the territorial question were not resolved, a peace treaty could not be concluded, and if that did not occur, Japanese-Soviet relations would not be normalized. Uno had made clear that Japan would welcome a visit by Gorbachev and wanted to make it a reality; however, if the Soviet side did not intend to work on the territorial question, the Japanese side would not work in the areas the Soviets proposed for cooperation. Then Gorbachev's visit would be just for conversation, which would be okay but not very successful and very regrettable.

The atmosphere improved at the May meeting when Uno visited Moscow. This time Uno came prepared to talk simultaneously about territorial and other issues. He spoke of the importance of an "expanded equilibrium" (*kakudai kinkō*) between the two countries.[56] In December Shevardnadze had asked for agreements in six areas relating to economic matters, the peaceful use of space, tourism, and environmental protection. Uno refused to consider any of these topics until the territorial issue was resolved. In May as a gesture of goodwill, he agreed to discuss the environment. Tokyo also reopened consultations—talks suspended almost a decade earlier—on maritime transport to move goods to Siberian trains en route to and from Europe. Moreover, rather than rejecting as an unnecessary clause Moscow's call for a declaration of friendship as part of a peace treaty, Tokyo agreed to consider a separate paper on this. Clearly, the moderates who wanted to encourage Soviet flexibility, in stages, had prevailed over the hardliners in the Gaimushō and the LDP who insisted on applying maximum pressure.

Kimura Hiroshi left no doubt of his association with the moderates.[57] He suggested five conditions for solving the Northern Territories problem and sounded positive about the prospects. In the Soviet journal *Novoe vremia* Kimura also appealed for Gorbachev to visit Japan, adding that a solution to the territorial problem does not need to be found beforehand, and that Gorbachev's visit will help.[58] From the leading Soviet academics came positive articles about pulling out Soviet armed forces from the area, and reconsidering long-standing objections to the U.S.-Japanese security treaty. After years of arrogance, Soviets were demonstrating their respect for Japan and for its Soviet specialists, whose articles now appeared in Russian journals and were being taken seriously.

The Pivotal Right of Center. Why had many Japanese on the right of center shifted toward the center beginning in mid-1987 and accelerating in 1988? Of course, changing Soviet policies helped convince some. Close cooperation with American and Soviet specialists may have played a role, too. In the spring of 1987 a joint U.S.-Japan study group began to bring together experts from the two countries. At first, the discrepancy in thinking was pronounced. As meetings continued and joint reports to both governments were prepared for early 1989, a convergence of viewpoints could be detected. Some members of this study group also had ties to the Trilateral Commission, which provided another venue for cross-national influence. Nakasone's "brains" also saw his views become clarified in the context of his meeting with Gorbachev and his Soviet visit. Of course, not all experts changed their views to an equal degree. Having visited Moscow often and personally learned in detail of Soviet new thinking, Kimura Hiroshi moved toward a centrist position faster than most.

In the middle of 1989 Japan faced a political crisis in which three prime ministers served in three months and the LDP unexpectedly lost control of the upper house of the Diet. If Moscow had been looking ahead to Abe Shintarō as Takeshita's successor and hoped to pursue personal diplomacy through Kanemaru after the Nakasone connection did not materialize, then it was a time for caution.[59]

Developments in bilateral relations over a year left a cautious mainstream group still doubtful that Gorbachev would do what was necessary but ready to pursue new opportunities, a pleased left-of-center group surprised that Japanese diplomacy had become more flexible but still not confident that this trend would advance, and a frustrated right wing certain that the Soviets were taking advantage of Japan without any intent to deliver. Within that group, there may have been some who actually worried that the Kremlin would deliver the four islands. According to one type of interpretation, some Japanese do not want to see a dramatic upturn in relations. They have formed a crisis mentality. They need an enemy. They dream of military power. They hope that Japan will not recover the islands until its military has revived.[60]

Japanese Soviet-watchers attentively assessed Moscow's motives in changing its approach to Japan from the time of the Nakasone visit. These analysts noted the effort to reconstruct Asian policy as reflected in Soviet journal articles during the summer of 1988, the new importance attached to relations with Japan, the shift in the Soviet Foreign Ministry to multidirectional diplomacy, and the heightened expectations about Japan's economic power and the Asia-Pacific region. They also stressed that when negotiations occurred in 1956 and 1973 there was a huge gap in power between the two countries, while today, in some respects, Japan's power is great. Raising Moscow's image in Japan is one of the goals of a changing Soviet diplomacy, they recognized. For all of these reasons, the Soviet approach has changed.[61]

Question 8: Will Perestroika Work?

When a barrage of articles from mid-1987 and books from late 1987 to mid-1988 addressed the question what is perestroika, they were usually asking if Gorbachev and the Soviet leadership were serious about reform or if the glow of change was simply cosmetic. Around the time of the Nineteenth Party Conference in June 1988, Japanese belatedly reached the conclusion that the Soviets are, indeed, serious. With the Nakasone visit in July (he went again in January 1989 with less fanfare), the Japanese public began to realize that the Kremlin is also serious about bilateral relations. The spell of thinking exclusively in terms of the Northern Territories seemed to be broken. In these circumstances, curiosity mounted about Soviet domestic events. Articles became more specialized and better informed in following the most recent internal Soviet developments. Japanese professors reported that students began to complain about the dearth of courses on the Soviet Union. At last, attendance in Russian language courses also rose from the minuscule figures of the past decade.

Japanese information came now from frequent personal contacts with Soviets who came calling, and especially from intensive visits by Japan's experts to the Soviet Union itself. As Itō Takayuki described the exchanges involving Hokkaidō University, Japanese found the Soviets human and easy to interact with at home, on picnics, and so forth. Unfortunately, he added, Japan lacks student exchanges—important since young people are the ones who have the courage to reach out to a foreign culture. It is as if policy makers do not trust youths; they fear ideological contamination. The burden to understand and interpret Soviet events based on the new contacts falls largely on a small number of senior scholars, he concluded.[62]

Signposts for Perestroika. Lacking a model for following the course of perestroika, scholars speculated about the arrival of a second or a third stage. They looked for signposts indicating an acceleration, a turning point. Through much of 1988 this approach kept its appeal, but gradually the tone changed. Increasingly, the focus shifted to the troubles wrought by the changes and how difficult they would be to surmount. Pessimism shifted from whether the Soviet leaders had the will to change, to whether the changes would not wreak havoc with no end in sight.

The Soviet Abyss. Japan is a country unaccustomed to economic dislocations and stagnation, to nationality rifts and violence, to political disorder and loss of control, and to a loss of historical roots and a search for a new direction. The closest it came to these experiences was after World War II, but then the choice of direction was in the hands of the occupation authorities, and quickly lines of authority were reestablished. Accustomed to order, Japanese tend to be easily unsettled by the prospect of an abyss, by the unknown.

The Soviet Union has plunged into such an abyss. Politics were changing abruptly almost month by month, leaving readers dazed about whether Gorbachev was defying the challenge of the conservatives at the top and about what the new Soviet-style parliament would be like after it is seasoned by trial and error. The economy deteriorated to the point that Japanese stopped taking the Soviet Union seriously as a country that can continue to function as a superpower. The nationality crisis continued to spread, tearing asunder the prospects for a cohesive response to almost every problem.

Visitors who returned to Moscow at the end of 1988 or in early 1989 saw mostly confusion and disorder.[63] Some found that Moscow reminded them of Japan right after the defeat. Democracy was ordered from above; reorganization reached all political and economic areas and even the society as a whole. Those in charge of the old system were being chased out, while the old history texts were cast away. Past opponents of the system occupied a heroic position. Shortages abounded along with a large black market. The people distrusted public authority. The biggest commonality may have been the abrupt shift in values, leading to confusion about the future.

Also common were articles pointing to desperate conditions. One person who went to the Soviet Union for a conference of writers of detective stories observed that he felt uneasy on the Aeroflot flight because of torn seats and white smoke emitted from the ceiling (the stewardess reassured him that it was steam, not the engine on fire). Then he found the water pipes busted in a third-class hotel. He missed neon signs to help to distinguish stores. He noticed lots of prostitutes. From these observations he concluded that there is no tomorrow for Gorbachev or for perestroika without first achieving rapid improvements in living conditions.[64]

Sociological Reductionism. Even authors who praise Gorbachev highly often doubt that Russians accept his style. Even more they doubt that reforms can work. At the bottom of their analysis is the view that the Slavic peoples of the country lack the character to take advantage of reform. The country is in a rut not only because of poor leadership, an undemocratic political system, a rigidly centralized economic system, and many other structural factors, but also because its citizens lack the values and education to work hard. One finds signs of a pervasive sociological reductionism in Japanese assessments of the prospects for Soviet reform, as in the earlier literature on what was wrong with the country in the Brezhnev era. The sustained skepticism of these years can be traced in part to this line of thinking.

Gaimushō Hope for Further Change. Until the autumn of 1988 there was some uncertainty about how responsive Gaimushō authorities were to internal changes in the USSR. In October 1988 Togō Takehiro, the new head of the Eurasian Department, set any doubts to rest in a radio interview.[65] He repeated Gorbachev's words that the Soviet Union is experiencing a second revolution, bringing fundamental change to political, economic, and social conditions and arousing the human factor. Togō observed that the personnel changes at the end of September, including Gromyko's ouster as president, were part of Gorbachev's determination to sweep out the conservative faction, which has remained in an equilibrium with the reformers. (Having so long focused on Gromyko as their adversary, Japanese naturally welcomed his departure as an important signal of a new look in Moscow. They also paid close attention to the later ouster of Ivan Kovalenko as the deputy in charge of Japanese matters in the Central Committee's International Department.) In this respect, Togō appears to be hopeful; yet he also warns that because perestroika is running into various obstacles, Gorbachev and his aides are alarmed. The lack of concrete success in the daily lives of Soviet citizens arouses a strong consciousness that unless perestroika is pushed forward the people will not follow Gorbachev. To enliven its economy, Moscow cannot turn back. Togō respectfully noted that the Soviet Union is a great power of the world through its military equilibrium with the United States and within the world has come to enjoy a great right to speak out. He also recognized Moscow's sincerity in striving to transfer money from armaments to civilian consumption through negotiated reductions with Washington. He foresees a time-consuming process before the results of the reforms become apparent.

On May 10, 1989, immediately after Foreign Minister Uno's return from his Soviet trip, Togō, who had participated in the third set of discussions of the peace treaty working group, again assessed Soviet developments.[66] He did so before an audience of 170 former ambassadors, business executives, and Soviet-East European affairs consultants. An edited version of his comments indicated that he felt that relations are moving ahead. Uno, he said, told Gorbachev that through the terms perestroika, glasnost, and democratization, Japanese are beginning to feel friendly (*shitashimi*) to the Soviet Union.

Assessing Soviet life, Togō pointed out that the people have completely lost the will to work. If limited to the current economic system, the Soviets fear they will end up a third-rate country. They despair that they cannot maintain their military power with quite backward science and technology. Being in Japan, it is hard to imagine the conditions inside the Soviet Union. In his three stays in Moscow from 1961, he added, he saw advances in housing and infrastructure, but basically the food and consumption levels did not change much. Now he went to vegetable stores and saw only onions with shoots growing out and other unsavory items. The butcher shops sell only one type of sausage and one type of meat. Everybody is lined up. While the USSR is called one of the world's superpowers, living is at an extremely low level. If in the next two or three years its economic system does not work, perestroika will not succeed. Gorbachev must now rush as quickly as possible to improve consumption, even by urgently importing from abroad. Yet, Togō added, Soviet economists say it will take six or seven years. He concluded that Moscow needs to stabilize international relations in order to advance its economic reform. In this context, policies toward Japan are changing.

Prospects for Perestroika. Soviet acknowledgment of lower GNP statistics and other incriminating data have encouraged Japanese confidence. It is now pointed out that the Soviet GNP in 1988 was lower than the Japanese level.[67] Suddenly Japan appears in the economic records as well as in everyone's perceptions as the second world economy.

While there is little outright optimism that the Soviets can soon turn their troubled situation around, there are Soviet-watchers who stress the positive changes that have been achieved. Shimotomai Nobuo continued to identify new advances such as parliamentary decision-making authority and rights to speak out even on military matters. Yet he also noted the gap between a rise in expectations and a consumer shortage and inflation, leading to a short-term crisis possibility. Others who see this no less strongly often argue that Japan should wait to obtain the best terms from a desperate Moscow. Shimotomai disagreed, saying that bilateral relations should advance since as Gorbachev's political base strengthens, there is an increase in the problems he can grasp. One must not easily fool with the theories that Gorbachev will lose power or the Soviet Union will self-destruct. After all, in China the reform faction with close ties to Japan has fallen. For two to three years an opportunity will exist because of Soviet domestic conditions. He added, Japan should, in a case by case approach, support perestroika and take a diversified stand on Soviet relations.[68]

Official assessments of the prospects for perestroika have been consistently gloomy. In August 1988 the director general of the information department in the Gaimushō identified three possible scenarios for the Soviet Union as it reaches its decisive stage.[69] He asserted that no specialists think that the first scenario—a successful economic reform—will occur. While the second scenario—a Khrushchev era repetition of the opposition defeating the reforms—is possible, more likely is the third scenario—a halfway political and economic reform with limited successes. Many of the projections in 1989 grew more doubtful as nationality and economic problems worsened.[70]

The debate over the prospects for the Soviet Union may have peaked in the spring of 1989. Special issues of journals and numerous articles asked, in one way or another, where the Soviet Union is heading. *AERA*, the weekly journal of the *Asahi shimbun*, presented a broad survey without general conclusions. *Sekai shūhō* included articles with a harsher message: socialism cannot cope with its problems; change does not mean improvement.[71] Nishimura Fumio, a central figure in the political analysis of the Soviet Union over a long period, described perestroika as groping in the dark.[72] Nobody knows what socialism is. In a June article asking if political reform will succeed, Ōkura Yūnosuke answered that the future is dark.[73]

In July, *Sankei shimbun* ran a series of impressions from recent Japanese visitors to the Soviet Union.[74] The conclusions were harsh. One company president commented that he was surprised that there had not been even a single step forward from his impressions twenty years earlier: the level of television technology had remained essentially unchanged. Lines were as long. Since perestroika started, the economy has deteriorated. The writer then pointed to Japan's extraordinary economic growth and asked which country will survive.

A Lack of Optimism. A "Soviet boom" in information aroused the Japanese public as it searched for insight into how the Soviet system is changing. Among Japanese Sovietologists, none seemed better able to understand the Soviet people than Hakamada Shigeki. Soon his books and articles were filling a void in coverage of the daily lives of the Soviet people. At the end of 1988 Hakamada's new book, *The Soviet Union about which We Want to Know More*, described the emergence of a crisis mentality first among Soviet reform intellectuals and then among others.[75] Soviets are realizing that their system is sick and are turning to other values in place of communism. He explained that in particular the existence of Japan has played a big role in shaking the Soviet worldview to its roots. Originally seen as a burnt down third-rate country without resources and unable to compete with a powerful, spacious, and resource-rich Soviet Union, Japan startled the Soviet people through its advance in the 1960s and 1970s. Its ability in the 1980s to battle the United States for number one in science and technology was a shock. The Soviet leadership, Hakamada explained, has been forced to reform because of the changing thinking of its citizens; the old monolithic control could not work. In his writings Hakamada never expressed optimism that the system was capable of making the reforms necessary to respond to the people. The more the Japanese were learning about Soviet life, the gloomier the prospects seemed for recovery. The idealism about Soviet recovery found among some circles in the West seemed almost totally absent.

The most that those with a flicker of hope could suggest is that Gorbachev will learn from prior mistakes and only now is beginning the fundamental reforms that are necessary. In other words, whether because of political opposition or inexperience, what preceded was not really perestroika. This viewpoint could be supported by an explanation of the errors that had occurred or by evidence showing why the most recent thinking reaches well beyond earlier thinking. Even authors taking this perspective in the spring of 1989 did not make a positive prognosis. They could foresee accelerated reform initiatives, but not a way to solve Moscow's problems. Meanwhile, most others were employing strong language such as "danger" and "crisis" to convey a sense of virtual hopelessness.

CHAPTER EIGHT

The Third Cycle, 1989–1991

Question 9: Is The World Witnessing the Death of Socialism?

ONCE CONVINCED of the deterioration of the Soviet Union, the Japanese people found new reasons in 1989 and 1990 to doubt the viability of socialism on a large scale. From the middle of 1989, world events first in China and then in Eastern Europe sent shockwaves through Japan. West Europeans, enthusiastic about bridging the Berlin Wall, could rejoice. Americans, preoccupied with human rights gains and military cutbacks, could feel vindicated. What was less clear was how Japanese would react. At last, they could look over the horizon to a new era, but in order to do so they needed to search first for guideposts on how to proceed. High on the list was figuring out how to interpret the many setbacks to international socialism. In reassessing socialism, the question of China's prospects loomed especially large.

In 1949 the victory of communism in China stirred many Japanese. Around 1960 the outbreak of the Sino-Soviet split and later in the 1960s the outbreak of the Cultural Revolution amazed many Japanese. In 1971 the breakthrough in Sino-American relations and soon thereafter in Sino-Japanese relations excited the entire nation. In 1978–79 the shift to a reform program in China along with new friendship ties aroused virtually a uniformly sympathetic reaction. For the fourth time in thirty years, a romance with China stirred Japanese guilt and hope. By the end of the 1980s a close bond with China was deeply fixed in the Japanese consciousness. There was no doubt that events in China could leave a deep impression.

In 1989 the combination within a few weeks of the Deng-Gorbachev summit, overshadowed as it was by student demonstrations, and the bloody crackdown on the reform movement in China produced one more in the series of intense responses to China. The old view was shattered that socialism could save China or, at least, would set the right course as it gradually yielded to a mixed reform system. Events in Beijing were interpreted as confirmation that communism is dying. Although Gorbachev fared well personally in comparison to Deng Xiaoping, there was little spillover toward a positive reassessment of Soviet prospects.

The immediate prospects of communism's collapse did not particularly excite Japanese hopes for a direct role in the disintegrating socialist bloc.

China's repressive state would not easily yield to student democracy or join with other states in the region to build a new order in East Asia. Caution and no major change of course was the preferred response. Eastern Europe seemed remote. As before, the debate about the future centered on the Soviet Union. Discussions about Japan's world prospects started from the changed Soviet role. Through the worldwide transformation of socialism, Japanese could sense a new identity for their own emerging superpower.

THE SINO-SOVIET SUMMIT AND COMPARISONS OF REFORM PROSPECTS

Normalization Poses No Danger. Official circles expressed no concern over the summit in Beijing. Sino-Soviet normalization is no more than a response to new Soviet-American relations, to common policies of economic modernization, and to other positive currents in the world. It is not directed against other countries. Slight hesitation could be detected, however, in the questions raised by Katori Yasue, who successively served as ambassador in each of the socialist countries from 1981 to 1987. How would normalization affect the Asia-Pacific region diplomacy of the two countries? Would Soviet troops no longer directed at China be redirected to the coast and become a concern to the United States and Japan?[1] Despite such questions, Tokyo emphasized the positive side of the Communist reconciliation, expressing trust in the Chinese. Japanese officials seemed to have confidence in Beijing, believing among other things that its huge appetite for foreign economic assistance and the vast sums promised in aid by Japan would be influential. In other words, close Sino-Japanese relations could be counted on as a good influence limiting adverse possibilities of the Sino-Soviet rapprochement.[2]

The new Sino-Soviet bond is not ideological. It is not a special relationship between socialist countries, but one additional case of peaceful coexistence among states in a world marked by improved East-West relations. It is not a real change from the "half-normalized" Sino-Soviet relations since 1982, nor is it directed at third countries. Japan can be calm about the Moscow-Beijing connection and need not reconsider its own diplomacy, explained a Gaimushō spokesman after the summit.[3]

The Japanese response to the brutality in China reflects a general principle of separating economics from politics, the major exception to which is Soviet policy. It also reflects guilt toward China from the war years, and fear that any criticism from Japan would only elicit fierce Chinese nationalism such as occurred during the Cultural Revolution. The Chinese people would recall the war, and their latent hostility to Japan would rise to the surface. Furthermore, Japan's response seems to indicate an emerging pan-Asianism stretching from Thailand to Korea, with Tokyo believing that it has a special responsibility to lead this region but in a manner that in no way suggests that it will impose its will on the group. Also, Tokyo is reluctant to venture into the lead when other countries in its region are cautious about condemning China, and it is worried about driving China into isolationism or even into the arms of the Soviet Union. Finally, Japan has refrained from incorporating human rights concerns into its foreign policy, and even now, as an international society emerges, it is reluctant to follow the American lead. In all of these respects, Japan's identity with the West must be balanced against its identity with the East and its special responsibility to China.

Ties Forged from Failure. Some Japanese commentators were less unflappable than the Gaimushō. In December 1988 Nakajima Mineo responded to the announcement of the Sino-Soviet summit with the assertion that this was a great turning point in the international political structure. He asked whether Japan's diplomatic strategy combining friendship toward China and toughness toward the Soviet Union, premised on the Sino-Soviet conflict, should not also take a big turn in 1989.[4] Many observers saw the new relationship as the end of ideological diplomacy, a sign of a new era of normalcy in relations. To the extent that the term socialism figured in the analyses, it was as a dying notion. As one heading in response to the summit announcement asserted, this marks the "defeat of the socialist economy."[5] The two countries were driven together by failure.

The student-led demonstrations in Beijing followed by the harsh crackdown in early June cast Gorbachev in a comparatively favorable light, yet strongly reinforced the attitude that communism is dying. As Mōri Kazuko asserted, for the Beijing students Gorbachev, the young and able leader, became the symbol of reform and democracy.[6] Nakajima said that Beijing's "bloody Sunday" invited a long season of disorder and repression. Yet he complained that the Japanese government had underestimated the democratic demonstrations from the start and then delayed in reacting to the tragedy of June 4. On June 6 Prime Minister Uno announced that because Japan, unlike the other Western countries, had experienced the Sino-Japanese War, it could not react in the same manner. When public opinion, including that of economic circles, responded negatively to this weak demeanor, the government began to express regret at what happened in China. This did not satisfy its critics. Nakajima called for tougher measures against the Chinese government, including positive steps to aid the victims, even suggesting that the vast sums of economic aid promised to the Chinese government should be reexamined.[7]

Another commentator went further, arguing that huge Japanese aid (75 percent of China's foreign assistance) makes China dependent and gives Japan leverage. Now Japan's hesitation allows China to drive a wedge among the advanced countries. This will isolate Japan. Japan must choose between American and Chinese ties. It should join with the advanced countries.[8]

Apart from the response to Chinese government oppression, there was interest in involving Japan in the movement of great-power normalization. From the left of center came the call for Japan to engage in "new thinking" now that both Soviet-American and Soviet-Chinese relations were normalizing. Japan was not on board despite the double détente—despite the new international environment due to Soviet-American and Soviet-Chinese summits. Japanese diplomacy must also break from its cold war mentality. It needs perestroika, said Mōri.[9]

Abandoning Romanticism about China. Analysts saw the return to despotism in China as a revival of Chinese tradition.[10] It is a country never ruled by law in which millions have been cruelly killed in past times. The main lesson from the events in June is that Japanese must abandon their romanticism (and their inability to see clearly due to feelings of guilt) about China. Idealism about socialism in the 1950s and 1960s had been reborn as romanticism about China. Now both have virtually disappeared in Japan, leaving the pessimistic conclusion that only by rooting out all aspects of socialism can hope be restored. For China, which has long been seen separately from Soviet socialism, this prospect now seems more likely, even if the current Chinese leadership is less inclined to act in accord with national needs.

On the left of the spectrum, one could detect only a faint voice of convoluted hope about the future of socialism. Yano Tōru contended that socialism is not dead despite what many are saying.[11] If a people's army massacres its own people, if the PRC suffers from a bankruptcy of thought, it signifies that leaders are trying to defend the logic of socialism. Gorbachev's call for a qualitative change in all areas of Soviet life and for a new revolution within the classical Marxist rubric, despite the fact that many people only half believe it, shows that there is a way out. Gorbachev sympathized with the demands of China's students. It is true that the image of the socialist system grows worse and worse, but there can be a second socialist revolution. The threat of socialism is not dead, nor is its force gone, said Yano.

From the Japanese left of center came the idea that China's reform has been blocked because its leaders neglected political reform in contrast to Soviet leaders. Moscow was now in the lead in a similar process—a process that is difficult and complex. Even though the old system will be completely transformed, this does not mean a transition to capitalism. In a world that is increasingly mutually dependent, other countries must show support for the reforms. Implicit is a warning that Soviet reforms may follow the Chinese path of June 1989 if the world neglects to support them.[12]

From the right came the counterargument that today's Tiananmen is tomorrow's Red Square. Indicative of this skepticism was an article by Uchimura Gōsuke, a specialist on Russian ethnography trained at the Harbin Institute in prewar Russian studies and held after the war for eleven years in Soviet internment. Uchimura argued that perestroika turned into a revolution to cast Leninism aside when it went beyond Gorbachev's plans. Presiding over the world's last colonial empire, Gorbachev faces a national liberation movement and has turned to Russian soldiers to repress it in Azerbaijan. Now the Russian leaders are as isolated as the Chinese. The only way out is the Tiananmen path. While chanting democracy, Russia would, in fact, establish perestroika with order. As an "enlightened" despot, Gorbachev would acrobatically ride the white horse of the KGB as he pursues a conservative path.[13]

There is simply no exit for socialist reform from the vicious circle of economic reform from above leading to political aspirations from below, which leads to the repressive reaction of militarized socialism, which, in turn, brings political confusion and economic stagnation and again necessitates economic reforms from above. The right of center and center agreed that socialism is self-destructing, but added that it is time to welcome the Soviet Union into the world order.[14] The shadow of its threat is diminishing. We are moving forward to the new international society.

The Image of a Developing Country. Some Japanese scholars had idealized Chinese socialism in the 1960s, but by the 1980s this was uncommon. Instead, many scholars considered China to be little more than a developing country, a species that must be treated with restraint. Even after the repression in June, many expected that eventually economic development would transform Chinese society and then politics. The implication is that Japan should show patience and continue to assist China's economic growth. If not, and if China became isolated, its people would suffer all the more at the hands of the government. Wait for the current student generation to climb to the top of the society in the twenty-first century; in the long run China will change. This same type of reasoning may eventually be applied to the Soviet Union. But for the present it is seen as socialist and not as a developing country, therefore its prospects appear less favorable. The Japanese know China better as a poor country from its presocialist past and have a critical view of past corruption and other problems that interfered with its development. If Japanese decide that socialism is dead, China's image spares it from being buried, but the Soviet image leaves it a corpse with little prospect for rebirth.

Contrasting Friendliness to China and the Soviet Union. China's popularity at the end of the 1970s was so high that almost 80 percent of Japanese said they felt "friendly" to it, and only 14 percent "not friendly."[15] Contrast these data to the figures of 8 percent "friendly" to the Soviet

Union and 84 percent "not friendly." A few Japanese writers have been intrigued by the question of why their fellow citizens like the Chinese but dislike the Soviets. Their answers are invariably rooted in history. Japanese cannot forget the favor of receiving culture and thought from China for over one thousand years, while they also cannot forget the historical threat from Russia and the Soviet Union. Authors in the 1980s also contrasted the sincerity of the Chinese they meet with the crude behavior of the Soviets. Specifically, they note Soviet bluster toward Japanese fishermen and their rights to fish. Invariably they also refer to 1945. As one writer asserted, Japan begged the Soviet Union to help obtain peace, but when the Soviets saw Japan's hopelessness they attacked without remorse, brutalizing the Japanese people. Reminding the reader that Japanese are grateful to Americans for their conduct at the end of the war, he concluded that there is not the least humanity in Soviet socialism.[16]

The West Wind Prevails over the East Wind. Hakamada Shigeki compares the American and Japanese images of socialism. He says that in March 1989, before the Tiananmen incident, President Bush had already abandoned containment of the Soviet Union and welcomed it into the international society as China had been welcomed earlier. In contrast, Japan still had an image of the Soviet Union as a "hard, socialist country" while seeing China as an ordinary country. Now China's image has changed. It is also seen as "hard." Hakamada adds that the younger generation cannot understand what attracted intellectuals and workers in the past to socialism and a planned economy. They do not know about the reactions to the early stages of industrial development and the Depression of the 1920s and 1930s, or Japan's fascination with a radically different worldview after the war, but only see a dead end for Marxism-Leninism as the west wind prevails over the east wind today. The negative image of socialist countries has intensified because Marxism-Leninism had a threatening theory of power and the state, assumed society could be completely manipulated, and believed that the world of spiritual and cultural values could be monolithically controlled as an independent entity. Changes in society increasingly defied these assumptions, leading to national decline.[17] Nothing Hakamada writes suggests that a revival is possible.

The Fall of Communism. Efforts to try to find defenders of socialism met with little response. On a late-night live television show ("Asa made nama terebi"), the moderator tried to elicit clashing views on what will be the future of socialism. In addition to the underdeveloped tradition of open confrontation between differing opinions, the results were affected by the hesitation even on the part of politicians from leftist parties to come to socialism's defense.

Some on the Japanese right referred to the massacre at Tiananmen as just what is expected from the vice of communism. To the extent that humanity permits it to remain, this kind of tragedy will be repeated. Optimism that the threat of communism is soon to disappear is dangerous, they added. Americans have been too soft on China and now are growing soft on the Soviet Union. Japanese, too, have overreacted to changes on the surface after Mao died. Borrowing some capitalist things has strengthened China's economy and the Communist system.[18] The obvious message is to deny the Communists such help and bring about their downfall more quickly. This is a message more easily applied to the Soviet Union.

The September 1989 issue of *Seiron* focused on the question, "Is Communism Dead?" One respondent asserted that communism has two special features—one-party dictatorship and a planned economy—that are indivisibly linked. The Soviets have tried some political liberalization, but their economy has worsened. The Chinese have, in contrast, liberalized their economy, but politics remains dictatorial. In a one-dimensional bureaucratic system, corruption is exacerbated by such a change. In response came the student demonstrations. Meanwhile, Soviet liberalization produced the independence movements of minorities forcibly absorbed earlier. Communist societies are torn by internal contradictions. Another respondent described the twentieth century as the period of the rise and fall of communism.[19]

In mid-August *Sekai shūhō* reported on the views of eleven specialists about the future of communism. The first report discussed a system emptied of ideology and economically dilapidated that can go neither forward nor backward. The second headline pointed to people who no longer respond to orders. The third likened Deng's actions in June to Stalin's in 1936. In both cases the leaders saw their country encircled by imperialist powers sending saboteurs, and the leaders feared domestic elements (enemies of the people) who would link up with them and destroy socialist power from within. Other authors wrote of corruption, nepotism, and privilege. Still others pointed to the severe despotism present in North Korea and Rumania. Among the authors, Inoguchi Takashi offered the fullest explanation why communism must die or fail. He mentioned that after seizing power the revolutionary party stopped halfway in the transition to a political party, thus it left undifferentiated political, military, policy, and information organizations. It still had the coloring of a military regime. Inoguchi also noted that socialist governments failed to make a transition from war to peace. This is bad for the economy and turns mass dissatisfaction against the regime. Vigilance against counterrevolutionaries leads to ignoring the opinions of the people. Now, either opposition such as Solidarity will take power or multiparty systems will advance.[20] As Iida Tsuneo wrote elsewhere, perhaps the biggest drama of the twentieth century will be the fall of the left occurring rapidly at century-end.[21]

The First East European Debate. After the summer debate inspired by Sino-Soviet and Chinese developments came a debate centered on the significance of Eastern European political changes. Many active participants in the debate about the Soviet Union took part. Japanese journals presented a wide range of scenarios. On the right, Teratani Hiromi, an academic long known for his negative depictions of Soviet life, asked if Moscow will stand by and watch as its control of Eastern Europe is lost. He implied that it will not. The Brezhnev Doctrine is not a thing of the past. Conservatives in the Soviet Union fearful of a spillover to their own nationalities would not watch idly as the tide of West European unity in 1992 sweeps Hungary and other East European countries along. Teratani suggested a continuation in the twelve-year cycle of Soviet repression. In 1956, 1968, and 1980 (against Poland's Solidarity), Moscow had stopped the reform drift. Now the cycle may be repeated in 1992.[22]

Sase Masamori was less willing to commit himself in his three-part series describing the splitting up of Eastern Europe. He stressed the diversity in the region and the new tense relations that were appearing, but he made no effort to predict the Soviet response.[23]

Surprisingly positive was Kawato Akio, head of the East European desk in the Gaimushō.[24] Known also as a moderate on the Soviet Union with a strong interest from his posting there in the gradual evolution of Soviet society, Kawato described favorable trends in an optimistic light as early as February 1988. He added that Japanese relations in the region are now very friendly. In Poland a public opinion poll found Japan first among the countries people like. There is now plenty of room to develop trade relations, and in international ties such as in elections for United Nations posts, East European countries are very favorably disposed toward Japan. Soon Kawato's optimism about the independence of Eastern Europe shedding communism in haste was confirmed by events. Few doubted the complete collapse of communism throughout the world, although many expected a lingering death for the nationalistic, Chinese variant.

Economic Collapse Is Not Enough. After Foreign Minister Nakayama's January 1991 trip to Moscow, the mood in Japan was somber. As the *Mainichi shimbun* argued, the confusion in the Soviet Union has thrown a screw into the machine of Japanese diplomacy. Timing had been crucial in the Japanese strategy—to play its economic card when Moscow most needed it for perestroika and new thinking. But with journals now trumpeting the collapse of perestroika, the Japanese government did not know where to turn. Ironically, having slowed progress in relations over the territorial question, the Gaimushō was now giving the world the unmistakable impression that it was showing a "sweet face" to the Soviets in order not to abandon all hope on the eve of Gorbachev's visit. Meanwhile, the idea that many had never really abandoned—of reform views on the Soviet surface representing more of a facade than a reality—resurfaced in Nakayama's reported view that what the new Soviet foreign minister, Bessmertnykh, said about not returning to the cold war was only a minority opinion in the leadership. The *Sankei shimbun* took a stronger tone, calling "Dictator Gorbachev" the main player in the last act of the economic and political crisis in his country. In the end he had fallen back on the party as his power base in the struggle against Yeltsin, who had charismatically brought together the hopes of the democrats but cannot match the military power of the conservatives. As Shevardnadze predicted, *Sankei* added, for a long time to come reaction and dictatorship will persist in the Soviet Union. Whereas the *Asahi shimbun* was reluctant to advocate any change in course, *Mainichi shimbun* and even more. *Sankei shimbun* saw a need to reappraise Tokyo's posture and the West's economic aid.[25]

With Gorbachev's turn to the right in the winter of 1991 and the eagerness of Chinese leaders to broaden cooperation with the Soviets on the Persian Gulf War and on party issues, Japanese confidence in the collapse of socialist economies was divorced from optimism on foreign policy matters. Loss of faith in regional cooperation with China was deepening, and concern over the latent Soviet threat remained. When on January 23, 1991, Beijing announced that Jiang Zemin would visit Moscow in the summer at the invitation of the CPSU, the timing could not but arouse concern.

Question 10: Is There a Japanese Perspective on Socialism?

At the same time as socialism was being declared dead in the summer of 1989, the JSP won an enormous electoral victory to deny the LDP a majority in Japan's Upper House. How could this supposedly moribund party with a platform full of clichés from the decades of Marxist idealism in the 1950s and 1960s make a comeback of such unexpected proportions? Few would have predicted it only a few months earlier. Most observers agreed that the results had nothing to do with JSP, except for the pleasing and nonideological manner of its chairwoman Doi Takako. The real cause was obviously the tarnished image of the LDP caught in the Recruit scandal and of its top leaders, who had profited handsomely from Recruit funds. Having just established an unpopular national sales tax, leaders were especially vulnerable to a charge of financial impropriety. Also, Takeshita's successor Uno had been caught in a sex scandal that played into the hands of the JSP's female chairperson, who appealed to a growing awareness of women's rights.

If initially socialism seemed inconsequential to the political arena, the aftermath of the election raised the question of what platform could unite the several opposition parties (excluding the pariah Japan Communist party) around the leadership of the JSP. Through the fall of 1989 the Japanese left was searching for a new approach to security, including a reassessment of the Soviet threat. Even earlier, dating back to the preparations for Doi's May 1988 visit to Moscow, the JSP had been seeking advice from Soviet experts on the left of center and the center. In search of a platform for electoral success, the question became clear-cut: was there an alternative Japanese approach to the Gorbachev reforms and new thinking that could rally the left or the center?

A Shriveled Curiosity? On the right of the spectrum, the answer was "No." Hōgen Shinsaku reminded Japanese that the JSP was founded on the spirit of socialism, of which the founding father is the Soviet Union.[26] In our era of high technology, socialism will soon be a shriveled curiosity. It has already turned into an anachronism. Can today's JSP country bumpkins conduct foreign exchanges or turn Japan into an international society? No, they would only demonstrate Japan's backwardness and isolate the country. While others found gentler ways of rebuking the JSP, they usually agreed that its foreign policy ideas fail to provide any reason to give it support. After months of tampering with its party platform in order to broaden its political base, the JSP was still perceived as hesitant about close military ties with Washington. In the February 18, 1990, election for the Lower House, the JSP did much better than other opposition parties but lost badly to a resurgent LDP. The JSP had failed to offer the people a positive reason to give it support. Yet, after the Iraq invasion of Kuwait and the LDP's lack of success in convincing the public of the need to dispatch SDF personnel as noncombatants, the JSP could claim to be closer to the antimilitarism or even pacifism of the population. It was not as isolated on foreign policy matters as some were predicting.

A Rebirth of Socialism? What kind of socialism will exist at the end of the Soviet reform process? Those who try to answer that question without rejecting the prospect of a socialist future repeat Gorbachev's vocabulary. Socialism from below will be based on respect for public opinion. Workers will be masters. Democracy will exist. At last there will be real socialism. The most vocal of the small set of Soviet-watchers who appear to believe in this rosy future are associated to some degree at least with the Japan-Soviet Society (NisSo kyōkai).

In 1987 this association prepared a book on perestroika, which began with praise for the historic achievements of socialism that capitalism could not match—equality of the sexes, liberation of peasants from the unequal land system and of workers from capital, guarantees of the right to work, no depressions or unemployment, and sufficient social welfare. Yet, they added, Russia was very backward in 1917, it was surrounded by capitalist countries, and its losses in World War II were enormous. While recognizing negative elements, the authors seemed to place most of the blame on circumstances beyond Moscow's control. Then, when discussing how the internal situation worsened from the 1960s, they laid the blame on the bureaucratic class's tenacious resistance. The rebirth of socialism was obstructed. Now, they added, Soviets have learned from these experiences and are only starting to do what is needed.[27] One chapter insisted that planning and state ownership are effective; therefore, socialism's superiority can be fully revealed by perestroika. A new stage of socialism will ensue. The authors of many chapters did not neglect to add that all capitalist countries face serious problems and today can find no way out of their crisis.

Fujita Osamu, the chairman of the association, concluded the study by reminding the reader of the great historical achievement of 1917 and the need to counter the American anti-Soviet strategy. The choice for Japan is between militarism demanded by the United States and pacifism consistent with Soviet new thinking. The Japanese people are threatened. They can improve their country by working hard for friendship with Moscow and for peace.

Even when the image of socialism had fallen in Japan, the association remained active. Now, its leaders insisted, the image is changing. Soviet events should lead the association to work harder. In doing so, they must counteract misperceptions. The Japanese people underestimate the Soviet economy. They have fixed opinions. There is still no peace treaty. The aim of the association is to achieve it and, with it, mutual understanding and friendly relations with Moscow.

In 1988, two hundred persons answered the call of the association to establish an institute of Soviet studies. They agreed to change their earlier methods. They too must rethink socialism. Confessing that they had remained silent about worker alienation, corruption, and other problems under socialism, they promised to do better. The problems, however, were not credited to anything inherent in socialism; deviations were responsible.[28] In early 1989 the new institute began to function, yet because of its members' reputation as unobjective supporters of communism and, in many cases, their long-standing association with the discredited JCP, it had a reputation as a fringe group. On some foreign policy matters, such as the June 1989 Tiananmen brutality, the JCP was so worried about "guilt by association" that it took by far the harshest line toward the Chinese Communists. Yet it clung to many notions of socialism that even the Soviets were jettisoning. The extreme left in Japan always seemed to be running a few steps behind. In February 1990 the decline of the JCP at the polls continued.

Even at the end of 1990, virtually no effort could be detected on the part of old-line Marxists to reexamine the history of socialism in order to explain the impact of perestroika. Fujita Osamu claimed that he was making such an effort, but he managed to add very little. At the same time that he reported new thinking about ownership, moving away from the 1930s' model and leading to a multilayered system, Fujita argued that a cleansed socialism must remain the leading sector.[29]

A Civil Society Socialism? In the journal of the JSP one finds a more realistic but relatively optimistic approach to socialism. Such well-regarded commentators as Shimotomai Nobuo and Satō Tsuneaki early in 1989 discussed problems in Soviet socialist reforms.[30] Satō recalled a 1984 article he wrote in a party publication in which he likened socialists to the rabbit napping while the tortoise knows where he is proceeding. Now he qualified this view. Stagnation existed, but with China taking the lead early in the decade and the Soviet Union from 1987 moving in the same direction, a new wave of reform has begun. Twenty years have been lost from the Czech incident. The Soviet economy is worsening. While other reforms are going forward, there is still an economic deadlock. But at last something is being done to overcome it. Shimotomai wrote that socialism based on a civil society is, in fact, possible. The image of the state has changed in the Soviet Union. There is a realization that unless the state depends on a civil society, perestroika cannot succeed. Shimotomai urged the reader not to underestimate the fundamental change in Soviet society.

A pair of articles in the same journal exposed the old thinking in the JCP about Gorbachev's reforms. One even suggested that the JCP leaders consider Gorbachev worse than Stalin because the party chairman Miyamato Kenji said early in 1989 that he regards Gorbachev's perestroika as the biggest error since Lenin's time.[31] Clearly, the JSP did not share the JCP's reaction and Miyamoto's defense of old-line socialism.

When the right was busy in the summer of 1989 gloating over the death of socialism, the JSP responded with nary a whimper. That was not their business any more; they proved that they could garner votes by capitalizing on the shortcomings in LDP-style capitalism.

In the aftermath of the July elections, opposition to the LDP coalesced around Doi and the JSP. A realignment of political forces was underway. A commission on the Northern Territories and Japanese-Soviet relations was created. As Gorbachev's position shifted away from traditional socialism toward social democracy, Japan's socialists were taking it more seriously. After all, the old JSP goals of disarmament and neutrality now seemed consistent with Soviet "new thinking." Also, there appeared to be a good chance to capitalize on criticisms of the LDP and Gaimushō for inflexibility, although as long as the parties on the left demanded extreme territorial concessions this would be difficult. Lacking its own Soviet experts, the JSP reached out to nonsocialists. It changed its name to the Japan Social Democratic Party. Yet cosmetic changes and Doi's appeal did not suffice. As the party declined, she resigned in June 1991.

A New JSP Platform? The JSP, as the LDP, is split into factions. Whereas both parties generate personal factions linked to the fortunes of individual leaders, there are subdivisions with ideological leanings. In the JSP these overlap more closely with personal factions. Doi is outside these ideological divisions, after being selected as chairman by a tottering party unable to reach agreement on the basis of its existing divisions. Among the socialist factions oriented toward foreign policy, there is one sympathetic to the Soviet Union and one leaning toward China. The pro-Soviet group is willing to settle for the return of two islands. The pro-Chinese group favors the complete return of the four islands. The official JSP position agreed with neither; it called for a return of the entire chain of Kurile Islands—a much tougher stance toward Moscow than that of the LDP or the Gaimushō.

For more than a year from the time Doi visited Gorbachev in May 1988, there was talk about adopting a new party line on the territorial question. After all, it made no sense for a position cynically taken a decade earlier to ward off accusations of being soft on the Soviet menace to be maintained by a party on record as opposing the Self-Defense Forces and the Japanese-American security pact. To win support from the center of the political spectrum, the JSP needed to accept, for the time being, the need for Japan's defense (which its new joint program of September 1989 did) and, at the same time, offer Moscow some possibility for a negotiated agreement on the territorial question. It needed not only to persuade the public, but also to find common ground with its potential coalition partners in the Lower House elections of 1990. The Kōmeitō and Democratic Socialist party (DSP) already favored a four-island approach. The obvious solution was for the JSP to join the LDP in backing the return of the four islands. Through careful wording the JSP might still distinguish its position slightly from that of the LDP, while doing nothing that would make it vulnerable to charges it was undermining unity crucial to pressing Moscow to yield.

Hesitation to reexamine the JSP Soviet platform must be attributed to two factors: (1) a new philosophy of winning votes without taking controversial stands, associated with Doi's personal touch; and (2) fragile balances among factions that could unravel and open a Pandora's box of disagreements in a party ranging from old-line Marxists to newly resurgent issue-oriented pragmatists. Doi's own words about the Gorbachev era revealed extreme caution. Meanwhile, the behind-the-scenes JSP discussion of perestroika suggested a positive outlook, bolstered by the borrowed Soviet vocabulary concerning contradictions in the system and the severity of the illness that must be cured.

The JSP's strong faction in sympathy with Brezhnev-era socialism was moving toward support for perestroika. Iwai Akira, its leader and the past chairman of the now disbanding Sōhyō labor confederation, saw his influence within the JSP decline. Some in this faction were at a loss, but perhaps they were no more flustered than the strong pro-Chinese faction in the aftermath of the June 4 brutality in China. The Inaguma group of former Trotskyites and ex-Communists was converging with reform Communists in the JCP and former Communists opposed to the one-man rule of the octogenarian Miyamoto and his refusal to accept the Gorbachev reforms. A new left was forming. Within the newly established Soviet Institute were reformers favorable to perestroika but hesitant to offend the old guard of orthodox JCP members and Miyamoto. Also, a young historians' group organized by Shimotomai Nobuo had a left-of-center orientation and involved some in the new left, while welcoming others from the center. Through leadership by Doi toward a new Soviet program, it seemed conceivable that many of these elements, excluding the genuine Marxist-Leninists, could find a common voice—a unified left-of-center opposition to the LDP. There was danger, however, that the left of center would be overshadowed within existing organizations by the barely converted old left, and that further fragmentation was inevitable. In the final analysis, if the JSP has no plans to bring back socialism, and the JCP after its resounding defeat in the latest elections is nothing more than a spent political force, one must conclude that socialism is indeed dead for the Japanese people.

Once the Lower House Diet elections of February 1990 had passed, interparty clashes erupted over charges of a continued Soviet military threat and its implications for Japan's defense. After the head of the Self-Defense Forces testified before the Budget Committee that the Soviet military threat remained as before (the codeword was now a "latent" threat) and Japan's position was to make no changes in course at this time, the heads of the JSP and Komeito took exception to this view. They said that Soviet change is real and it is time for Japan to change its defensive plan. Japan is out of step with its allies, and it lacks an approach to extend the easing of world tension to the Asia-Pacific.[32] The opposition parties were suggesting that the LDP was using the notion of the "Soviet threat" as a means to its own ends. This minor dispute in the spring anticipated the autumn special session of the Diet, where the LDP could not win its way on sending noncombatants to the Persian Gulf.

Question 11: What Does the End of the Cold War Signify for Japan?

Perhaps more intensely than anywhere else in the world, in the winter of 1989–90 Japanese were debating the meaning of the collapse of communism for the world order. Many cautiously welcomed the new era. They expected Japan to be a major beneficiary and looked forward to a fundamental realignment of the world. Recent publications suggest a world in disequilibrium, which needs to be set right. The military factor will diminish, led by Moscow's shift to economic priorities. Bipolarism will give way to wider integration, but also to more regionalism as Asia follows Europe in becoming an arena of coordinated economies and even polities.[33] These and other Japanese responses emerged in a short time span as events in East Germany, Czechoslovakia, Rumania, Bulgaria, and the Soviet Union itself, ended the monopoly of power by the Communist party.

For Japan, along with the new future orientation came heightened expectations that Moscow must negotiate with Tokyo not only the fate of four small islands but also the future security of Northeast Asia. As the entire character of Europe was being transformed, Tokyo could now look ahead to a rethinking of the character of the Asia-Pacific region.

Within the Gaimushō, former heads of the Soviet desk Hyodo Nagao and Shigeta Hiroshi commented on regional security on various occasions in 1988, complaining that the press exaggerates the impact of the INF and that the mistake should not be made of anticipating a change in Japan's situation.[34] The East-West conflict is very deeply rooted. The danger of war continues. Rather than achieving a thaw in Soviet-American relations, what has occurred should be described only as managing the conflict. Hyodo assessed the Moscow summit in the spring of 1988 as producing no big surprises. The Soviets had been pressured into concessions by the Reagan military build-up, by Western unity including Japanese support for this build-up, and by the fear of SDI. This did not mean, however, that the essence of Soviet strategy had changed. Even in the summer of 1989 similar views could be heard from the Gaimushō, although they were finally being seriously challenged from without and even from within.

By the beginning of 1989, the direction of Soviet diplomacy toward the Asia-Pacific region had become a subject of debate. One journal invited nine commentators to give their views, and wide differences of opinion could be seen.[35] Kamiya Fuji still argued that we overstate Soviet changes toward Japan. Fundamentally, there is not so much change, and toward the Asia-Pacific region there is no change at all. Nagai Yōnosuke added that the hot war continues in Cambodia, and there are no signs of new thinking toward the region. Saeki Kiichi conceded that Moscow now realizes the need to face the region in a new way and is eager to find a strategy to reduce the huge gap between its military and economic presence, but it still has no new thinking toward Japan. Egashira Kazuma, Nakajima Mineo, and Hakamada Shigeki disagreed to varying degrees. Egashira cited the allure of Japan's economic power, which is pulling Moscow into a positive approach. Nakajima spoke of Moscow chasing a dream. Despite real changes in Moscow's approach since the time of the Vladivostok speech, Moscow remains an outcast in the region while its diplomacy in Europe is flowering. It is eager to make an Asian breakthrough too. Hakamada was more cautious, noting that Soviet international affairs experts had been shocked only in the last one or two years to learn concretely of the economic successes of the Newly Industrialized Economies (NIES) and ASEAN countries, including advances in high technology. Conditions are still lacking for a full reassessment; Gorbachev needs to gain more power over his rivals, Hakamada indicated.

New Thinking toward Asia. Leading the way in assessing the new thinking toward the Asia-Pacific region was Akino Yutaka. His article of March 1989 makes a strong case for reconsidering the cautious Japanese response.[36] First Akino notes that Gorbachev actually renewed a line of thinking begun under Andropov. Its roots are relatively deep. Second, he explains step-by-step over three years how Soviet thinking about the world has changed through a new foreign minister, a personnel shuffle, and a continued growth in awareness of realities through diplomatic activities. Akino disagrees with those who claim that the Soviet approach to Asia remains unchanged. He mentions Gorbachev's unpublished May 1986 speech to Soviet Foreign Ministry personnel in which he called for a rapid change toward Asia. Akino identifies many of the figures who are changing Soviet thinking, offering details of why and when new ideas emerged. He concludes that there has been a great transformation in Soviet perceptions. Others on the left of center or the center such as Shimotomai were also reviewing Soviet debates in support of a similar conclusion.

The debate remained largely at the level of "Has the Soviet position changed?" or "Is Moscow serious?" until the summer of 1989. Japanese were mostly interested in whether the Kremlin would agree to return the four islands, not in what more general approach to the Asia-Pacific region might evolve. In May the scope of thinking may have been enlarged by both the Sino-Soviet summit and the Gaimushō's agreement to consider a paper about the promotion of peace along with the territorial question in the deliberations of the joint bilateral working group.

Moscow sought a broadening in the context in which Soviet-Japanese relations were being discussed. Territory relates to security, and security means a regional approach. Also, Gorbachev's announcement in Beijing of the withdrawal of 120,000 Soviet troops from the Far East (making more concrete an earlier pledge to reduce forces in Asia by 200,000) caused the Gaimushō to acknowledge that the Soviet position toward the region did show some positive change. In August the appearance of a largely non-Communist government in Poland further stimulated thinking about Soviet tolerance for unexpectedly new approaches to regional security. If Eastern Europe could depart from the Brezhnev doctrine, why would Moscow insist on old arrangements in Northeast Asia?

At the forefront of the debate was the question of how different are conditions in Europe and Asia. The pessimists emphasized the existence of sharp contrasts. They said Europe is simpler because it is divided into two regional groupings; the complexity of all the two-country disputes in the belt from Korea to Singapore will defy resolution. Pessimists also argued that in the European arena ground forces matter, and Moscow enjoys military superiority from which it negotiates. In contrast, the Asia-Pacific clash focuses on naval forces in which the United States is superior. Moscow has realized since the Vladivostok speech the difficulty of applying a European security approach to Asia. Others asserted that the Soviet Union is a European country economically, and in the Asia-Pacific area it is only a military power. How could it expect to play a major role in the region if it did not rely on its military muscle?

In late August 1989 the JSP called for international discussions about the general security situation in the Asia-Pacific region. Eager to bridge its old concerns for peace and independence with centrist demands for security and interdependence with the United States, the JSP drew attention to the new opportunity for a comprehensive solution through multilateral negotiations with Moscow. Opinions divided about whether Moscow had become a trustworthy partner ready to be included in a mutual dependency structure or if it was a latent enemy still interested in world hegemony. One group on the right favored an increase in the Japanese military for balance in the Far East, while a majority preferred to rely for support on U.S. military power, and a small minority dreamed of doing neither in the near future after Soviet agreements were reached. The very hope for an agreement on security implied a shift from U.S. dependency to multidirectional foreign policy, including an Asia-centered regional component. Of course, all scenarios depended on an interpretation of Soviet motives and some calculation of the future Soviet role in the region.

Throughout the 1989 debate on regional security, idealists scarcely made their voices heard. Soviet speculation about a combination of untapped Soviet raw materials and land from the world's last vast frontier, plus Chinese labor from the world's largest population, plus Japanese money and technology from the world's capital-accumulating giant, plus South Korean entrepreneurship from the most dynamic of the NIES seemed like no more than a pipedream to the Japanese. Visitors to the Vladivostok-Nakhodka-Kharbarovsk region returned with skepticism that there were any profits to be made. Security considerations could not be resolved on the flimsy expectation of a major new regional economic situation.

Whereas Europeans had been deeply troubled in the 1980s about the threat of war, Japanese were not. They thought that as long as they had the American security umbrella, they were not vulnerable. Moscow's turn inward to resolve domestic troubles and its shift toward economic diplomacy were reassuring. Support for notably increasing the military budget fell to 11 percent of Japanese respondents in 1988 from about 20 percent early in the decade.[37] Moscow could not capitalize on fear nor on anticipated savings since Japan expects no "peace dividend" from a modest military budget.

At the first meetings of the Soviet-Japanese peace treaty working group there was a pronounced tendency to talk past each other. Officials were concerned about making unilateral concessions that could not be retracted and might have been better used later as bargaining chips. So much Japanese attention is focused on the ministerial and deputy-ministerial meetings that concern must be given to not creating false impressions or unduly raising expectations.

Both Soviet and Japanese expectations for a breakthrough in relations were low in the late summer of 1989. Gorbachev was scarcely expected to open the territorial and World War II Pandora's box by generosity toward Japan at a time when the Soviet hold over its own Baltic states and parts of Eastern Europe was cracking in response to similar nationalistic demands. Also, Soviet reformers seemed to have little leverage in the midst of their country's economic crisis. At the same time, the Kaifu leadership offered only an interim solution to political uncertainty in Japan. It did not seem sufficiently in control or experienced in foreign affairs to respond to a Soviet initiative. Moscow was waiting for elections to determine the fate of the LDP and, if it won, to produce a stronger leadership. But in the fall the situation abruptly changed. As on many other issues, Moscow decided it should move quickly; Gorbachev set the date of 1991 for his long-rumored trip to Japan. That imparted a new sense of urgency to bilateral relations and to Japanese inquisitiveness about the future.

After Gorbachev's Sverdlovsk speech of April 1990, Sugimori Kōji commented that once every two years Gorbachev goes to Siberia to make an important statement on Asia. In the Vladivostok speech of 1986 he accepted China's proposals, and soon there was rapid normalization. In the 1988 Krasnoyarsk speech he yielded to U.S. concerns on regional military matters and stressed the political significance of the Seoul Olympics, leading to diplomatic relations with South Korea. The clear Sverdlovsk message is aimed at Japan, added Sugimori. Although the Japanese mass media interpreted the reference to the 1975 Helsinki Accords' acceptance of the results of World War II as a rejection of Japan's territorial demands, the Helsinki document also recognized that boundaries can change peacefully. This speech sets in motion the comprehensive negotiations proposed when Abe visited Moscow in January and will end, predicted Sugimori, in a quick breakthrough as did the other two speeches. Japan should jump at the chance because Soviet economic cooperation— a vast market for Japan, natural resources, an intelligent population, the creation of a North Pole ring with new prospects of global significance— will play a great role in solidifying Japan's global structure.[38] It is not insignificant that this article appeared as part of the first issue of a new monthly journal on the "super-scenario" for the coprosperity of Japan and the Soviet Union, under the heading "Buying the Soviets."

They Need Us More than We Need Them. By the time Gorbachev's visit was announced in late September 1989, the Japanese government and foreign policy experts had settled down to wait for further initiatives from Moscow. Both the cautious optimists such as Kimura Hiroshi and some in the newly influential Gaimushō moderate group and the unpersuaded pessimists such as Sase Masamori along with still wary Gaimushō Soviet veterans agreed that Moscow needs Tokyo more. While they differed on how much encouragement to offer in the preliminary negotiations (would this strengthen the hands of Soviet reformers? would it signal a lack of Japanese resolve?) and on how much pressure to apply (would it be counterproductive? would it awaken Moscow to the costs of its intransigence?), they converged in thinking that Moscow would have to take the initiative.

Kimura explained that Japan is secure and economically successful after restructuring in the 1970s.[39] Its only concern in Soviet relations is the return of the Northern Territories, the demand for which is not diminished by time. Tokyo can wait. Perhaps Moscow can get by somehow without Japan, but it, in fact, has a great need for Japan's cooperation. Otherwise it would be difficult for the Soviet Union to become a real member of the Asia-Pacific community, Soviet economic stagnation would worsen, the fall toward a second- or third-rate country in the area of high technology would continue, and the tempo of development of the Baikal-Amur Mainline (BAM) railroad structure and the coastline would be greatly slowed. The real balance sheet of power relations is in Japan's favor. According to the cautious optimists, if the laws of inertia and custom govern Moscow's calculations, logic will not win out for a time. But in the end it will. Sooner or later, Moscow needs to return the islands.

While some observers were not as sanguine as Kimura and interpreted the advances in negotiations of 1988–89 as insignificant, Kimura traced a path of hopeful compromise proposals. He cited ideas for joint use, rental, special economic zones, and other proposals. Already in 1956 Moscow was willing to return two islands; in the intervening years, Japan's bargaining position has improved. Moreover, any Japanese government would be in danger of falling if it accepted only two islands or a variation of that formula. Moscow realizes that it has no alternative.

Many Japanese foreign affairs experts doubt Kimura's view that Moscow gains enough from handing over all of the islands to make it worthwhile.[40] They do not take as seriously the possibility that the floating of reform proposals will lead to further concessions or that the power of the Soviet reformers will increase and enable them to deliver. Furthermore, the prospects of Japanese goodwill and positive cooperation by the government, business circles, and the nation are not seen as sufficiently tangible benefits to entice Moscow. Some who were skeptical may have anticipated that if the current wait-and-see mood shifts more decisively in the direction of pessimism, perhaps Japanese patience would give way to pressure tactics. The momentum of preparations for Gorbachev's 1991 visit was sufficient to forestall a turn in that direction.

Following the September 1989 announcement that Gorbachev would visit Japan in 1991, Japanese quickly began to debate whether this signified that Moscow was preparing to return all four islands. By October, Soviet Japanologists, reformers, and diplomats were practically tripping over each other on Tokyo's airwaves and interview circles. Some sought to dampen expectations of one-sided concessions. Dmitri Petrov of the Institute of the Far East visited Tokyo in October and stressed that while Gorbachev could make some concessions, circumstances such as ethnic demands for autonomy inside the Soviet Union make it difficult to meet Japan's demands. He added that only progress based on compromises from both sides on a draft peace treaty would favorably affect the territorial issue.[41] But the momentum was moving too fast for such warnings to be taken seriously.

Soon a frenzied pace of diplomatic activities had begun. By late October it was clear that Yakovlev's November visit to Japan would be followed by Abe's January visit to the Soviet Union, then Shevardnadze would arrive in Tokyo in March. Meanwhile, the peace treaty working group would hold its fourth meeting in December. Such intense preparations for the Gorbachev visit more than a year in advance were interpreted as a sign of the Soviet leader's personal emphasis on relations with Japan. Some commentaries did not neglect to warn that Soviet efforts to shape Japanese public opinion were mounting. They also suggested that in response the Gaimushō was adopting a threefold strategy of hardening the attitudes of the public, strengthening Japan's international position, and simultaneously advancing diplomacy with Moscow.[42]

Courting the Japanese Superpower. The Soviets had some success in firing the imagination of Japanese about the prospects for a new era. Arriving in Tokyo in November with the message that a breakthrough in bilateral relations is necessary, Soviet number two Yakovlev objected to Japanese insistence on the principle of the indivisibility of politics and economics by saying that he likes doctors who do not simply rid the patient of one disease (the territorial problem) but cure the whole body. He reached out to leaders in the LDP, seeking to move beyond the intransigent diplomatic channels. Yakovlev tantalized the Japanese by calling enigmatically for a "third way" to solve the territorial problem.[43]

Now that the Berlin Wall had fallen and the Bush administration had promised positive assistance for Moscow, the calls in Japan were mounting for a new Soviet policy. They were accompanied by a rising optimism in media editorials that the results of the Yakovlev visit were the starting point for a new Japanese-Soviet relationship,[44] and by a sudden urgency for forming a worldview appropriate to the new world currents. Communism was collapsing; the question of Japan's response now rose to the fore.

While one response within the government found Yakovlev's call for a "third way" a conciliatory posture,[45] the official response was that it was nothing more than a restatement of the Soviet position in favor of a comprehensive improvement in relations.[46] The media split in its response too. *Sankei shimbun* referred to this Soviet "smile strategy" as an effort to raise Japanese expectations.[47] It noted Gaimushō concerns that the respect shown to the imperial household through Yakovlev's call on the emperor may have been aimed at moderating Japanese alarm about the Soviet Union, and that as Japan considers a five-year plan for defensive preparedness the Soviets sought to impress Japan's opposition party leaders that the spending would be unnecessary.

The fall of 1989 saw a parade of prominent Soviet visitors arrive in Japan: along with Yakovlev, Andrei Sakharov and Yuri Afanasyev attracted the most attention. Their visits impressed at least one *Sankei shimbun* editorial board member as a sign of the remarkable rise in Japan's standing in economics and international politics. According to his newspaper, Soviet leaders hoped to explore the prospect of a big return from Japan for concessions on the islands and for a public relations dividend.[48]

Security Overshadows Territory. Commentators on Gorbachev's planned visit discerned that beyond the bilateral question of territory, an outline was likely to emerge for security in the Asia-Pacific region as a whole. Of course, the United States, China, and other Asian countries must be involved as well.

The announcement of Gorbachev's planned visit in 1991 renewed the criticism by Japanese reformers that the Japanese government's diplomacy remained mired in old attitudes. While the Soviet side was at last preparing to broaden concern for the end of the cold war to negotiations about disarmament in the Far East and to link this to a peace treaty with Japan, Tokyo, they said, could not look beyond the return of the four islands. According to Satō Kikuo, just as through the Brezhnev era Moscow saw Japan as no more than a dependency of the United States of no necessity for a military and ideological great power, Japan saw and still sees the Soviet Union as unnecessary for its own economic prosperity. Moscow's Japan image has turned 180 degrees, but Japan's Soviet image has not turned half of that. Although Japan well appreciates rapid changes in the Soviet camp, as before the theory of the Soviet threat is tenacious, and the danger that the Gorbachev regime may fall momentarily is also widely felt. With these attitudes, the Japanese side is slow to pursue a breakthrough in relations. Satō contrasts the strong supportive statements of Thatcher, Mitterand, and others, as well as the bold breakthroughs between Sadat and Begin or Gorbachev and Reagan, with the bystander approach of the Kaifu leadership.

Economic Aid. Satō proposes a "decisive, realistic approach" based first on political leadership, then on support from the Gaimushō, economic circles, and opinion leaders. Discussing alternatives recently proposed in Japanese and Soviet publications for handling the islands, Satō objects only to the cold war mentality of the Japanese side. He calls for linkage—an exchange of territory for economic and technical assistance. Any subsequent economic aid that Japan gives to the Soviet Union must be presented as "a symbol of appreciation and gratitude to the Soviet move." To assure Moscow that the deal is guaranteed, he proposes that the United States serve as the "ideal mediator."[49] Others in Japan are more reticent to involve Washington so deeply in an issue that presents Tokyo with an opportunity to boost itself as an independent world power.

In late 1989 after Gorbachev had expressed his intention to visit Japan in 1991, Japanese became more forthright in discussing the sensitive topic of a quid pro quo. Speculation centered on what would constitute reasonable compensation for the four northern islands, and what formula could mask the barter element to make the deal acceptable. As Ōkura Yūnosuke, a former Moscow correspondent, explained, there must not be "any hint of monetary compensation."[50]

The Economic Lobby. Moscow has tried to create a business group in Japan strongly interested in Soviet ties. It had some success in the 1960s and 1970s but lost many of its preferred targets for economic reasons related to Japan's restructuring after the 1973 oil shock and to decreased need for raw materials in a buyer's market, and for political reasons after the Afghanistan deployment of Soviet troops and Japan's imposition of economic sanctions. Trade recovered after the low point of 1985, but not enough to meet Soviet expectations.

From time to time business groups sent large delegations to Moscow to try to expand ties. Moscow's list of desired projects did not remain constant, but it also failed to find many takers. Two particular goals stood out on the list: a mammoth program to develop the Soviet Far East and Siberia and rising hopes for the attraction of joint ventures. In the middle of 1989 Japanese interest in both remained slight.

In August Kawai Ryōichi, chairman of Komatsu and head of a committee from the Keidanren business federation, led a large group to Moscow. Many went with the attitude that the recent Soviet focus on the Far East and Siberia is unrealistic. There simply is insufficient infrastructure to make the economy of that region profitable. Apart from some minor coastal projects, little could be expected of the Japanese there. The delegation was prepared to discuss nearly a thousand joint-venture projects, but only a handful had previously been launched, and newly liberalized Soviet legislation was not expected to increase the figure beyond a modest level of mostly small projects. Businessmen complained of ruble inconvertibility and products not up to international standards of competition; they set modest sights on serving the domestic Soviet market.

Kawai also serves as vice-chairman of the Sino-Japanese Council of Keidanren. Experienced in investments in planned economies, he appreciates the frustrations of Japanese businessmen who have dealt with the bureaucrats who dominate in large projects. For a time there seemed to be a growing feeling in Japan that the Soviet European region may be superior to China in infrastructure, ability to utilize advanced technology, and knowledge of modern management; yet anxieties about bureaucratic interference remained, and then hopes were overwhelmed by anxieties of chronic disorder.

The Japanese government has guaranteed loans to China and provided an extraordinary amount of financial assistance. Until the Northern Territories are returned by Moscow, the government will offer no guarantee to business investors there. It does not stop them from pursuing profits, but the national climate of linking economics to politics cannot be encouraging. There is no sign that business prospects are sufficiently favorable that a strong interest group seeks to pressure the Japanese government to help out more. While guilt toward China left from the war era produced a consensus on the need for economic help, there is no guilt toward the Soviet Union. Some Japanese see a West German parallel as both wartime guilt and a greater Soviet threat induce business deals that the Japanese will not match.

Speaking in West Berlin on January 9, 1990, Prime Minister Kaifu announced an aid package to Hungary and Poland to "help bring about a new order." He asserted, "The moves toward reform in East Europe will affect not only the European scene but the basic structure of the current international order as well, and thus will have a significant impact on the stabilization of the Asian-Pacific situation." Then, he added, "Japan, as a leading member of the industrialized democracies, is expected to play a major role not only economically, but also politically." Kaifu appeared to be linking the breakup of the postwar Yalta order at both ends of the Soviet Union, while dangling economic aid in the form of loans, guaranteed investments, and encouragement for private-sector involvement in joint ventures such as the Suzuki plan to build Hungary's first car factory, announced on the same day.[51]

From the July Houston summit of the seven industrialized nations through the Gulf crisis beginning in August, Japan's summer of 1990 provided a test of multipolarity in world affairs. Kuriyama Takakazu, the administrative vice-president for foreign affairs in the Gaimushō, scored the new, more assertive diplomatic role favorably, noting success in persuading other participants in Houston to accept Japan's renewed aid to China and its accord with the United States in opposing, for the time being, aid to the Soviet Union. He explained that through financial aid Japan is likely to meet the challenge for its new global responsibility in the Middle East crisis. But Kuriyama's call on the United States to get "rid of its postwar superpower mentality" while Japan sloughs off its "postwar mentality" failed to address the concern that Japan's responses to China, the Soviet Union, and Iraq were sufficiently divergent from the international consensus that Americans could not rely on Japan's new mentality to relieve it of some of its special burden. At the same time, mention was made of the suspicion that through the contrast in its aid programs to Beijing and Moscow, "Japan is trying to develop its own sphere of influence in Asia," and that by calling off his first planned trip to the Middle East, Kaifu was failing to make an "active contribution to the creation of a new international order."[52]

In the late summer of 1990 the Japanese public was mesmerized by the emotional saga of a Soviet boy named Konstantin who, after being burned in Sakhalin, was sent to Sapporo in Hokkaidō for skin grafts and other medical care. This story helped arouse an outpouring of sympathy and charity for the Soviet people. In the midst of this drama, Shevardnadze spent three days in Tokyo laying the groundwork for Gorbachev's April 1991 visit. The *Asahi shimbun* remarked on how the Soviet foreign minister, who along with Secretary of State Baker is the world's busiest diplomat, for three days pursued the feelings of the Japanese side who hosted him. He set a "soft mood," afloat, the paper said.[53] The LDP was now earnestly engaged in exchange visits, beginning with a delegation of about sixty Diet members later in September. Asian security questions would now become a central concern in negotiations, with an emphasis on confidence-building measures. Shevardnadze stressed the need for relations based on trust, discarding notions of a hypothetical enemy. Cooperation in responding to the recently erupted Middle East crisis over Iraq heightened awareness that Japan seeks more from Moscow than islands. At the same time as the visit, there was a report that a highly placed Soviet Japanologist, Valeryi Zaitsev, called at a conference in Vladivostok for the return of three islands, omitting only the largest and most northerly island of Etoforu. Clearly, hopes were rising in Japan, as seen in the reported reactions of business leaders, but talk of a historical turning point came mostly from the Soviets, while there was still caution in Japanese government responses. As before in the five-year drama of waiting for Gorbachev, movement centered on atmospherics rather than on concrete positions. Not without reason, Shevardnadze concluded that the "climate is now completely different."[54]

Long before Gorbachev traveled to Japan, talk began about the "cherry blossom summit." Creating the right mood seemed to occupy even more public attention than making the necessary concessions. After all, except for a few academics there seemed to be no one prepared to present concrete alternative proposals in order to weigh their merits. So many ideas were raining down on the public from Soviet sources, while so few specifics were being revealed by the Gaimushō that the question of whether one should succumb to optimism or pessimism was very difficult to determine. When winter arrived, however, the Soviet reformers grew silent while the bright imagery of the cherry petals had flittered away.

By October 1990 the perceived Soviet position, as relayed to Abe and explained by prominent Soviet spokesmen, was to return two islands and arrange a formula for continued progress on the other two. Such a formula would have to "save face for both sides." The new Soviet ambassador, Liudvig Chizhov, insisted that only an atmosphere of trust would make a solution possible.[55] Clearly, Moscow was seeking a psychological breakthrough. Japan's recent official recognition that there is no longer a Soviet threat must now be developed into a spirit of cooperation, including openness to Soviet integration within a developing regional program for development.

Waiting for Gorbachev, Kimura Hiroshi anticipated an unprecedented historical event with an accompanying emotional outpouring.[56] He explained that the return of the Northern Territories must be linked to economic aid on a considerable scale, on a par with purchasing the real estate of Hawaii and Guam. The price should be seen not so much in strategic or economic gains for Japan, but for its psychological or symbolic significance. As former prime minister Satō often repeated, not until the return of Okinawa and the Northern Territories would the postwar era end. Through an injection of confidence with know-how to support a market economy, Japan can make a real difference in resolving Moscow's economic crisis. In return, Japan should gain an admission that Stalinist expansionism was a mistake, which helps to create a clean slate for a new era, built on a new structure for Soviet-Japanese relations. In other words, the high emotional pitch is warranted because of the effect on Japan's psychological liberation.

Trial Balloons. The mood of late 1990 was uncertain. On the one hand, the diversity of Soviet public statements intensified. Just about every Soviet Japanologist or visiting official had his own compromise proposal for the Northern Territories. On the other hand, none of the top officials or advisers and no Soviet Foreign Ministry channels offered any clear-cut confirmation that a solution at all likely to be acceptable to the Gaimushō would be proposed.

The Japanese "wish list" for Gorbachev's visit was growing. Instead of one present (territory), many should be offered. There should be a turning point to resolve in a humanistic manner the bilateral problem of the Siberian POWs, including a full accounting and an apology by the Soviet leader. There should be an admission of wrongdoing in the Soviet violation of the neutrality treaty in August 1945. There should be a retraction of the Soviet statement in 1960 reneging on the negotiated understanding that Moscow was prepared to return two islands in return for a peace treaty. Except for the prize present of the islands themselves, the others represented no material loss but an attitude of contriteness and a recognition of Japan's just complaints.

By the end of 1990 the Northern Territories were seen as a global problem—even analogous to the Berlin Wall prior to the fall of 1989. With the tearing down of the wall came German unification, agreement on the security of Europe, and acceptance of the Soviets as a member of the European community. With the return of the islands to Japan would come the end of Japan's abnormal postwar status, a giant step toward a new security arrangement in the Asia-Pacific region, and Soviet access to the greatest credit-bearing country. Gorbachev's visit to Japan was not simply a bilateral matter. As Shimotomai Nobuo explained, it was a global matter, and, moreover, expectations inside the Soviet Union were extremely high.[57] Satō Kikuo was similarly emphatic in predicting the dramatic impact of Gorbachev's visit on the Asia-Pacific situation, linking it with the South Korean-Soviet establishment of relations and the projected Japanese–North Korean normalization in breaking the cold war in the region and opening a new page in history.[58]

As others in late 1990, Satō urged a broad historical vision in solidifying bilateral relations. First is needed a platform for negotiations based on trust, wiping away feelings of antipathy. Satō added that Shevardnadze, Primakov, and Yakovlev had all made statements in the fall suggesting that the possibility was extremely remote of an official Soviet attitude change in favor of returning the islands. Yet he did not take these at face value. A few billions of dollars from Japan might appear as an injection into the crisis-plagued Soviet economy, a kind of barter as in the case of West German assistance.

High Soviet expectations for Japan's cooperation in the transition to a market economy offer reason for hope. In turn, the tenacious mistrust felt by Japanese can be swayed by heartfelt Soviet abandonment of the victor's consciousness from World War II, including an expression of regret about the suffering of Japanese held prisoners in Siberia from 1945. At his parting news conference on August 15, Ambassador Solovyev indicated that such an expression regarding past history is needed. At the same time, the Japanese side should shed its feeling that the Soviets in 1945 behaved like a burglar at the scene of a fire. Satō added that the Middle East situation has revived in some Japanese business circles dependent on petroleum products and raw materials, such as the automobile industry, an urgent concern for diversification of supplies for fossil fuels. This raises the necessity of participation in the development of Siberia, even though the majority in economic circles still believe that such investment would be akin to throwing large sums of money into a ditch.[59] From the world of business appeared an article about the "treasurehouse of resources" that had risen to the surface in the Persian Gulf crisis. Big business attention was concentrating on the development of the Soviet Far East to the point one journal asked whether, when Gorbachev arrives in Japan, the priority for the Japanese government will be the Northern Territories or development.[60]

From before the Houston seven-nation summit, where Tokyo was the most resistent to aiding Moscow, to December, when Japanese were asking if their country should be the only economic power to refuse to help the Soviets in their food crisis, a debate intensified about how far Japan should deviate from the principle of making politics and economics inseparable. German Prime Minister Helmut Kohl personally appealed to Kaifu Toshiki in a June letter to help integrate the Soviet Union into the world economy, Gaimushō official Owada Hisashi asserted in August that the return of the islands was not an absolute condition for aid, Prime Minister Kaifu's three interviews in Soviet publications showed a shift toward a "carrot" diplomacy holding out a vision of Japanese technology and capital as the tow truck for economic development linking Siberia and the Soviet Far East to the Asia-Pacific region, and by December a Japanese journal revealed that Kaifu was ready to help despite resistance from the Gaimushō.[61] There was now talk of parallel progress in economic cooperation and territorial talks.

Isolationism. Edamura Sumio, appointed ambassador to the Soviet Union in June 1990, explained that as one of the advanced countries, Japan could not treat Soviet relations simply on a bilateral plain. It bore responsibility for the fate of world politics and the world economy as a whole.[62] This professional diplomatic judgment contrasts with the shift toward isolationism among the people.

In September 1990, 56 percent of Japanese (compared to 70 percent of Americans) answered that the Soviet Union had become a trustworthy country, up from 43 percent a year earlier. The gap in Japanese-American perceptions persisted. The majority of Japanese (58 percent compared to 41 percent of Americans) still saw the Soviet government as not very friendly and felt a Soviet military threat (62 percent compared to 36 percent of Americans).[63] Such doubts lowered hopes for activism.

Indicative of the spirit of pacifism was an editorial in *Hokkaidō shimbun* on November 2 asserting that Japan should do nothing in Iraq. This would help to prevent war. Japan should not side with the United States. Only the LDP—but by no means all of it—stood behind the principle of an active world role to stop Saddam Hussein and prevent another such leader from appearing. The Gaimushō similarly identified itself with respect for the United Nations charter and a mixture of pragmatism in working closely with the American-led coalition centered at the United Nations and of morality in meeting international obligations.

Among the explanations for the cautious responses to the Persian Gulf crisis, at least four suggest long-term isolationist tendencies. First there is the view that postwar socialization in schools has taught freedom without obligation. It has meant not only a rejection of the military, but also a denial of authority other than that embedded in organizations close at hand. Critics charge the Nikkyōso, a leftist teachers' union long at loggerheads with the Ministry of Education, with inculcating in the generation now in its forties and fifties and, to a lesser degree, in the younger generation too an instinctive anti-internationalism. Under this influence, the media is also seen to be placing peace above principle.

Second, there is the view that the postwar (or, some add, more long-term) vacuum in universal values has yet to be filled. Mercantilist businessmen and self-interested politicians operate with immediate considerations in mind. Pragmatists, even in the Gaimushō, lack a philosophy or set of principles for setting a future course. In the prewar era, officials and politicians had already been preoccupied with evading criticism. This led to avoidance of direct assertions of principles and reliance on indirect means and playing with words in order to make slight shifts in laws or constitutional interpretations less vulnerable to attack. Inaction is also justified by narrow legal arguments, avoiding the need for politics based on debates about principles. Emotionalism on the left and the right have hindered the emergence of a strong center.

Third, the opposition political parties seem to be driven mostly by fear of a repetition of the militarism of the 1930s and 1940s. They have been reluctant to respond to changes around the world, including virtually no distinctive reactions to the Gorbachev era. Out of touch with a modern, middle-class society and an integrated world based on capitalist economic prosperity, they appear afraid to face the new era.

Fourth, there is what might be called anti-Americanism, which is more open now that the Soviet threat has diminished. Tokyo should not let Washington determine its course of action. Some on the right buttress this thinking with a definition of national interest in support of Arab interests as opposed to Israeli ones. Many on the left stand on the postwar peace constitution. Both views lead to inaction in the Persian Gulf. Women have given considerable support to this avoidance of confrontation.[64]

A confident Japan on December 4, 1990, agreed to provide about 100 million dollars in medical and other aid to a desperate Soviet Union, even prior to any resolution of the territorial dispute. As a Japan of the West, its support affirmed a commitment to the cooperative regional spirit of rewarding Gorbachev for his efforts to build a safer and more humane world. As a Japan of the East, its support recognized Soviet efforts to diffuse tensions in the Korean peninsula and demonstrated constructive attitudes toward creating a favorable atmosphere for the April summit. As a Japan of the world, its offer of assistance suggested that global needs took precedence over bilateral leverage. Ironically, that same month Gorbachev turned abruptly to the right, forfeiting further claims to charitable aid.

In early 1991 the journal *Sekai* asked individuals to comment on Shimotomai's proposals on how Soviet-Japanese relations could be broadened. In these proposals, there was an appeal for changing Japanese thinking, which had linked the signing of a peace treaty to the resolution of the territorial problem and left the initiative entirely in Soviet hands. Referring to the new international environment, Shimotomai called on Japan to act: to provide more humanitarian aid including credits; to invest in the long-term equipping of the Soviet market; to offer know-how; to keep the SDF at the lowest level needed for safety while pursuing confidence-building measures; to agree to temporary approaches to the islands such as Soviet demilitarization there and to guarantees of permanent residence there to Soviets who desire this; to develop citizens' exchanges; to deepen joint historical consciousness through meetings and joint textbooks; and finally, to treat bilateral relations in a global vein, especially by creating for the Asia-Pacific region a new strategic framework similar to that adopted for Europe, by working to protect Siberia within the context of global environmental problems, by striving for regional economic development of the Japan Sea environs (the Soviet Union, China, North Korea, South Korea, and Japan), and by gradually incorporating the Soviet Union formally into the regional economic institutions.[65] Here we see a reform agenda in contrast to the caution of the political establishment.

Wada Haruki's position in early 1991 was even stronger. Gorbachev's visit was Japan's chance for the future.[66] Through it Japan could get out from under the American shadow and gain international responsibility commensurate with its economic power. It would become whole again after forty-six years. Adopting an appropriate compromise position on the territorial issue, leading to the return of two islands plus cooperation and future prospects for the other two islands (what Wada has been calling the "plus alpha" approach), is Japan's best hope.

Question 12: Will the Soviet Union Survive?

In the final months of 1989 and into 1990, Japanese pessimism about Gorbachev's prospects reached a new high. Strikes, ethnic clashes, secession movements, economic disintegration, and other domestic troubles became the mainstay of news from the Soviet Union.

Where will Gorbachev's changes lead the Soviet Union? In the late fall and winter of 1989–90, in the face of the remarkable transformation of socialism in Eastern Europe, analysts became increasingly future-oriented. They granted that there was no turning back to the old system even if Gorbachev should lose power. Reforms had already exceeded Gorbachev's plans. The future was in the hands of the people. Hakamada Shigeki responded with five scenarios for the future of Gorbachev's regime: (1) a compromise with the people who do not want frantic reform and with the conservatives; (2) Polandization through a revolution from below; (3) conservatives restoring order with authoritarianism after a time of economic disorder and nationality conflict; (4) continuation of trial-and-error perestroika; and (5) Gorbachev forcefully pushing perestroika from above.[67] By agreeing to aid perestroika, the Bush administration is linking Soviet domestic politics and foreign policy and may be tipping the balance from the third to the fifth scenario, concluded Sasaki Tōru. Hakamada was less hopeful.

The December 1989 issue of *Voice* carried a series of articles answering the question of where the Soviet Union and Eastern Europe are going.[68] Looking back on the year 1989, some observers remained unpersuaded that communism had changed fundamentally. For instance, Iida Tsuneo argued that if the Gorbachev system is shaken, all can turn quickly to bubbles. He added that changes so far amount to loosening the binds; this offers no guarantee for the future. Condemning the command economy does not make it simple to replace it with a free economy. The verdict is still out on where communism is heading.

Accusations that the Soviets had not changed their spots since 1985 were still common in the second half of 1989. For instance, Kurakawa Masato's book, *The Pure Lies of the Pure Red Country*, describes the Soviet logic and worldview as one deception after another. Kurakawa finds evidence in the continued defections of famous cultural figures who then criticize the system harshly. Émigré confessions fill his study.[69]

By the fall of 1989 Japanese observers had concluded that nationality policy constitutes an enormous test that must be passed before perestroika can proceed. Both are linked by the unleashing of initiative from below. While the unrest aroused by the former undermines the stability demanded by the latter, only by satisfying many of the radical ethnic demands can the energy of the grass-roots level be adequately aroused. In the local elections from the end of 1989 to the spring of 1990, further distancing from Moscow and the Communist party could be expected. Despite the fears of social unrest, there is simply no alternative if reforms are to progress. In the case of the Baltic states, independence itself had become linked with the revival of the Soviet Union. Japanese as well as other people of the world were watching to see if Moscow would pass this difficult test.

It became common to list alternative scenarios for the future of Soviet nationality problems. The ideal in these analyses was pluralistic coexistence similar to the European community, preserving international order through a peaceful solution.[70] But observers doubted that the rational Gorbachev had the answers for the irrational emotions of the rising tide of nationalism. The word "crisis" now often arose in conversations with Soviets.

In August 1990 Boris Yeltsin visited Kunashiri, one of the four islands, and listened to the opposition of its residents to the return of the territory to Japan. He then opposed the return himself. This heightened Japanese awareness that any settlement would have to satisfy the Soviet residents of the islands. Articles and documentaries on Japanese television showed Etorofu and Kunashiri as islands with unpaved main streets and scarcely any signs of development. Reporters found people eager for joint ventures with the Japanese and for free movement, or even for both countries to cede sovereignty, but opposed to yielding their land and even worried about where they would live next.[71] The issue of Soviet survival also impinged on the question of authority and popular support to deal with Japan.

Moscow's Need to Revive Japanese Interest. After the funereal mood of mid-1989, Japanese interest somewhat revived in doing business with the Soviet Union rather than waiting for it to die. With Moscow's encouragement, interest was piqued by a massive natural gas field discovered off Murmansk, and a planned Soviet exhibition on the application of military technology to civilian needs. Soviet officials considered new ways to lure the Japanese into investing in the Far Eastern region and in smaller-scale joint ventures. Meanwhile, the tolerance shown in Moscow for a non-Communist regime in Poland strengthened the impression that an evolutionary path could be found for modernizing socialist countries.

The full thrust of the debate about the end of the cold war and the decline of the Soviet Union is presented in chapters 14–16. In the first months of 1990, as the Gorbachev era was reaching the end of its fifth year, Japanese were intensely exploring the future. At last, they could detect the light at the end of the postwar tunnel that had narrowly confined their vision. Gorbachev was coming, East European communism had collapsed, the Soviet Communist party had agreed to give up its monopoly over power while Gorbachev would assume the newly strengthened powers of the presidency, Germany was close to reunification, the LDP was elected to lead Japan into a new era, and negotiations were beginning with Washington to resolve troubling bilateral problems. Conditions were set for Japan to look ahead to its future role as a superpower.

In 1990 there was no dearth of analyses of the collapse of the Soviet Union—economically, ethnically, and politically. Its sinking economy, independence-seeking nationalities, and much reviled leadership came under close scrutiny. Pessimism abounded, but not the foreboding that the breakdown would ultimately cause serious damage beyond the Soviet borders. Perhaps the economic nadir would bring the Soviet people near famine, or ethnic unrest would create a virtual state of anarchy, or Gorbachev would lose his mandate to run more and more of domestic life. For Japan's emergence in a stronger world role, none of these forces would be very damaging. The Soviet decline opened the way for Japan's climb, but cautiously and step by step, not by leaps and bounds.

The Meaning of Statesmanship. Caught in a showdown over Lithuanian independence, Gorbachev in the spring of 1990 could not be expected to risk the support of those worried about the collapse of Soviet borders by responding generously to Japan's territorial demands. Would Japanese leaders find an interim solution that might make the 1991 summit a success? On April 23, Kanemaru Shin of the Takeshita faction broke ranks with the unswerving advocates of four islands at once as the entry point for normalization by calling for at least two islands to be returned. Even though the Japanese public will accept only four, starting with two could produce a breakthrough in relations, he explained. The *Asahi shimbun* report of the speech said that Kanemaru had met altogether three times with Primakov, who told him that he would tell Gorbachev of this suggestion. It also mentioned the danger of Japanese isolation, which may have prompted this proposal, and that Primakov had hinted early in the Gorbachev era that Moscow might be willing to part with two islands. Yet the newspaper added that the LDP has only opened a debate in response to the fire lit by the announcement of Gorbachev's visit. The official party position remained that there was no change in the call for four islands at once, and that the Soviet occupation of all the islands is illegal.[72]

Just as Japanese optimism was reaching its peak, a survey by *Nihon keizai shimbun* revealed just how far thinking had changed. As of December 7–10, 1990, 56.4 percent of respondents stated that they trusted Gorbachev, while only 20.3 percent said they did not. For every one person who did not expect progress in April on the territorial question there were four (72.4 percent vs. 18.3 percent) who did. Mostly they anticipated a step-by-step approach, but as many as 30 percent foresaw the simultaneous return of all four islands.[73] Only one day after Kyodo News Agency reported on this survey, however, it noted that the Soviet Defense Minister Dmitryi Yazov asserted that Moscow will not give up the islands.[74]

In the second half of January 1991, when Foreign Minister Nakayama visited Moscow in the hope of making progress toward the April summit, Japanese considered perestroika to be at a crossroads. Soviet troops had already killed fourteen Lithuanians and were poised to storm the separatist power centers in the Baltic. Reform associates of Gorbachev were following Shevardnadze's example of weeks earlier by leaving their posts and publicly denouncing the swing to the right. While Japanese sources expressed various regrets, the overall impression conveyed was not strong support for Soviet reformers but a preference for compromise and stability. As the *Asahi shimbun* editorialized, in the Baltic both sides should use restraint, while on economic and social matters the first priority was discipline and a restoration of order. Rather than perceiving a polarized situation, the editorial stressed the intermediate category of technocrats such as Prime Minister Pavlov.[75] One sees here a parallel to the Japanese reaction to China's 1989 crackdown on reform. The prevailing assumption is not that Western-style human rights demonstrations and reformist critiques will quickly settle the future course of socialism. Rather, it is the expectation that stable technocratic leadership can gradually, in an orderly fashion, build a new order. This outlook reduces both the euphoria of optimism when reformers are most vocal and the depths of pessimism when their power is sinking fast.

To many observers, the Soviet threat had shifted from an expansionist monolith to a self-destructing, fragmented country. The real global danger had become the breakup of the Soviet Union. It followed, for those to the left of center, that Japanese aid was necessary not only for humanistic reasons but also to reduce the sources of world unrest.[76]

The Carrot or the Stick. On January 31, 1991, a brief clamor followed the statement by Artem Tarasov, the cooperative movement leader, that Gorbachev had made a secret deal with the Japanese government to return the four islands for twenty billion dollars.[77] Rumors of the "carrot" approach reached a peak as desperation was spreading that no solution would be found.

When reliance on the carrot to entice the Soviets seemed to be failing early in 1991, Kimura Hiroshi was quick to declare what the "stick" signifies. He first explained that Russia has long been caught in a European complex, and Gorbachev, who has used the phrase "European common house" sixteen times, shares it. Now the Asia-Pacific age is arriving, but the Soviet Union cannot join. Japan blocks its entry until it pays the admission price by returning the territories. Lots of countries in Asia and Africa face famine and are more deserving of Japanese assistance than are plump Soviets, added Kimura. Without the return of the islands, the Japanese nation will feel its security threatened. With the return, however, it will feel gratitude and will offer its thanks in economic terms, in the Eastern way. At stake is a nationality's pride. A nation that remains calm about the loss of four little islands would, in the end, lose all four of its big islands, warned Kimura. Japanese do not only chase after goods and money. The islands are not an economic plus, but a sign of the nation's resolve, of its backbone.[78]

On the eve of Gorbachev's visit, *Asahi shimbun* reminded its readers in a series of articles of Washington's scheme to draw Tokyo into the cold war and into conflict with Moscow. The paper stated that in 1956 John Foster Dulles had threatened Japan's leaders that the United States would annex Okinawa if Tokyo did not demand all four northern islands from Moscow. Pointing to State Department documents as evidence, the paper stressed that foreign pressure (*gaiatsu*) is at the root of the problem. One article ended with the warning that now, even after the cold war structure has changed between the United States and the Soviet Union, the United States's existence remains important in the Japanese-Soviet territorial question.[79] The *Asahi shimbun* series on the Northern Territories, which appeared simultaneously with Kimura's *Sankei shimbun* interview series, demonstrated how the issue had again become politicized.

Reviewing the postwar history of Soviet negotiations by Japan's business circles, Suzuki Keisuke sought to entice Moscow. If the Soviets could only overcome their current chaos and could make amends with Japan, they could become part of a "Northeast Asia common house." With the removal of Japanese distrust toward the Soviets, business would respond with new projects. Its "watch-and-see" attitude would give way to cooperation east of the Urals. With concerns heightened about the future of the Persian Gulf region, the energy prospects of the Soviet Union are appealing to Japan.[80] The message to Gorbachev was unambiguous.

Bold Soviet Japanologists who had encouraged Japanese to expect a compromise were no longer optimistic. Indeed, Giorgyi Kunadze wrote in a Japanese weekly that Gorbachev had lost the remaining trust of the Soviet people. He warned that Tokyo should now resist aiding Moscow if a Soviet dictatorship would agree to Japanese terms. Such aid might finance the dictatorship for a few years, but later Japan would have lost the friendship of the Soviet people. Helping Soviet dictatorship in return for the islands would lead to a crisis in future Soviet-Japanese relations.[81] At about the same time as Kunadze's statement was issued, *Yomiuri shimbun* reported on a December poll of one hundred Soviet Japanologists, revealing that only seventeen opposed returning any islands, while about half favored returning at least two.[82]

The center of the political spectrum gave up hope for perestroika early in 1991. Hasegawa Tsuyoshi referred to the January 13 crackdown as a "mini Tiananmen incident." In his opinion, the Thermidorean reaction had begun. Anticipating various scenarios, he expressed alarm about a future that is completely opaque.[83]

At the beginning of March the possibility of Soviet compromise on the territorial question appeared to have been ended. Soviet diplomats stated clearly in interviews that the political situation was not favorable. The sharpening conflict between Yeltsin and Gorbachev exerted a big influence, especially because Yeltsin had switched to oppose the return of the islands after listening to their inhabitants. One article concluded that the Japanese side was shocked by this turn of events. Gorbachev's visit was coming at the worst possible time.[84]

Kimura Hiroshi concluded that after six years of Gorbachev a second era was beginning. In this new era Gorbachev relies on military force, has lower power and prestige, and turns to bureaucrats rather than reformers. He also finds himself more isolated from the West, but because Japanese are not very concerned about human rights and think mostly about territory, Gorbachev can go forward with his plans to visit.[85]

PART THREE

The Building Blocks for Perceptions

CHAPTER NINE

Views of the Russian Heritage

POPULAR ACCOUNTS in the 1980s settled on the deep recesses of Russian history to explain Soviet expansionist foreign policy. Amateur historians took their turns at tracing the psychological continuity of the Russian outlook on the world. Applications of this analysis reappeared in far-flung contexts, for example, in Arai Hirokazu's doubtful response, after the signing of the INF treaty, to American cooperation with the Soviet Union. He said that we must be wary of illusions. Relaxation of tensions based on activating Soviet society may take generations. The tradition of a closed society, in which the people's will is not reflected, has persisted through hundreds of years of Russian history.[1] In other words, the true Russia is what matters, not the transient images of today. The true Russia is at best a passive populace, or perhaps worse, an aggressive and untrustworthy nation. That it shows no signs of changing was the message found over and over again in Japanese writings. The problem is as much the people as the government.

Japanese are accustomed to characterizing other nations in terms of personality traits observed or imagined over a long span of history. While these traits may not be immutable, they are often accepted as stereotypes assumed to persist unless evidence to the contrary appears. Explanations of their origin center on geographical conditions at the time of a nation's emergence or on the long-term historical environment, including the pattern of interaction with other nations and of state formation. From far back in history, a mentality takes shape, exhibiting both regional and national features. Japan's mentality was generated by regional Confucianism and by the formative era of the Yamato state; later it was solidified by the centuries of gradual evolution. National mentality can change to some degree, as in the postwar democratization and internationalization of Japan. Russian character also stands to benefit from these contemporary forces, but for the present their weakness helps to account for the deep impact of forces out of the distant past. The contrast between eighteenth-century Russia and Japan is relevant today in part because the modernization of each nation is deeply rooted in its past.

THE FORMATION OF THE RUSSIAN WORLDVIEW

Itō Kenichi, Arai's former colleague at the Gaimushō, writes often about the long historical perspective needed for analyzing Soviet foreign policy.

He explains that the behavioral continuity between the Soviet period and imperial Russia is a function of the character of the people, their national traditions, and their deep-seated national aspirations.[2] Itō traces the origins of each of these back to natural conditions of geography and climate, arguing that their impact endures; neither modern Russia nor modern Japan abandoned its basic philosophy as a result of the Russian Revolution or the Meiji Restoration. Once formed, a nation's fundamental outlook is very difficult to transform. By implication, he is arguing that Japan is fortunate in its heritage while Russia is not.

The Hunter Type of Society. Itō's argument about a hunter society can be quickly summarized as follows. Local conditions in Russia led the early, weak, and scattered nomadic peoples to flee the steppe for the forests of the tundra in times of danger and then, as in 1480 when the Mongols were ousted, to venture back out into the open spaces. Character was formed in the hidden recluses of the forests and also in the alternation between two contrasting environments. Lacking natural lines of defense, and even more vulnerable when found in the open expanses of the steppes, Russians felt exposed. They looked to territorial expansion as their best protection. Environmental conditions led them to place their faith in expansionism and eventually in ideological messianism, giving Russia the role of savior. Yet this did not degenerate into suicidal folly before well-armed neighboring states.

The hunter type, as Itō labels it, respects the strength of its opponent, builds its own strength in preparation, and seizes opportunities to attack weak nations. Gorging itself on small and poorly defended prey, it grows more powerful. Such a state is distrustful of any negotiating partner, since it assumes a world divided into hunters and hunted. To succeed it relies on numerical superiority. What it lacks in quality, it makes up for in tenacity.

The Russianization of Marxism meant that the culture remained largely unchanged after 1917 despite the adoption of an ideology born elsewhere. Stalin's character—immoral, lying, silent—is the epitome of this heritage. Itō doubts that the Soviet mentality will shift away from this hunter type.[3]

Itō's analysis includes a number of explicit and implicit historical comparisons. He explicitly observes that Russia is distinct from the West. Russia lacked the rationality that Western Europe acquired from Roman law. Furthermore, Itō asserts, the Byzantine heritage of the inseparability of church and state in the person of the emperor left Russians disinterested in fundamental human rights. In fact, he contends, Russia is close in background to the Mongols. Village communalism, not individualism, resulted from, among other causes, the Mongol rule. The Mongols also affected Russia's diplomatic approach characterized by insincerity and an uncompromising style. Having itself experienced the threat of Mongol invasions in the thirteenth century, Japan is prone to a negative reaction through guilt by association with this extreme form of militarism and cruelty.

As a result of these traditions, Western Marxism was perverted. The native revolutionary thought of the Narodniki brought to the fore romanticism about village communalism and low expectations about the mature consciousness of urban workers, as well as high hopes for revolutionary heroism by a vanguard dictatorship, which eventually evolved into a bureaucratic system to control the people. Itō concludes that this Russian heritage is so firmly embedded and dangerous that the entire fate of humanity is at stake.[4] Implicitly, he seems to be describing a country in many ways the opposite of historical Japan, long isolated from the outside, with many natural internal lines of defense, and aware that only quality, not numerical superiority, will enable it to succeed.

The Siberian Lens. The well-known novelist Shiba Ryōtarō has also written often about the unchanging Russian traditions.[5] The argument is close to Itō Kenichi's line of analysis. He too finds Russian absolutism to be rooted in Asian nomadism and expansionism, originating in the Mongol influence. From these early times there existed an unhealthy suspicion of foreign countries and a latent desire to conquer them. Through the lively prose of a best-selling author, the case against Russia's historical foundation reaches a large audience.

Serious historians find many errors in this line of analysis, which, they say, is drawn largely from primitive, prewar sources. But they concede that it has had a wide impact in Japan, where people are accustomed to believing in close continuity with their past and to finding negative elements in the spiritual world of the village.[6] Japanese are predisposed to identifying historical roots for the behavior of modern nations in popular culture and in the worldview of ordinary citizens.

Shiba acknowledges that he sees Russia through the lens of Siberia as opposed to Europeans who have seen it through the lens of European Russia.[7] Russians swaggered across Siberia, wreaking destruction on the small tribes they encountered. Russians sold the furs, which they collected through this conquest, for European muskets to subdue the natives. Ivan IV was followed by Stalin, the cannon became a rocket, and Russians continued to resort to weapons, without mercy, in forcing other peoples to join their multinational country. Shiba suggests that it is not easy for Japanese to understand the Russian control system, which is similar to that of the Mongol khanates. Owners had the power of life and death, restricting all freedom of movement. This led not only to a pattern of coercion, but also to a tradition of heroism not found in Japanese society. Russia stands for a dangerous form of behavior in the tradition of the Siberian adventurers and the Mongol armies.

Hōgen Shinsaku carries this line of argument to its extreme. He recounts Russian history over many centuries in the worst possible light. At night the Russians would drink with the Siberian tribes they visited and have a good time. The next morning they would burn down the village, kill yesterday's friends, and head further east. Russians have always been treacherous. A single person is likable when drinking and boisterous, but he is also deceitful. Hōgen explains that Russians have multiple sides to their character, but, above all, that character is aggressive, leading to expansionist policies and a "hateful" country.[8]

Nomads from within and Without. Shiba Ryōtarō points to Russia's very young history from the fifteenth or sixteenth century to explain the character of its people. Barely out of the wilderness, where they had lived dispersed in the forests and still close to the dark historical stage of nomadism, Russians could not achieve the civilization typical of a fixed, rural society and then engage in the gradual state formation found throughout the civilized world. There was no Great Wall built because there was no rural society to protect nor any way to mobilize large numbers. The Mongols showed almost no human sympathy, leaving Russians feeling victimized, with their embryonic cities destroyed. Despite borrowing from neighbors to create bureaucratic organizations, Russia's loss of time under the Mongols meant that a city culture could scarcely develop. Russia's leaders followed the Mongols in their belief in the efficacy of gunpowder. They saw farmers as nothing more than animals to command. Dependence on one supreme ruler—the tsar—was excessive. Shiba contrasts these conditions with those in Japan, where farmers were owners and lords could not buy and sell even their own castles. Japanese lords actually had to rent land for estates from the townsmen.[9] In short, Russia failed to develop the complex society of the West or even of Japan.

Crude Russia Met Mature Japan. In Shiba's view, imperial Russia became fixated on Japan as a source of supplies for the development of Siberia. Russians had trouble believing, however, in what they learned about the island country to their east. Japan, Shiba insists, was a more mature society, economically and culturally. It had less inequality than China, India, and other Asian countries, and the masses enjoyed good opportunities to obtain wealth.[10] A crude and backward Russia faced a relatively just and mature Japan.

This assessment of Russian backwardness and envy, Shiba assures the reader, is not anti-Soviet. He is reporting the facts, not his emotions, since he is actually predisposed to admire Russia. He confesses that he liked Russian novels when young and expects that were he able to visit old Petersburg he would be moved to tears. He also dissociates himself from those who can find justification for Japan's Siberian Expedition after 1917. Russia's shortcomings do not excuse Japan's own excesses. Unlike Itō's more sweeping condemnation of Russians, Shiba suggests that nice

Russians (despite the backwardness of their country) turned into not-so-nice Soviets after 1918.[11] However that may be, the bottom line in Shiba's analysis is that the expansionist traditions carried over. What is objectionable about the contemporary Soviet Union can be traced back to Russian national character in its formative period.

Modernizers or Slavophiles. Japanese discovered from Dutch sources on Russian history the model of modernizing reforms to help a country catch up to the West. At the end of the eighteenth century, along with the crisis consciousness from Russia's hovering presence not far to the north, which aroused a widespread awareness of the need for a sea defense policy, came a much fainter but perhaps, in the long run, more significant appreciation for modernizing reforms following the example of Peter the Great. Russian history set an example—although not wholly a positive one since the reforms advanced haltingly—for Japan to follow.

Having missed the Renaissance and the Reformation, Russia did not produce a full civil society or true capitalism. Not only its distinctive traditions, but also its retarded development limited its adaptability in our times. Yet, according to Morimoto Yoshio, Peter the Great introduced a new atmosphere, resembling early Meiji Japan.[12] Newspapers appeared, a Western-style calendar was adopted, various types of schools were founded, translations of foreign writings appeared, and studying abroad was encouraged. Peter dreamed of making Russia a world power. Nevertheless, at the same time as Russia was importing Western culture and technology, Peter was building the basis of a centralized bureaucratic system and placing religion completely under the personal control of the tsar. One leader by himself could not adequately reform Russia, which remained embedded in traditions hostile to modernization. Peter's approach drew from contradictory traditions and left a fragile foundation for the future.

Pan-Slavic thinking figures as a negative force in Japanese commentaries. Morimoto highlights the attempts of those who subscribed to this current of thought to sanctify Russian history and to glorify the village community, merging into one essentially indivisible entity mankind and god as well as the individual and society. In opposition to advocates of Westernization, its believers sought to save Slavic tradition from the sicknesses of Western individualism, rationalism, and internationalism. In the Soviet era Stalin represents the Slavic faction, while Gorbachev's lineage can be traced to the Westernizer faction. The old worldview continues to reappear, complicating Russia's modernization at each step in the process. Few Japanese authors have yet tried to explain how such a powerful historical force can now be dislodged. The serious historians avoid simplistic national-character arguments, while the popularizers who are fond of them are unlikely to probe deeply into the historical record.

Kimura Hiroshi starts his 1980 book, *The Soviet Union and the Russians*, with an impression of the bad manners observed in the "northern bear's" bluster in 1976 following the defection of a Mig-25 pilot who flew his plane to Japan. The crass pressure only hardened the feelings of the Japanese people, he insists. But then he warns Japanese not to let their dislike cause them to remain in ignorance. The tendency since the Meiji era of studying countries that serve as models for Japan must yield before the national interest to be prepared in disputes and negotiations. Kimura cites as an example Ruth Benedict's study of the political culture of the Japanese in World War II, which facilitated America's smooth occupation and subsequent friendly relations. He warns that current fragmentary impressions of Soviet life coexist with more developed knowledge of the ideology and the system roughly as water and oil coexist, without mixing.

To achieve a multi-angled, human approach, Kimura stresses the roots of national character. The absence of natural boundaries, the low precipitation making agriculture unpredictable, the forest origins, and the severe winters combined to form a distinctive mentality. The people came to think that they could not prove victorious; they could only defend themselves in daily battle with an unjust heaven.[13]

Kimura is careful to distinguish the intelligentsia from others, and also the masses who are Russian in character from the elite who are Soviet. Given their tenacious Russian historical characteristics, the people liked Stalin more than Khrushchev; they are inclined to a strong leader. They are also nationalistic. Thus, authoritarianism, expansionism, a brusque negotiating style, and gigantomania or a desire to be number one are all linked to the weight of history.[14] One result is a willful neighbor that makes no effort to understand the feelings of others.

THE ECLIPSE OF TRADITION

As the Gorbachev reforms accelerated, the explanations centered on a relatively unchanging national character seemed increasingly out of touch with reality. It became necessary to rethink the relationship between past and present. In the last days of 1989 Morimoto, borrowing heavily from Kimura's work and Western sources, took a close look at the distinction between Soviet and Russian with the objective of understanding the prospects for perestroika in a nation limited by Russia's traditions. Morimoto directly confronted the widely accepted thesis that the Soviet system is essentially a reincarnation of deep-seated negative characteristics of the Russian heritage, and, as a result, little can be expected of Gorbachev's reforms. Having to do battle not only with the decade-old facade of Brezhnev's stagnation and the half-century-old edifice of Stalin's com-

mand economy and authoritarianism, Gorbachev faced an even more tenacious foe in the foundation of Russian's millennium of national traditions antagonistic to modern reform needs. Morimoto's analysis recapit-
ulated the nature of this most serious threat of all and how it might be
overcome.

The Socialist Surface and the Russian Essence. Morimoto Yoshio's
book starts with an analogy. A storm blows through the great forests of
Siberia. It furiously shakes the high treetops but does not budge the tree
trunks at their roots. Likewise Gorbachev by himself, no matter how
strong the winds he unleashes, cannot easily change Russia's backwardness and national traits. Yet where the movement of geological plates has
been occurring, an earthquake could cause enormous changes in the forest. The author describes how forces building beneath the surface may, in
due time, shake the system beyond any of the storms of the past.

Morimoto depicts the two faces of the present-day Soviet Union: the
socialist, public surface (*tatemae*) and the national, private essence
(*honne*). As is customary in Japanese analysis distinguishing between
tatemae and honne, the latter is what matters most. In hotels, shops, and
offices one encounters the uncivil, public Soviet, while social contacts
with individuals, one by one, bring out the kind and cheerful, private
Russian. Morimoto adds that Japanese deportment also differs from office to entertainment spot, but he insists that the Soviet gap is enormous
by comparison. Separated from the mainstream of world history, Russians are distinctive in ways very difficult for outsiders to comprehend.
Especially for island people such as the Japanese, the continental character of Russians is puzzling. They are tenacious and patient. At times they
are gentle and relaxed, but at other times they are given to emotional
outbursts and not easy to manage. A harsh system of control evolved over
these insubordinate subordinates. Given to anarchism and yet aware of
the need for a firm order, they were inclined to a cult of the tsar and later
of Stalin.

Morimoto adds that Soviet behavior is more understandable from the
viewpoint of Russian particularism than as a manifestation of socialist
ideology. In any case, the two faces of Soviet and Russian are fused into
one. Both are in the process of transformation. Already, along with urbanization and communications, national character and modes of
thought are changing at great speed. Gorbachev's reforms have accelerated these changes. Both Soviet and Russian traits need to be swept away.

Morimoto explains that Russians learned from their severe climate to
remain stoic (*nichego-ism*) in times of difficulty. "If winter is here, spring
cannot be far behind," they reasoned. They have a plains character:
cheerful, intemperate, and so forth. They also have a forest character:
engrossed, ascetic, and mystical. More than other peoples, Russians jump

from one extreme to the other. Morimoto depicts the mir or village community as the base supporting the imperial government by squeezing the serfs, and, at the same time, as a simple democracy conducive to cooperation and self-protection of the serfs. Evil egalitarianism grew out of the lack of individual property rights and the regular repartitioning of the land. Neighbors looked coldly on the lone individual who worked enthusiastically as someone who violates the group's rule. The community was not under a chairman or an accountant, and it lacked written decisions. The collective farm of the Soviet era has altered the old organizational form, but it preserves the village community and its traditional human relations of *giri* and *ninjo* (duty and human sentiment).[15] Structural continuity kept old ways of thought inimical to modern incentives from fully disappearing.

Similar themes appeared in other books comparing Russians to Soviets. They argued that Russians are humans, while Soviets are almost inhuman and represent the cold application of power. Vodka is important to the Russian. Geography contributes to his generous nature. But Russians also demand strong leaders and are ready to follow orders unquestioningly. To them liberalism means anarchism—something to be avoided.

Also similar to Morimoto's argument was the description of Russian national character provided in a 1977 book by another correspondent, Kimura Akio.[16] While on the surface (*tatemae*) the national character is socialist, underneath it is Russian in essence, says Kimura. The Russian has a *nichego* spirit, forbearance enough to wait out Napoleon. The negative side, however, is the lack of drive for international competition, a result of the passivity and laziness induced by the long winter wait in the countryside. Also, the history of serfdom and absolutism have left a lack of initiative at work. Compounding this problem, the two-day work week and four-week vacation became widespread in the 1960s. If holidays are added, one-third of the year is spent out of work—an enormous amount of time off, as seen from Japan in the 1970s. Moreover, workers commonly slip away from their jobs one or two hours early on Friday. Along with these criticisms, Kimura also comments on the human warmth, friendliness (in contrast to the English), and optimism (in drink and song) as well as patriotism of the Russian people. The Russian character has its appealing side, even if the effects seem scarcely conducive to modernization.

Nakamura Yoshikazu is among those Japanese, particularly from the generation educated in the first two postwar decades, who express admiration for the Russian people. As one of the editors of the 1989 reference work, *A Dictionary to Know Russia and the Soviet Union,* he contributed many articles on Russian national customs. His description of the Russians bestows lavish praise on the artistic genius of the people ranging from literature to music and ends with the statement that in other fields of the arts and of learning the contributions to world literature are also remarkable.[17] Increasingly, this generation, which had initially admired Soviet creativity too, has been obliged to blame the Soviets for suppressing the Russian vitality in their heritage.

In contrast, others insist that the Russian national character has merely been used by the Soviets, without changing it. They imply that those who think otherwise are really suggesting naively that Stalin betrayed Lenin as well as the Russian people. In their view, Lenin did the betraying. He was a product of Russia. Only by fixing the blame where it properly belongs will Japanese be able, at last, to cast aside all romanticism about Russia and socialism and perceive clearly the enduring threat that faces them. In fact, the battle to overcome romanticism has long been won. Japanese are inclined to see the dark side of Russian character, but not to attribute as decisive a role to it as some would like.

A Vertical Society to an Extreme. Contrasting the Japanese way of thinking based on trial-and-error, which leads to moderate reform, and Soviet national character with its tenacious and excessive concern for security and its unease when a long-term outlook is not established, Morimoto Tadao (not to be confused with Morimoto Yoshio) concludes the two peoples have worldviews at opposite extremes. Using a term often applied to Japanese society, he finds the USSR with its nomenklatura system a vertical society to an extreme, leading to rampant personal alienation and concealed conflict relations. These differ from the familialism forged in Japan's corporate society. In response to such centralized controls, Soviets could only turn to sabotage as a way to get ahead by forming vertical and horizontal human relations of their own.[18] Yet Morimoto also finds change in progress in the Soviet consciousness. The country has lost its romanticism and high idealism and is growing accustomed to Gorbachev's realism as the basis of a new worldview.

Prospects for an Earthquake. According to Morimoto Yoshio, the old Russian behavioral principles made modernization and democratization, that is, perestroika, virtually impossible.[19] In the prerevolutionary era a feudal society had long persisted; it was bifurcated into muzhiks (instead of farmers) and officials. Until the 1930s there was no proletariat either. Normal evolution of social classes did not occur. Yet much has occurred during the era of Soviet rule. At the end of this century, Morimoto finds, a modern citizenry is quickly evolving. Soviet society is changing fundamentally. Even if the Gorbachev regime were to fall, the society would not return to its earlier form; after some years a second perestroika would occur. On the basis of this analysis, Morimoto concludes that even when winds of change are slow to blow down the old order, conditions for an earthquake may be building below the surface of that order. This conclusion is supported by a review of recent generational changes.

Four Postwar Generations. Morimoto identifies four generations: (1)

the Stalin generation now over age sixty-five, whose formative years in their late teens and twenties occurred during the 1940s, is retiring from society's front line; (2) the Khrushchev senior generation, which absorbed the renewed humanism and democratization of the anti-Stalinist mood in the 1950s, has become the nucleus of perestroika, beginning with its standardbearer, Gorbachev; (3) the Brezhnev middle generation, which is most numerous, remains rather cool to perestroika; and finally, (4) the Gorbachev younger generation with its three sacred treasures of foreign-made jeans, sneakers, and audio equipment, its intoxication with rock music, and its high spirits about beauty contests, has no fascination at all with Communist ideology. Each generation has almost completely repudiated its father's era. Information on advanced countries is pouring into the Soviet Union. Japanese refer to their own younger generation as *shinjinrui*, or a "new race." In the Soviet Union, too, a new race has been born, perhaps more shocking to its elders than in Japan. The tempo of history is likely to intensify further. When the *new race* becomes the nucleus of Soviet society, it is possible that a new type of society will become fully mature. This is the conclusion about how society will overcome heritage in determining policies and their outcome.

Defeats Spark Reform. Morimoto finds a pattern in Russian history of reform, rejection, and reinvigoration, with successively shorter intervals. He detects a series of diminishing gaps between abortive reforms and the popular response necessary to reinvigorate them. From Peter the Great to the Decembrists, one hundred years passed. From the emancipation of the serfs to the Russian Revolution, fifty-some years went by. From Khrushchev to Gorbachev, the interval shortened to twenty years. Morimoto adds that fifty years in the last century cannot compare to a duration of twenty years in our era of world economic change propelled by the rapid development of science and technology. For example, in computers the Soviet Union during these past two decades has fallen more than two generations behind.

Morimoto also injects the observation that the lesson of Russian history is that wartime defeat induces change. The most recent demonstration of his point is that in the first half of the 1980s Russia was essentially defeated in Afghanistan, and this, in turn, stands as a symbol of defeat in the cold war. Accelerated world change, shortening gaps between reform needs and their realization, and the impetus of defeat all buttress the conclusion that successful reform is close at hand.

When Japan was occupied by the American army, modernizing reform was pursued by absolute power from above with the aim of democratization. Gorbachev's situation parallels this, but the Soviets lack the democratic experience of the Americans who held power in Japan. Moreover, the Soviet goal of pluralism through one-party control is logically contradictory. Morimoto concludes that the prospects for success are not as promising in the Soviet case; yet in raising the parallel he is suggesting that the positive foundation that worked in Japan could also lead to change in the Soviet Union.

According to Morimoto, Japan's northern neighbor has long been balanced between the backward, medieval, despotic system of its past and the modern, capitalist, Western-style society that offers hope for its future. After rapid modernization parallel to Japan's from the 1870s to 1910s, communism and especially Stalin caused a reversion. This result was facilitated by the extremely strong backward elements supporting Russian capitalism, such as a revenue base heavily reliant on vodka taxes, a policy of enriching the country and building a strong military primarily through exports of grain (even in famine conditions), overreliance on foreign capital, and village community ownership of land coupled with a semiserf system of rural organization. Having progressed initially before 1917 and now benefiting from the aspirations of some postwar generations that have come of age during times of reforms, the Soviet Union is poised to move decisively toward modernity. Tradition is not immutable.

Traveling to the Soviet Union in April 1990, Katsuda Kichitarō found Moscow similar to Japan two or three years after its wartime defeat. Inefficiencies, shortages, inflation, and human desolation were his strongest impressions. People had forgotten how to laugh. Moreover, conditions were close to anarchy. With this introduction, Katsuda informs the reader that the five authors of his book are not connected to the mass media in Japan. They are, he insists, persons labeled "hawks" or "anti-Communists," and they entitle their volume *Theory of the Collapse of the Soviet Union*. Katsuda equates the conditions of the whole country in 1990 to the situation found after the Chernobyl accident. He explains that to defeat the Mongols the Russians adopted their rulers' control system of Asian despotism, leaving a deep imprint on the political culture. The essence of Russian history is expansionism. (He charges that former prime minister Ōhira had told Japanese reporters after the Afghan invasion that Russia is essentially a defensive country.) Given this tradition, continuing to the 1980s, it will definitely be difficult to overcome the opposition of the military and others to perestroika. In this respect, he equates Gorbachev to Alexander II, who also fell into the trap of reforms from above. The future is under a thick fog, we are told. The past imposes severe limits on the present.[20]

Japan and Russia Differ Fundamentally. While many parallels are found between Japan and Russia, Japanese are firmly convinced that the differences are more significant. Morimoto volunteers that the Russian people are one of the world's most difficult peoples to govern. At times they are unrestrained and anarchic. They look to powerful one-man rulers who resort to violence and despotism. Russian history represents un-ruliness and arbitrariness to an extreme. In contrast, Japanese history, even at its most militaristic, is not depicted in terms of unruly mobs and arbitrary despots. Adding up the victims of Soviet socialism over the twenty-three years of full Stalinism—from collectivization, forced fam-ines, purges, political imprisonment, wars, forced migration, and so forth—Morimoto concludes that Roy Medvedev's figure of forty million is a low guess, while a figure exceeding fifty million deaths would be a high one.[21] Such wanton destruction of life registers the high price ex-acted by Russian traditions.

The national psychology of welcoming strong control persists, ex-plained Hakamada in late 1990. But the people also now prefer the capi-talist system to the socialist one, an attitude only expressed by the intelli-gentsia in the 1960s. Change is occurring, even if deep-seated attitudes endure. Hakamada wonders if Gorbachev is not overlooking the psychol-ogy of his country, adding that the Soviet leader acts as if he were running a Western country. Reformers also have the illusion that Western things can simply be transplanted in their country. On the contrary, the result is confusion since the Soviet Union lacks the orderly consciousness of a civil society, Japan's traditional consciousness, or China's commercial society consciousness.[22]

Cutting Russia Out of the Soviet Future. Morimoto Yoshio concludes with the question whether the day is coming when the Soviet Union will no longer be Russia.[23] To do so, it needs to democratize to avoid falling to the level of a third- or fourth-rate country. It must form a civil society, on the basis of which political democracy eventually leading to multiple parties can be constructed. This will enliven the economy through free competition. Also, Moscow must accept the liberation of territories from imperial control. Each of these processes is rapidly unfolding, although with uncertain consequences. The positive scenario envisions that revolu-tion from above by Gorbachev will lead to mass trust manifested in elec-tions and then to revolution from below through responsible behavior. This is a difficult transition, which creates golden opportunities as well as dangers of instability threatening the entire world. Unlike earlier com-mentators, Morimoto is cautiously optimistic that national heritage can be overcome.

Bringing Russia Back into the Soviet Future. From the viewpoint of those who regard Russia as likable and the Soviet system as loathsome, the path forward requires letting Russians behave as Russians. Let them reassert the traditions that they have been denied. Former Ambassador Niizeki Kinya explains that he quite likes Russians, who are simple and not in the habit of putting on airs.[24] If the villain has been the Soviet system, then removal of its yoke offers hope for the future. Yet Niizeki does not go so far as to suggest that Russia has a good historical foundation for modernization. Even those Japanese with a romantic impression of nineteenth-century Russian vitality have not proposed a strategy for its revitalization in the twenty-first century. A new Russia as part of or separate from a revamped Soviet Union is not associated with the national traits suitable for economic competitiveness.

The Geographical Angle. Japanese see the Soviet Union from a distinctive geographical angle. They see it as a neighbor. To some, Russia is a neighbor that does not belong. The Russian outlook is so unbalanced in favor of its European side that it should be seen as a interloper in East Asia with no standing. Others recognize the Soviet Union as a genuine Asian country. For instance, one source commented on the vast scale of a country comprising 17 percent of the world's land and then added that Russia is three-quarters in Asia.[25] Geographically its claim to standing in Asia should be secure.

The same source suggests that the USSR be seen as having an East-West and a North-South axis. On the second axis are placed the relations between Russia and Central Asia. Unlike other approaches that see Europe and East Asia as the decisive international forces, with the Soviet Union in limbo between them, the counterargument is made that Islamic and Central Asian ties could be consequential too. In one country, we find encapsulated the world's divisions between East and West and between North and South. At the start of the 1990s the true West, found, above all, in the Baltic states, is trying to assert its independence, and the true South, situated primarily in Central Asia, is expressing its hostility to domination. Implied in this argument is the idea that there is a Russian core, seen as the North, that must be better identified. There is also an implicit message about bilateral relations. There remains the East, in which Japan ambivalently seeks to play a leadership role and at the same time keeping its own identity largely at a distance in the West. Determining the significance of the East for the Soviet future will be one step toward resolving the uncertainty about Soviet identity. Regions, however confused the labels, are important in Japanese thinking about national character and its effect on world development.

There is a tendency to dismiss the Soviet Union as a world power because it cannot be easily classified in the dominant regional categories used by Japanese. Without socialism as the basis for classification, regionalism with its inherent historical background rises to the fore. Russia emerges as a hybrid and as a country increasingly set apart. This is a source of negativism because the stereotypes of Russia's past are almost all that is left to guide predictions about further development.

Absorbing World Culture. Igeta Sadoyoshi, a specialist on Dostoyevsky, returned to Japan after a five-month stay in Moscow in 1989 exhilarated by the fascinating cultural life.[26] He described the ferment since 1987 from simultaneously absorbing cultures that originated all over the world and through the entire twentieth century. The Soviet Union has now become the site of an experiment in cultural competition. Igeta compares the excitement and openness of Gorbachev's glasnost to past exhilarating experiences in Japan when the country's isolation was ended after 1853 or when its values were transformed in the postwar years. Baltic and other minorities are looking to Catholic, Protestant, and other cultural influences, while Russians are also seeking their own identity through international cultural interaction and revival. An image emerges of a blend of past Russian culture and the best of current international culture, shaping a new identity.

If analysts weigh internationalization or convergence of generational change heavily, they can find reason to predict the rejuvenation of the Russian people. This remains a minority perspective. It is the very lack of receptivity to world culture that is assumed to keep Russia in suspension between West and East. The heritage that diluted Peter's reforms, that brought Lenin's revolution and Stalinism, and that led to arrogant militarism and expansionism remains the biggest stumbling block to a successful Soviet future.

In 1990 the separation of Russia from the Soviet Union through Yeltsin's conflict with Gorbachev and the parliamentary declaration of sovereignty aroused intriguing questions about the meaning of Russian identity. The centralized Soviet state was exhausted, while a resurgent Russia was arising within the context of republics searching for the limits of their sovereignty and a Communist party in the midst of its own ethnic and ideological fragmentation. In this state of flux, Japanese also became more open-minded about the meaning of Russian identity until the start of 1991, when again the dark forces of the past seemed to overwhelm the forces of reform. When at midyear Shevardnadze led in the formation of the Democratic Reform Movement and Gorbachev welcomed it, some of the caution began to dissipate.

CHAPTER TEN

Views of Soviet Development

WITH THEIR catch-up psychology dating from the 1860s, the Japanese weigh success in economic development heavily in their judgment of another country and its people. At times they have also been attracted to promises of social justice combined with rapid growth. Especially troubled in the 1920s and again in the immediate postwar decade by lingering poverty and inequality in their own country, many Japanese envisioned Soviet socialism as an alternative path with some promising features. But since the 1960s this motivation has rapidly disappeared. The main stimulus for studying development of Soviet history is now clearly to understand that country's potential as a superpower.

Careful research to ascertain the true circumstances of Soviet development began in earnest at the start of the 1960s. In addition to the economy itself, investigators studied the political history and social organization of the socialist system, especially in its formative period. They searched originally for an overall grasp of the socialist model, but increasingly for a specific prognosis about the Soviet economy. Building on the results of these studies, recent analysis has turned to assessing the course of perestroika and its prospects for success. From historical roots and vague ideals, scholarship has turned to immediate prospects and inherent flaws.

DEVELOPMENT IN RUSSIAN HISTORY

The Forbidden Fruit. In the occupation period, after censorship had been lifted, the once forbidden fruit of revolutionary history became the favorite diet of historians. Implied in the new writings was the question troubling many intellectuals: "Why did Japan not have a revolution and spare itself the ignominy of the 1930s and 1940s?" Russia had not succumbed to militarism or been defeated in the world war; therefore, its revolutionary path seemed vindicated. Study of Russian history developed as an appendage to the history of the Russian Revolution; historians looked back to earlier periods to determine how Russia had made the transition from there to here. As discussed in chapter 9, a similar retrospective approach in the 1970s and 1980s led to the search for the roots of Russian military expansion. In the search for the sources of revolution, there was a tendency to praise the people and blame the system. This produced a

mixed assessment, offering both scope for scholarship and outlets for ten-
dentious assertions.

The early studies of the Soviet Union in the first half of the 1950s reveal
a community torn between two extremes. One article would proclaim the
Soviet Union a democracy, cite Stalin and Lenin, and reproduce some
high-sounding jargon from other Soviet sources. Another would cite
Western criticisms of the lack of freedom and even of the fascist character
of the Soviet system, expressing dismay at the suffering of the Soviet people. Those not firmly on one side or the other often threw up their hands
and complained of the impossibility of drawing objective conclusions.[1]

Through the 1950s and early 1960s a sympathetic image of Russian
history often appeared. Rather than appearing as an aggressor, Russia
was presented as a victim. Often invaded in history and their cities
burned, the people had developed a will to defend themselves. Even in
difficult circumstances, they believed that they would not lose. The Russian people built their economy and culture to help stop the invaders.
Drawing on European culture, they reached a high level of development.
Rather than seeing Russia as the successor to hunters, nomads, or Mongols, some sympathetic observers of this early postwar era remarked admiringly that increasingly the "democratic intelligentsia" set the tone for
that country.[2] They even glorified Russia as a unification of Europe and
Asia into one culture.

The postwar field of Russian history became a target of increasing self-
criticism. This mood within the field clearly surfaced in review articles
appearing throughout the 1960s, for example, in the annual reviews published in the journal *Shigaku zasshi*. The early research was faulted for
weak methods, shallow evidence, lack of depth or originality, and uncritical acceptance of Soviet historical studies originating in the Stalin era.
Japanese became acquainted with the forces of history à la Marx and
Stalin. They learned through vague conceptual terms, mixed with no
more than a smattering of historical evidence. Their understanding of
development was largely limited to statements about the need for a revolutionary movement to mobilize social classes or to overcome the block-
age of capitalism in a society still partially feudal in nature. Along with a
diagram of the moving forces of class conflict, they learned primarily
about socialist and revolutionary thought. Given the dearth of sources
available to academics, it was easier to present what Plekhanov said
about Russian capitalism than to analyze the empirical evidence of social
history.[3] These were the self-criticisms about the state of Japanese writings on Russian and Soviet development for almost two decades after the
war.

Critics objected that in place of empirical scholarship, value judgments
abounded. Historians became participants in a general debate among in-

tellectuals about contemporary politics, unfolding in the polarized context of selecting which worldview postwar Japanese should adopt. By showing sympathy for peasants and workers and the movements on their behalf, historians of Russia were trying to prove that they were on the side of the Japanese people too—that they did not have reactionary consciousness. For many, to study Russia was a way to show solidarity with the socialist model and to leave no doubt about one's opposition to prewar Japanese militarism and postwar American imperialism and its collusion with the Japanese right.

Turning Points in Interpreting Development. Historians recognize 1962–63 as a turning point in the study of Russia.[4] Under the twin prodding of Khrushchev's 1956 speech (soon followed by the Soviet suppression of the Hungarian uprising) and the subsequent Sino-Soviet split, genuine research on Soviet history began. Russian history began to poke out from beneath the shadow of the Revolution. If either the Stalin system or the post-Stalin one was bad, then historians were obliged to find the causes of its emergence. The new wave of historians critically reexamined intellectual history associated with the revolutionary era and looked also at the community structure (*kyōdōtai*) of the peasantry,[5] in this way transposing themes popular in the study of Japanese history to find explanations for the course Russia took in 1917 or 1928–31. They became self-conscious about historiography, shifting from ideological extracts to substantial documents.[6] In this context, translations of Western scholarship exerted an increasing impact. Yet it was assumed that Japanese scholarship of Russia has its own traditions and remains, for the most part, an autonomous field.

From 1968 there was talk of another turning point. Prior to that time studies concentrated on revolutionary thought. Now they were turning toward other themes, including the history of the economy and of foreign policy. Max Weber's ideas began to provide an alternative to Lenin's.[7] A thousand-page study of the Russian Revolution by Eguchi Bokuro is seen to have marked the end of an era. Already his successor at Tōdai, Wada Haruki, had become recognized as the foremost authority on the early twentieth century; while Wada had solid credentials on the left because of his political activism and his admiration for the revolutionary movement, his more flexible outlook and tolerance for diverse approaches as long as they are based on primary sources was leading to a more professional and specialized scholarship. The Soviet move into Czechoslovakia and the violent last hurrah of the Japanese student movement in 1968–69 combined to reduce sharply interest in the Russian Revolution.

For the next two decades studies of Russian history gradually improved. The earlier turning points turned out to be mostly adjustments in course, as the traditions of studying nineteenth-century revolutionary thought (despite the addition of non-Bolshevik views) did not readily yield to such diverse interests as the study of Peter the Great and Ivan the Terrible or research on enserfment. Scholars were slow to fill in gaps in historical coverage, to provide overall images, or to realize a dialogue between Marxists and non-Marxists. Yet in the 1980s interests were broadening to include religion, the liberal and reform movement, the women's movement, banking, and diplomacy.[8] These topics did not displace the established favorites, but they did diversify and deepen the overall scholarship.

Recent Self-Criticisms. In 1985 Shiokawa Nobuaki reviewed Japanese studies on Russian and Soviet history.[9] He found that in the 1950s a slow start had been made in utilizing primary sources and taking an objective approach. He observed that even in the 1980s Japan was without a regional studies approach; disciplinary boundaries were strict, and research lacked breadth or an overall view. Japanese studies of the region remained isolated from foreign scholarship. Without émigrés and good research opportunities in the Soviet Union, Japanese do not easily understand the culture they are studying, and language skills are affected. Recently, he noted, there has been a change of generations as the postwar leaders such as Kikuchi Masanori at Tōdai and Kimura Shoichi and Toriyama Shigeto at Hokkaidō University are passing on, leaving scholars in their forties and fifties at the helm and bringing quite a few in their late thirties into the limelight. Shiokawa warned, however, that there are very few younger historians to carry on; the 1970s and 1980s did not produce a large crop of entrants into graduate programs. Despite this shortage, the transition to youth was accelerated with the need to adapt to the new opportunities of the Gorbachev era. Shiokawa and others in his generation (roughly the late thirties in 1985) rose to the fore.

Shiokawa's 1990 review article in a Soviet journal stresses the rise of the new left, originating in the student movement of the 1960s, as a force in the study of Soviet history. Faulting the Japanese government for a lack of enthusiasm for Soviet studies, leading to complex conditions of research ranging from insufficient funding to a meager scholarly exchange program, Shiokawa credits the young enthusiasts with largely overcoming such obstacles. From the second half of the 1950s to the mid-1970s, the field was divided among diverse types of Marxists: there were Trotskyites, Maoists, Italian Communists, market socialists, and those who joined Karl Marx to Max Weber. Then, just as English and then American influence spread, with convincing scientific results from non-Marxist scholarship, the young new left was rising to the fore. Studies of the history of social thought at last faded, while social history of the *Annales* mode became popular, with concentration still focused on the mid-nineteenth century to the mid-1930s. Shiokawa adds, however, that Japanese historians remain independent as part of a three-way dialogue with the USSR on one side and the West on the other. The critical voice of the new left is still evident in Shiokawa's concluding remark that anti-Soviet policies of the Japanese government and attacks by rightist forces must be blamed for the concept of the "Soviet threat" and the fanning of negative emotions among that part of the population knowing almost nothing about the Soviet Union. Yet he adds that Sovietologists who long devoted their energies to history are now turning to the contemporary era.[10]

Kimura Hiroshi added to the chorus of complaints about inadequacies in the study of Russian and Soviet history, objecting to the rigid approach, the narrow research focus, the difficulty of finding library sources in Japan, the isolation from international scholarship, the dearth of studies of political and military relations and of sociology and geography, and the hesitation to express one's independent views.[11] A popular complaint is to object to the one-sided preference for studies of Russian social thought from the 1860s to the 1920s at the expense of well-rounded history or of research on other periods. Kimura is careful to note that, in spite of lingering problems, notable progress has been achieved. The Gorbachev era has heightened both the progress and the self-criticisms aimed at overcoming shortcomings in the field.

Unidimensional Writing. A 1986 book by Kikuchi Masanori entitled *The Myth of the Russian Revolution* restates the simplified version of Russian history against which many professional historians have been struggling.[12] It explains that one has to turn to tsarist history to find the birth of absolutism. In opposition to an ignorant aristocracy, Ivan IV had made himself God's representative and strengthened his authority while forging a national identity through victories in wars. His standing was enlarged because the bourgeoisie remained weak and the simple people believed in the tsar as God. The result was serfdom, a backward system, and the masses beseeching the tsar for salvation from their lords. Terror, torture, and a sharp division into a privileged class and the masses, who were forced to work, were the dismal state that preceded the revolution. Backwardness predated 1917. Yet there was a way out. The Russian intelligentsia realized that, in comparison to the advanced West, they could make no breakthrough in their country's backwardness as long as they were under the tsars. At the same time, the common people, who were illiterate and accustomed to an egalitarian community, looked for salvation in progressive thought.

Wada Haruki's 1987 review of Kikuchi's book encapsulates the rising consciousness of the need to break with the postwar historical tradition.[13] Wada expresses his disappointment that although more than a decade had passed since the founding of the Russian History Association and its criticism of overreliance on explanations of Soviet history drawn from sources in the Stalin era and of translated history, Kikuchi has not done adequate research and does not properly understand the sources he uses. Wada devotes twenty-seven pages to specifying the historical errors that he found. Higher standards of scholarship are now expected.

While foreigners rarely examine Japanese writings on Russian history, an exception is I. A. D'iakonova's 1989 review article on Japanese historiography of the 1905 Revolution.[14] She finds that the quality of work improved in the 1980s, drawing on more primary sources. She also welcomes the fact that the Japanese often disagree with Western historians such as T. von Laue, who minimize the revolutionary nature of the events. They do not accept the "conservative Western dogma." Her conclusion is that there are more than a few original works, although she regrets that Japanese interest seems to have fallen during the period of Soviet stagnation when new sources were hard for both Soviets and Japanese to find.

Nakayama Hiromasa's monograph on the role of foreign capital in Russia's economic growth before 1917 was praised in 1990 by the Soviet reviewer D'iakonova not only for its in-depth statistical analysis, but also for its comparative approach. She singles out comparisons highlighting the similar timing of modernization in the two countries, for example, the simultaneous introduction of the gold standard. The reviewer adds that, at last, the ongoing perestroika of Soviet historiography opens the possibility for research on comparative-historical themes in a broad chronological framework similar to the best works of foreign colleagues. While praising the Nakayama book as a model worthy of translation, she regrets that its comparisons did not reach further.[15] Other advances were occurring in Japanese historical studies of special interest to the Soviets, among them the 1990 five-volume history of the Russo-Japanese War by Kojima Noburo. Recent Japanese scholarship on historical and contemporary Soviet affairs is also appearing increasingly in English, often as monographs, as part of jointly authored books, or as articles.[16]

Some Historical Themes. The village theme figures widely in Japanese studies of Russian history to the 1930s. Similar to postwar research on Japanese rural history, scholars are searching for the roots of the civilization, for the consciousness of the masses. They show their sympathy with the people and, in most studies, the great cost borne when collectivization wiped away the spiritual world of the village. Village studies link man and nature; they show how traditional values are displaced. Solzhenitsyn's message about the loss of old village values resonated well with Japanese who follow Russia, as did the revived interest inside the Soviet Union in the village prose of the 1970s and the ecology movement of the early Gorbachev years.

In comparison to Western studies of Russia, Japanese have been slow to find merit in the liberal or capitalist alternative. They have shown less interest in reformers such as Tsar Nicholas II's minister Stolypin. Convinced of the desperate conditions of Russian backwardness, they have taken it more for granted that a revolution was essential. Their heroes have been the Russian narod suffering at the bottom of society, not the emerging bourgeoisie seeking reform from society's intermediate ranks. Only recently, as discussed in chapter 11, has interest in "civil society" become a central part of scholarship, working back from the contemporary era to a presocialist path of development.

Setting aside empirical research on the question of the success of the Soviet model of development until the 1980s when it could be simply concluded that the model is a failure, academics turned to the formative stage of Stalinism. They debated the alternatives available in the 1920s for Soviet development and the factors that led by the early 1930s to Stalin's administrative model. This scholarly tradition endured to the late 1980s.

DEVELOPMENT IN SOVIET HISTORY

The Origins of Stalinism. Taniuchi Yuzuru's 1962 book, *Soviet Political History*, established the tradition of empirical scholarship on the 1920s that has remained the strongest field in Japanese historical work on Russia and the Soviet Union.[17] He examined contradictions in modern development related to the persistence of an earlier village structure. In the process Taniuchi analyzed debates on industrialization, data on village elections, and other evidence concerning the power structure. Japanese historians date the beginning of genuine Soviet studies in their country to the publication of this book.[18]

In 1986 Taniuchi completed the fourth and final volume of what is considered his monumental work on the formation of the Stalin regime. As his reviewers note, he laid the cornerstone for the foundation of Soviet studies in Japan, trained many of the younger historians at Tōkyō University (Wada specialized on the period through the revolution, Taniuchi on the period following the revolution), and set an example in the critical examination of primary sources that helped emancipate scholarship "once dominated by preconceived notions and ideological dogmas."[19] In his books in the 1960s Taniuchi analyzed the class structure in the countryside and found that communal relations prevailed, not class struggle. He also concretely examined the details of individual social strata and social organizations through 1927.

The four-volume project carries the analysis forward to understand Stalin's relations to the countryside from 1928 to 1930. The major contribution is in elucidating the bottom levels of the political hierarchy in the countryside and showing the degree of change between Leninism and

Stalinism. In his view, much of the original idea of Bolshevism was still kept alive in the 1920s, when the party was part of society, not part of the state. Abolishing the rural communes in the course of collectivization, the state became assimilated to Russia's backwardness. Yet, however bad the situation from the early 1930s, through transforming the villages, a way out of that backwardness might still be found. Implied in this approach is the possibility that normalcy could return without abandonment of socialism. Taniuchi still expressed this optimistic view of socialism's potential a quarter century after his first major work.

Regardless of their views about the future of socialism, historians admired the quality of his research. Three joint reviewers concluded in 1988 that "Taniuchi's work not only towers as the pinnacle of accomplishments by Japanese scholarship on the Soviet Union, but indeed is unrivaled throughout the world."[20]

Shiokawa Nobuaki's review of the Taniuchi "masterpiece" offers effusive praise together with specific qualifications. It ends with the observation that Taniuchi's view of the state reflects the outlook of those who spent their youth under the imperial system and their adolescence in the postwar turmoil. It is different from the outlook of the postwar generation. Understandably, when political scientists of Taniuchi's generation perceived in Japan the absorption of rural communal elements into the imperial system, he found a parallel process in the Soviet state in the 1930s. The postwar democratic intelligentsia were confident of their own political philosophy. While many others gradually grew silent as time tempered their views, Taniuchi is the rare case of someone carrying on. He produced a classic of almost impossible difficulty, insists Shiokawa.[21]

Within the younger generation, too, interpretations of the transition to Stalinism produce differences of opinion. In a dispute between Shiokawa and Shimotomai one finds evidence of the importance of studies of the pre-Stalin era in resolving whether socialism has a future without Stalinism and whether the legacy of the revolution is worth continuing.[22]

Lenin Is Guilty Too. Japanese intellectuals in the first two postwar decades were nurtured on the classics of Marxism-Leninism and, even after Stalin fell into disrepute, many retained lingering sentiments about Lenin. Inoki Masamichi recalls that even in the 1920s at his high school in Kyoto, not a few students worshipped Lenin as god-like, although he avoided this fate because he read Kant before starting on a book by Lenin and quickly realized that Lenin's materialism was extremely simplistic. Thirty years later, Inoki wrote a short biography of Lenin, concluding that despite being a first-rate strategist, Lenin had serious shortcomings in his personal life (such as one instance where he humiliated his wife) and was ignorant of rudimentary politics and sociology (e.g., when in his last year he favored expanding the Central Committee to include many workers then employed in industry, expecting this to counteract bureaucratization, when it actually opened the way to Stalin's dictatorial system). The glow has faded from Lenin's image in Japan. Probably few would disagree with Inoki's comment at the end of 1989 that Lenin bears a large responsibility for the Stalin era.[23]

The last refuge for at least somewhat positive images of Soviet history was the coverage of the 1920s before Stalinism was imposed from above. By the late 1980s this type of romanticism had lost its allure to all but a small number of older researchers, including Taniuchi, who still found some merit in the early ideals of socialism.[24] A new wave of interest in Soviet history in response to the Gorbachev era ranged through previously neglected themes such as Khrushchev and Brezhnev era problems of reform, but with no other objective than to show why development had slowed and then stagnated.

The Shift to a Contemporary Focus. By 1988–89 many Japanese specialists on the origins of Stalinism felt vindicated that their research themes had become the center of internal Soviet debates. Now Soviet reformers were reexamining the 1920s and 1930s to understand the internal logic of how their malfunctioning system had been born or, as Butenko phrased it, how Stalin had seized power from the workers.[25] To rid themselves of this system, reformers were making studies of its emergence, already looking back from perestroika. Japanese scholars were relying on their knowledge of the past to interpret the present in contrast to Soviet reformers who were relying on their knowledge of current Soviet problems to look back for early causes. Naturally, they were also closely following Soviet historiography, explaining how recent products of glasnost shed light on many historical topics, including issues of Japanese-Soviet relations.

In a typical year in the early 1970s, about fifty Japanese articles and perhaps a few books were published on what is called contemporary (*gendai*) Russian history. The three most popular themes were the revolutionary movement (where Wada's influence was strong), the theories of Lenin and his colleagues (where old-style Marxists prevailed), and the transition to Stalinism (where Taniuchi's school prevailed and studies gradually moved forward to look at the 1930s). Research conditions remained inadequate. There was much talk of breakthroughs widening the scope of inquiry, although the range continued to be rather circumscribed. Many advanced students from the 1960s generation, who entered the field at its peak, eventually continued their research abroad: Hasegawa Tsuyoshi at the University of Washington, Kimura Hiroshi at Columbia University, Hakamada Shigeki at Moscow State University, Shimotomai Nobuo at the University of Birmingham, Shiokawa Nobuaki at Australian National University, and Kuromiya Hiroaki at Princeton University.

All but Kuromiya, sooner or later, turned to writing about Soviet developments in the 1980s, some while continuing scholarship on the earlier Soviet system or Russian history. The result is that many of Japan's new generation of Gorbachev watchers are well-versed in early Soviet history. As Shimotomai observed in an international collection of articles on recent Soviet historiography, "Soviet history is recovering from the realm of mythology," and now a real understanding of it is important because of its profound impact on the history of humankind in our days.[26]

MODERNIZATION

In the early postwar years the assumption that socialism accelerated economic development was widely accepted among Japanese intellectuals. Capitalism had produced the prewar Depression, while socialism had constructed an industrialized Soviet Union able to defeat Germany and then to rebuild rapidly after the war. By the early 1960s three factors contributed to a reassessment: (1) Soviet self-criticisms accompanied by improved Western scholarship showed that Soviet development was one-sided and problem-ridden; (2) Japanese success in postwar development made the socialist alternative less appealing; and (3) Western scholarship and, for a time, modernization studies intensified their influence on research methodology for Russian history.

In 1963–64 modernization studies from the United States gained a new following: Cyril E. Black, whose scholarship increasingly bridged Russian history and modernization studies, taught summer school in Hokkaidō; the national association on Russian history made modernization its principal conference theme, and the annual review articles on the field paid considerable attention to the topic.[27] There was also a critical response that modernization theory overlooks class relations, exaggerates the will of the elite, underestimates the masses, is insufficiently concrete, and may even be ahistorical by placing nineteenth-century Russia with contemporary less-developed countries. Some argued that modernization is impossible without the revolutionary movement. The challenge of the new approach—a sharp departure from the prevailing interest in revolutionary movements and revolutionary thought—may not have led to much direct emulation in Japan, but it coincided with what was called a qualitative change away from the old derivative Soviet approach to an independent scholarly outlook,[28] including some attention to comparisons between Japan and Russia and to the process of economic development. Japanese historians looked more intensely at the developmental process of modern Russian society.

Arguments popular in general studies of Russian history were transposed into the literature on modernization, sometimes with comparisons drawn to Japanese history. Katsuda Kichitarō finds Russia to Peter the Great and Japan to the Meiji era similar, since both were developing some elements of internal modernization.[29] But, Katsuda adds, the two countries, as other underdeveloped countries, began modernization, for the most part, in response to outside forces. Both countries had to absorb European civilization in order to modernize, causing friction with traditional civilization, mental instability, agrarian proletarianization and abject poverty, and other social ills. Modernization from above remained incomplete. In reaction to the alien culture and to changing social conditions, Slavophiles and Japanese romantics embraced a cult of the people, and, out of guilt, sought to be of service to them. Yet Japan managed to close the spiritual and cultural gap, in part through rapid diffusion of primary education. Lacking a strong bourgeoisie, despite the remarkable expansion of higher education, Russia instead created an intellectual proletariat of unemployed or anticapitalist persons without hope for the future. Differences in educational development led the countries in different directions. The many internal imbalances coupled with a reactionary regime above led in Russia to interest in Marxism, which offered the intellectuals a vanguard role in leading the proletariat to an industrial society and socialism. The passion of the victims of early capitalism and the nature of Russian backwardness combined to bring revolution to the country as part of modernization.

The Resumption of Soviet Modernization. In defense of Soviet prospects, a kind of modernization perspective was invoked in the years of stagnation before perestroika. This view, as expressed by Kikuchi Masanori, describes the poor preconditions for modernization in Russia, praises modernization against great difficulties before 1917 and also the modernizing achievements afterward, and sees some basis for a renewal of the process ahead. Kikuchi finds similarities between the tsarist and contemporary stages of modernization: the country lacked city freedoms, the people were tightly controlled compared to the West, the state sought to borrow foreign technology without foreign culture and morality, a monoculture export economy (then grain and now oil) evolved, agricultural and industrial Russia were divided, a rich state operated in a poor country, and the persistence of absolutism conflicted with pressures for economic reform. This double image belies the notion that the revolution interrupted the course of modernization.

After 1917, the Soviet Union became competitive with the United States in only sixty years and became first in the world in the production of many goods. Yet the large-scale units of Soviet production and services and the very hierarchical social structure contrast sharply with Japan and do not well serve current needs. Localism and nepotism contradict the need to separate fathers' and sons' careers in a modern urban society.

Respect for intellectuals as producers is lacking. Technocrats do not recognize human rights. These and other conditions leave the masses apathetic. Despite these problems, Kikuchi finds hope that more than half of all party members have technical or higher education. He concludes that the system can continue to modernize; it will not collapse.[30]

While there are many Soviet specialists who identify themselves as economists, few have made empirical studies of the Soviet economy in any phase of its development. The early interest in modernization theory in the mid-1960s may have helped to deflate the balloon of utopian thinking, to diversify research on pre-1917 history, and to steer a younger generation toward the social history of the 1920s and 1930s, but it did not produce economic historians, sociologists, or even historians of the long-term Stalinist industrial transformation to the 1950s or 1960s. Perestroika breathed new life into development studies, as Wada Haruki explained in 1989.[31] Japanese became interested in the relationship between a mature industrial society and democracy. As Soviet society rose from 20 percent urban in the 1920s to 50 percent in 1961, it was reaching the level of Japan in the early 1950s when social conditions for democracy were ripening. Now the Soviet Union is about two-thirds urban, about as Japan was in the early 1960s, recalling the tremendous changes toward a consumer and information society that came to engulf Japan.

Comparative Socialism. As disillusionment with the Soviet Union among intellectuals grew after 1968, the older generation of Marxist economists found an outlet in what was called comparative studies of socialism. They could continue to concentrate on the level of theory and to find positive models of socialist development. In the process, they rejected the implications of convergence between capitalism and socialism in modernization theory. Iwata Masayuki wrote about Yugoslavian worker management, Nakanishi Osamu turned to comparisons of socialist countries, and an association for the study of socialist economics (Shakaishugi keizai gakkai) provided an alternative to the more conservative Soviet and Eastern Europe Association (Soren Tōō gakkai). Finally, the failure of the Solidarity movement at the beginning of the 1980s and chronic problems in the Soviet Union and elsewhere led some of the left-leaning economists such as Satō Tsuneaki to become more doubtful about socialism in general.

In early 1988 Satō predicted the fate of perestroika five years ahead. He explained that Soviet misjudgment at the time of the oil shock of 1973 and the rapid development of NIES left it with a huge technological gap. Like China, it may have lost about twenty years and can only hope to recoup by turning outward. Satō likens perestroika to the New Deal of the 1930s and predicts that it too is the only way out but offers no quick solutions. The shock suffered by the Soviets is comparable to the shock of the Depression. With the middle class of educated specialists as his power base, Gorbachev can advance.[32]

Convergence. Some analysts find parallels between Japan's reforms from 1945 after the stultifying controls left by the Meiji system, which for a long time could not be overturned despite a maturing society and Gorbachev's reforms breaking away at last from the Stalinist system.[33] In their view the Soviets will now follow Japan's lead and rely more on human resources and on wider international cooperation to gain access to technology and apply it. Because of their large research establishment, they may have some success. Yet specialists on the economy such as Kaneda Tatsuo expect a considerable delay in the Soviet transition since in the new era of the information society, personal computers and other technological challenges to traditional centralization are essential. Without necessarily acknowledging it, these specialists have returned to the arguments of modernization theory and of convergence theory. Moscow can accelerate its modernization by adopting the policies common to the major capitalist industrial powers. The opportunities are there, even if the effects may be diminished by residues of Soviet socialism and by inadequacies in human resources. Economists tend to weigh the convergence factor more than other specialists.

THE STATE OF THE ECONOMY

Consumer Life. Presentation of details on Soviet consumer life has recently become fuller and more balanced. For example, Nakayama Hiromasa, who after a ten-year absence returned in 1988 for the academic exchange to live in Moscow, reported topic by topic on how conditions had changed.[34] He noted that the atmosphere in stores remained essentially as before, although spacious stores had opened in new districts. Housing had improved, but not in a striking way. When a household is able to obtain a separate apartment it is still a great source of happiness. New outlying districts that were helping to meet the housing need are not provided with comparable snow clearance or transportation. In small cities the wait for a telephone might last twenty to twenty-five years. Clothing has clearly improved over a decade earlier. Styles resemble Japan about thirty years before; Westernized youths wear jeans and mini skirts. Nakayama bemoans the near disappearance of black bread. This is the level of detail that offers Japanese a vivid impression of the diversity of change and of the "Westernization" of society.

Stories about technological backwardness cater to the Japanese inclination to dismiss the Soviet Union as a second-rate country. For instance, *Yomiuri*'s thoughtful investigative reporter Kojima Atsushi wrote in mid-1989 about Soviet telephones and perestroika. He described not only desks with up to eight telephones depending on rank, but also a communications system of unimaginable backwardness for the present-day Japanese.[35] For the technologically conscious Japanese it is difficult to take such a backward country seriously.

Kanamori Hisao, the director of the Institute for Soviet and East European Economic Studies (SOTOBO) and the Japan Economic Research Center, traveled to the Soviet Union once or twice a year from 1985 to determine if perestroika would succeed. In July 1989 he summarized his conclusions.[36] He said that perestroika is not currently succeeding. Inflation is serious, some consumer goods are unavailable, and income inequality is widening. The situation is due to: (1) the three misfortunes of falling oil prices, Chernobyl, and the Armenian earthquake (it was as if Japan had been hit simultaneously with the oil shock and the Great Kantō earthquake); (2) policy mistakes; and (3) one-sided stress on legal changes while neglecting the importance of changing consciousness. Despite these reservations, Kanamori disagrees with those who call the economic reform an outright failure. Freedom of speech brings Soviet dissatisfaction into the open, but there is much exaggeration. Even with the new sugar rationing, Moscow residents will be entitled to more each month than the average Japanese consumes. Soviets have more meat and milk than Japanese have. Now Moscow will cut its huge budget deficit, increase consumer goods, and adopt a very different Thirteenth Five-Year Plan. The people are now involved! The right course has been chosen. The economy will advance.

Kanamori's conclusion represents a minority view. Most Japanese sources are doubtful about short-term economic prospects. A much more decisive break with the socialist planned economy is needed to persuade even the relative optimists, while others are skeptical that structural change alone will work before the Soviet people themselves are disabused of their socialist bad habits through a long-term process.

Economic Crisis in 1989. One late 1989 article on the "death knell" of communism explained how Japanese accustomed to a good service system find the Soviet system bad to a "frightening degree." Citing example after example of material shortages and poverty, laced with comparisons to Japan, the article notes the comment of a visiting Japanese economic critic that in Russia stores are not a place to sell things. They are just for storage.[37] This is typical of the denigrating coverage that, even before the economic collapse of 1990, suggested an almost hopeless situation for the Soviet economy.

The sinking Soviet economy has been widely covered by Japanese sources. For example, Mori Akira, a language student who spent the first half of 1989 in Moscow, on his return wrote a detailed description of the worsening consumer economy, noting that Soviets first coming to Japan are startled by the department stores and the Akihabara electronics cornucopia.[38] To extricate itself from its economic crisis (along with the nationality problem, labeled the "double crisis"), Moscow would likely turn to Japan for help. As Hasegawa Keitarō wrote in December 1989, Gorbachev hoped to gain a strong endorsement for his leadership and his economic reform program at the Twenty-Eighth Party Congress in the summer of 1990 and then to use it as a launching pad for visiting Japan in early 1991 and obtaining Japan's indispensable aid.[39]

Hasegawa reached a large Soviet audience in *Izvestia* with his combination of trenchant criticisms of the state of the Soviet economy (the crisis would last at least two to three more years and would not be finally overcome for about ten years) and direct parallels with the Japanese catastrophe right after World War II. In 1949 Japan liquidated subsidies for firms and in the process cut its deficit and inflation and made firms responsible to owners and not the state. Hasegawa concludes that Japan can become a good example to the Soviet Union, especially by showing that success results from the enormous sacrifices borne by the people through hard work.[40] With such words of encouragement for the applicability of the Japanese model, Hasegawa also appeared often in the Japanese media in 1990.

Economic Forecasting. Satō Tsuneaki wrote in mid-1989 that glasnost is proceeding beyond expectations as seen in the parliamentary elections, new thinking has brought startling developments in foreign policy, but the third element in the troika of initiatives, economic perestroika, is at a dead end or worse has entered a danger zone.[41] Financial deficits and inflation have risen to the surface, and acceleration of the technological revolution and then reform of the economic system have been tried and found wanting. Living standards are worsening. Falling oil prices, lost revenues from the anti-alcohol campaign, the cost of Chernobyl and the Armenian earthquake, and urgent expenses to improve neglected social capital all overwhelm the consumer economy. Moreover, Satō stressed the contents of Gorbachev's economic strategy itself as a determining factor. In the current plan, capital accumulation was increased at the expense of consumption. This does not mean, however, that the prognosis is bad.

Now, Satō found, the strategy is beginning to change. Consumption funds are rising, foreign goods are being urgently imported to raise consumption, conversion from military to civilian demand is occurring, and other realistic strategies are evolving. Moscow must describe objectively the entire sick state of its economy, preparing white papers by neutral economics experts, and find a program aimed at rehabilitation, even if immediate growth is sacrificed. Otherwise, there is a danger of ignoring the bridge from the past to the future and rushing blindly into a market economy. Along with warnings about the short-term difficulties ahead, Satō left the reader with some hope for the long term.

Two Options. In the spring of 1989 the author using the pseudonym Saga Tōru published a book on the Soviet economy concerned with the question "will it revive or not?" In it he describes in detail the causes of stagnation, the past efforts to overcome its manifestations, and the problems facing perestroika. Raising the issue "for whom is the economy?" he dissociates himself from the view that the Soviet people stop loving their country because of their poor material conditions. Saga reminds the reader that in Japan, too, the question is raised about who benefits from prosperity to the extent that there are not improvements in confined housing and backward infrastructure. Also, present-day Japan deemphasizes the pursuit of spiritual values in the midst of its material prosperity. People cannot live by bread alone.[42] Although the Soviet problems are acute, they are not unique.

The author depicts an economy plagued by bottlenecks, which only in 1988 did reform measures start to address. The conditions faced by Gorbachev are extremely unfavorable. Yet Moscow's decision to internationalize is based on the reality that as the technological revolution is sweeping ahead in the West, it is losing its place as a superpower. Internationalization is essential for Moscow: to be able to export industrial goods, to stimulate domestic competition through imports, to open Siberia for development, and to become part of the dynamism of the Asia-Pacific region. But its economy is not ready for competition on the world market.

The outside world must decide how to respond. So far there are no Soviet guarantees about reducing its excess military presence in the Far East or returning the Northern Territories. Is Moscow now not sufficiently aware, however, that without outside technology and capital, it cannot achieve the international mutual dependent relations that Gorbachev advocates?

The two options apart from an extreme anti-Soviet response are to provide economic aid on a large scale or only to do what is necessary to avoid unnecessary confrontation based on ideological reasons. The risks of the first response are great. The backwardness of the Soviet infrastructure makes the costs enormous. Also, the lesson of the Russian Revolution's repudiation of foreign debts should not be forgotten. Should the West bear both the burden of military competition and assistance? The West has a favorable bargaining position because without its aid the Soviet position will deteriorate year after year. The author leaves it to the reader to choose one of the options, advising that the response should be based on a sober calculation of pros and cons. In any case, he concludes that the foundation of the postwar world structure is collapsing with the decline of the Soviet economy.[43]

The Size of the Soviet Economy. The case that Japanese were underestimating the Soviet economy was made by Kanamori Hisao in a *Chūō kōron* article.[44] He argued that the 1987 Soviet GNP was really about 50 percent higher than Japan's and about half that of the United States. Acknowledging the complexities in such estimates, Kanamori offered several reasons for positive expectations. First, there is the problem of relying on foreign travelers' assessments. Traveler accounts now paint a horrendous picture, but they overlook differences between socialist and capitalist economies. Travelers pay high prices for items that are cheaply available to Soviets: meat, bread, services, and housing. They do not notice how Soviets can manage on low incomes. The Soviet people do not have luxury, but they can get by. We should not trust our first impressions. Second, there is the danger of overemphasizing consumption. We overlook the huge levels of investment. Third, there is the lack of awareness of how much expertise is now available to set problems right. Moscow now has good and influential economists who appreciate the country's real problems and can offer appropriate solutions correcting past mistakes. Fourth, there is the error of misjudging the will of the Soviet people. Already strong support can be found among the intelligentsia. Lately, the freedom of meetings and academic discussion in Soviet intellectual circles surpasses that in Japan, added Kanamori admiringly.

At the opposite extreme, Morimoto Tadao, who heads another economic institute called Torei, reported in March 1989 that the 1987 Soviet economy was really only about 20 percent of the American figure and 40 percent of the Japanese one.[45] Moreover, what is produced is not very good. Steel is of poor quality and leaves the Soviet economy without international competitiveness. With its economy in shambles, Moscow has a crisis mentality, fearing that in the twenty-first century it will become a third-rate country. From this, Moromoto deduced, Moscow will have to return the Northern Territories or suffer the consequences of inaction, that is, give up its hopes of developing the Soviet Far East. Clearly, this thesis of economic desperation works in Japan's favor.

Between the two extremes, which still directly confronted each other in early 1990, three viewpoints were most in evidence.[46] From official circles and many on the right it was common to hear that Japan should not underestimate the Soviet economy. It could still support a superpower military machine for a long time to come. Morimoto's figures could lull Japanese into overconfidence. On the contrary, there is no reason to expect a return of the islands out of desperation. From left-of-center specialists came the view that Soviet economic troubles are more severe than

Kanamori indicates. Moscow has a reasonable chance to recover based on proposals of reform economists, but a long and difficult transition lies ahead.[47] While the desperation level does not force Moscow onto its knees before Tokyo, it provides a favorable opportunity to secure cooperation. Most Japanese seem to be closer to Morimoto's view than to Kanamori's. Moscow is weak and its economic deterioration will weaken it further. Japan can wait because the gap between the two countries is quickly widening. This conclusion, reenforced by doubts that the Soviet people will respond positively to perestroika, leaves most Japanese in no hurry to make concessions or to contemplate an important place for the Soviet superpower in the future world order.

The Response of Japanese Business. Business circles were asking what the Soviet reforms mean for Japanese industry. In one 1988 report it was argued that Soviet-Japanese trade is stagnant compared to European and American trade with Moscow. The report pointed to toughened export restrictions after the 1987 Toshiba affair and said that the problem is really U.S.-Japanese relations and irrational impediments demanded by the American side.[48] Now that the Soviets stress the Far Eastern region it should be possible to advance Japanese-Soviet economic relations. The emphasis is on favorable prospects for Japan, but with cautionary notes.

Most business circles did not share this rosy assessment. Doubting that the Soviet economy would soon recover or that profits from the Far Eastern region are close at hand, they preferred to wait. Negative forecasts for the Soviet economy placed a brake on Japanese interest in expanded relations.

Rare optimists such as Tsutsumi Seiji found that colleagues in their firms remained skeptics. Tsutsumi lectured in Moscow about how Japan had risen from the ashes after 1945, with the implication that Russia could do so too, utilizing Japanese managerial methods. Yet he acknowledged that his countrymen remained doubtful.[49] Among the doubters was Hachiya Minami, who responded to a 1989 reorganization unifying three Soviet chemical ministries as merely the replacement of one bureaucratic machine with another. He reminded Soviet readers that Japanese ministries are fundamentally different because factories are not maintained within their structure.[50] It would take a thorough reform to get such Japanese to take Soviet prospects seriously.

Agriculture under a Red Signal. Kaneda Tatsuo in early 1988 offered a relatively hopeful long-term forecast for Soviet agriculture, while suggesting that short-term obstacles are numerous.[51] If the epoch-making new policies continue for five or ten years, Kaneda predicted, there might be a revival of agriculture as occurred earlier in China. Because of the large-scale mechanization and the great dependency on outside inputs in Soviet agriculture, he did not expect a copy of the Chinese model. Yet the

Soviet desire to remain a superpower into the twenty-first century drives it to sacrifice its existing system and principles. Agricultural reform is a vital link in the advance of the entire economic perestroika. Kaneda expected the leadership to see the reforms through and, to some degree, to heal the severely diseased system. He found in the mixture of small-scale groups of workers and family farms the possibility of a change to fluid forms of management similar to the agricultural cooperatives in Japan.

Kaneda Tatsuo's 1990 book on agricultural perestroika ends with a surprising message for a Western audience. Reviewing the process of change and the thinking of the Soviet people, Kaneda concludes that since Russia has a tradition of village community (kyōdōtai) and such consciousness endures to some degree, conditions are now favorable for a new collective organization. This is the road to socialism managed by the people. A village cooperative movement could bring about the revival of agriculture, even to the degree that the Soviet Union in the twenty-first century would rise as a model for cooperative agriculture around the world.[52] This optimistic ending about a rapid improvement of food supplies through the introduction of a new economic mechanism does not directly appeal to the widely successful Japanese examples of rural cooperatives, but it is consistent with a strain of thought in Japanese studies of Soviet and Japanese history that views the democratic and egalitarian roots of the historical village community as a positive force for modern development.

Contingent Assistance. At a conference in Sapporo in early 1988, Soviet specialists debated how far their country should shift from a planned to a market economy in order to optimize its reform. Japanese joined the discussion too. Mochizuki Kiichi presented a view from the old-line left, warning of the dangers of a great shift to a market economy and affirming the continued importance of central planning.[53] That is a view not often heard these days in Japan.

Mochizuki continued in 1988 to make excuses for the Soviet economy. Caught in the arms races in which one side's excesses lead to excesses by its opponent, Moscow devoted too much of its GNP to its military. If Japan spent 10–15 percent of its GNP in this way and faced COCOM restrictions, would it have been able to build its current prosperity? Mochizuki found that even if Soviet goods are not trendy, they are longlasting. Moreover, its total employment, low working hours, substantial social welfare fund, and end of exploitation of man by man present positive features even if it is behind in some areas. It is behind because in 1917 it was internationally isolated and subjected to wars, losing about ten years at the start and another ten years in the 1940s. Moreover, Naziism aroused a violent fear and distrust of capitalism, leading to the postwar drive for military parity. Yet now realism exists, and restrictions by the

West and Japan stand in the way of socialism realizing its true potential. Vast resources, high-level scientific basic research, and changes in investment, management, and pricing policies can develop along the deep roots of the past two decades of attempted reforms.[54]

Mochizuki reminded Japanese in August 1989 that the Soviet side is now sweetening the conditions for entrance in the world economy, and that various countries are advancing into the Soviet market aware of its enormous latent demand. He added that the Japanese response is relatively slow. It should display leadership and work hard to strengthen mutual understanding and goodwill through the development of economic relations.

Much less optimistic than Kaneda or Mochizuki is Sawa Hidetake, a recently retired reporter from *Sankei shimbun*. Sawa's study of Soviet agriculture offers little hope. He talks of only an "advance under a red signal." The farmers will not respond to what is offered. The postscript to the study adds that the twentieth century will bring the funeral for communism.[55]

JAPAN'S ROLE IN THE
FUTURE SOVIET ECONOMY

The Soviet Union has grandiose dreams of what might be accomplished in Siberia and its Far East. Siberian lumber, South Yakutsk coal, Sakhalin oil, vast port construction could all become part of tens of billions of rubles of investment—even adding up to a 230 billion ruble price tag by the year 2000 if Moscow's 1987 plan materialized. Yet Japanese remained virtually unmoved. They do not share these dreams. Tokyo only grudgingly began to mention its willingness to examine economic cooperation after a peace treaty is signed, although by early 1989 at least one Japanese journal began to speculate that a deal was at last possible.[56]

Complementary Economies. Morimoto warns that Japan can lose money if it does not know the Soviet Union. This is not because the Soviet Union is some kind of economic superpower—a fixed and erroneous idea in the West based on a vastly exaggerated estimate of a GNP that Morimoto places only fourth in the world, at about France's level. Rather, profits can be won by responding to the Soviet push to convert its economy and to Soviet leadership in selected fields of basic research. To become competitive, Morimoto adds, Moscow must abandon its military superpower status and turn with intensity to the service sector. Its extreme poverty, with workers' income even lower than it is in developing countries and an impending rapid rise in obligations to pension holders, leaves it no choice. Not long ago Japanese housing was disparagingly referred to as "rabbit hutches." Morimoto suggests that the Soviet Union can hardly be considered a great power when citizens spend half their money on food and live in housing that is worse than rabbit hutches, with persons in their twenties perceiving the housing shortage even more acutely than the food problem. The world's first socialist country has reached a dead end—a conclusion supported with comparisons to Japanese economic achievements. Nevertheless, the Soviet Union is in the forefront in some fields of basic research, such as man-made diamonds, in which Japan does not even have independent research. Morimoto concludes that Soviet basic technology can dock with Japanese applied technology, creating possibilities for new advanced goods.[57] The two countries are mutually complementary.

The Rim of the Sea of Japan. One school of thought takes the prospects for economic relations between the Soviet Far East and East Asia seriously. Represented by Kanamori Hisao, this school welcomed Gorbachev's Vladivostok speech in July 1986 for its recognition that the Far Eastern region must become largely self-sufficient of the distant Moscow-centered economy and must instead become closely integrated into the Pacific region economy. It saw more substantial evidence of serious intent in 1988 following the formation in March of the Soviet Domestic Commission on Economic Cooperation with the Asia-Pacific Region led by Evgenyi Primakov. Although most Japanese were skeptical of the Soviet Central Committee's July 1987 "Comprehensive Far East Plan" calling for more than 230 billion rubles in investment to the year 2000, some at least found it, however unrealistic, to be a clear signal of a new commitment to economic relations with Asian countries.

By 1989 they noted the expansion of Sino-Soviet and Soviet–South Korean trade as signs of a regional economic emphasis that was likely to involve Japan. Not only is the Soviet Union committed, China is eager to boost development in Manchuria, South Korea seeks diversity to lessen dependence on the United States, and Japan plans as part of its Fourth Nationwide Comprehensive Development Plan to reduce concentration in the Tokyo area especially by promoting new industries along the Japan Sea facing the mainland of Northeast Asia. There is now a convergence of economic interests.

Kanamori also was optimistic because of the high degree of economic complementarity among Soviet materials, Chinese and North Korean labor, and Japanese investment potential. He disagreed with those who conclude that natural resources are not needed by Japan. As economic growth is recovering following the oil crises, he saw demand increasing for timber, nonferrous metals, coal, natural gas, and petroleum. Eventually Japan is likely to import processed timber and foods. The new Soviet seaport of Vostochnyi, the anticipated designation of Nakhodka as a special economic zone, and the prospect for joint ventures in shipbuilding, vessel repair, and sightseeing are all identified as reasons for optimism. The fact that the five countries along the rim of the Sea of Japan are at different stages of economic development while being very close geographically is, in Kanamori's opinion, a cause for high hopes for multilateral trade.[58]

A series of concentric circles can be extrapolated from the emerging geographical reasoning among some optimists. The Japan Sea rim forms the core of a larger East and Northeast Asia sphere of interest, which, in turn, broadens to an Asia-Pacific region, and finally to a world economy. Distinctions between East and West or socialism and capitalism, as earlier conceived, fade before this conceptualization. Yet the Soviet Union only figures into the primary zones of cooperation as a fragment of a larger political entity. Connections between economic and political geography remain vague.

There were more audible voices on the right urging Japan not to bail out the Soviet economy. By letting it sink further, Japan would come out best in the end. Some wondered what the rush was to negotiate a deal trading economic assistance for the four islands, when Moscow's need for Tokyo's help would only intensify over the next decade. Among them were those who wanted to do nothing until the Soviet Union collapsed.

Closer to the middle of the political spectrum, opinions generally favored contingent assistance. If Moscow made sufficient concessions on the islands, Tokyo should help the Soviet economy. If perestroika proceeded to create adequate conditions for foreign investors and signs of economic recovery, Tokyo should encourage them. Japan's bargaining position reflected economic power politics. Since it was not laced with much idealism, Japan could be expected to drive a tough bargain.

By the latter months of 1990 the Soviet economy was collapsing, desperate plans for shifting to a market economy were being adopted, and interest in Japanese economic cooperation was rising. The press reported the impression that Soviets in important posts were all beginning to study Japanese.[59] Under the heading "To Learn from Japan's Economy," the *Mainichi shimbun* mentioned that the first Japanese to lecture at the central planning agency, Gosplan, drew five hundred listeners.[60] The first Soviet "White Paper on the Japanese Economy" ranges widely in covering the postwar recovery, policies toward inflation, the government's role, the banking system, and labor relations. As the five-hundred-day Shatalin plan for converting to a market economy rose to the center of attention in September, the Japanese-style model played a big role, according to news reports.[61] Such hopes faded quickly when Gorbachev sided with the centralizers in rejecting the Shatalin plan and other market-oriented reforms. Only in July 1991, when Gorbachev was considering the Yavlinsky reform program to attract massive foreign aid, did the Japanese model draw renewed attention.

CHAPTER ELEVEN

Views of Soviet Society

MARXIST-LENINIST social class approaches, antithetical totalitarian approaches, and ethnographic approaches have come and gone in Japanese writings, leaving remarkably little insight into the attitudes of the Soviet people. They have proven to be largely deductive or ill-informed about contemporary social change. Recently, general sociological, social psychological, and modernization approaches have been introducing new terms of discourse. The state of Soviet studies is changing quickly. In the Gorbachev era a new sociology of the Soviet Union is emerging in Japan, even if the discipline itself has so far had little to do with this advance.

The Social Class Approach. The social class approach concentrated on forces of history as abstractions. This meant relying on official statements or ideological excerpts for appreciation of the elemental forces of Soviet society. With this approach there was no way to detect the true feelings of the Soviet peasants toward collectivization or of Soviet nationalities toward assimilation policies.

The Japanese left was long obsessed with social classes and social movements as part of a grand theory of social change. It sympathized with the Bolshevik Revolution and with Stalinist "scientific" theories about the objective forces of history. Omitted altogether from the leftist analysis were the Soviet people as individuals—their aspirations, their frustrations, their way of thinking.[1] It was assumed that so-called cultural variables were no more than a diversion, likely to lead to an erroneous understanding of history.

Desirous of learning from a genuine socialist country, postwar Japanese on the left found that, without the reins of powers in their own country, there was little that they could directly apply. One exception was education, where a leftist teachers' union wielded considerable influence. In the postwar years there was a surge of interest in Marxist teachings and of translations from Russian. For instance, the writings of N. K. Krupskaya, Lenin's widow, were translated in eleven volumes.[2] Through educational reforms, socialist policies benefiting the masses might be applied. In practice, this meant that teachers were free to espouse the principles of the social-class approach, but this did not lead them to delve deeply into Soviet life.

The Totalitarian Approach. The totalitarian approach describes an oppressed population controlled by fear alone. One source explains that the

Soviet people were ready to be liberated in 1941.[3] When German soldiers arrived in World War II, Ukrainians greeted them with bouquets and kisses. Yet the Germans squandered this goodwill when they treated the people like dirt. Hitler tried to rule a vast area by military force alone. He also made strategic errors; he behaved as if he were a military god. An opportunity was missed with this callous approach to the Soviet people.

Hōgen adds that while Japan is changing greatly, almost nothing seems to be changing in the lives of the Soviet people.[4] This was a view before Gorbachev's reforms intensified, consistent with totalitarian theory about an oppressed people but not informative about the diverse interests and opportunities that helped sustain the system or about the intensifying grievances that would soon undermine it. To the end of the 1980s for some on the right the Soviet Union still constituted an evil world with no escape from its forthcoming collapse.

Writing in 1987, Nasu Kiyoshi pictures a dark world without hope, charity, or love.[5] The Soviet people are almost unanimous in wanting to end the existing system. They live like slaves or cattle. This system, he says, will soon collapse. Reforms cannot help.

Suzuki Toshiko set her task in 1979 to depict objectively the everyday life of the Soviet people.[6] She mentions good points, such as the availability and quality of preschool education, and not such good ones, such as the advantages that go unfairly to the powerful. Such impressionistic, firsthand accounts were supplemented by popular translations of American books of the 1970s such as Hedrick Smith's *The Russians*. These books were richer in information and qualified notions of totalitarianism.

The Ethnographic Approach. The ethnographic approach provides many details on the customs of a population, for example, on what they eat, drink, and wear. It is a step forward because it challenges Japanese to appreciate Soviet citizens as a people with their own distinctive habits, eating "shashlik," drinking "kvas," and pausing to enjoy "mushrooms" while engaging in the popular pastime of "walking." The recent *Dictionary to Know Russia and the Soviet Union* does an excellent job in covering such ethnographic details.[7] Yet this is no substitute for appreciating Soviets in terms of universal categories such as youth and women, which have been underutilized in Japanese coverage. Ethnography meant identification of what is unique in the Soviet way of life (often based on conditions of an earlier era) without finding changing patterns of behavior and relating them to universal aspirations.

THE NEW SOCIOLOGY

The new sociology of the Soviet Union contrasts with the old pseudo sociology drawing largely on generalizations about national character or deductions from totalitarian theory. The new approach draws from modernization theory through the analysis of the long-term transformation of a society—the rise of a mass society. It focuses on discrepancies between the political system and the needs of a modern society in the new information era or the age of high technology. Concurrently, the new studies point to the consequences of a command economy, separating the outcomes in various areas of life. They often have an applied orientation. How are different social classes and groups responding to perestroika? What are the social roots of a new civil society? Rejecting ideology as an adequate explanation for the conduct and attitudes of Soviet citizens, the new "sociologists" (none formally trained as such) have discovered Soviet society. An enormous gap in Japanese perceptions of the Soviet Union is now being filled.

Few Japanese have paid attention to social aspects of the Soviet Union, to the daily lives of the citizens. They have seen it, above all, in military and political terms. Yet, as Shiokawa Nobuaki explains, industrialization, urbanization, and mass education are major accomplishments that should not be overlooked. To understand the prospects for perestroika, one should use the perspectives of cultural anthropology and the sociology of religion to study a different culture, adds Shiokawa.

Shiokawa describes a society of many contradictions, opposing interests, and pluralism. Now that Soviet politicians and theoreticians are awakening to this reality, it may be possible to find appropriate responses. The author discusses the effects of glasnost on social activism and on law, which he says Japanese have not been noticing. He reviews Soviet discussions of subcultures, social deviance, AIDS, ecology, and nuclear energy, finding a wide range of opinions. He then examines school bullying, elitist schools, part-time female labor, and minority policies. These are issues that have been almost totally overlooked in Japanese coverage of the USSR, he contends. What also stands out in his series of articles is the emphasis on the commonalities between Soviet problems and the "diseases of advanced societies." Perhaps Japan is an exception, he interjects, but then he suggests that Japan is only late in getting infected.[8]

THE SOCIAL PSYCHOLOGICAL APPROACH

In the 1970s it was the Japanese right that introduced Russian national character into the study of the Soviet Union. As seen in chapter 9, their goal was to show how it was either the root of Soviet evil or the victim of Communist oppression. Not until the Gorbachev era did Japanese on the center and left of the political spectrum bother to respond seriously to this challenge. Finally they discovered that they needed to include the Soviet people in their equations analyzing prospects for change. The first step was to introduce reform thinkers as individuals and describe their heroic struggles aimed at building a brighter future. Soon analysis turned also to the attitudes of various social groups, drawing on a wide range of evidence.

The Japanese have a fascination with explanations of their own distinctive human nature, whether offered by foreigners or by observers from within Japan. It should not be surprising that this interest in perceptions of national character should spread to views of other peoples. As public opinion polls reported year after year that the Japanese dislike the Soviet Union more than any other country (with the possible exception of North and, for a time, South Korea), a thriving literature appeared on why the Japanese have these feelings. In addition to examining sources of tension in the development of Soviet-Japanese relations, these popular studies often described characteristics of the Soviet system and people that were repulsive.[9] Having studied in the Soviet Union for five years and returned there frequently to meet friends and learn more about the society, Hakamada Shigeki reacted against the one-sidedness of this literature. Since the beginning of the Gorbachev era, he has also sought to supersede the simplistic predictions of success or failure for the reform program with an analysis rooted in an understanding of the reactions of the Soviet people. He argues that popular consciousness matters in both foreign and domestic policies. As an example of the former, Hakamada looked at the history of Sino-Soviet relations, including problems of misperceptions between the revolutionary enthusiasts coming to the Soviet Union from a newly victorious China and the leisure-oriented Soviet youth of the post-Stalin era.[10] In studying the latter, he concentrated on the receptivity of the Soviet intelligentsia and masses to Gorbachev's reforms.[11]

Hakamada's agenda, to some degree, derives from Gorbachev's own perceptions as well as from personal conversations with Soviet intellectuals. It is more than a response to the state of Japanese scholarship. Gorbachev and leading Soviet reformers have called for activating the human element. They have stressed the need to change the attitudes and behavior of Soviet citizens, often referring to social psychological factors that must be changed. Hakamada's goal is to understand those factors that Soviets complain have scarcely been studied. He conducts this search with obvious affection for many Soviet friends and for the spiritual world in which they are found.

In one of his most popular articles, "The Misunderstood Soviet Union," Hakamada complains that Japanese perceptions of the Soviet Union are removed from reality. He cites such examples as: (1) the myth that the Soviet economy is planned, when in fact Japanese firms are better able to plan for the long term; (2) the comparison of Americans as pragmatists and Soviets as ideologists, when the reverse is true since many

Americans are idealists in their private life and their approach to politics while Soviets are usually cynical realists; and (3) the view that managers are powerful, when in practice workers do much as they wish, knowing that in an economy short of labor they can easily find another job.[12] Others before him have sought to puncture misconceptions; what makes his pursuit different is the emphasis on developing an overall perspective centering on the microworld in which people find themselves.

Hakamada is concerned with the mental barriers to change. One finds in his writings little optimism about the prospects for perestroika. He recognizes that mental barriers are not easy to change by reforms launched from above.

THE THEORY OF CIVIL SOCIETY

People may accept communism when they know little about it or when they find themselves in troubled or underdeveloped conditions. As the socialist system matures and society develops, support will diminish. There is no compatibility between the interests of a modernized population and the socialist system. This is the message of recent Japanese writings.

In the first half of the 1980s, negative views of the Russian heritage often implied some degree of compatibility between it and socialism. As discussed in chapter 9, Japanese often found Russian character well suited to the Communist system. Japanese had difficulty identifying with the Soviet people as victims. Lately that has changed as they realize the strong aspirations among the Soviet populace for a new order.

According to this line of thought, the Soviet people are ready for a civil society that makes the state subordinate to the people, but socialism only offers one-party dictatorship. Convergence on a foundation of socialism is impossible. Only pluralism and multiple parties can resolve the impasse by dispersing altogether with the socialist system. Partial reforms, as attempted in the Soviet Union to date, do not correspond to social needs and will lead to a crossroads: abandon the system or let the society regress at great cost. Modernization produces a civil society, which requires a democratic system.

Can a civil society coexist with a one-party monopoly on power? Many Japanese seemed to doubt the viability of this combination, while seeing the prospect of a compromise. Uda Fumio's 1989 book questioned both a return to the old conservative path as well as a complete shift to a civil society as some reformers desire. Instead, in his third scenario an equilibrium would eventually be achieved between the one-party monopoly and the civil society.[13] Shimotomai Nobuo took a similar intermediate position, with optimism about the prospects for socialist pluralism.[14] He argued that despite the complete breakup of the old system, the country would not turn to capitalism. The revolution is over; mutual dependence with the international society is needed. The outside world can further this prospect by providing support.

Shimotomai Nobuo described the contemporary Soviet Union as an industrial civilization without a civil society. Although optimistic theories of the 1950s had supposed that Soviet democratization could be achieved on the basis of urbanization and industrialization, the Brezhnev era showed that the changeover is more complex. Revolution from above, as occurred in the 1860s and 1960s, needed to be accompanied by some separation of power and the rise of citizens' movements. What Stalin had taken away in the 1930s must now be restored to Soviet society and expanded.[15] Shimotomai seemed to see this happening under Gorbachev.

Hakamada Shigeki discusses the relationship between national traditions and the civil society. Production relations little changed from the 1930s are incompatible, he argues, with the increasingly complex society of the 1980s. The former, based on orders from above, arouses antisocial behavior, cynicism, and low labor discipline in a population with a high cultural level. The centralized economy that built an industrial society and served the emergency conditions of wartime and postwar recovery outlived its usefulness. Administrators kept trying to move people around like chess pawns, while workers simply walked away when a manager became a little strict. They could get away with it because of a labor shortage. Corruption became so pervasive, beginning with local party bosses who behaved like mafia heads, that many came to see honest workers as fools. Under these circumstances, Soviets turned away from public life and the workplace to "my-homism." A new approach had to begin with the new values of the Soviet people and break the old reliance on a strong hand from above. This is the reality of Soviet life that Hakamada feels the Japanese public has not understood.[16]

Hakamada warns that a civil society cannot emerge easily, as it might in Hungary, which has a tradition for it. While reform intellectuals may be ready, the psychology of the Soviet masses and the bureaucrats is not. A turning point has occurred, but a long time will be needed.

A Coalition of the Dissatisfied. Hakamada explained that there are many forms of dissatisfaction in a socialist country. Rarely have they led to a political crisis. In the past they were not linked to each other. The dissatisfactions of nationalism, religion, and intellectual life were separate from the material dissatisfaction of the masses. Dissidents were isolated. Now horizontal solidarity has been born. Glasnost provides the information to make this linkage possible.

A Mass Society Facing Limits. Saga Tōru reminds Japanese that Soviet life is changing. This is not a one-time change of the Gorbachev era, but a gradual change from the 1950s. A mass society is taking form. This was delayed because of the authoritarianism in Russian history, which lacked the urban, democratic character of Western cities after the seeds of a similar evolution were stamped down by the Mongols. The wounds of serfdom, which came later, are still not erased from the minds of the people. A dual character emerged: outward acceptance hides inward opposition to authority. The state did not develop as the creation of the citizens; it became a threat. In this respect, the Russians resembled the Japanese who lived under a feudal system to the 1860s.[17]

Saga adds that a great change in society has now occurred, as it did previously in Japan. A class of Soviet citizens exists. Rising educational levels, living standards, and urbanization have produced this effect. A Western living style has spread to a broad stratum of intellectuals. Onetenth of the population has received higher education. The more highly educated young are no longer fearful, and glasnost encourages them. A civil society is developing, but central control remains deeply rooted in some areas. Also, people need time to become accustomed to self-administration. The transition resembles what has occurred in Japan through the industrial revolution.

Popular images of Russian society as grey, monolithic, and controlled dissolve with increased familiarity, adds Saga, in a transparent reproach to one-sided Japanese thinking. In fact, the Soviet people are hard to control. They have increasingly diverse interests. They are also losing trust, turning to illegal acts and selfish concerns. There has been an explosion of informal associations. How far can the civil society evolve under one-party rule? Problems are intensifying; economic reform is difficult. The society is becoming destabilized because of the persistent limits on change. Gorbachev has opened a Pandora's box. Until the system changes, the contradictions with social development will increase. This is Saga's pessimistic short-term conclusion.

Hakamada finds in the March elections of 1989 the buds of a civil society.[18] The prerevolutionary intelligentsia, he observes, saw itself as a special class. Then, through much of Soviet history, the party and masses joined together to suppress the intelligentsia. Now for the first time shared values with the masses prevail. The intelligentsia has a burning interest in political and social reforms, and the masses showed their similar thinking in the elections. The removal of this class barrier is of enormous significance in Russian history. It is also a contrast with Chinese history, where leaders do not use the intellectuals against the bureaucracy and have not mobilized criticism of the bureaucracy from below except in the anti-intellectual Cultural Revolution. Yet Hakamada is far from sanguine about Gorbachev's chances to ride the new coalition to success. He finds an allergic reaction to the Soviet leader inside his country because of the worsening consumer shortages. In fact, Hakamada concludes that the psychology of the people is still a more serious barrier to reform than bureaucratism. The civil-society perspective is insufficient without a social-psychological dimension, his work demonstrates.

SOCIAL FORCES AND SOCIAL PSYCHOLOGY

In Hakamada's analysis there are, excluding nationalities, three principal social forces: the masses, the intelligentsia, and the bureaucracy. Gorbachev's appeal is largely to the intelligentsia and foreign observers, but not to the masses, and especially not to the local party committee members and others in the bureaucracy. There are three social psychologies rather than one. The masses appear as a swing group, who along with the conservative officials can be frightened by sudden shifts in policy. Gorbachev equates his perestroika with a revolution, yet he seeks to have it carried out by the established channels of authority. The very people on whom he relies are the ones who are psychologically opposed to the changes. Hakamada refers to this as a "revolution without revolutionaries." He also writes admiringly of the strong attachment of the Soviet intelligentsia to spiritual values; aware of this orientation to art, literature, and the world of ideas, he rejects a Marxist structural approach to this group and also the prevailing Japanese skepticism that there is anyone to admire in Soviet society.[19]

Hakamada's respect for Soviet intellectuals is seen in his praise of their European spiritual tradition. He mentions their craze for art books and foreign literature, and their treatment of Pasternak and Mandelstam as saints. The contrast is with excellent students in Japan who are anti-intellectual and materialist, setting their sights on the business world. Hakamada is careful to add that the critical intelligentsia is not representative of the Soviet masses.

Hakamada's most general point may be that ideology and political speeches have little to do with the attitudes of the people. Focusing on the concrete circumstances of the Soviet population who are tired of speeches that are not translated into reality, of political talk in general, he says, they want deeds, not words.

A second point that pervades Hakamada's analysis is that the psychology of a population, or better the masses, is long-lasting and difficult to change. Research on it is the key to predicting the effectiveness of reforms. In part, he equates social psychology with tradition, commenting that the Soviet people lack a tradition of commercialism found in China.[20] This is one reason why the entrepreneurial spirit has not burst forth on the streets of Soviet cities as it has on Chinese streets. In mentioning the weakness of individualism in Soviet history, Hakamada expresses concern about the dearth of democratic traditions in a socialist country. He concludes that perestroika is not a salvation. Inertia prevails in the Soviet population, and a long period will be needed to overcome it.

Hakamada's third point is that the success of socialist reform based on the current strategy is doubtful. A reform strategy that demands short-term material sacrifices and greater discipline and sobriety in the hope of long-term prosperity and leisure benefits, Hakamada asserts, is not winning popular support. The masses do not trust promises. They are increasingly fearful of unemployment and inflation, which are now widely considered in the mass media to be necessary elements of reform. The psychology of the people is such that only immediate material gains, especially to alleviate the serious shortcomings in food, lodging, and medical care, would be effective. The people's support is indispensable in order to change work habits, but, whatever the merits of the reforms to date, they show no signs of winning this support. Half-measures even heighten dissatisfaction by raising expectations.

Reacting to the coal miners' strike in August 1989, Hakamada observed that, consistent with the March election results, the boundaries are beginning to collapse between the isolated intellectuals and the masses who had distrusted their liberalism. Real liberals exist in the Soviet Union. Citizens' movements organized first in the Baltic states are spreading to Moscow and elsewhere. Their activities in pursuit of fundamental human rights and self-determination for separate nationalities verge on those of political parties. From the start, they gained widespread support from intellectuals, and now they are reaching a broader urban audience. In contrast, Hakamada adds, Japanese liberals are all intellectuals.[21]

Hakamada studies the living Soviet Union more through personal experiences and images reported by friends than from the printed word. He links the prospects for change to popular feeling about the existence of a crisis. In his personal observations of the 1960s, Hakamada found leaders successful, as they had been earlier, in conveying a sense of crisis, of a people victimized, threatened, encircled by capitalism. In contrast, the new alarm focuses on an internal crisis. Gorbachev surrounded himself with "brains" who knew the Western world well and already had a sense of impending crisis. They knew that national strength was not a question of more land, greater natural resources, and a bigger military. Among other things, it was Japan's economic and technological successes that came as a great shock to them, changing their thinking. Hakamada finds it ironic that in the 1930s Japan along with Nazi Germany had a big influence on Stalin's psychology, heightening his fear of enemies as seen by the fact that millions of those purged were called Nazi or Japanese agents, and now in the postwar era the psychological impact of Japan is huge in breaking down Stalin's system.[22]

Interested in one people's perceptions of another, he asks why the Soviets were negative to the Chinese in the years of the Sino-Soviet split, why the Japanese are negative to the Soviets in the 1980s, and why the Soviet people are strongly pro-Japanese in the Gorbachev era.[23] In each case, he looks for answers in the psychological state of the audience and in comparisons of two societies. Believing in the absolute value of economic growth and unaffected by Japan's export offensive elsewhere in the world, Soviets admire both Japan's achievements in technology and its way of life.

In his late 1988 book aimed at filling in gaps in what Hakamada calls the strange, unbalanced Japanese knowledge of the Soviet Union, he looks more deeply at the worldview of Soviet reform intellectuals. First noting that in the mid-1960s Soviets looked down on Japan from the heights of socialism at the same time that the Japanese progressive intelligentsia still had a tendency to beautify the Soviet Union, he finds first a gradual change from the late 1960s as Soviets opened their eyes to the changing Japanese economy and technology and then a shock to the very roots of the Soviet worldview in the 1980s as Japan battled the United States for number one in these areas. On top of this shock came the shock of the surging NIES rapidly overtaking the Soviet Union and threatening to sink it to the level of a third-rate country by century's end.[24]

There is now some interest in the comparison of Japan's postwar development and perestroika. Both are seen as abrupt departures from a militaristic, nondemocratic system. In both cases, there was a shock and a realization that borrowing and dependence on the West are essential. Moreover, both reform programs concentrated on decentralization and invigoration of social activism. Hakamada notes that Soviet reformers are now comparing decentralization of enterprises and land reform in postwar Japan with their own situation. Even as a political model, Japan has attracted attention. Japan's LDP factions guarantee a degree of pluralism, suggesting that a kind of Soviet one-party pluralism may be possible if it too can add institutionalized factions.

Hakamada also considers the barrier of acute nationalism, which has now erupted. He explains its recent appearance in several ways. In World War II, there was sense of common destiny among the Russian people, which was kept alive in textbooks afterward. It was not until a younger generation turned to jeans and rock that there was a sharp break from this thinking. Second, Stalin's ideology talked of bourgeois nationalism and relied on terror; only from the West in recent decades have Soviets learned that one of the most important human rights is the right of minority nationalities. Third, for a long time Soviet citizens were preoccupied with finding enough to eat. It was not until they satisfied to a degree the basic material needs that nationalist identity intensified. Hakamada mentions as his fourth point that Marxist-Leninist ideological education made the unifying concept of the Soviet man a part of national consciousness. After the 1960s the ideology was losing its impact in the midst of growing experimentation with new values and diversification. Religious, individualist, traditional, and other values gained ground. Gradually nationalism and religion became linked as the pillar in the new thinking. Perestroika opened the way for the new consciousness to explode to the surface.[25]

Hakamada challenges the idea that the Soviet people are collectivist. Citing surveys in both countries, he suggests that 80 percent of young Soviet parents prefer home rearing to preschools, while 80 percent of Japanese want their children in schools at this level in order to foster their collective nature.[26]

In his 1987 book on socialism in the Soviet Union, Eastern Europe, and China, Hakamada finds parallels between Soviet party ideology and Japanese Confucian thought. Both Tokugawa Japan and modern socialism employed internal passports and other controls intended to be strict, suggesting more commonalities than contemporary societies have with the Soviet Union. Moralism and views distant from reality and the actual lives of the masses in each case led to rationalism and efforts to return to the original spirit of the thought. Japan's reforms in 1787 following the Tanuma years of stagnation parallel the reforms following Brezhnev. Yet Hakamada warns that Matsudaira Sadanobu, who followed Tanuma, aroused dissatisfaction and could not cure the illness of the time. He had to resign after six years. Reforms brought a relaxation of social discipline and at the same time more bribery, corruption, economic disorder, and selfish pursuits. Matsudaira's asceticism resembles Gorbachev's; a society does not easily oblige its leader.[27]

Gorbachev's successes in diplomacy and in domestic information and culture are more impressive to foreigners than to Soviets, adds Hakamada. In actual life Soviets have not yet felt perestroika, he observed in early 1989. The people have not climbed on board. Accustomed to unfulfilled promises, they do not pay attention to words. What they see around them are longer lines, higher prices, and tightened discipline from the abortive anti-alcohol campaign and closer monitoring in the workplace. Soviets in favor of perestroika now warn that it may take five to ten years for a breakthrough. It is being held up by the conservative faction and the huge bureaucracy. Japan, too, has found that it is difficult to achieve administrative reform, as has China with its shorter history of Communist bureaucratism interrupted by the Cultural Revolution.

Social Backwardness. Shiokawa Nobuaki finds that prerevolutionary Russia lacked Max Weber's entrepreneurial spirit, and, after the long withering of initiative since the 1930s, it will be even harder to achieve it now.[28] In this respect its situation is different from that of other modernizing countries. But in other respects the differences are not great. Perestroika, argues Shiokawa, must be seen in a wider context. Socialism is more backward than capitalism, but they exist in the same era and have common problems. While we should examine differences resulting from historical traditions and the distinctive socialist system, the similarities will help us to understand Soviet problems and prospects.

Recent problems in education as a channel for social mobility, as severe as they are, do not suggest backwardness compared to the West. Women's labor-force participation is first in the world, and, whatever the problems debated, this is not an area where the Soviet Union is behind the West. In health, Central Asia has a remarkably low level, but not all of the country is so far behind. The problems of an aging population and the financial burden of free medical care on health insurance are similar to other countries. Ethnic conflicts are also erupting worldwide. Formerly backward areas have recently achieved industrialization, urbanization, and mass education, which bring the new type of ethnic conflicts and a stronger national identity to the surface. In short, a lot of the Soviet troubles are pretty much the same as the diseases of highly industrial societies.

Of course, in certain ways the country is behind. Elsewhere social problems arose early in industrialization too, but the Soviets pushed the process and did not pay much attention to the problems. Now the Soviet Union is not yet fully into the high-technology information revolution. This phase qualitatively changes an industrial society.

A Sick Society. A 1989 book on the Soviet and East European family system points to many features that must appear remarkable to Japanese who are accustomed to the other extreme. It notes the heterogeneity of birthrates by nationality (Japan is homogeneous), the low life expectancy (Japan's is the highest), the early age of marriage even while pursuing higher education (uncommon in Japan where only late marriage is socially acceptable), and the high divorce rate (Japan's is moderate). The book explains that many Soviets have only one child because the environment for raising them in a relaxed manner is absent. If the mother is to concentrate more love on the child, her burden in and out of the home must be reduced. Also, the male role has become unclear, leading to alcohol, domestic violence, and the destruction of the family—another contrast with Japan. The authors fault the Soviets for underestimating the role of the family.

After noting these general comments in the introduction, the book proceeds to analyze the results of a questionnaire administered to experts in and out of each country in the region. The coverage is broad, for instance identifying the favorite pleasures of the city population as eating out or inviting friends to eat at one's home; going to a play, concert, movie, and so forth; and enjoying nature. Figures are given to show that one in six is an alcoholic or chronic drinker, but also to show that more than fourteen million children use summer pioneer camps. This study's wide coverage fills in gaps in the Japanese literature although it is not at the level of methodological depth or specialization to be notable by international standards.[29]

Generalizations about the sick Soviet society are not hard to find. Morimoto Yoshio is more optimistic than most about the future but does not hesitate to pinpoint problems in the present. He describes a divorce rate so high that it competes with the U.S. rate for first place in the world. In the Soviet case, moreover, alcoholism is the main reason. Soviet citizens thirst so much for alcohol that the average male stood in line for seventy or eighty hours to purchase it while the anti-alcohol campaign was in operation until late 1988. Morimoto also identifies the world of connections (*kone*) that interfered with meritocracy in Soviet society. Under a strict government and economic system, life became manageable through a network of exchanges—a community of connections.[30]

Large-scale-ism. Often discussions of Soviet conditions highlight what is opposite to Japan. Voicing this contrast, Kikuchi Masanori refers to macro versus micro approaches; Japan has many small businesses, the Soviet Union has fewer, larger ones. He points to the presence of 100 times as many farm units in Japan, 20 times as many industrial firms, and 4.5 times as many service establishments. The Soviet area is 60 times that of Japan, which compounds these differences.[31] Clearly, Japan's small-scale fragmentation is unlike the Soviet pattern. By extension, geographical breadth creates one type of human nature, visually identified as anarchistic and requiring strong leadership using command methods,[32] while the confined Japanese learned how to control themselves.

Spirituality. The dismissal of national traditions, including religion, strikes Japanese as a sure prescription for trouble. Given their own acceptance of national traditions as the root of their country's modern success, Japanese responsiveness to Gorbachev's tolerance for a revival of religion as a source of spiritual values should not be surprising. At the time of Gorbachev's meeting in the Vatican with the pope, Hirooka Masahisa discussed the Soviet effort to fill in the spiritual emptiness of its citizens.[33] Not only do Japanese admire economic success, they assess nations for the fabric of social order based on voluntary compliance accompanied by a firm sense of morality associated with productive lives. In this respect, Japanese clearly judged Soviet society to be a failure.

To the extent that Communist party control means one-man dictatorship, the appeal in Japan is definitely eroded. The Japanese government as well as most large firms follows the principles of collective leadership and regular rotation of office. This almost faceless exercise of power stands in sharp contrast to the lifetime tenure and cult of personality in one socialist country after another, and even in Japan's own JCP. There is no mistaking Japanese apprehension about the violation of safeguards protecting group interests and the dignity of each member, appropriate to seniority and position in an acknowledged hierarchy. For a Japanese, such usurpation of power verges on being uncivilized.

Contrasting the Japanese way of thinking based on trial and error, which leads to moderate reform, and Soviet national character with its tenacious and excessive concern for security and unease when a long-term outlook is not established, Morimoto Tadao concludes that the two people have worldviews at opposite extremes. Using a term often applied to Japanese society, he finds the USSR with its nomenklatura system a vertical society to an extreme, leading to rampant personal alienation and concealed conflict relations. These differ from the familialism forged in Japan's corporate society. In response to such centralized class controls, Soviets could only turn to sabotage as a means of resistance and to self-defense mechanisms as a way to get ahead by forming vertical and horizontal human relations of their own. Morimoto also finds change in the Soviet consciousness. The country has lost its romanticism and high idealism and is growing accustomed to Gorbachev's realism as the base of a new worldview.[34]

By the summer of 1989 the tone was turning pessimistic about Gorbachev's ability to ride out the pitching and rocking of the storm besieging his domestic policies. Reviewing the natural disasters, accidents, and bloody ethnic confrontations that followed one after another, the impoverished living conditions, the scathing criticisms of the party, the huge coal strike in July, and the enormous costs of the settlement, one article concluded that opposing policies that could threaten Gorbachev's position did not yet exist, but that on all sides perestroika was running into trouble.[35]

After the events in the spring of 1989 it was natural for interest in Sino-Soviet comparisons to increase. Hakamada finds one silver lining behind the Chinese clouds: at last Chinese youths have restored their morale after turning cynical and materialistic after the Cultural Revolution. The same is true, he adds, for Soviet students who are enthusiastic about politics after breaking away from the narrow careerism of recent times. Physics students read voraciously about literature, society, and politics. In the sparkle of their eye one feels a seed of salvation for a system that does not seem to have a future.[36] While other Japanese are predicting the death of communism without qualification, Hakamada is cautiously describing the revival of a spiritual life that may lead to a future that sheds communism.

East, West, and North. The devastated economies of the Soviet Union and Eastern Europe face massive rebuilding in the 1990s. Japan's willingness to provide economic assistance on a large scale offers hope to them. Yet Japan has come to symbolize hope in another sense. When Pope John Paul II met with Prime Minister Kaifu on January 13, 1990, he was reported as saying, "One thing I have to ask you is that the diligence of the Japanese people be introduced in these countries." He expressed concern that Eastern Europeans might instead learn "countervalues like egoism, hedonism, racism, and practical materialism" from the West.[37] In a continent torn between Western secularism and Communist nihilism, Japanese traditional values appear as an attractive alternative even if Soviet prospects for adopting Japanese values appear very low.

CHAPTER TWELVE

Views of Soviet Politics and New Thinking

Mayumi Itoh

IN THIS CHAPTER I draw both on my interviews in late 1986 with nearly one hundred Japanese Sovietologists and international affairs experts or officials and on Japanese publications of the following years to identify responses to Gorbachev-era political reforms and to new approaches to foreign affairs. The stages of Japanese responses and some of the ongoing debates have already been traced in part 2. Here I expand on the reasoning found among different segments of the political spectrum as views about the Soviet capability to change became less pessimistic over the six-year period. The evidence reveals a mixture of views; deep-seated skepticism about the capacity of socialism to change grudgingly yields to reflections about relentless transformation either producing domestic chaos, as the pessimists predict, or leading to some kind of a postsocialist order at home and a period of responsible Soviet behavior abroad, as the optimists suggest. The pessimists predominate, although through 1990 qualified optimists were gaining ground on some issues, including on Gorbachev's genuine commitment to reform and on the end of the Soviet threat to the world and to Japan.

THE POLITICAL SYSTEM

Reforms within the System. Skepticism prevailed through 1987 in the Japanese interpretation of Gorbachev's perestroika. The majority, ranging from the right to the center, were deeply distrustful of "economic perestroika," regarding it as merely "reforms within the system," but not "reforms of the system." It would fail, due to triple constraints: the systemic constraint (ideology), the organization constraint (vested interests of the bureaucracy), and the personal constraint (Russian political culture). Gorbachev could not override the system. Nor would he really try. What Gorbachev was trying to do was to save socialism, not to abandon it.

A small number on the left took perestroika at face value and supported it as a means to strengthen a system that is still viable. Most on the left, however, along with some on the right of center and the center, adopted a wait-and-see attitude, which contrasted to the vocal opposition toward Gorbachev's "propaganda" and the warnings against the Soviet threat still highly publicized from the right.

As the focus for perestroika shifted from the economic to the political dimension and dramatic developments occurred one after another, Japanese came to perceive that Gorbachev's program was not intended for some cosmetic change but for a real restructuring of the system. The left of center spoke out increasingly in 1988, convinced that Gorbachev realized that economic perestroika was impossible without political perestroika. Especially after the March 1989 Soviet elections, opinion shifted firmly behind the prospect of radical change. But this did not give rise to much optimism about the outcome.

A Pandora's Box. For the most part, Japanese assumed until 1988 or 1989 that Gorbachev could not and would not override the dictates of the party monopoly of power. One reason for this conclusion is that most subscribed to "the conservative view that admits only an actual change as evidence of change and that dismisses conceptual change as mere rhetoric."[1] This reaction may be particularly strong in Japan, where the public is known not to place much confidence in sweet talk or glibness.

Many focus on how the situation has worsened in reality, predicting unlimited chain reactions. They argue that the authorities cannot control the process they have set in motion, that Gorbachev has opened a Pandora's box. They reason that the legacy of socialism is destructive or that multinational empires have little hope of survival after forceful control is relaxed. As Japan learned in 1945, the age of imperialism is over.

By 1989 skepticism about willingness to act was yielding to the view that the crisis is so serious that the leadership must go forward with actual change, but it will be fiercely resisted. Although critics eventually admitted that Gorbachev initiated a bold decentralization policy to revitalize the Soviet system and decrease the power of the party organization and bureaucracy, they doubted, above all, that Gorbachev could control the resistance of the nomenklatura. As a former *Sankei shimbun* journalist stated at the end of 1988, Gorbachev's domestic perestroika has not shown any credible results due to the strong resistance from the middle echelon of the political structure.[2]

Privileged Pluralism. In mid-1989 Sase Masamori took note of a changing political climate through the Congress of People's Deputies, in which the radical group, led by Boris Yeltsin, called for the repeal of Article 6 of the constitution, which stipulates the leading role of the party. Sase regarded the formation of this group as the virtual birth of an opposition party in the Congress and the Supreme Soviet, a harbinger of a plural party system. He also noted that the notions of right and left seem to have been reversed: those who advocate political pluralism, who used to be regarded as reactionaries, now identify themselves as "leftist radicals." This, in turn, means that those who adhere to "the party's leading role," who had claimed to be going along with the progress of history, should be labeled as "rightist conservatives," whereas "reformers from above," including Gorbachev, should be called "centralist opportunists." Implied in this classification is the notion that Gorbachev and other leaders are half-hearted reformers who will pull back before the difficult challenge of really making the system different.

Doubting that Gorbachev, who in 1989 more than once stated that "socialist pluralism" would suffice, would accept the radical reformers' request for the relaxation of one-party rule, Sase dismissed "socialist pluralism" as sham pluralism. It does not accept genuine pluralism. Furthermore, were it to work for a time, it would suffocate essential discussions on alternatives to socialism. Since nonconformist pluralism and nonsocialist pluralism will be put outside the framework of this limited pluralism, Sase coined the phrase "privileged pluralism."[3] Sooner or later Gorbachev's "opportunistic" attitude will have to face a trial, and, Sase implied, it will fail.

An Enlightened Dictator. One possible outcome would be a dictatorship. Earlier speculation resurfaced that this was the Soviet leader's ambition. When Gorbachev carried out sweeping changes in the party organization and in its personnel in late 1988, Kimura Akio described these as a step toward establishing Gorbachev's dictatorship. Agreeing with Andrei Sakharov, Kimura cautioned against the centralization of power in one individual and the arrival of a second Stalin.[4] Some journalists suspected that Gorbachev wanted to become an "enlightened dictator" legally through revision of the constitution. Although by mid-1989 the power of the president was to some extent limited by the Supreme Soviet, they doubted at first that the Supreme Soviet would be able to criticize the president in reality. In the face of party bureaucrats they expected that Gorbachev would have to use undemocratic measures to realize democracy. He would become a dictator in the name of democratization, as Peter the Great was a dictator in the name of modernization.[5] Given the intrinsic contradiction of decentralization by means of centralization, observers subscribe to the axiom that absolute power would corrupt absolutely. The future of Soviet democracy remains grim.

Only 10 Percent of Perestroika. After the overwhelming victory of Boris Yeltsin in the election to the Congress of the People's Deputies in March 1989, a journalist articulated the widespread view that it is premature to "expect" that perestroika would advance by this. Ōkura Yūnosuke calls the election only "10 percent of perestroika," noting that the constituencies in which more than three candidates ran were merely 10 percent of the total. He likens Gorbachev's perestroika to that of Khrushchev, whose reforms failed because he began to fear the pace of the thaw and restrained his liberalization. While permitting the publication of *One Day in the Life of Ivan Denisovitch*, he banned *Doctor Zhivago*, which is more moderate. In this and other ways, he lost the support of intellectuals. Party conservatives seized the opportunity and ousted him.[6]

The True Test of Glasnost. Many authors asserted that glasnost is quickly reaching its limit; for instance, in August 1989, Yoshinari Taishi said that glasnost brought about unexpected pitfalls for Gorbachev. As it revealed the dark history of the Stalin era, an unlimited number of new facts were uncovered, one more damaging than the next. Implicit in these views is that Gorbachev is unwittingly digging his own grave. Yoshinari concluded that no fundamental reform is possible without glasnost, and if Gorbachev intends to proceed with true glasnost, he should accept political pluralism, which is irreconcilable with one-party rule. Once he reaches this point, he will have to limit glasnost.[7] Few suspected that, in fact, the one-party monopoly would fall victim to the reforms in 1990, but they did anticipate the center's retreat from political reform in early 1991.

Kimura Hiroshi (not to be confused with the political scientist of the same name), the specialist in Russian literature who translated Solzhenitsyn, maintains that glasnost should be the "touchstone" of Gorbachev's perestroika. Kimura thinks that debates in Japan seem to be out of touch; both the optimistic and the pessimistic schools exaggerate the nature of perestroika. In Kimura's opinion, Gorbachev's perestroika is not at all a grand human experiment on how and whether socialism will survive, but it is just a process of social change that tries to transform an abnormal society, due to the distortions since the revolution, into a normal one.[8] For this, Kimura says, the civil liberties obtained through glasnost are an absolute requirement. Testing glasnost is the same as verifying perestroika. In Kimura's opinion, glasnost seems to have ushered in genuine freedom of expression in Soviet literature, as exemplified by the release of Boris Pasternak's *Doctor Zhivago*, Evgenyi Zamyatin's *We*, and George Orwell's *Nineteen Eighty Four*. As one Russian writer said to Kimura, "life became severer, but merrier." Nonetheless, Kimura notes, in late 1988 Solzhenitsyn remained taboo. Speculating that Gorbachev might have had to make a compromise with some conservatives to carry out the massive reshuffling in the Central Committee at the end of September in which Gromyko was ousted, he is hopeful that all that was lost was a "hasty thaw." The thaw will continue in any case.

Kimura made the publication of Solzhenitsyn's *Gulag Archipelago*, which denies the Communist ideology, the true test of glasnost before its release at a meeting of the Politburo on June 29, 1989.[9] With that decision, one more Japanese observer was finally persuaded that Gorbachev was prepared to carry perestroika forward to its completion. The still vocal group in 1989 that perceived Gorbachev as an "opportunist" was being challenged by more and more analysts persuaded that he is a genuine reformer eager to turn his country into a "normal" society.

Those on the Japanese right observe political perestroika through skeptical eyes. They maintain that it is incompatible with one-party rule. In February 1990 when Gorbachev led the way in accepting multiple parties, some on the right still doubted that Communists would relinquish their monopoly on power. Many others, however, were now convinced that Gorbachev would use the strengthened powers of the presidency to build a broader power base. The central issue was shifting from whether Gorbachev was for real to whether genuine reforms could actually work in the Soviet setting.

Instability of Control by Backward Rulers. Some Japanese think that the non-Russian republics' demand for independence from the Soviet Union will lead to the collapse of the Soviet Union. They think that Gorbachev's democratization will lead not only to the collapse of Communist party rule in the satellites in Eastern Europe, but also, through ethnic conflicts, to collapse in the Soviet Union itself. One writer states that the Soviet Union only "reclaimed" the territories that Russia previously had taken from ethnic groups by force. Lenin and Stalin seemed to think that they could unite those ethnic groups by socialism, but they failed. Throughout history, powers that controlled heterodox ethnic groups collapsed when the people under their control caught up with the ruling group economically and culturally. In the case of Russia, it was unreasonable from the beginning for it to control ethnic groups that had higher standards of living and culture. Given these historical facts, Ōkura predicts that the Soviet Union will eventually have to break up into pieces.[10]

Many observers think that Gorbachev is playing a dangerous "tightrope" game. Those on the right basically remain skeptical that he can succeed. They maintain that real systemic reforms are impossible since Gorbachev cannot override the framework of the system. Seeing a stalemated situation in the Soviet Union in 1989–90, they seem to be even more convinced that their assessments are coming true.

Critics conclude that Gorbachev is in a no-win situation: If his perestroika does not succeed and the system remains intact, the Soviet Union will eventually collapse through economic default. In turn, were Gorbachev's perestroika to succeed, political pluralism would flourish, and this means the demise of communism. Were the independence of ethnic groups to be allowed, it would mean the collapse of the Soviet empire. Thus, starting from any scenario, they find no chance for the country to survive as the vanguard of communism. In essence, the skeptics about Gorbachev's reforms are "optimists" about the collapse of the Soviet Union.

Compromise to Fill a Power Vacuum. Those in the center admit the potential significance of perestroika; it contains the seed of fundamental changes, as well as the seeds of self-destruction. They also feel that their perceptions have been vindicated, as more Japanese to the right of center have come to acknowledge that Gorbachev's intentions for reforms are genuine.

For Hakamada Shigeki the key to the Soviet political future is the process of filling the power vacuum resulting from the weakening of the Communist party. Local-level changes in personnel, organization, and law are not ready to replace the party organization or to prevent anarchy. Hakamada praises the courageous determination to cast aside the party monopoly, and he expresses the hope that the spreading confusion accompanying this will prove not to be destructive but rather to be the creative birth pangs of a new society.[11] Here one finds cautiously hopeful agnosticism at the center of the Japanese political spectrum about a transition deemed necessary for Soviet reform, but still seen as very dangerous for stability.

Even if there is a power vacuum it does not mean that there will not be stability of leadership at the top. In the midst of doubts that Gorbachev could remain in the top Soviet post, Kimura Hiroshi, the political scientist, explained why the possibility of his ouster was slight. First, he observed that unlike artists and academics, the survival of politicians is not so directly connected to their success. Often one splendid achievement is sufficient to keep power. Second, Gorbachev knows how to compromise. He cleverly balances forces on the left such as Yeltsin and those on the right including Ligachev.[12] Kimura expects there to be stability of Soviet leadership in the near future. This also seems to be the prevailing assumption in Japanese decision-making circles. There seems to be a near consensus that the election in March 1989 followed by the selection of Gorbachev as a new-style national president marked a positive shift in political perestroika.

One scholar sees the election process as a means to shock and "sift out" the conservatives in the party and the state bureaucracy who doubt perestroika. In the opinion of Nishimura Fumio, Gorbachev first tried to consolidate his power by resorting to the traditional method that every Soviet leader has used, control of the party organs, but he failed because the newly appointed officials had a background similar to the old members. Then he devised the strategy to replace the Central Committee, the de facto decision-making organ, with the revised Supreme Soviet as a new decision-making system.[13] Seeking a normal society capable of international competition, he is turning now to a normal political system as the only stable base for such a society.

Disciples of Khrushchev. Suzuki Hironobu defines the main support for Gorbachev as the last generation of the Stalin era, who, both well educated and highly motivated, can be found within both the nomenklatura and the general society. Among the enthusiastic supporters are reform intellectuals, journalists, and specialists in the think-tanks on international relations. However, the intellectual reformers cannot actually implement the reforms. In contrast, the majority of the nomenklatura strongly resist perestroika, having Stalinist mentality and being accustomed to authoritative, directive government and a controlled economy.

The leading support for Gorbachev ironically belongs to some minority groups in the nomenklatura. First there is the group of ambitious party and state bureaucrats, who intend to be promoted by removing the human connections formed under Brezhnev. They support Gorbachev only as a strategy to achieve their promotion and their ambition; therefore, there is no guarantee that they will remain in the Gorbachev camp if perestroika fails. The second group of Gorbachev's supporters are conscientious bureaucrats, who are worried about the stalemate and corruption of their country.

While the conservative leaders are "disciples of Stalin" from an earlier generation who were chosen and promoted by Stalin in the personnel vacuum resulting from the massive purges, Gorbachev and his supporters are "disciples of Khrushchev" who formed under de-Stalinization. They understand that, in the context of the advance in mass and higher education in Soviet society, control has to shift from human connections based on political allegiance to a more impersonal system employing the merit system. In Suzuki's opinion, the Soviet nomenklatura produced the reformer Gorbachev and has proved it retains vitality.[14]

Revolution from Below. Those on the left of center regard the election of March 1989 as a "turning point" that made perestroika a "revolution from below." In the opinion of Shimotomai Nobuo, the leadership recognizes the irreversibility of perestroika. The reform will not just stop at rationalizing institutions. It is systemic reform, requiring a redistribution of political power.[15] Shimotomai thinks that, in terms of development and change in the political system, the Soviet Union since 1988 has shown a dramatic evolution comparable to the "revolution from above" in 1929–30 that established the Stalinist system.[16]

Those to the left of center regard the election of the members of the Congress of People's Deputies as undeniable proof of drastic political perestroika. They do not subscribe to the conservative view that dismisses changes in concept as mere rhetoric. In Shimotomai's opinion, the "conceptual revolution" comprises by far more momentous changes than any sudden changes in policy not endorsed by conceptual change. This is the more so not only because conceptual revolution precedes behavioral revolution, but also because a gigantic mechanism operates to control concepts in Soviet society, and it had earlier led to the sacrifice of people who tried to protect traditional ones.[17]

Shimotomai admits that economic reforms have not yielded visible results. The important point, however, is that the economic difficulties have led to reforms in different areas: political reform, the reevaluation of history, glasnost, the emphasis on consumer goods in economic reforms, new thinking in foreign policy, and military reform. All these have shown new development that extends beyond mere reforms. What started out as a "revolution from above" has shifted to a "revolution from below." The reform range expanded from politics and economics to the human mind. Perestroika has been transformed into a change in people's consciousness and behavior, a change in the political system, and even a change in world politics.

Shimotomai divides Soviet elites into three categories. First, conservatives saw perestroika as a reform to restore order and strengthen discipline. Second, passive reformers identified perestroika as a method to improve the economy and productivity. Third, radical reformers thought perestroika should move ahead to a "social revolution" that involves a shift of political power. In the first half of 1989, "social revolution" finally became decisive. A landslide change is taking place in people's consciousness and behavior. The core concept of this revolution is pluralism, which exists at three levels: pluralism of opinions, pluralism of profits, and pluralism of politics. "Pluralism of opinions" has made progress due to glasnost and also religious policy. "Pluralism of profits" emerged with the recognition of cooperatives, joint-stock companies, and private ownership of capital. "Pluralism of politics" (behavior, structure, and organization), specifically pluralism of the party, became the focal point of political perestroika. In this political transformation, Shimotomai finds signs of the institutionalization of "civil society."[18]

"Northern Ireland" Type or "Scotland" Type? Contrary to a generally held view that regards ethnic uprisings negatively as a factor for the disintegration of the Soviet Union, Shimotomai sees them as a manifestation of the "rise of the people," as another ramification of political perestroika. According to Shimotomai, it is wrong to think that this issue will lead to the failure of perestroika. Rather, this occurrence is a positive outcome of perestroika. It is a normal and wholesome phenomenon. Indeed, Soviet authorities favorably view the People's Front. There are common aspects between the decentralization movement by ethnic minorities and Gorbachev's decentralization of the economic organization. In the summer of 1989, Shimotomai held that it remained to be seen whether the movement would intensify centrifugal forces and lead to calls for independence (the Northern Ireland type), or would accept political, economic, and cultural pluralism and uniqueness (differences) and maintain unity of the state

(the Scotland type).[19] His opinions continued to evolve as the centrifugal forces gathered steam.

By late 1990 Shimotomai was dividing Soviet leaders as follows. On one side was Prime Minister Ryzhkov, who favored drawing on the merits of Western countries as a means to follow a new socialist path. In the middle was Gorbachev, who advocated a Northern European type of socialist democratic path. On the other extreme was Yeltsin, who called for the abandonment of socialism and a transition to the capitalist path. Their support in these choices varied by generation. Youth in their twenties or younger disproportionately favored the capitalist path, the middle generation agreed with Gorbachev's choice of democratic socialism, while the elderly tended to prefer socialism. Differences by occupation were also noted, with state farmers, pensioners, and long-term unemployed most eager to keep the Communist party in the leading role.[20]

"The Beginning of the End" or *"The End of the Beginning"*? Those on the left maintain that the Soviet Union is heading in the right direction, for essentially the same reasons as those on the right cite for their predictions of collapse. They think that the Soviet Union is undergoing a painful process of transformation from a Communist country to a democratic socialist country; it is right in the middle of hard labor in the birth of democratic socialism. They tend to believe that Gorbachev will muddle through the difficulties and finally succeed.

In contrast to those on the right who argue that Japan should not aid Gorbachev's perestroika, those on the left of center consider wishful thinking about Gorbachev's fall or the self-destruction of the Soviet Union irresponsible. Instead, they suggest that Japan should use its "economic card" to help maintain the pace of perestroika, given the prospect that perestroika will fall into a short-term crisis due to the gap between the rise in the expectancy level and the shortage of commodity goods and inflation. To do so is necessary for world security and democratization, especially now that the Chinese reforms have stagnated.

The major difference of opinion is in how to conceive perestroika: Is it the demise of the Soviet Union and the loss of communism ("the beginning of the end"), or is it a rebirth of the Soviet Union as a democratic socialist nation ("the end of the beginning")? Expectations are colored by the position of the observer in the political spectrum.

FOUR TESTS OF NEW THINKING TOWARD JAPAN

Various authors have identified at least four tests to see whether Gorbachev's new thinking is real vis-à-vis Japan. The first test is the territorial issue. As seen earlier, in the first cycle, Gorbachev's basic attitude on the issue was not different from that of his predecessors, and the only glasnost that Foreign Minister Shevardnadze revealed in 1986 was that the Soviet Union would not object if the Japanese raised the issue. Later, progress was made, but before 1991 Japanese refused to raise their hopes high that this test would be fully passed.

The second test came in 1986 when the Soviet Union lifted an eleven-year ban on the ancestral-grave visits to the Northern Territories by the former islanders. It is an important Buddhist custom to visit graves in August. It turned out to be only to the Habomai and Shikotan islands, however, and the more distant Kunashiri, not to mention Etorofu, was to remain off limits. In addition, the Soviet Union imposed visas for the visits. Further, it demanded a Russian visit to the graves in Japan of the war prisoners of the Russo-Japanese War! All of a sudden, Russians demanded to visit graves that they had forgotten for more than eighty years. This measure was perceived as a device to maneuver Japan into de facto acceptance of the Northern Territories as Soviet. That Gorbachev could propose such an anachronistic and artificial reciprocity indicated to some observers that the Soviet conventional wisdom with its quid pro quo attitude had not changed. Visits to other islands later became possible, and even the graves of the postwar POWs who died in Siberia were being identified and opened to visitors. This test was at last likely to be met.

The third test is Gorbachev's visit to Japan. Despite repeated invitations by Japan and Gorbachev's stated interest in going, no concrete date or itinerary was set up until the fall of 1989. For several years the Japanese took this inaction as evidence of continued neglect. With one announcement this test seemed certain to be met.

The fourth test was whether Gorbachev would oust Ivan Kovalenko, deputy head of the International Division of the Communist party in charge of Soviet policy toward Japan for decades. The Japanese foreign policy elite argued that Kovalenko, in addition to Gromyko in his capacity of foreign minister, whose ouster was warmly greeted, shared responsibility for the high-handed and coercive policy toward Japan. Insofar as he remained in the office, Soviet policy toward Japan would not change. Finally, in late 1988 he was, indeed, ousted.

In our first cycle, failure on all four tests led the Japanese to conclude that Gorbachev's "new thinking" toward Japan was merely rhetoric. As the rest of the Western countries were hailing Gorbachev's new thinking, Japan was perceived as being left behind in resisting the changes. In retrospect, however, the Japanese sense of benefiting little from Soviet changes had a basis in reality. The fact was that Japan ranked low in the Soviet foreign policy priority list. The first priority was, of course, the rapprochement with the United States and Europe, and then came China. Japan seemed to be at the periphery of Soviet interests.

Belated Signs of Change. Only in the second cycle did the Soviets belatedly begin to show substantial signs of new thinking toward Japan, expressing more flexible opinions on Soviet-Japan relations. The new views found in Soviet journals were closely followed by Japanese experts. Some Soviet scholars stated that there were three major difficulties in bilateral relations: the territorial issue at the bilateral level, the "Soviet threat" at the regional level, and the Soviet evaluation of the U.S.-Japan security treaty system at the global level. To achieve a breakthrough in Soviet-Japan relations, it is necessary to acknowledge the existence of the territorial issue, to remove the "enemy image" of the Soviet Union deeply rooted in the Japanese fear of the Soviet threat, and to change the Soviet evaluation of the U.S.-Japan security treaty system. Soviet spokesmen and Japanologists not only admitted the existence of the territorial issue, by 1988 proposing joint possession of the Northern Territories and increasingly other compromises to assuage Japanese feelings; specialists also were acknowledging that the Soviet view of the U.S.-Japan security treaty was anachronistic. In this area they made a quick about-face, even suggesting the importance of the treaty for regional security. With some progress on each test, the officials in the Gaimushō acknowledged that Soviet attitudes had begun to change in the summer of 1988, which coincided with former prime minister Nakasone's visit to Moscow.

In the third cycle, a series of statements seem to indicate that a turning point in the Soviet foreign policy toward Japan might have finally come. Although the first test (the territorial issue), which remains the most difficult and important one, has not been passed, the Soviet Union had begun to show more flexible attitudes and was making efforts to grope for a solution as a way to improve relations. For example, in his visit to Tokyo in November 1989, as the head of the delegation from the Supreme Soviet, Aleksandr Yakovlev, suggested a "third way" for the solution of the issue. By this, Yakovlev implied that the Soviet Union and Japan should work out a compromise formula.

Another example was that, in January 1990, Moscow announced the creation of a Japan-Pacific Research Center under the Institute of World Economy and International Relations of the Soviet Academy of Sciences. This center was to examine approaches to a breakthrough in Soviet-Japanese relations. Seven out of the ten original projects concerned policies toward Japan. Unlike the Kovalenko era, sympathetic expert guidance would inform judgments about Japan.

Gorbachev's visit to Japan was finally announced in the fall of 1989 to take place in early 1991. Although the biggest tests—territory and summitry—remained to be passed, many Japanese analysts found reason for optimism in the developments of the third cycle. This mood continued to spread until January 1991, when a political turn to the right revived negative images about Soviet intentions and lowered hopes for Gorbachev's visit. With the deterioration of the Soviet reform climate early in 1991, many old doubts resurfaced about the Soviet political system and its foreign policy implications.

GLOBAL NEW THINKING

In the first stage of the Gorbachev era, a majority saw in Gorbachev's new diplomatic style, such as "smile diplomacy" or "multipolar diplomacy," no fundamental change in Soviet global objectives. The consensus on the short-term objectives of his disarmament proposals was that they were aimed at reducing the very heavy external burden so as to concentrate on perestroika and to contain the SDI. The majority, ranging from the right to the center, regarded Gorbachev's long-term objectives as his "peace offensive" to split the West. Multipolar diplomacy was intended to use Western money and technology to aid perestroika and at the same time to weaken the U.S. alliance with Europe and Japan. Analysts urged caution: without the help of the West, the Soviet Union would collapse, so Japan should just watch for that to happen. Conversely, a minority on the left of center and the left took Gorbachev's initiatives at face value as genuine efforts for disarmament.

Signs of Cost-Effective Diplomacy. In the second cycle, as the INF treaty was signed and Gorbachev expanded new thinking in foreign policy, observers were divided again on how to interpret his initiatives. The majority agreed that the stalemate in the economic reforms forced Gorbachev to turn to new thinking in foreign policy, as it had forced him to shift the priority of his domestic perestroika from economic to political reforms. Perestroika could not succeed without the capital and technology of the West and a reduction in the burden of military expenses. In essence, domestic economic reform requires stability in international situations; Gorbachev needed to earn points in foreign policy as a lever to promote domestic reforms and to compensate for his unpopularity in the domestic scene.

Many did not think that the Soviet long-term objectives had changed, and they still regarded Gorbachev's initiatives as part of a "peace offensive." Die-hard skeptics held that the Soviet Union under Gorbachev has not abandoned its global objective of world revolution. Insofar as the Communist ideology represents the raison d'être of the Soviet Union, the Kremlin cannot abandon the ideology. Thus, the "new détente" is merely a time-saving device for domestic perestroika. These and other observers differed on how to interpret Gorbachev's new thinking in foreign policy: Is it tactical change (change in style) or strategic change (change in substance)?

Analysts adopted various phrases to convey the essence of new thinking. Former ambassador Katori Yasue referred to it as the "refined peace offensive."[21] Togō Takehiro, also in the Gaimushō, stressed Gorbachev's need for stability in international relations as part of domestic policy, producing "cost-effective diplomacy."

Togō saw Soviet withdrawal from Afghanistan as an example of this type of diplomacy. The Afghan invasion not only had caused problems domestically but also had isolated the Soviet Union in the world. The military burden was enormous. Togō concluded optimistically that the same sort of new thinking would have a positive effect on the negotiations for the reduction of conventional forces in Europe.[22] Some on the right of center, who had held "it-remains-to-be-seen" attitudes in the first cycle, have come to find real perestroika in Soviet global policy and now support the new thinking. At the end of 1989, when the collapse of the cold war system in Europe became evident before everybody's eyes, the Japanese government clearly abandoned its unyielding skepticism toward the Soviet foreign policy objectives. Coinciding with Gorbachev's announcement of a date for visiting Japan, the collapse of communism in Eastern Europe opened Japanese eyes to prospects that earlier seemed beyond belief.

De-ideologization. In 1989 Morimoto Yoshio cast doubt on the skeptical views that the Soviet Union will revert to power politics since the change in Gorbachev's foreign policy is only a means to facilitate domestic economic reforms. Rather, he stated that the new Soviet foreign policy will bring about international relaxation of tensions and interdependent cooperative relations.[23] In the words of Akino Yutaka, another scholar, the Soviet democratization drive signified the "radicalization of perestroika." Paradoxically, the difficulty of radicalizing domestic perestroika effectively resulted in the radicalization of its external arm: perestroika in foreign policy. Recognition of the internal enemy against perestroika made the existence of the external enemy seem less important. As a result, the content of the "new thinking" began to change in substance. The new concepts—"nonoffensive defense" and "reasonable sufficiency" in security—the denial that Moscow serves as the center of socialism, the reliance on economic diplomacy, the acknowledgment of a balance of interests, and the supremacy of human values—all mark a departure from class conflict toward "de-ideologization."[24]

Asymmetrical Parity. Akino Yutaka also analyzed how Soviet foreign policy changed significantly under Gorbachev. First, change occurred in the concept of peaceful coexistence since 1987. Now the concept is applied not only, as in the past, to the countries that have enemy relations with the Soviet Union, but to all countries. In other words, with the Soviet recognition that capitalism is not going to fall, it is natural that the old concept of peaceful coexistence with the West, previously considered temporary, is no longer applicable. With his need for real cooperative relations with capitalist nations, Gorbachev seeks "positive" peaceful coexistence. In military doctrine, "nonoffensive defense" signifies the non-preemptive use of nuclear weapons, and "reasonable sufficiency" means reduction of offensive conventional armed forces. The latter yielded the concept of "asymmetrical parity," a contribution to the INF agreement and to negotiations aimed at the reduction of strategic nuclear forces by 50 percent.[25]

To "Humanize" International Relations. Those on the left of center welcome the new thinking as a totally new development in Soviet foreign policy. Offering a comprehensive analysis of Gorbachev's foreign policy, Shimotomai identifies three stages: first, from March 1985 to mid-1986; second, from late 1986 to mid-1988; and third, from mid-1988 on. The first stage was marked by the replacement of Gromyko by Shevardnadze. The main objective of the first period was the rapprochement with the United States, as exemplified by the U.S.-Soviet summit in the fall of 1985. The new-thinking diplomacy began, along with the indirect denial of the Gromyko diplomacy, in the second stage. The INF Treaty was signed and took effect, and the basic concepts of new thinking were proposed, such as the emphasis on the Asia-Pacific region, the "common house of Europe," and the "nonoffensive" military doctrine based on reasonable sufficiency. In the second period, however, the new-thinking diplomacy only coexisted with the Gromyko diplomacy because the priority was still on the United States, and the new concepts remained just concepts. In contrast, the third stage marks a clear denial of Gromyko diplomacy and the real birth of new-thinking diplomacy. Since 1988, this initiative has shown realistic development, as exemplified by unilateral disarmament, the Sino-Soviet summit, the support of spontaneous reforms in Eastern Europe, Gorbachev's approach to the NIES in East Asia, and multipolar economic diplomacy. At last, these initiatives have begun to draw a belated response from the Bush administration, added Shimotomai in August 1989.[26]

Nakano Tetsuzo points out that Gorbachev had the new political thinking in mind even before he assumed power in 1985. He traces the origin of the new political thinking to Gorbachev's speech as chairman of the Soviet Foreign Affairs Committee to the British Parliament in 1984 in which Gorbachev talked about "world interdependence." From this the notion of the "common house" of Europe derives. It is a significant coincidence that the need for new political thinking was recognized by a Soviet leader in England in 1984, the year about which George Orwell wrote in his depiction of a totalitarian state. The new political thinking is based on Gorbachev's idea that a nuclear war should not be fought, and that security requires mutual dependence with the ultimate objective of humanizing relations among nations.[27] For Nakano, the new political thinking is deeply rooted in changes in human values; mutual verification of security is not possible with mutual distrust but must rely on trust in universal human values.

If the JSP regards the new thinking as "an effort to reach Karl Marx," to quote Nakano, the JCP regards it as the denial of Marxist-Leninism—the "worst mistake since the death of Lenin": new thinking is nothing more than "old opportunism"; so-called respect for "human values" is really the abandonment of historical materialism, the submission to nuclear threat, or even evidence of hegemonism. Chairman Miyamoto Kenji stated that Stalin, Khrushchev, and Brezhnev all made mistakes; however, none of them had ever denied historic materialism, class conflict, or its dialectic solution. General Secretary Fuwa added that the mistake of new thinking is its denial of class conflict in the name of the supremacy of human interests, and its denial of national liberation and of people's conflict in capitalist nations. Nakano shook his head in disbelief at the "fossilized thinking" of the JCP.[28]

The skeptics on the right refuse to abandon their deep-rooted distrust of Soviet global objectives. They are prisoners of their ideology. The optimists on the left of center broke the taboo and began to speak out, finding fundamental changes in the Soviet worldview and its concept of human values. This dichotomy appears most vividly in views of military policy. Despite Gorbachev's bold initiatives, the majority of military strategists refuse to abandon their skepticism, while a few are reacting with high hopes.

NEW THINKING IN MILITARY DOCTRINE

The "New Munich Accord." In the midst of the worldwide applause for the INF agreement, those on the right stood isolated, critical of the INF treaty. They thought that the United States should not have agreed to remove its INFs in Europe. The Soviets wanted the treaty only because they were desperate to remove U.S. cruise missiles and Pershing IIs from Europe and to nullify NATO's "flexible response" strategy, combining strategic, tactical, and conventional forces and the West's qualitative supremacy.[29] Second, they argued that the significance of the INF treaty was exaggerated, given that the number of warheads to be eliminated is only 3–4 percent of the total. Third, the abolition of the INFs actually lowers the threshold of nuclear war and thus endangers the world, with a higher possibility of all-out nuclear war.[30] One military strategist calls the INF treaty a "new Munich Accord." In Nakagawa Yatsuhiro's opinion, due to the extreme edge in conventional forces in Europe, the Soviets could still enjoy military superiority without any possibility of the central command mechanism in Moscow being destroyed instantly. The deployment of the U.S. INFs had meant that limited nuclear war in Europe would leave U.S. soil a "sanctuary." This would have been the worst nuclear war for the Soviets. Washington has now destroyed the best deterrence against the Soviets,[31] playing into their militaristic ambitions. This was the warning heard in early 1989 before the collapse of communism in Eastern Europe and the Soviet-American agreement on conventional forces.

Nakagawa Yatsuhiro notes that there are three major problems with the Japanese mass media. First, it exaggerates "Gorbachev's disarmament" while neglecting "Gorbachev's military expansion." Second, it does not analyze the effects that disarmament could have in destabilizing the military balance. Third, it avoids questioning the substance of Gorbachev's "disarmament" proposals. Nakagawa concludes that Gorbachev might be a strategic genius who can make flexible use of disarmament, military expansion, and propaganda for the Soviet long-term objective of global military superiority.[32] Another analyst deplores the atmosphere in which those who speak for the arrival of a new "détente" are called intellectuals and pacifists, while those who see through Gorbachev's tricks are labeled hardliners against the Soviets and hawkish.[33]

Officials in the Gaimushō differed in their evaluation of the INF Treaty. On the whole, they were positive about what had been accomplished but wary of future prospects. Shigeta Hiroshi, the Soviet desk head in the mid-1980s, said that the INF treaty had a dramatic significance. It was the first agreement for real disarmament to abolish deployed nuclear weapons rather than arms control to set a ceiling for future production of nuclear weapons like the SALT treaties. Shigeta considered optimistic, however, the hopeful mood created by the negotiations to cut strategic nuclear weapons by 50 percent, to reduce conventional weapons, and to abolish chemical weapons. These negotiations did not mean a "thaw in U.S.-Soviet relations" or a "change from confrontation to dialogue," as claimed in the mass media. Rather, they presupposed a confrontation and were concerned with controlling it. To verify such an agreement would be very hard.[34]

Hyodo Nagao, the Soviet desk head in the late 1970s, also said rather doubtfully that the significance of the INF treaty was greater for the Soviets. The Soviets made big concessions in abolishing SS-20s in Europe just because they are desperate in the face of the consolidation of Western power. As late as July 1988, he said that although some aspects have been changing dramatically because of perestroika and glasnost, the nature of the Soviet military strategy toward the West has not shown any signs of change, and we should not be misled by the new détente mood.[35] Two years later it was Hyodo who became the head of the Eurasian Department and an important figure in bilateral negotiations.

A Fat Military of Low Technology. Maruyama Hiroyuki thought that the massive reduction of Soviet military power—military perestroika—was a "product of a compromise" between reformers in the military, supported by Gorbachev, who advocated reasonable sufficiency for defense, and the conservative military leadership, which advocated a traditional offensive military doctrine. The compromise was made because the military leadership was aware of the problem of the "fat military of low technology." The means to military-strategic parity had shifted from quantity to quality.[36]

In a similar vein, Nagai Yōnosuke did not think that the military was at odds with Gorbachev's disarmament proposals. Rather, it was the military leadership that had advocated the shift in the military system from a "heavy-thick-long-big" type to a "light-thin-short-small" type based on high technology. The goal was modernization of the military. Furthermore, Nagai noted, the military leadership might be far ahead of Gorbachev's new thinking. Due to the development of satellites, a "transparent revolution" had taken place in which both sides were now exposed to each other. Given this reality, the military may have found no problem in accepting verification. Nagai added that the reduction in conventional forces is not likely to be as appealing to the military. The rank-and-file personnel could be converted into a civilian labor force, but the officers with their vested interests would pose problems.[37] Takizawa Ichirō explained, in the same vein, that some think that the military is against perestroika, whereas others think that "the rivalry between the party and the Soviet military is exaggerated," and that the military actually supports perestroika.[38]

Unlike many others, Hasegawa Tsuyoshi thought that the new thinking was an attack on the military. This includes criticisms of the privileges given to the military in the distribution of resources, the denial of von Clausewitz's theme that war is politics by other means, and glasnost unveiling the secrets of the military. The most important change is the demotion of the military by the acceptance of reasonable sufficiency as opposed to the earlier emphasis on parity.[39] Hasegawa's centrist position seemed to gain more adherents as time passed.

For Hakamada, the enormous military expenditures cause Gorbachev to be serious about relieving the economic burden as much as possible. To view Gorbachev as a messenger of peace who does not rely on the military at all, however, is optimistic. As long as the Soviet Union is a nation, even Gorbachev cannot override the logic of the nation. Thus, the Soviet Union will continue to modernize its military, along with the West. Nonetheless, it will not employ an expansionist policy as in the past. Gorbachev knows how the West distrusted the détente under Brezhnev and that he cannot get economic, scientific, and technological cooperation from the West should he embark on a similar military expansion.[40]

Tokyo Can Deal with Moscow. Togō Takehiro, the director of the Eurasian Department before Hyodo, took note that the Soviet Union began to realize its long-term mistake of neglect of the Asia-Pacific region. In response to new interpretations in Soviet publications of July 1988, Togō said that they reflect the fact the Soviet Union has failed in its Asian policy and has not shown any substantial achievement in the region even two years after Gorbachev's Vladivostok speech of July 1986. The Soviet Union has lost leverage toward the region because it had no presence in the region except a military one.[41] This view from the Gaimushō implies Soviet recognition of its own weakness before Japan, and willingness to negotiate from that basis.

No Common Asia-Pacific House. On the question of how to interpret the intentions of the Krasnoyarsk speech in September 1988, in which Gorbachev made enthusiastic approaches to the newly industrializing economies among Asia-Pacific nations, former ambassador Katori cast doubt on its objectives. Although he gave some praise to Gorbachev's multipolar diplomacy, which is concerned with military and political diplomacy as well as with economic and cultural diplomacy, Katori noted the contradiction that Gorbachev called the Soviet Union a part of the "common house of Europe," on the one hand, and an "Asia-Pacific house," on the other. He considered that the Soviet Union was intrinsically a European nation and had done nothing for the Asia-Pacific region except by its military presence. It is evident that Gorbachev used such rhetoric because he wanted to expand the Soviet sphere of influence into the Asia-Pacific region, added Katori.[42] In other words, he was not persuaded that Moscow was prepared to negotiate realistically as a consequence of its weakness.

Moscow's Japan and NIES Shocks. For some observers, the Soviet response to the region was not just a question of weakness. Hakamada Shigeki evaluated Gorbachev's multipolar diplomacy toward the Asia-Pacific region positively. He said that the Soviet Union had suffered a "Japan shock" (shocked by its economic recovery and prosperity) during the 1960s and 1970s and recently a "NIES shock" (shocked by the economic development of Korea, Taiwan, Singapore, and Hong Kong). Within the region, only the Far Eastern part of the Soviet Union is left behind. In response, Moscow's approach toward the region shifted from ideological to pragmatic. This is a positive development.[43]

To summarize, reviewing the first four years of Gorbachev's perestroika, Katō Masahiko, an NHK commentator, stated that Gorbachev's new foreign policy philosophy, based on "interdependence" and "global problems," is fundamentally different from the traditional Soviet diplomacy, based on "international class conflicts." The West did not take it seriously in the initial stage, regarding Gorbachev's slogan as merely propaganda or a "peace offensive" while expansionistic foreign policy in Afghanistan and the "Soviet threat" were publicized. However, the new-thinking foreign policy has achieved a miraculous success in these four years. The successes include the U.S.-Soviet agreement on mutual military inspections, the INF treaty (the first nuclear arms reduction), the withdrawal from Afghanistan, and the unilateral cut in conventional armed forces. He also noted that the new thinking had changed the nature of the Soviet military doctrine as well. It assumes that security in the nuclear age is guaranteed not by deterrence but by interdependence, and not by military measures but by political measures. A traditional offensive military doctrine has been converted into a defensive one, based on the concept of reasonable sufficiency.[44]

It was only at the end of 1989, when the collapse of the cold war system in Europe became evident to everybody, that many Japanese reconsidered their unyielding skepticism toward Soviet foreign policy objectives. But until the Northern Territories issue is resolved, nobody expects much Japanese action to help the Soviets.

PART FOUR

The Soviet Debate and Japan's Future

CHAPTER THIRTEEN

Patterns of Perceptions

DESPITE past accusations from the extremes of the political spectrum, there is no indication that restricted or distorted information accounts, to any notable extent, for current Japanese images of Soviet socialism. In the first half of the 1980s, information may often have seemed one-sided, for example, excluding the human dimension of Soviet life, but even then it was possible for the alert reader to fill in many of the gaps. Increasingly in the Gorbachev era, Japanese sources have expanded their coverage, offering ample factual material and thoughtful interpretations to permit informed judgments. One-sidedness faded as the middle of the spectrum diversified and deepened its contributions to the political debate. A democracy, Japan was not plagued by serious problems of news bias.

Readers could follow day-to-day developments visually on television and, in greater depth, through the overlapping contents of multiple newspapers—sources with virtually a universal reach and a high news content. For relatively educated readers searching for more analysis, perhaps no other country provides a wider array of weeklies and monthlies, eager to broaden their popularity by expounding novel explanations for the latest political currents. The Japanese public could also turn to dozens of new books each year ranging across the political spectrum, or to scholarly quarterlies and occasional publications with specialized analyses of the patterns of Soviet change. Once Soviet affairs were grabbing headlines, the Japanese people were bombarded with an abundance of information capable of changing their opinion.

Compared to American popular coverage, Japan has no single paper with the authoritative range of the *New York Times* nor the fine differentiation into specialized journals for original scholarship and translation, but its up-to-date exchange of interpretations is unsurpassed. An entire national community keeps informed and contributes fresh ideas in a manner more timely, more widely disseminated, and more interactive than in the United States. A true national debate has progressed over most of the past six years.

Many individuals did rethink their attitudes toward Soviet socialism, but few appear to have made an abrupt change. Gradually the extremes tended to collapse toward the middle. Some on the extreme right became less alarmed about the Soviet threat and more hopeful that Tokyo could deal with Moscow. Among the small numbers remaining on the extreme left, the bloom of idealized socialism faded under Gorbachev's withering exposés. The right of center grew more optimistic about the improved international environment and about new bilateral relations, parting company with the extreme right. Meanwhile, the left of center became less critical of the Gaimushō's intransigence toward the Soviets, and more assertive as its expectations were rising. Gorbachev gave a human face to socialism, rendering it less frightening and even rather pitiable. Month by month, Japanese watched these changes and reacted to them.

THE CYCLE OF CHANGING IMAGES

In chapters 6–8 I observed over a six-year period twelve successive popular themes, divided into three cycles. The first cycle, lasting roughly two and one-half years, was Japan's awakening. In comparison to Western Europe and the United States, Japan was slow to awaken to the radical character of the Gorbachev era. There was little predisposition to idealize the prospects for Soviet transformation or to take seriously Soviet rhetoric calling for change. These are signs that Japanese were pragmatists more than idealists. They were relatively satisfied with the status quo over the short term rather than rushing to find a way to overturn it. Furthermore, they were accustomed to reacting cautiously to international events, not to playing an active role. It took a long time and a lot of hard evidence to convince the Japanese people that something important was happening.

The period of uncertainty also was prolonged by a propensity to skepticism. It took as long as one to one and one-half years after the INF agreement was reached in late 1987 before confidence climbed high that Japan, too, would gain from the new course of Soviet diplomacy and reform. Japanese were slow to trust the Soviets and even to feel fully confident that Washington was, on the whole, acting in the best interests of Japan. It took special efforts, beginning in the summer of 1988, to address Tokyo's own concerns before the Japanese people felt adequate reassurance.

From about the middle of 1989 a new level of confidence could be detected. It is not the euphoria found among West Europeans that at last the cold war is behind them, nor the enthusiasm among Americans that Gorbachev can be trusted. In Japan the confidence is less emotional and more closely tied to gradual, long-term trends. This is none other than the self-assurance of a country that need not bother with immediate negotiations because history is on its side. Responding to bilateral prospects and to global trends, Japanese are beginning to discern a new order. Through this newfound confidence shine the rays of a new worldview.

The Sequence of Each Cycle. More than anything else, the international spotlight galvanizes Japanese into active reexamination of their own views. In the opening of each of the first two cycles and to some degree the third too, Japanese grew concerned that their country's thinking was isolating them from the United States and other allies. They became introspective out of a concern that Japan was out of step. This occurs because of the long-standing habit of closely following what others say about them. What they heard was not necessarily flattering, although the criticism remained quite muted as long as Japan appeared to be a secondary player. Are Japanese irresponsible freeloaders without principle, neither contributing their share to the defense of the free world nor much concerned with moving ahead to a new era? That worrisome question was beginning to be heard. Introspection also resulted from self-doubts. Japanese often judge themselves harshly. What is wrong with us, they wondered, that our views are so negative, while other nations think differently? Such reactive thinking is by no means uniquely Japanese; as the flow of information in our shrunken world continues to accelerate, we are likely to become ever more alert to the opinions of other nations. Japanese hypersensitivity is ahead of its time.

The second stage in each cycle led to concern for what the new international trends mean for Japan. In fact, there were remarkably few suggestions proposed for changes inside Japan. Analysts debated the objectivity of their information and the appropriateness of their attitudes, not the nature of their society or, until 1990, the level of their military budget. While the LDP had trouble at the Upper House polls in July 1989, and in February 1990 it still faced a rather strong JSP in the Diet after the elections to the Lower House, nobody suggested that the Soviet issue or the collapse of communism abroad contributed to voter discontent. When Soviets debated China in the 1970s or Chinese debated the Soviet Union in the first half of the 1980s, domestic reform had constituted the hidden and primary agenda. In contrast, Japanese debates started with the assumption that there was no lesson to learn for the domestic agenda in their country. Reform must look elsewhere for models or, more to the point, must look within Japan and must proceed cautiously, centering on unfairness rather than inefficiency, in order not to tamper with success. Yet there was a stimulus to thinking about how to "internationalize" Japan.

What aroused the country the most were the bilateral problems of Japanese-Soviet relations and, by extension, the international implications of how these problems are handled. Problems of divided countries can be found around the world. Often they concern huge territories, large national populations, and highly charged issues such as divided families. Japan's claim to the Northern Territories involves only small amounts of territory and no Japanese nationals currently there, although small numbers of survivors and descendants settled in Japan. The issue is important for its symbolic value. On the surface the bilateral dispute is over four small islands. In fact, it is about Japan's place in the world order. Debates have concentrated on bilateral questions in connection with the changing international environment. To the extent that they have a domestic Japanese component, concerning what the Japanese people should do, the focus is the internationalization of the country. While focusing on small, scarcely habitable islands, the Japanese public was really searching for Japan's place in a changing world.

Almost as an afterthought, each cycle eventually got around to looking closely at what was happening inside the Soviet Union. At times Japanese attentively followed the prospects for perestroika and for Gorbachev's leadership, but, apart from the international consequences, it did not seem as if results were terribly important. This may be due to a predisposition to judge national prospects as a reflection of deep-seated cultural heritage rather than short-term human rights policies, or due to a stress on international economic competitiveness based on the quality of the work force and management rather than on the limited themes of perestroika reforms. Yet, as the saga of an embattled leader and a collapsing economy and empire reached an ever higher pitch, public concern with the Soviet domestic scene was finally climbing.

Old Soviet Hands Out of Cycle. At its peak in the first half of the 1980s, the group of Soviet desk veterans in and out of the ministry wielded authoritative influence. A simplistic image of the "evil empire" justified deferring to government-trained experts who urged unanimity and centralized leadership in the struggle. In 1985–87—the first cycle—this group remained assertive, warning that (1) the West is gullible before a "charm offensive"; (2) Japanese opinion must remain firm, particularly in support of the "entry approach" to the islands, which precludes consideration of other issues until the Kremlin hands over Japan's territory;[1] and (3) perestroika is primarily a cosmetic change that does not affect the real Soviet system or Soviet motives. In the second cycle of 1987–89, the voices of this group gradually dimmed. At the start, even from within the Gaimushō, criticism of the INF agreement could be clearly detected, and warnings against public susceptibility to "Gorby mania" were still frequent. Only when serious bilateral discussions on the Northern Territories commenced did the Gaimushō quiet its internal doubters. Nonetheless, their pessimism was still evident. Until the last moment, they vociferously rejected the idea that perestroika might succeed in producing such unexpected offspring as a parliamentary opposition or private farmers.

In the third cycle, from 1989 to 1991, the Gaimushō Soviet experts confidently expected their outlook to be confirmed, but they found unexpected twists. At last there was a chorus of voices chanting in harmony that socialism is dead. Firmness to Moscow was finally paying off in more desperate Soviet proposals for returning some territory and paring the

Soviet military. Japan was moving close to the top, while the Soviet Union was apparently collapsing. Yet, despite confirmation of their wildest dreams at the beginning of the decade, their satisfaction was diminished. The Gaimushō had turned to moderates to work out a deal with the Kremlin. Gorbachev was often not resisting change but leading it. The battle still needed to be fought against the growing numbers abroad and at home who welcomed the Soviet entry into an integrated world on terms that appeared too soft to many Japanese. There was pressure for concessions to conclude a deal on the Northern Territories when some insisted that Japan's position was strong enough not to have to yield much ground.

The old-line Soviet experts clung to the essence of containment theory, awaiting a new opportunity to achieve it. As long as the territorial problem was not resolved, their chances remained good. Shunted to the periphery within the Gaimushō, they could expect through the normal course of reassignments to reassert authority over Soviet affairs early in the 1990s. If the moderates could not regain the islands through their flexible approach, the old Soviet desk hands were prepared to introduce a tougher line.

Writing in early 1990 under the pseudonym Otemachi Saburō, the Gaimushō official Tamba Minoru expressed his pessimism about the course of events. He warned of naive persons who expected too much from Gorbachev's 1991 visit. He asserted that what some see as signs of moderation are merely reflections of glasnost. At the negotiating table the Soviets remain very hard.[2] Many in this camp felt vindicated by the Soviet retrogression at the start of 1991. To optimists both inside Japan and abroad, they could insist that Japan's professionals had been correct all along.

Synchronization of Calendars. Soviet-Japanese relations are troubled because the two countries have been seeing events through different frames. For the Japanese, the present cannot be seen apart from 1945. For the Soviets, the two countries should be ready to start fresh. Yet the Japanese are not the only nation reminding Moscow of the unfinished business of history. In the second half of 1989 the message was coming loud and clear from the Baltic states and Poland. The way the wartime legacy was handled in these places sets a precedent and establishes a new way of thinking about the relevance of the wartime era for the Soviet people. Accustomed to discovering the ghost of Stalin everywhere in their domestic system, Soviets should not be surprised to find it in the international arena too. Ironically, a reverse problem of synchronization operates in Sino-Japanese relations. It is the Japanese who wishfully look at the present as a new age bereft of historical baggage, while Chinese cannot overlook the history of the 1930s and 1940s. A clear difference, however, is that the Japanese feel guilt toward China and can offer much assistance to assuage this. The Soviets do not feel guilt toward the Japanese and have only the islands to offer. In each case, a large perception gap produces friction in bilateral relations.

Another difference is that when Japanese look at China, they see the great past of a country that they know well and subsume socialism into that; when Japanese look at the Soviet Union, they split it off from its past or project the Soviet era back into the past. Japanese have tended to see an inverse relationship between the United States and China in the 1950s, and between the Soviet Union and both the United States and China since the 1960s. Being anti-American meant being pro-China, and later being anti-Soviet meant being pro-China or pro-American. As the Soviet threat diminishes, Japanese are being forced to reassess their sympathy for China (it is declining) and their dependence on the United States (it too is declining, but slowly and with some ambivalence about whether it may not still serve a very useful purpose at home and abroad).

THE BATTLE FOR PUBLIC OPINION

Psychological Dependence. Critics remain unconvinced that a mature citizenry is already making appropriate, informed decisions. The problem, in their view, is not familiarity with the facts. While the level of knowledge is far from ideal, as early as October 1986, before the blitz of coverage of Soviet reforms, 61 percent of Japanese knew the name of the Soviet capital, 52 percent knew that Gorbachev is the Soviet leader and a like number could identify its flag, 12 percent could recall that the ruble is the currency, and 7 percent could accurately estimate the population.[3] No doubt specific knowledge has been growing. The real problem, according to critics, is that Japanese lack a value system or a mindset to process the information and to draw independent conclusions.

This line of criticism took several directions. First, there was the view that Japanese were accustomed to seeing the Soviet Union through the eyes of the United States. They were not used to thinking for themselves. Second, there was the related impression that Japanese were educated to regurgitate facts rather than to search for creative syntheses of the details. New information is not readily transposed into new conclusions. Third, one can find the view that intellectuals in Japan are closed and passive in their thinking. They do not make a major effort to get to know the thinking of another nation, particularly the Soviet Union. Indeed, they wait to be guided by the bureaucracy. Representative of this viewpoint, Hakamada Shigeki suggests that even in the midst of the current "Soviet boom," there exists a danger of "unbalanced consciousness" or "strange knowledge." Ideology stands in the forefront, but the society is somewhat overlooked.[4] Finally, all of these doubts coalesce in the two-sided historical argument that Japanese personality development remains stultified because of the absence of the democratic traditions of the West emerging over centuries and because of the psychological trauma from the war only forty-some years before. The critics charge that the Japanese people lack principles, they are subject to stereotypical thinking, they are not realistic, and they are not internationalized. Faith in the Japanese public generally takes the form that they are not easily made gullible. They will not be swayed. In the fall of 1990 even the LDP leadership learned this lesson when it found public opinion resistent to new thinking about active Japanese involvement in the Persian Gulf crisis.

The Impulse for Independence. One remedy for the existing ailments in public thinking is to take a fresh look at international security through independent Japanese eyes, opened by the Gorbachev era. This was the message of Doi Takako's arguments in the election debate on February 2, 1990. While Prime Minister Kaifu Toshiki asserted that there is no crisis in the relationship between Tokyo and Washington, which he argued is primarily a security relationship, Doi referred to the relationship as "very difficult" and to the security treaty as "a negative factor" that is too rigid.[5] Whereas the close election in July 1989 for the Upper House of the Diet scarcely hinged on any international issues, the February 18, 1990, election broadened from the issues of the unpopular 3 percent sales tax pushed through the Diet in early 1989 and the still fresh scandal of political financing to the questions of managing Japan's security and its relationship to Washington. Gorbachev's initiatives had induced Japanese to begin to rethink their psychological dependency, but the LDP won with the minimum amount of rethinking. Doi's "rethinking" had turned out to be little more than warmed up old thinking by Japan's socialists.

In April 1989 the Japanese alarm about American Japan-bashing may have climbed to a new high, which seemed only to intensify over the following months. An article on the trouble due to Washington's new demands concerning Japan's joint production of the FSX plane referred to the "yellow peril" theory.[6] It complained that unfair American criticism now was extending beyond trade to objections to Japan's culture. George Kennan's containment imagery is now being applied to Japan. American polls now show the Japanese economy is a much bigger threat than the Soviet military. Japanese closely follow American thinking, especially the noisiest of criticisms, about their country.

Japan Needs to Do Its Own Thinking. The sentiment has arisen that Japan needs to rely on its own assessments of the Soviet Union. The government official using the pseudonym Saga Tōru wrote in 1989 that the tendency to believe blindly in the opinions of European and American specialists is a problem. Although they gather a lot of materials, their conclusions are sometimes one-sided and exaggerated or intentionally distorted due to policy considerations. He adds, we must build a base for doing our own investigations, doing our own thinking, making our own decisions. In the prewar era Japan's South Manchuria Rail Company Research Bureau conducted the top-class Soviet research in the world, recalls the official. Should not a similar situation prevail again?

The same author also warned that Japan should not simply brag about its victory in technology and economics. Japan needs to shoulder an increasingly large responsibility as it faces the twentieth century. It is necessary to look back at contemporary Japan's civilization as a spiritual support to match the individualism, rationalism, and Christian morality of Western civilization to this time. It would be wrong to rush unthinkingly into the twenty-first century, leaning one-sidedly on technology the way a child might brandish a weapon.[7]

This and similar proposals assume that Japan has its own viewpoint and its own spiritual civilization to present as an alternative to the West. Furthermore, they find that the dichotomy between active technological leadership and passive security dependency is becoming too simplistic. Even though socialism has failed as an alternative to Western values, this does not mean that Japan cannot emerge as the leader of another, more modest spiritual system, building on Western values for the most part, with much to offer the world in the next century.

Perceptions in Transition. The period 1985–91 appears as a time of transition in perceptions. At the start, Konstantin Chernenko was the conservative Soviet leader hesitant to depart from the traditions of his mentor Leonid Brezhnev, Ronald Reagan was the American leader whose view of the Soviet Union had changed little from the time earlier in his first term when he referred to it as the evil empire, and Nakasone Yasuhiro was the Japanese leader bent on strengthening Japanese patriotism while preserving close ties with the United States. Insufficient hope for Soviet change left the established postwar way of thinking in Japan largely intact. Even after Gorbachev replaced Chernenko, it would take time to revise Japan's decidedly negative views of the Soviet Union. Although Nakasone played a leading role in the transition to a new phase and was anxious to accomplish more, there was close temporal correspondence between the end of his tenure as prime minister in the fall of 1987 and the first big shift in Japanese thinking.

By the second half of 1987, enough uncertainty had been created that Japanese were earnestly debating how the Soviet Union was changing and what implications would follow. Gorbachev's perestroika and glasnost were steadily deepening into an irreversible shift in the very nature of socialism, Ronald Reagan had become optimistic about reaching agreement on intermediate nuclear forces and working together closely with

Gorbachev on other issues, and the Japanese public was pushing ahead of its cautious leaders—officials in the Gaimushō and Prime Minister Takeshita Noboru—in assessing prospects for change. The second cycle was marked by uncertainty with no clear outcome in sight. Although skepticism was noticeably giving way more than half a year before Takeshita resigned in the spring of 1989, the Japanese leadership remained cautious. A dying emperor, a paralyzing political scandal, and a hesitant prime minister with little international exposure or charisma were compounded by genuine uncertainty about Soviet intentions.

The spirit of the new Heisei era could not be immediately defined when Emperor Akimoto succeeded his father on February 1, 1989. Elections in July revealed unexpected depths of dissatisfaction with the status quo. At about the same time the progression from Soviet parliamentary elections to open debate in the new parliament offered new assurance that glasnost was for real. Most important, the collapse of the familiar guideposts for international socialism and superpower relations stunned the Japanese into rethinking their place in the world. The year 1989 will go down in history for the downfall of communism (no less in China, where the bankruptcy of the one approach to reform socialism that had seemed to be successful led to worldwide disillusionment). It also marks the rise of the new worldview of Heisei Japan.

Closing the Ideology Gap. Japan has reached superpower status in advance of its citizens' consciousness of the responsibilities of leadership. This is granted by countless intellectuals who seek a solution in closer acquaintance with foreign societies. The reasons for the time lag in understanding and responding to the world may be traced to: (1) the lingering Tokugawa assumption that political knowledge was reserved for appropriate officials; (2) the sustained censorship and misleading propaganda through 1945; (3) the pragmatic orientation of catching up, in which so-called practical knowledge takes precedence; and (4) the highly charged ideological views of those responding to these conditions and perhaps to other aspects of life in Japanese society. After World War II, the trauma of defeat and lack of trust between the government and the intellectuals polarized thinking. While soon nearly all Japanese came to see themselves as middle class, their way of thinking only gradually shifted from the extremes to middle-class concerns.

Changing views of the Soviet Union enable one to trace the shifting outlook of both the left and the right. The significance of the Gorbachev era may be a final and abrupt disappearance of the ideological gap between the two sides, although on the far right and far left there remained some unwilling to accept this breakdown. Communications with academics normalized as study associations became more diverse in their membership; curtains between academic factions were dropping with the fall of the Iron Curtain. Ideology is now almost universally disparaged as a barrier to knowledge. A middle-class consciousness bespeaking a common sense of community is spreading.

The Gorbachev era has prompted official circles in Japan to recognize that their country faces the biggest transition in international conditions during the postwar era. In June 1989 Watanabe Taizō, the director general of the Information Department in the Gaimushō, interpreted the new era. He explained that the retreat of Communist ideology, which should not be exaggerated, furnishes one reason, and the relative decline of the United States in political and military as well as economic power provides a second. Japan is now facing high demands for burden sharing. It is greatly affected by the transitional era. The significance of nonmilitary problems is rising. Watanabe expresses concern that West European society is being fragmented by varied responses to the relaxation of Soviet-American tensions.[8] This emphasis on Western unity as a goal suggests that coordination should also guide Japan's response to the new era.

A different view of ideology and bilateral prospects is also present. Objecting to some Japanese who need the Soviet enemy to sustain their dream of military power and prefer to fan the flames of a crisis mentality in the hope of never resolving the islands questions, Nakazawa Takayuki finds hope in the language of Soviet Foreign Minister Shevardnadze during his visit in December 1988. Along with others to the left of center, he asserts that it is not correct to keep all issues hostage to the territorial talk. Three elements in Shevardnadze's remarks especially excite his interest. First, the use of the term "humanity" as many as twenty times without any use of "communism" or "socialism" signals a shedding of ideology in international relations. Japan could look forward to world relations in which ideology would be absent. Second, the Soviet official's respectful view of Japan as a country with a rich culture and tenacious traditions points to a state of appreciation for Japan's distinctiveness. At the same time, Japan is seen as a model for the Soviet open door to the whole world, dealing with all, borrowing a lot, and sharing much with the world.[9] As some Japanese look ahead to their country's new world role, they welcome this kind of attention.

Respect in International Affairs

Japan's Value Is Not 1 Percent of That of the Soviet Union. The memoirs of former ambassador Niizeki Kinya appeared in two volumes in 1988–89. Having studied in Riga at the end of the 1930s, served in Berlin during the war, been involved in the planning in 1945 to try to obtain Soviet help to end the war, played an active role in the negotiations to reestablish relations in 1956, served as ambassador in the early 1970s during the best period of Soviet-Japanese relations since 1917, and headed the Japanese Institute of International Affairs as it expanded research on Soviet studies through the 1980s, Ambassador Niizeki has a remarkable vantage point. His view of the Yalta agreement is indicative of official thinking. It was a victory for Soviet diplomacy, coming at a time in February 1945 when Soviet troops were favorably situated only eight kilometers from Berlin as opposed to a distance of four hundred kilometers for American and English troops. Roosevelt was in bad health and had become extremely tired after the long trip to Yalta. In a hurry to conclude the negotiations, he overlooked the State Department's proposal and, based on erroneous thinking, swallowed Stalin's demand for territory belonging to Japan. Churchill was excluded from the secret negotiations on the Far East. In these many ways, Washington mishandled the Yalta negotiations and came away with a bad agreement. From this line of reasoning, it is not hard to extrapolate to more recent concern that American presidential diplomacy is not up to the standards needed to protect Japan's interests in negotiations with Moscow.

Niizeki presents some concrete examples of Soviet arrogance and rudeness to the Japanese. He makes it clear that in 1945, three million Japanese soldiers carried out the fastest and smoothest disarmament in world history, not spilling a drop of blood of the allied soldiers. Yet the Soviets ignored this and kept proceeding, killing 80,000 soldiers and taking about 600,000 POWs to Siberia. Then, in March 1956, in the midst of negotiations, Moscow made a unilateral declaration of fishing limits. Other "fish shocks" followed over the years. When Khrushchev met with Japan's agricultural and fishing minister in 1958 he took the extraordinary step of denigrating Prime Minister Kishi for most of the time, while spending only five minutes of the one-hour meeting on the fishing problem. Khrushchev once referred to Japan as having only volcanoes and earthquakes. Later, Soviets placed Japan's value at one one-hundredth of the Soviet Union's. In Party Congress speeches through 1966, Japan was lucky to receive one passing reference.[10]

The Gaimushō well recalls these and other signs that Moscow did not take Japan seriously. Despite Gorbachev's Vladivostok speech and later elaborations on the theme that Moscow now respects Japan, Japanese still see their priority in Moscow's eyes as low and await more tangible proof. They seek respect. They equate the cold war with a lack of respect.

RESPECT IN INTERNATIONAL AFFAIRS

A Respected Superpower. Japanese are beginning to wonder how they can convert their country's economic might not only into a source of pressure to recover the Northern Territories but also into a building block for the respect and authority customarily granted to a superpower. Of course, Japan's foreign aid program, which is now easily the largest source of civilian economic assistance in the world, can be expected to raise the country's standing in the Third World. Its cautious response toward China in the summer of 1989, supportive of stability above democracy and continued economic development above pressure for political change, may keep its pursuit of a common regional position with China on track despite that socialist country's lurch backward toward Communist dictatorship. As the atmosphere of confrontation between East and West diminishes in Southeast Asia after the settlement of the Cambodian fighting and in Northeast Asia as the Korean conflict becomes less volatile, Japan can more readily become the regional leader. From this region, it seeks through cooperation what it could not gain by military might and occupation half a century earlier—a coprosperity sphere that enhances Japan's world leadership. Yet superpower relations will also have a lot to say about the degree of respect that Japan enjoys.

One can expect that future international tensions will, at times, force Japan to choose between its two partnerships with Asia and the West. As long as the Soviet Union is a potential threat and China is an uncertain supporter of regional stability, Japan can be expected to side with the West on most major issues. Yet, to some degree, its values will be in conflict with both sides. Loyalty may take precedence over principle, economic stability may take priority over democracy, consistency may be preferred to idealism, and, as seen in the cautious response to the Iraqi invasion of Kuwait, caution may supersede leadership. When these preferred values are at the forefront, Japan may find it hard to earn the respect of the United States and some European nations. The way it handles relations with Moscow offers an early test of such differences.

Restoring "National Dignity." On the right are individuals who have sought throughout the postwar era to instill patriotic values. They want youth to believe in their country, its symbols, and its special mission. Increasingly in the past two decades, they have joined with many others (particularly in the older generations) in deploring the narrow, materialistic values of young Japanese. To them it is almost a matter of salvation that young Japanese retain the work ethic and distinctive values associated with an orderly society. Confusion about the Soviet Union threatens to eliminate a source of clarity in popular thought. Some on the right think that an appropriate response is to reassert the evil of Soviet socialism, illustrated by examples that are particularly meaningful to the Japanese public.

Moscow's repatriation of POWs in the late 1940s was a slow and sporadic process, with little explanation to the Japanese about the long delays. While there were also delays in bringing back the millions of Japanese stranded across Asia and especially the largest numbers left behind in China, the Soviet POWs became the focus of attention by 1948–49. The concern was not only the uncertainty of return for hundreds of thousands and the conditions of harsh forced labor that they faced in Siberia, but also the "red refugees" returning brainwashed by the Soviets. Coming off the boats, some hit the ground singing the Internationale and making "agitator" speeches. When two thousand returnees were polled after their return in 1949, 86 percent said they had good feelings toward the Soviet Union, 14 percent normal feelings, and 0 percent bad feelings. These were not isolated results, although the previous poll (52, 26, and 20 percent) has been less pro-Soviet and revealed less readiness to abolish the imperial institution (52 versus 76 percent). Yet the effect of "brainwashing" was usually short-lived. While 20 percent entered the JCP, after three months at home only about one in seven remained very active.[11]

Suetsugu Ichirō, who became active in the movement to help the returnees, describes the postwar Siberian forced labor of POWs as unprecedented in history. It was criminal activity that cannot be forgiven. Moreover, suffering families received no news. When the news agency TASS issued misleading statistics that threatened to leave many POWs unaccounted for, the suffering families pressed their complaints. A movement had begun with the slogan "A Loving Hand to the Refugees." After a sit-in before the offices of Soviet representatives seemed to spark a renewal of the repatriation, support grew.[12]

Suetsugu describes how one postwar movement led to the next. His group sought Japan's revival and independence. In 1950–51, in the midst of street demonstrations, they fought for the right sort of peace treaty. Then there was the question of building up the Self-Defense Forces. Supporters on the right found the Japanese government too timid. They struggled also for amnesty for so-called war criminals. While not fully winning some of their battles, they continued to be active. After the United States agreed to return Okinawa, the foremost goal became the return of the Northern Territories. Suetsugu's personal advocacy was well-known for many years. In late 1988 he increased his visibility by writing a series of opinion columns for the conservative *Sankei shimbun*. In November, on the eve of Shevardnadze's visit, he wrote as many as seventeen columns. There is no doubt that he is intensifying his personal role in trying to bring the islands back to Japan. In his career over more than four decades, one sees a persistent interest in restoring national dignity.

The POW issue resurfaced in October 1989 in *Asahi shimbun* when one writer criticized textbooks and the Mombushō for not treating the experience of Japanese soldiers in Soviet camps after World War II, and another responded by noting examples of coverage in these books while adding details about the rewriting required by the ministry before final wording was approved.[13] The Ministry of Education is not failing its conservative supporters.

One new Japanese approach to the POW issue was the tendency from 1989 for those who had been held in Siberia after 1945 to return forty years later for a visit. A newspaper series outlined the train route and described the new spirit of bringing home a Soviet military cap for memory's sake. It also recalled one returnee's memory of a Soviet girl's remark that the food for Japanese soldiers had been better than what was available to Soviets. Viewing his old room, the returnee said that here is his second native place. Such memories mingled with tearful visits to graves and recollections of those who had died. The POW experience is even described as an international exchange that allowed the Japanese amidst their suffering to know the gentle Russian people.[14] Such sentimentalism contrasted with the more widespread impact of efforts to show the injustices of Stalin's forced labor.

Respect through Others Learning from Japan. Soviet leaders were slow to convey to the Japanese their country's shift from arrogance to admiration toward Japanese society. After Gorbachev's Vladivostok speech, admiration for Japan's economy became increasingly noticeable.[15] Yakovlev's November 1989 visit went further, when he told Nakasone that there are points in Japanese worker relations from which Moscow should learn a lot.[16] He spoke of the mysterious side of Japan, as Americans do who marvel at Japan's successes and strive to learn its secrets.

Aleksandr Yakovlev is described as a Soviet leader who recognizes Japan's distinctive political and economic culture.[17] He considers it the country of the twenty-first century. With this appreciation, the Soviet drive to improve relations is likely to bear fruit. Moscow will make concessions, it is argued. When Yakovlev and other reformers lost power in Gorbachev's lurch to the right of early 1991, one casualty was Soviet flattery and its impact on the Japanese.

One of the factors that was beginning to pique Japanese interest in Soviet thinking is their realization that the Soviets were turning to Japan as a model. After believing for years that Soviets look down on their country, they were pleasantly surprised to learn in the late 1980s of a more favorable attitude on the part of the Soviet public and of the reform groups that have gained influence. Hakamada Shigeki first noted this in 1987 based on his close contacts with Soviet reform thinkers.[18] In late 1989 Kimura Hiroshi developed the theme by pointing to five aspects of the Japanese model of interest for Gorbachev's perestroika. He listed economics, technology, national security, foreign policy, and domestic politics.[19] In late 1990, as described in chapter 8, the Soviet white paper on Japan and the mounting fascination with Japan's achievements briefly suggested a stampede of enthusiasm for Russia's successful eastern neighbor.

Japanese sources have many times ordered the major countries in terms of their priority to Moscow. Always Japan was well down on the list, below China and below Western European powers. Hints that Japan's turn is coming or that only recently has its priority been rising are taken as evidence that Moscow's reordering of priorities—its realism—remains incomplete.

At the end of 1989 Shimotomai Nobuo wrote that the time has arrived when relations with Japan have become Gorbachev's next diplomatic problem. Relations with Europe have turned around, American ties are advancing, stagnation has set in with China, and this leaves only Japan.[20] On this, as on other issues, Shimotomai is at the optimistic end of the political spectrum. Others, however, were beginning to sing the same refrain in 1990.

The media took note of high-level Soviet admissions that the feelings of the Japanese people had been hurt by the Northern Territories situation. It is important to consider mutual perceptions and to achieve understanding of each other, the Soviet official V. I. Borudin told the Japanese when he accompanied Yakovlev to Japan in November 1989.[21] Appeals for showing respect for public opinion in the other country as the basis for advancing the dialogue could be widely found in the Japanese media.[22]

We can speculate that there is a connection between receiving respect and realism from Moscow and reducing deference to and dependency on Washington. Japanese are interested not only in the hierarchy of military and economic power, but also in the less tangible hierarchies of political and cultural power. Their success over the past four decades gives them the confidence to aspire to more than economic power. The Soviet Union is the obvious and immediate target that has stood in Japan's way. Whether in supporting Japan against the Soviet Union or as the next and more serious target of readjustment, the United States will also be tested by this process.

Social Sciences at Fault. By late 1989 some Japanese had accepted the notion, popularized in America, that we have entered an age when ideology does not matter. The yardstick of pro-Soviet or anti-Soviet no longer applies, asserted the journal *Sekai shūhō*.[23] To use it risks misjudgment. To achieve de-ideologization requires overcoming some existing barriers to objectivity.

As communism collapsed, some Japanese on the right were asking why the illusions of Soviet-style socialism long impressed old left intellectuals who played a central role in the social sciences within Japan and still are numerous. How had they misjudged the Soviet Union, Eastern Europe, and China for so long, even referring to the Soviet "liberation" of Eastern

Europe in the 1940s? Noda Nobuo of Kyōto University argues that, as one reads about "the path to slavery," increasingly the depravity of the social sciences in Japan can be seen. Now research must be conducted in a different way, he insists.[24] Others less interested in settling a score accepted the basic argument that the social sciences needed to be strengthened commensurate with Japan's new world role, and that it would be necessary to make explicit some safeguards for objective scholarship.

Language as a Tool for Understanding. In November 1989 a newspaper reported that a "boom" had begun in Russian language courses and the sale of self-study language cassettes. This is the first surge in popularity since 1961 when Yuri Gagarin circled the earth in space. Previously, enthusiasm came from those who wanted to read nineteenth-century literature in the original. Now interest can be found in both students and company employees of a wide age range looking for career opportunities. Opportunities to learn about Soviet character and traditions are widening, and mass media coverage of perestroika is arousing interest.[25] The article does not fail to mention that the overall numbers, while a sharp rise over figures from a few years ago, are still small. Without language competency and direct contact with Soviet life, accurate understanding will be difficult, according to many academics.

Morality in World Affairs. The Japanese people are increasingly guided by the same moral authorities as other developed nations. The resounding reception given to Andrei Sakharov when he received an honorary degree from Keio University in October 1989 shortly before his death was indicative of his moral stature among educated Japanese youth. Admiration in late 1989 for East European and Soviet human rights aspirations also seemed to rise to a new high.[26] Although the human rights theme had not previously been as dominant in Japanese appraisals of socialism as it had been in the United States, the images of 1989, from Chinese students packed into Tiananmen Square awaiting a bloodbath to Rumanians bravely standing up to a dictator's final massacre, created a new wave of empathy for the people battling for their rights. Even if human rights values are not as central as in some Western countries, they are gaining in popularity. In this way, the Japanese are likely to gain international respect.

INTERNATIONAL CONSCIOUSNESS

At the end of 1989 Japanese were asked by the *Yomiuri shimbun* if reform in socialist countries would be useful for disarmament and a relaxation of world tensions in the 1990s.[27] One-quarter found it very useful, 45 percent found it quite useful, 15 percent found it not very useful, 1 percent found it completely useless, and 14 percent did not answer. At the same time, 84 percent (43 percent strongly and 41 percent somewhat) welcomed the reforms. While 86 percent answered that they are familiar with the tearing down of the Berlin Wall, 65 percent said that they knew about Soviet perestroika, and only 37–43 percent were aware of the various democratic changes in Poland, Hungary, and Czechoslavakia.

Cautious Optimism. The public clearly preferred a cautious response by Japan; while 19.5 percent said their country should positively assist the Soviet Union and Eastern Europe, 64.2 percent called for careful examination of the situation, 7.0 percent preferred no aid, and 9.4 percent did not respond. Asked their view of the Malta summit, which some recognized to be the end of the cold war era and the start of a new period of cooperation, 37 percent said they highly value it, 43.8 percent somewhat valued it, 8.4 did not much value it, 0.8 did not value it at all, and 9.9 did not answer. The best informed were the most positive. While barely two-fifths of respondents strongly welcomed the democratization and liberalization, of the 37 percent who were aware of Hungary's abandonment of communism, 62 percent were strong supporters. Surprisingly, respondents below the age of thirty reacted coolly; fewer than 30 percent strongly welcomed the reforms as opposed to 42.5 percent for respondents as a whole. Almost 70 percent of supporters of the LDP and DSP agreed that socialism has reached a dead end, while only 50 percent of JSP and Kōmeitō supporters concurred.

The *Yomiuri* results show a wariness about predicting reductions in world tensions. The newspaper identified the Tiananmen incident in China and the persistence of the Northern Territories problem as reasons for a lack of confidence about Asian peace. Interestingly, the sex gap is huge—only 18 percent of women expected the recent developments to be very useful for a relaxation of tensions as opposed to 34 percent of men. As seen in other surveys related to the Soviet Union, Japanese women are more cautious.

The paper found the lack of genuine enthusiasm (37.1 percent only) for the Malta summit to be another sign of wavering about whether European developments will be extended to Asia. The enthusiasts formed one faction. Those who were enthusiasts about the summit numbered three-fifths of the total who strongly welcomed the reforms, three-quarters of those who thought the outcome would be very useful for the relaxation of world tensions, and two-thirds of those who wanted Japan positively to assist the reforming countries. The lukewarm backers were another faction, who viewed the summit and the prospects for relaxation more or less positively, while considering aid cautiously. As opposed to Western Europe, Japanese consider themselves distant from the new developments and reluctant to act, although the generation in their twenties is slightly more ready (24 percent) to extend aid, and LDP supporters (17 percent) are least likely to be part of the positive faction for aid, in comparison to 24 percent within the JSP, JCP, and Kōmeitō. The responses reveal cautious optimism; most figures do not indicate real exuberance or very hopeful reactions, but they do show the continued advance of positive thinking.

As the cold war was being declared at an end, *Asahi shimbun* released a joint Asahi-Harris poll showing that Japanese trailed Americans in their optimism about the relaxation of tensions after the Malta summit. While 65 percent of Americans predicted a considerable relaxation in East-West relations, 54 percent of Japanese were similarly impressed. It was not that Japanese believed that there would be no change (28 percent as opposed to 30 percent of Americans), but that they favored other responses or did not answer. From the time of the INF agreement two years earlier, the Japanese positive response had jumped from 35 to 54 percent as the negative response slipped from 50 to 28 percent. The American negative response had only dropped from 45 to 30 percent. The gap between the two nations was narrowing.

Trusting the Soviets. Asahi shimbun also found that 43 percent of Japanese now believed that the Soviet Union had become a trustworthy country, as opposed to 34 percent in 1987, while those who disagreed dropped from 46 to 36 percent (about the same as the American drop, from 40 to 31 percent). Trusting responses were at last in the lead, but still not close to the 55 percent level registered by Americans in 1987 or the 62 percent level now indicated. Fewer than half of Japanese were prepared to express such trust, and in the generation aged sixty and older only 33 percent were trusting in comparison to a high of 72 percent for Americans aged sixty-five and over. Wartime memories differ in the two countries.

Over two years, Japanese managers had made the most abrupt switch from a below-average 33 percent trusting to a well above-average 52 percent. Hokkaidō residents had also changed their minds; previously only 24 percent were ready to trust their Soviet neighbor, and now 57 percent were trusting. Most vulnerable to the Soviet threat, these northerners also have the most to gain from economic ties. Access to fishing grounds long served as a lure. As additonal hopes were raised, Japanese on this northern island were converted into the strongest supporters of the new opportunities. In the summer of 1990 an agreement on ferry service to Sakhalin finally brought a step forward in economic ties.[28] At the other end of the country skepticism persisted: only 36 percent of Kyūshū residents trusted the Soviets at the end of 1989. Tokyo and the Japan Sea areas closer to Soviet territory also saw more optimism than the more distant Osaka area.

The Asahi-Harris poll in December 1989 revealed other differences in

Japanese and American thinking about issues in East-West relations. While respondents were generally similar in attitudes about the probability of success for perestroika (17 percent negative, 57–59 percent a little), only 10 percent of Japanese saw a great change for success compared to 21 percent of Americans. In both countries, males and white collar employees were more positive. Japanese tended to see the cause of the reform of communism in Eastern Europe as much in low living standards (41 percent) as in the lack of freedom (40 percent), while Americans concentrated on political freedom (48 percent to 30 percent). Younger Japanese focused more on the economic side (50 percent), while younger Americans were especially aware of freedom. Older Japanese were more reluctant to attribute the reforms primarily to economic motives. When asked if in the near future change toward democratization would resume in China, Japanese were evenly divided in their response (43 to 42 percent), while Americans were optimistic (55 to 36 percent). The informed groups in Japan most optimistic about the Soviet Union tended to be most pessimistic about China.

In June 1990 *Yomiuri shimbun* reported on the second binational poll on Soviet-Japanese relations.[29] Compared to the winter of 1989, Japanese had a more favorable assessment of relations (good or very good, 24 percent vs. 13 percent, and bad or very bad, 25 percent vs. 40 percent). The friendship gap was narrowing. As Soviet views turned somewhat sour (a change from 77 to 73 percent feeling friendly and from 10 to 18 percent not feeling very friendly or feeling dislike toward Japanese), Japanese views grew a little rosier (from 25 to 29 percent friendly and from 67 to 61 percent not very friendly or feeling dislike). The perception gap remained. The newspaper stressed the positive changes as Japanese responded to Soviet changes and the announced Gorbachev visit, but it noted that Soviets reacted to the discrepancy between improving Soviet-American relations and little changed Soviet-Japanese relations. Japanese also continued to perceive a Soviet military threat (serious, 27 percent; to some degree, 50 percent) and the territorial dispute as an obstacle. On the Japanese respondents' wish list for a successful summit, 68 percent put the Northern Territories, 48 percent a peace treaty, and 40 percent a fishing agreement, while only 24 percent noted a relaxation of Asian tensions, 20 percent cultural exchanges, and 18 percent economic cooperation. The Japanese public continued to look at the Soviet relationship primarily in terms of immediate bilateral political and symbolic concerns rather than in the context of regional and global relations or of economic and cultural concerns.

A Kyodo-TASS binational poll at the end of October showed more favorable feelings toward the Soviets. Now 42 percent of the Japanese were favorable and only 34 percent unfavorable. The previous joint poll of early 1987 had shown only 18 percent favorable. In late 1990, Japanese were also optimistic about the Gorbachev visit; 64 percent expected a settlement of the territorial dispute.[30]

Judging Japan Comparatively. The Japanese self-image often contrasts with images of other countries. Only China's 56.6 percent approaches Japan's 70.4 percent for a wonderful culture and tradition. West Germany at 43.4 percent is second to Japan's 72.8 percent for superior technology. Japan is also first in high economic power with 55.7 percent, ahead of America's 40.6 percent and West Germany's 18.3 percent. The most startling contrast is good domestic order—64.2 percent in Japan versus 7.8 percent for second-place China. While only 15.3 percent say that Japanese can be trusted by other countries, that is still double the level of trust for the United States in second place. Even in protecting freedom and rights, Japan is number one at 41.9 percent versus 30.1 percent for the United States. Japan works hardest for the realization of world peace (34.7 percent versus America's 13.9 percent), but not for modernization (28.4 percent versus China at 41.4 percent and Korea at 40.4 percent). One detects here concern for Asian competition. Understandably, only for the heading of strong military power does Japan trail at just 5.7 percent. In what group of countries does Japan belong? Respondents preferred Europe, America, and the advanced country group at 48.8 percent, but they also chose the Asian countries at 26.9 percent or neither at 16.4 percent.[31]

Ranking Japan's Priorities. The Japanese ranking of the major countries of the world in terms of their priority for Japan's diplomatic activities related to peace and security is recorded in a national poll. Asked to choose up to three countries, only 2.5 percent of respondents picked Central America, African, or East European ones. In December 1981 and again in January 1989, two countries were on top: the United States with 72–73 percent and China with 59–64 percent. These are the two primary concerns of the Japanese people. In 1981, not long after the 1979 oil shock, Middle East countries were third at 29 percent; by 1989 they had fallen to sixth at 10 percent. Western European countries held rather steady at 21–18 percent, although slipping from fourth to fifth place. Apart from the fall of the Middle East, the major changes over the decade were the sharp rise of the Soviet Union and Korea. The former climbed from 20.7 to 38.4 percent, settling indisputably in third place rather than its earlier fifth place ranking. At last Japanese were taking Soviet diplomacy seriously. Korea jumped from 9.1 to 21.5 percent or sixth to fourth place; now two of the top four were East Asian countries.

Polls also examine the international consciousness of Japanese. In May 1988 the NHK asked respondents what contacts they had with foreigners. Ten percent had worked with a foreigner, 9 percent had made friends with a foreigner, 8 percent had corresponded, 5 percent had a family member or relative enter into an international marriage, 3 percent had a foreigner stay in their home, and a equal number had been sent abroad for work of at least one-month duration, while 1 percent had studied abroad. The highest figures were 38 percent having spoken with a foreigner and 21 percent having traveled out of the country. Many Japanese follow foreign news: 46 percent are interested in accidents and events, 42 percent in world politics and economic work, 37 percent in the living and thinking of foreigners, and 16 percent in foreign history (below sports, travel, fashion, and culture). Television is the prime source of information, but 66 percent of respondents rely on newspapers too (83 percent of those who follow politics and economics), and 33 percent rely on magazines, while 12 percent rely on books. Most contacts are with Koreans, who comprise over 80 percent of "foreigners" in Japan, normally having been born there. Asked where they would like to visit, Japanese place the United States first and leave the Soviet Union completely off the top ten on the list.

The United States is seen first as having strong military power (60 percent), then high economic power (41 percent), superior technology (32 percent), and protection of freedom and rights (30 percent). The Soviet Union is seen almost exclusively in the image of a strong military power (72 percent), while only 18 percent note superior technology, 13 percent add a wonderful culture and tradition (14 percent for the United States, 57 percent for China), 10 percent and high economic power, and 7 percent see it as working hard at modernization (12 percent for the United States), and 5 percent as working hard for world peace (14 percent for the United States). Only 2 percent credit the Soviets with protecting freedom and rights.

Japanese do not trust other countries. The United States scores first, with 8 percent saying they can trust it, West Germany is next with 7 percent, China has 6 percent, and Korea, the Philippines, and the Soviet Union are last at 1 percent. In 1988 the Soviets scored better than the Americans in maintaining domestic order (7 to 2 percent). By 1991 Soviet disorder must have changed this result.

Images of Internationalization. In the fall of 1989 Tamamoto Masaru discussed what internationalization is. He said it is a search for national identity, for the meaning of Japan's history from the Pacific War to the present, and for a new orientation in the world.[32]

The mood in Japan at the start of the 1990s is that Japan stands on the threshold of a new era, in which it will have to emerge, at least part way, from out of the shadow of the "pax Americana" to assume an active role as an "internationalized" society. This proposition has become a cliché of Japanese political commentaries; it has acquired unprecedented popularity both because of domestic concern over recent international developments, such as Soviet-American negotiations, and because of heightened pressures from the outside world. From the major world capitals Tokyo is being bombarded with essentially the same message, appealing for "internationalization," even though the specific contents of the appeal are often contradictory. Washington seeks cosmopolitan world citizens, who will purchase more foreign products and bear a larger burden of defense costs. Moscow calls for "realistic" and "respectful" internationalists, who will give up their "bystander" status in response to a changing superpower that is eager for Japan's cooperation. Beijing desires repentant and generous Japanese who are mindful of the history of their region and eager to heal its wounds through joint economic efforts. Compounding the problem, each of these capitals appears increasingly confused about what it really wants from Japan. Many images of an "internationalized" Japan have been proposed to suit the national interests of other countries, but not much attention has yet been given to what sort of "internationalization" is likely to arise out of the worldview and the interests of the Japanese people.

Controversy can be found about why Japan should internationalize. Is it because the United States insists on it (as it has through the 1980s) as a way to share burdens and to make trade fairer? Is it the correct response to the end of the cold war—an outcome sought by Moscow and much of the global community—to enlist Japan's vast economic resources in support of a new world order? Or is it essentially an indigenous response to Japan's own frustrated aspirations at failing to achieve a comprehensive peace and a proper place in the world for more than four decades? Evidence on Japanese views of the Soviet Union supports the third option. Wariness of Soviet intentions was a principal factor that kept Japan from internationalizing adequately before. Now Japan is gaining its release to internationalize on a large scale, within limits resulting from U.S. uncertainty about sharing superpower authority, Soviet hesitation about making a deal with Japan, and East and Southeast Asian worries about the revival of Japanese domination.

The Outcome of Internationalization. If the impetus to internationalize comes primarily from within, the outcome is likely to reflect Japan's internal aspirations. These vary across the political spectrum. Two contrasting views best represent the vocal community.

The extreme right consists largely of those concerned with moral education, national dignity, the Soviet threat, and international influence. Many in this group are suspicious of Washington and hostile to Moscow. Nakasone is different, not because he does not share many of their aspirations, but because he welcomed a close bond with Ronald Reagan and optimistic overtures to Mikhail Gorbachev as the means to achieve these ends. Apprehensive about losing Japan's long-standing "Russian complex," some speak of the need for "healthy alarm."[33] They fear that internationalization threatens to make Japanese defenseless.

The left of center and center march to a different agenda. Their notion of internationalization centers on Japanese society more than the Japanese state. The Japanese people must become international citizens, sharing in the human rights values of the West and forging a civil society to keep the state from reverting to wartime excesses. Similar to the far right, this part of the spectrum does not want isolation or narrow mercantilism. Yet their scenario leaves less room for an assertive Japan.

At the end of the 1980s, the existing disarmament movement reasserted its opinion that Japan should take a leading role in structuring international peace. As Diet member Utsunomiya Tokuma reported in the journal of the Utsunomiya Disarmament Research Institute, Japanese sovereignty had remained only half formed because of the security pact with Washington and American armed forces seemingly permanently stationed on Japanese soil. Citing the unusual courage of LDP politicians in the 1950s who had championed peace and resisted Washington, the article suggests that the new disarmament mood following the INF agreement should revive this thinking.[34] Antipathy to the Persian Gulf War gave a temporary boost to this cause, but the decisive outcome achieved by the armed intervention of the West marginalized those who sought peace through compromise.

Internationalization can be embraced by various groups on the political spectrum, each with its own qualifications. On the left, objections to prewar nationalism are expressed in many forms. The target is Japanese nationalism. On the right, the target is cosmopolitanism. If that develops, Japanese lose their own identity and become rootless. To resist this, they must know the heritage of the East, to be firmly grounded in their national and regional traditions as a step toward well-rooted internationalism.[35]

Genuine Understanding and Shared Values. While Japanese frequently call for greater mutual understanding, they may not actually show much interest in understanding other societies, especially the Soviet Union. The old left was satisfied with a dogmatic application of formulas, and the new right is too nationalistic to empathize easily with the needs of others. The right of center leans toward pragmatism, as business interests set the tone for a market-oriented approach. The left of center focuses on social problems, but it does not show much sign of philosophizing about their origins and effects. Some critics contend that it does not have a sense of culture. In the Japanese response to Gorbachev it is not easy, except in the writings of centrists such as Hakamada and a few historians on the left with a long-standing interest in Russian culture, to find an appreciation of Soviet literature, art, or ways of thinking. If there is a European or Western "common house" in value orientations, then it would seem as if American and Soviet reform intellectuals are under its roof without many Japanese.

Soviet collectivist values have failed in the past two decades to withstand the twin forces of Brezhnev era self-interest and cynicism and Gorbachev era self-criticism and idealism. Japanese group-centered values have also been challenged, especially by rapid modernization and Westernization of youth culture. Yet the traditional Japanese values do not face an atmosphere of self-doubt and crisis. Moreover, they are truer reflections of the attitudes of the educated community than were Stalinist-imposed values in the USSR. Convergence with the West on human rights concerns, individualism, and the dangers of a strong state may be proceeding faster in the reform community of the new Soviet Union than in Japan, although the basic elements of such values have become more widely disseminated in Japan and the opposition to them is much weaker than in the Soviet Union.

Trilateral Perceptions. By the second half of 1990 Japanese had recognized not only deep changes in Soviet thinking, but also multiple imbalances in the imagery of two of the three major powers toward the third. *Asahi shimbun* surveyed American and Soviet attitudes toward Japan and found that when asked to identify one salient item, (1) only 5 percent of Americans as opposed to 39 percent of Soviets chose the Japanese standard of living being high; (2) as many as 17 percent of Americans regarded Japan as aggressive, 13 percent as exclusionary, and 28 percent as overpopulated in contrast to 1 percent of Soviets on each item; (3) twice as many (34 vs. 17 percent) Soviets described the Japanese economy as efficient. Clearly, Soviet images of Japan were positive. The same survey found that Soviet images of America were more positive than Japanese ones. Soviets exceeded Japanese in believing that the United States has a high living standard (36 to 5 percent), that Americans succeed through hard work (17 to 7 percent), and that the United States has developed science and technology (15 to 7 percent); while Japanese exceed Soviets in seeing the United States as a free society (29 to 14 percent), as a society degenerating from a lot of crime (23 to 2 percent), as a place where the difference between rich and poor is great (10 to 4 percent), and as a country where there is racial discrimination (7 to 1 percent).

Reviewing these survey results, Shimotomai noted that Soviet-American thinking agrees on the priority of disarmament, while Japanese-American thinking agrees on first of all resolving trade frictions. But Soviet-Japanese opinion does not share any common goal. The Japanese side seeks disarmament first, while the Soviet side wants expanded trade and advanced technology above all. He pointed to the fact that Soviet-

Japanese distrust is not yet wiped away completely, while at the same time Japanese-American relations are worsening. The article was entitled, "The Enemy Image Lurking in the Shadows."

Shimotomai took note of the fact that 46 percent of Japanese wanted the American military to withdraw from the Asia-Pacific region. Only 37 percent did not think so (the corresponding American figures were 26 percent for withdrawal and 69 percent not thinking of it). He concluded that the end of the cold war is bringing a tendency to isolationist pacifism rather than a desire for great-power status.[36] While more Japanese objected to the idea that the Americans and Soviets should still fill the role of international political leaders (24 percent compared to 15 percent of Americans and 12 percent of Soviets), the majority (65 percent, more than the 60 percent in the USSR but less than the 82 percent in the United States) seemed content with this status quo of two world leaders. Americans had the strongest status quo outlook on the future, but even Japanese did not, for the most part, advocate an alternative.

The Japanese sense of victimization was reflected in questions about the friendliness of one government toward another country. Among the Japanese respondents in late 1990, only 24 percent found the Soviet government friendly as opposed to 58 percent not very friendly and 5 percent antagonistic. While 37 percent of the Japanese found the American government friendly, 44 percent saw it as not very friendly, and 7 percent as antagonistic. Japanese continued to see their country as beleagured. Compared to Americans and especially Soviets, they were not very worried about the danger of a future nuclear war (12 percent deeply worried in Japan, 22 percent in the United States, 47 percent in the USSR). They did not succumb to hopelessness but felt enough anxiety to maintain their drive to normalize their country's standing.[37]

Creating International Citizens. A question facing Moscow in the late 1980s and increasingly other great powers as well is how to involve the Japanese public in the pursuit of a more ideal world. How can they turn into international citizens with responsibility for solving world problems? So far, the Japanese people seem less susceptible to external public relations and less involved. The younger generation in particular passes through the narrow bottleneck of "exam hell" crammed with facts, but with little curiosity. In comparison to the academic successes of two or three decades back who, whatever their myopia about socialism, were exposed to the world's literary classics and philosophies, the *shinjinrui* or "new human race" takes a narrow outlook. Men concentrate on building business careers. Women are more internationalized than before in hobbies, fashion, and music, but avoid politics and world issues. Youth and now many in their twenties and thirties have little knowledge of the reality of World War II. As one newspaper article in August (the month of deepest remembrance because it recalls Japan as a victim) 1989 stated, "Our generation does not know about Auschwitz." While an exhibition about it seeks to bring some awareness, there is no exhibition at all on Japanese war crimes in Asia. Could Japanese groups mount one? The paper reported, "As things stand now in Japan, we couldn't. It would just be too dangerous."[38]

Enduring Pessimism. The pessimists warn that bilateral relations are grim and are unlikely to change in the foreseeable future. They are deeply rooted in history and in differences in national character. It is not only in the late 1980s that the mood of bitter rivalry prevails; even in the second half of the 1970s before détente had collapsed there was a malaise in relations more serious than many observers detected. As Anatolyi Dobrynin, Soviet ambassador to Washington, reported to the chairman of Japan's Democratic Socialist party in July 1978, among all the bilateral relations the Soviet Union has, the worst are with Japan.[39] Cognizant of the cold relations between the two countries, M. S. Kapitsa used the term "refrigerator" to describe them.

Japanese pessimism about the return of the islands stems from several reasons. At first, when Gorbachev was newly in power, the principal reason remained a "negative image of the Soviet leaders and Soviet people as expansionist, abrasive, and unsympathetic." There was nothing in their character or past behavior that might lead them to hand over territory unless forced to do so by superior military power—an inconceivable outcome. Later, when Soviet-American relations were advancing, Japanese adjusted by seeing Soviets as less stubborn and more rational. Yet pessimism was rooted in the belief that Soviets would only make concessions in response to great power massed against them and to the prospect that a growing gap would leave them well behind. Eventually, observers began to see changes in Soviet values, conceding that Soviets were desperate for a better life and might act out of that impulse. Now pessimism centered on the belief that the economic gains from territorial concessions to Japan would be insufficient to sway Moscow or that the costs in revanchinist demands from others would indirectly exact too high a price. This type of pessimism is more qualified and can be more readily contradicted by changing evidence both about Soviet flexibility and about the Japanese readiness to respond with an attractive offer. The three cycles correspond to these three prevailing attitudes. In the final cycle, the extreme right still clung to the first or second attitude, while some in the center and left were beginning to go beyond the third attitude and anticipate a more optimistic outcome based on changes in each country. In early 1991 pessimism was again deepening.

CHAPTER FOURTEEN

Strategy toward the Soviet Union

SINCE AGREEING to the resumption of diplomatic relations in 1956, Japanese have shown persistence and patience in waiting for conditions that would bring full normalization, including a peace treaty, to Soviet relations. With firm American military support, Japanese have felt secure. With superior rates of economic growth and increasing economic ties to the Asia-Pacific region, they have felt that time is on their side. With the Kremlin's increasing diplomatic isolation and ineptitude in appealing to Asians and especially to the Japanese public, there seemed to be little reason for Tokyo to take the initiative. In 1985 the Japanese strategy remained to insist on Soviet acknowledgment of the existence of the territorial question and then on Soviet willingness to make restitution, while avoiding any hint of Japanese disunity, overanxiety, or premature concessions.

The high degree of consensus and continuity in Japan's handling of the Soviet question would suggest a well-crafted strategy for managing bilateral relations. Furthermore, the virtual absence of clear statements about how to respond to various contingencies or to progress in negotiations leaves the impression that the strategy remains intentionally vague, in order to yield as little as possible before the Kremlin makes some major concessions. Discussions in Japan about strategy did not often produce an open clash about differing options. (The exception was the argument in 1986–88 between the so-called entry and exit approaches about whether the Northern Territories question must be resolved as a prerequisite for warmer relations or could be postponed as an outcome of such relations, but the exit advocates remained a tiny minority, mostly on the left of center.) Japanese debates normally revolve around fundamental questions for understanding what to expect or what intentions the other side has. The protagonists appear to have been more concerned about the strategy for proceeding than about the short-term negotiating tactics.

THE MILITARY FACTOR AND SUPERPOWER STATUS

Is the Soviet Union a superpower? Will it remain a superpower for long? Does Tokyo have flexibility in its dealings with Moscow, or must it rely on Washington's superior superpower status? These are some of the fundamental questions that are discussed in the search for guidelines for a Soviet strategy.

Weighing Military and Economic Strength. In recent times Japanese have looked at the world primarily through the prism of economic development and technological change. They admire dynamism and advances on the frontiers of technology. Proud of their own successes over four decades, they extrapolate the methods they used to their images of other countries. Eyeing the future, the Japanese people anticipate a mixture of integration and competition in which international advantages will depend even more on domestic social strength. Japan's strategy toward other countries will depend in large part on their willingness to accept the rules of the new world order.

In times when the threat of war does not seem very distant, the Japanese grudgingly incorporate military might into their calculus of international strength; they did so for the Soviet Union into the mid-1980s. Seeing it as a kind of monster, a notable minority unmistakably credited it with superpower status. In recent years the monster image has faded. Lacking a sustained interest in military power, many Japanese are no longer taking Moscow seriously as a superpower of any kind. By the economic standard foremost in their calculations, the Soviet Union has dropped out of the superpower running. Carried to an extreme, as in the 1989 estimate that the Soviet Union's GNP, properly adjusted for black market exchange rates, is about equal to France's and 40 percent of Japan's,[1] this approach simply dismisses the USSR from Japan's principal concerns. Even if official circles are more restrained in dismissing Soviet military power for the foreseeable future, they share the image of economics first and of a "rusted superpower" reliant on outdated industry unable to stand the wear of time.

In contrast, Americans judge national powers as much by their military might as by their economic strength, until recently usually weighing the former more heavily. Obviously, this has obliged Americans to take the Soviet Union extremely seriously. Recently, Americans are relenting in this concern, to the dismay of others. Along with some Gaimushō Soviet experts, there are Americans who are becoming alarmed about public overconfidence. They still believe that for decades ahead the USSR will remain one of two military superpowers capable of making continued infusions of high technology with military applications. Given its financial handicap, they may acknowledge, Moscow cannot expect to narrow the technological gap of at least five to ten years. Yet even as this gap widens, there may only be grounds for long-term confidence, not for short-term complacency.

If the military factor still matters and the most that can be expected is a managed equilibrium somewhat in America's favor, the Japanese right of center concluded in 1989, the cold war will not end. East-West military competition will continue. For some time Moscow will no longer behave as an opportunist ready to become involved in Third World conflicts for geopolitical advantage. The world will become safer. There will be no threat to Japan. Yet the Soviet Union will remain a superpower. It would be unwise to relax one's guard very much in the event of a Soviet change of direction or a sudden Soviet decision to seize some golden opportunity. Great Russian nationalism is the sort of seething force that could explode in a new direction. By 1990 hopes were rising, but not without continued doubts.

In mid-1990 Inoki Masamichi well expressed mainstream Japanese thinking. Responding to the Twenty-Eighth Party Congress, he asserted that the Soviet Union has lost the cold war, that Gorbachev has abandoned socialism in favor of universal human values and a private property system, that from 1987–88 the Soviet Union has plunged into a crisis stage, that, responding too cautiously, Gorbachev has lost decision-making power and Yeltsin along with other radicals had reason to jump clear of the Communist party, and that the Soviet future is now unclear. Inoki added that blind belief in power and force whether by Japanese militarism to 1945 or by the Soviet military superpower creates a system whose feet are made of clay.[2] This is recognition that the Soviet threat is receding, but no illusion that the Soviets will follow Japan's postwar lead in thoroughly shifting priorities.

The Third Industrial Revolution. When economic development in the advanced capitalist countries reached a new level as the 1970s began, the socialist system, which had begun to crack in the second half of the 1960s, fell into a crisis. The system was unsuitable to the needs of the new era. Japan entered the first information revolution in the 1960s and 1970s, beginning to shed its industrial society partly under the influence of the "Nixon shock" and the "oil shock" of the early 1970s. A comparable Soviet shift is only now taking place under the impact of other shocks. Japan's second stage of the information revolution from the second half of the 1970s to the 1980s, including microcomputers, fax machines, and intelligent buildings, has advanced rapidly. Now the Soviet Union has much to do to catch up, including ridding itself of its obsolete socialist system, explained Aihara Minoru in 1989.[3] According to this logic, it was only a matter of time until the Soviet collapse turned the world from an era of confrontation to one of cooperation. Whether the new international era is labeled the third industrial revolution, the information age, or something else, the conclusion is the same—socialism is unsuitable and must give way if the USSR is not to be left further behind. Military power cannot long persist if economic vitality is lost. This conclusion is central to Japan's worldview.

Much of the Japanese political spectrum seems already to have decided that the Soviet situation is too desperate for the country to retain not only a monster or opportunist attitude, but even for it to persist as an ordinary superpower. Japanese need only wait as this fact sinks into the Soviet public's awareness. In the meantime, the best means of deterrence is closer Japanese-American military cooperation in high technology, such as anti–submarine warfare and the other areas of joint development announced on March 27, 1990.

Washington's Demand for Dependency. In the scenario of continued Soviet-American military competition, the American-Japanese relationship retains an important military dimension. Japan will still feel dependent on the U.S. military, although less so. As a country with few raw materials and inadequate food supplies, Japan may also feel an imbalance in economic dependency. In the face of trade tensions, this also would add to Japan's reluctance to challenge the established American hegemony in relations with the Soviet Union. The East-West framework would endure, with Japan subordinate. As a result, Japanese policy toward the Soviet Union would be deeply influenced by Washington's perceptions and interests. The day of the independent Japanese superpower would be far off.

Some analysts argue that since 1945 Washington's interest has been to slow the improvement of Japanese-Soviet relations and economic ties. Still concerned about the revival of the Soviet potential as a military equal, Washington would persist in pressuring Tokyo to use restraint. It would be the driving force. Tokyo would not jump into the lead but would cautiously follow Washington's example. After all, the gains to be found in the Soviet Union are but a fraction of the value of the American connection. Those who take this view cite the Toshiba case in 1987 as proof that even at a time of improving Soviet-American relations, Washington could not tolerate Tokyo pushing ahead onto the fragile territory of superpower relations. Is American sensitivity merely the wounded pride of a petulant power unable to accept the reality of its own decline, or is it the legitimate concern of the country that is most cognizant of the costs of military laxity? Even those Japanese who grant the latter are likely to find some credibility in the former. In any case, it is unlikely that Japan, which has prospered in the cold war era, will unilaterally take risks in rushing to overturn it.

Japan needs a world strategy for the coming era, explained Itō Kenichi in mid-1988. It needs a larger picture of world history befitting a great power. For Itō this includes more burden sharing with the United States and also more realism about strengthening Japan's high-technology defensive power, including nuclear weapons. The Soviet nuclear threat will remain; it could seize Hokkaidō with its huge military superiority, while the United States might be tied down by simultaneous turmoil in Europe or the Middle East. Talk of a postnuclear era should not lead to the illusion that such weapons will be completely eliminated nor, added Itō, should it deflect awareness of Japan's genuine military needs.[4]

Itō's late 1990 book argued that in the wake of the Iraqi invasion of Kuwait it was clear that Japan's leadership and the nation as a whole lacked a clear vision of the post–cold war world. In place of narrow legalistic thinking on how to proceed, they need strategic thought looking beyond Japan's oil supply to the structure and logic of the new world order. Itō equated the cold war with a "Third World War." Even though not a single tank volley sounded nor a drop of blood flowed, the West won and liberated Eastern Europe. Just as Germany and Japan had themselves rejected their old systems after the Second World War, the Soviet Union is doing this now. The main battlefield was the economy. Economic power is decisive in today's politics. Iraq will realize this truth too, insisted Itō, assuming that economic sanctions would run their course.

Itō argued also that the "Third World War" had been unnecessary. It occurred because Stalin was an imperialist, who left for his successors the wounds of imperialism in the postwar division of Europe and in the occupation of the Northern Territories of Japan. Now the victors should show magnanimity to the Soviet Union, the loser of the cold war, in order to build a lasting peace. Economic power should also decide the new structure for Asia, but to conclude that generosity is already warranted is to show ignorance of the current situation in Asia, where Stalin's injustice persists toward Japan.

Iraq, added Itō, is pursuing nineteenth-century classical national interests against a world of twenty-first century enlightened national interests. Yet the battlefield is actually the stores of Iraq, affected by economic sanctions and the gasoline stands of the rest of the world. The United States is the power that stood in Iraq's way. Itō wrote that it has been popular of late to look down on the United States and to talk of the twenty-first century as Japan's century, but how can a people unwilling to shed blood or sweat to maintain order gain such a role? Disagreeing with some Japanese scholars who think the security treaty with the United States is no longer necessary now that the Soviet threat is fading, he saw it as combining the forces of two great economic powers and now deserving of restructuring to give it new life in nonmilitary cooperation.[5]

Itō equated the impact on Japan of the Iraqi invasion and the world response with the impact of Perry's black ships arriving in 1853. The slumber of the forty-five years of postwar "pacifism" is like the slumber of the three hundred years of the closed Tokugawa system. In each case Japan at first tried to follow the letter of old customs and laws and not to think deeply about the changes occurring on a world scale.[6] Itō was equally contemptuous of the debates and mentality of each of these eras, even reaching into the LDP today. Politicians lack strategic thinking. Itō's book includes views ranging from Ishihara Shintarō's saying "no" to the United States to Doi Takako's pacifist socialism. Itō disagreed with both of them, urging that Japan, which is now at a turning point, join the United Nations' efforts. He regretted that it is not yet able to respond to a rapidly changing world.

The Iraqi Crisis and Realism. As Itō made clear, when Iraq invaded Kuwait in August 1990 and aroused a united response in favor of economic sanctions as well as American-led military encirclement, Japanese and other nations were obliged to rethink some of their assumptions about the new era. Clearly, the military factor still matters, reducing Japan's independence to the degree it cannot survive without security for its exposed oil supply lines. Unmistakably, it was Moscow and not Tokyo that played a role second to Washington in exerting influence on the international response. Apparently it was Tokyo that stayed somewhat on the periphery while interlocking interests drew the world's powers closer together. Japanese also observed that the United States was bending to the reality of a complex world, which demanded cost-sharing military build-ups, United Nations' resolutions, and armed units from as diverse a range of countries as possible. The world had changed, but this did not give Tokyo as much leverage over Moscow as some had expected.

Measured Cooperation. When Gorbachev spoke hopefully of "expanded equilibrium" concerning Soviet ties with the countries of East Asia, Japanese spoke cautiously of "measured cooperation."[7] The West should act collectively and respond positively, in a limited way, to desired changes. The Japanese side should not press its advocacy for the Northern Territories loudly because that might prove counterproductive, for example, by provoking a strong patriotic reaction among Russians. At the same time, Japanese should keep the larger military picture in mind. They should ask why a weak economic power should oppose the combined resources of the United States, Western Europe, China, and Japan, which have more than five times its economic base. A lot of restructuring of the Soviet military is needed to satisfy Japanese who start with this logic.

No Consensus on the Future of the Soviet Military. There is a group of Japanese Soviet-watchers concentrating on the armed forces. In the February 1989 issue of *National Defense*, three of the six articles focused on the Soviet Union.[8] One article discusses economic capabilities, showing on a chart that over two-thirds (68.5 percent) of the Soviet government budget goes for defense as opposed to 5.8 percent of Japan's and 37.4 percent of America's. Looking ahead to the policies needed for perestroika to succeed, the article predicts military opposition. Another article studies the results of a Soviet poll on attitudes toward conscription. It shows a declining interest in serving.[9] A special issue of another defense journal in October 1988 looked at Soviet questions such as military force and ideology and party control of the military.[10] In this journal the articles are not in any way alarmist. There is a range of opinions, indicating the absence of a consensus on the future of the Soviet military and Japan's response.

PSYCHOLOGICAL FACTORS IN INTERNATIONAL RELATIONS

The Future Role of Military Power. The U.S. Christmas military intervention in Panama only three weeks after the Malta summit between Bush and Gorbachev signaled that even in the new atmosphere of cooperation Washington would use its military might to resolve regional problems. Military strength and its unilateral use were not irrelevant to the new world order. This could be interpreted as a reassertion of the U.S. claim that superpower status based on military strength still counts for a lot. Japanese hesitation to support the Panama intervention could be understood as the outlook of a different kind of superpower, which, as Foreign Minister Nakayama Tarō told the General Assembly on September 26, 1989, was looking forward to "a major transition from discord to dialogue, from conflict to cooperation." In 1989 Japan took initiatives to strengthen the financing of UN peacekeeping operations. It was eager to extend cooperation to settle regional conflicts and to promote nuclear nonproliferation and a ban on chemical weapons. During the same UN visit, Nakayama announced the agreement for Gorbachev's 1991 visit to Tokyo, adding that Japan-Soviet relations are moving "from confrontation to dialogue and cooperation, like U.S.-Soviet relations."[11] Optimism about the prospects for duplicating Washington's breakthrough with Moscow did not necessarily mean identical thinking about how far the shift from military to economic power should proceed in resolving international disputes.

Yet short-term actions belied long-term reasoning. The Japanese doubted that an era of peace was on the horizon. As if to reinforce their point that détente means little in the Asia-Pacific region, the Self-Defense Forces in August 1989 announced a build-up of tanks on Hokkaido. This is the first line of Japan's defense—the front line in the event of a U.S.-Soviet war. The article well suited the view in some official circles that tensions with the Soviet Union will increase in the time of so-called détente.[12]

Japan's Defense Needs. A debate about future Japanese defense needs came into the open in 1989. The position that in the new era of détente Japan can revert to its minimalist position of the 1960s or early 1970s can scarcely be detected. Instead, the disputants differ over whether this is a time notably to increase military readiness or merely to stick to the recent course of gradual build-up. Given the continued growth in the might of the Soviet navy in the northwest Pacific, argues one group, Japan should strengthen its defenses to the north. Believing that American military strength brought Moscow to make concessions on the INF, they may hope that Moscow will look at long-run changes in the military balance as it cuts back and Japan expands and decide that this is an opportune time to seek a preemptive negotiating strike to limit the future of Japan's military growth by taking away the Northern Territories psychology. On the other side of the debate are those who see no Soviet intention to build up their forces in the region and do not find any reason to make any new response. Consciousness of Japan's severe budget gap, affected in 1989 by the fragile status of the unpopular sales tax introduced in April, makes any untoward growth in the SDF unlikely. Indeed, the plan approved in late 1990 for the defense budget over the following years lowered the annual rate of growth to about 3 percent.

The transition to superpower status is not an easy one for a country made allergic to military engagement beyond its nearby waters by the domestic and regional memory of World War II. Caution comes from opposition parties whose negativism is still cloaked in the mantel of the militarily restrictive constitution, from LDP factions each jockeying for credit for one of their own number emerging as the prime minister who leads the country into a new global role, from a bureaucracy accustomed to cautiously balancing the budgetary growth of one ministry as opposed to another, from global business anxious not to alienate large-scale partners in any country, and from a diffident citizenry unaccustomed to demanding quick and tough government action as a matter of principle. After the Iraqi invasion of Kuwait, Prime Minister Kaifu responded slowly and, seemingly, more to American pressure and impatience than to what seemed to be the national interests of a country highly dependent on Middle East oil. In Japan's responses to new Soviet thinking about the Asia-Pacific region and bilateral relations there was also a pattern of procrastination, and uncertainty about the locus of leadership. Kaifu, together with his patron Kanemaru and Kanemaru's rising protégé Ozawa, seemed inclined to more vigorous leadership, while the triumvirate of the 1980s consisting of Takeshita, Abe, and Nakasone appeared to be divided and inclined toward political infighting.

In the spring of 1990 a genuine debate in the Diet and the media followed the SDF's white paper insisting that the Soviet threat continued and calling for a substantial rise in the military budget. Apart from the negative responses from political parties on the left, the Kōmeitō disagreed, urging that the defense budget be limited, while within the LDP Kanemaru was known to be critical of the failure to take Soviet changes seriously. The Iraqi invasion of Kuwait in August had the effect, however, of relieving the growing pressure to downplay the role of military force in world affairs.

THE ECONOMIC FACTOR

Japan's confidence in its economy and that of the NIES in its region grew by leaps and bounds in the 1980s. This should not be surprising. The Pacific trade deficit between the United States and these five countries totaled twenty-one billion dollars in 1980. By 1987 it had climbed to eighty-nine billion dollars. Japan sought to lead the capital-rich East Asia against the land- and resource-rich Soviet Union. Extensive resources no longer impressed the Japanese after their success in overcoming the oil crisis in 1973.

Using Japan's Riches. The far left had difficulty pondering this enormous wealth. There remained only the residue of the poverty-inspired postwar idealism of neutrality and progressive service to a lasting peace for mankind. In any case, it was difficult to detect proposals to help world socialism or the Soviet Union. The left of center took an internationalist position based on economic aid. Keeping the military budget low and avoiding nationalism, Japan could gradually emerge as the quiet, generous superpower. The Soviet Union could be expected to benefit, especially from the increasingly generous proposals of late 1990 and early 1991.

The right of center expressed a more wide-open internationalist position. Japan would assume a new world role, expanding its military slowly as a means of gaining more leverage. It would be a Western power, morally siding with the West and supporting SDI and other joint military endeavors. Its foreign policy experts and think-tanks would be more closely integrated with those in the West but would develop a distinctly Japanese worldview. Based on its economic might, Japan would become an equal partner with the United States.

The right of center is prepared to break with Japan's past roles as a merchant nation quiet about its principles and without backbone toward Washington, a neomercantilist nation that separates economics and politics. As is first being demonstrated toward Moscow, Japan's economic power will be used for political ends.

A Low Level of Trade. Observers were beginning to look closely at the prospects for Soviet-Japanese trade as the possibility of a diplomatic breakthrough rose in 1989. They explained that from the early 1980s to the present, Soviet trade had fallen from 2 to 1.5 percent of Japan's total trade because of: (1) Japan's insistence on a return of the Northern Territories, which led to making politics and economics inseparable; (2) cautious adherence to COCOM restrictions on Japan's high-technology exports after the 1987 Toshiba Machine incident; (3) Japan's reduced interest in Soviet oil and raw materials due to world market conditions; (4) the inflated value of the yen; (5) the tightening of credit to Moscow following the Soviet entry into Afghanistan, allowing few new projects to be established; (6) the dearth of Soviet hard currency due to fallen oil prices; (7) the negative conditions in the Soviet Far East due to a shortage of infrastructure and labor. Yet for the Soviet Union, Japan is the third leading trade partner after West Germany and Finland among Western industrialized countries, and 1988 brought a record 5.19 billion dollars of two-way trade. This was made possible by the high yen value of exports of steel, machinery, and equipment, and also by price rises for Soviet marine and wood raw materials. The outlook on the future appears to be pessimistic despite repeated comments by Soviet economists that trade between the world's second and third economic powers is far from the level it should be.

A Japan Sea Economic Community. Even taking these circumstances into account, Ogawa Kazuo finds reasons for optimism about future economic relations. Improved East-West relations are expected to stimulate economic cooperation. Given his domestic difficulties, Gorbachev must advance on his new diplomatic path. COCOM restrictions are falling. Soviet economic ties are advancing in East Asia with China, Korea, and Taiwan and in Southeast Asia too. Moscow is rethinking its diplomacy with Japan, which will lead to expanded trade. The Japanese government and industrial circles are taking the initiative under the new conditions found in Northeast Asia, even raising the possibility of shifting beyond bilateral to regional approaches in many fields. Japan's great power in economics, industrial technology, capital, and human resources leads to expectations that it will display its leadership. The formation of a Japan Sea economic community reaching to the Soviet Union, China, South Korea, and North Korea is no longer just a dream. Moscow is moving ahead with plans to develop its Far East, for which Tokyo's help is indispensable. Ogawa concludes that it is also in Tokyo's long-term interest to respond positively.[13]

Developments in the Soviet Union aroused Japanese regional interests. In the port city of Niigata there was talk of a plan for the Japan Sea circle, linking the Soviet Far East and Siberia, Manchuria, Korea, and Japan in a lively economic and cultural exchange. Far from the centers in Moscow, Beijing, and Tokyo, this belt could give a boost to regional economic development. The mayor of Niigata made his third trip to Vladivostok in the summer of 1990 and heard of plans to open the Soviet port as the window onto the Asia-Pacific region. A movement was building to invite

"Gorby" to the city as excitement rose over the prospects of "outer Japan."[14]

Business Hesitation. There simply is insufficient infrastructure to make the Soviet Far Eastern economy profitable, responded most Japanese experts. Apart from some minor coastal projects, little could be expected if sound investment were planned. The Japanese delegation to Moscow in the summer of 1989 was prepared to discuss nearly a thousand joint-venture projects, but only a handful had previously been launched, and newly liberalized Soviet legislation did not increase the figure beyond a modest level of mostly small projects. Businessmen complained of ruble inconvertibility and products not up to international standards of competition; at most they set their sights narrowly on finding a small niche in the domestic Soviet market.[15]

The Japanese government guarantees loans to China and provides an extraordinary amount of financial assistance. Until the Northern Territories are returned by Moscow, the government will offer no guarantee to business investors. It does not stop them from pursuing profits, even if the national climate of linking economics to politics cannot be encouraging. There is no sign that business prospects are sufficiently favorable that a strong interest group seeks to pressure the Japanese government to help out more. While guilt toward China left from the war era produced a consensus on the need for economic help, there is no guilt toward the Soviet Union. As of June 8, 1990, of the 1,792 joint ventures registered in the USSR, only 33 were Japanese (compared to 241 from West Germany and 202 from the United States).[16] Some Japanese see a West German parallel to their country's conduct in China as both wartime guilt and Soviet anxiety induce business deals with the Soviets that the Japanese will not match.

Hakamada has linked Japan's China boom from the early days of the "open-door" policy to its Siberian bust of the Gorbachev era. Once burned by drawn-out and unprofitable dealings with the still bureaucratized joint-venture operations in China, the Japanese business community was reticent to repeat the experiment in the Soviet Union. In this and other ways mentioned previously, Japanese viewed their contacts with Soviet socialism through a Chinese prism.

Beating the Koreans to the Soviet Market. The school of bilateral optimists starts from two assumptions: that Gorbachev is committed to a breakthrough with Japan and that Japan has much to gain from an improved relationship with Moscow. For evidence of the former they turn to Gorbachev's statements—for example, on July 22, 1988, to Nakasone that he would do whatever was needed to improve Japanese-Soviet relations, or on September 16, 1988, at Krasnoyarsk that he can well see the possibility of a breakthrough in relations. From the time of his Vladivostok speech in July 1986, the Soviet leader has identified Japan as a power of first importance, as the focal point for Moscow to play a role in the dynamic Asia-Pacific region, as a remarkable success story in a short time since World War II, and as an example for its nonnuclear international policies and for its people's tremendous energy. As time passed, the Soviet evaluation of Japan rose, encouraging some Japanese to expect commensurate breakthroughs in policy.

Soviet long-range vision, according to Morimoto Tadao, foresees that within one hundred years the Asia-Pacific region will become the center of the world economy and world politics. Because of Moscow's many possibilities for opening its Far East, Japanese business can have high hopes in such areas as establishing infrastructure, reequipping the fishing industry, processing lumber products, producing foodstuffs, and serving the tourist industry. It follows that the Soviet Union will become a huge market for the twenty-first century. Will Korea be first in the development of Siberia? Similar to Japan, it is without resources, and it is even more dependent on trade because of its narrow domestic market. Moreover, Korea also faces the pressure of "bashing" from foreign trade frictions. It is now competing to replace Japan in export markets. Its foreign policy is based on realism. Japan must pay close attention or it will be outmaneuvered, as occurred two decades earlier in the American breakthrough with China through ping pong diplomacy. The advance of Soviet-American interests also threatens to isolate Japan. These are Morimoto's warnings to his countrymen.[17]

A Technological Mismatch. Hoping to draw the interest of foreign businessmen, Moscow in late August 1989 listed fifty-nine items of industrial technology, including advanced military and space high-tech items, open for international commercial ties. The response in *Nihon keizai shimbun* was that while Soviet science may be first-rate, its technology is third-rate.[18] The listed items are technologies from which Japan graduated two generations earlier. Japanese business circles failed to get excited about Soviet hopes for cooperation in technology.

VARIED OBJECTIVES ALONG THE POLITICAL SPECTRUM

The Right. The American right, for a time represented by Ronald Reagan, can deal with Moscow. Its concerns are international tensions, military build-ups, and human rights. Moscow appeared ready to meet most of Washington's demands in these areas. The Japanese right may be less prepared, in the long run, to welcome the Kremlin as a partner. Its immediate concern about four islands may be just the tip of a still concealed iceberg. The Japanese right is not likely to be satisfied for long with reduced world tensions, managed military expenditures, and Soviet civility. In Japan there is the feeling it is hoping for more. This is not an idealist longing for a more perfect world. It is rather a long-term expectation for a different world order without the Soviet and American superpowers on top. The far right is seeking a stronger military, a sharper break with the postwar order, and a new nationalistic identity stressing Japan's uniqueness and its cultural superiority. Improved Soviet-American relations on the one hand diminish the appeal of its rallying cry against Moscow and, on the other, strengthen its call for greater independence of Washington. If pessimism about the return of the Northern Territories were to grow, following increased expectations from 1988 to 1990, the right would be handed a golden opportunity. It is biding its time for a new stage of anti-Soviet rhetoric along with a partial decoupling of Japanese-American relations from the cold war track of opposing Moscow.

Sase Masamori prefers the American catchword "containment" to the Soviet catchword "new thinking" to explain recent diplomatic successes. It would be hasty to abandon containment policy, he adds, because it is the means to further success. There is a danger that catchwords can cause misunderstanding; therefore Japanese must not judge Moscow by the catchword "new thinking."[19] Sase also finds the term "détente" objectionable. It signifies public relations successes for Moscow, while expansionist ambitions are retained. It means stealing technology. Sase proposes the term "conditional détente" to reflect these suspicions.[20]

Japanese veterans of Soviet talks seem to have a cyclical view of bilateral relations. In the first wave of 1954–56, Moscow trumpeted "peaceful coexistence." In the second wave of 1971–73, it called for "détente." Since 1986 or 1987 a third wave has come accentuating "new thinking." Japanese-Soviet talks gather momentum in each wave, hopes are inevitably raised, but, in the final analysis, the Soviets, driven by a nineteenth-century political philosophy, insist on keeping what they have once won by war and never releasing it again. The main question for many on the right is not whether negotiations will finally prove fruitful, but how long the third wave will last.

In 1987 many Japanese were hesitant to discuss divisions on the right of the political spectrum. They stressed the unified goal of returning the territories and restraining the Soviet military. By 1989 one often could read or hear about the forces on the extreme right opposed to the INF as well as to flexibility of any sort in negotiations with Moscow. If the Kremlin did not return the four islands and if negotiations reached an impasse, what would the reaction be on the right? Kimura Hiroshi mentions Japan's arch-conservatives along with a group in the United States who do not necessarily want the Soviet Union to return the territories. They fear that the Japanese nation would, to a degree, turn toward sympathy with the Soviet Union. The theory of the Soviet threat would lose force. Soviets would appear as people. These responses would undermine the political agenda of the arch-conservatives, Kimura warns.[21]

If no settlement with Moscow is reached, Kimura's "arch-conservatives" will lead in continued attention to the danger to Japan's security. They may argue that the four little islands endanger the security of the four big islands (Hokkaidō, Honshū, Shikoku, and Kyūshū, the main body of Japan). They will push for faster budget increases for the Self-Defense Forces either in close cooperation with the United States, which has sought the same, or to distance Japan somewhat from the United States, which may appear in a more negative light because of its excessive cooperation with the Soviet Union or its economic harassment of Japan. The Soviet threat seems to be the only hope for the right to build Japan into an "all-around" superpower.

The right wing would like to play on a psychology that has been fostered since the late 1970s. The cold war era requiring military alertness is not over, they insist. There is no peace treaty. All the prosperity Japan has been able to achieve is in jeopardy. The younger generation must not forget the living symbol of Japan's humiliation. As long as this issue is before the Japanese public, the threatening pacifism of the postwar era and the dangerous notion that Japanese should play a special role in creating a peaceful nonnuclear world can be held at bay. Anti-Soviet attitudes are the key to the battle for the minds of the Japanese people.

Sono Akira laid claim to expertise as former ambassador to West Germany in responding to the drama of Eastern European events of late 1989. Moscow had a strategy to win the cold war, he insisted, the very existence of which was now being hidden in the shadow of the new mood of friendship. The tearing down of the Berlin Wall did not signify to Sono, drawing on his more than fifty years as a Soviet-watcher, a real departure from the long-term strategy. Rather, Gorbachev was giving highest attention to rebuilding his nearly bankrupt socialist country and to keeping the flame of Communist revolution lit. Temporary humiliation must be accepted, while awaiting a chance to go on the attack when the "crisis of capitalism" finally occurs. Meanwhile, Moscow is developing a powerful information offensive. It is also shifting the financial burden of support for Eastern Europe to the West. Soon the West would appear to be the villains objecting to the unification of Germany. Neutralization of Germany would mean the breakup of NATO, leaving American forces far away while the Soviet army would remain just west of Warsaw able to exert psychological pressure after the West had lost its sense of security and could not soon restore its defensive strength. Moscow would import capital and technology from the West, transferring the costs of its economic recovery elsewhere, while playing on intensifying conflicts among America, Japan, and Europe. Sono could find no cause for relaxed vigilance.[22]

If Moscow returns the islands, an enormous psychological shift could occur inside Japan. Antipathy for the Soviet Union may not be very deep. Although the image of the Soviets as robbers who stole Japanese land creates strong distrust, it could be replaced. This worries some on the right.

Voices on the right call for the Japanese to assume responsibility for their own defense. The idea from 1945 to now—that their country can simply leave the Soviets to the United States for protection—is inadequate. The legacy of postwar silence about the Communist threat by intellectuals has still not been adequately dissipated. This lack of alarm is referred to as "low consciousness."[23] Those who cried out against it in the mid-1980s remained concerned as the Gorbachev era unfolded because they feared that most Japanese were now taking the Soviet threat less seriously.

It is common to add to this argument that Japanese should not take the attitude that they will just use their money while the United States dirties its hands with military power. Japan has its own national interest. The West is subject to division. Only Japan can make the Soviet Union take it seriously.[24]

In the fall of 1990 Nakagawa Yatsuhiro warned that those searching for a "third way" to solve the Soviet-Japanese disagreement, in line with Yakovlev's call a year earlier, were, if not actually linked to Soviet propaganda work, naively serving its aims. The mass media's racket about Soviet softening on the territories was completely mistaken since no official Soviet source had spoken of returning land. He asked why Japan should pay for islands illegally occupied. Rather, the Soviet side should pay for use of the territory over the past forty-five years, and for lost fishing income for Japan. If it pleads a lack of money, it can transfer additional islands in the Kurile chain instead. Since Gorbachev was willing to "sell" East Germany, perhaps he would sell southern Sakhalin and the northern Kuriles. According to Nakagawa, the minimum sign that Moscow is serious about new thinking and that its expansionism is over is the immediate, unconditional return of the Northern Territories. Since the July 1990 Houston summit, this has become a condition for Western economic cooperation and a litmus test being observed by the world. The Soviet style appears to have softened, but its basic posture is unchanged.

The situation is reminiscent, says Nakagawa, of 1955–56 when Prime Minister Hatoyama betrayed his nation's interests; again Japan is in danger of succumbing to Soviet propaganda. Then Moscow was desperate to remedy its error in not signing the San Francisco Treaty and make sure that it could maintain a vast espionage and Communist command staff in

Tokyo. Now the Soviets are desperate for economic help. Only by being insistent can Japan succeed. Abe and Ozawa speak in a compromising tone in the manner of Hatoyama, in contrast to the earlier tough diplomacy of Prime Minister Yoshida Shigeru toward the Soviets. It is a sacred duty, added Nakagawa, to hand the land of one's forefathers to one's descendents. If Japan fails on the little four islands, the Soviets will grow ambitious for the big four from Hokkaidō to Kyūshū. To call for the return of the Northern Territories is to defend the Japanese archipelago. Even if Western countries see Japan as stubborn now, within a decade when the Soviet-American honeymoon has passed, they will respect Japan, Nakagawa insists.

Itō Kenichi and Sase Masamori were slow to be convinced of the seriousness of the Soviet intent, but by late 1989 and 1990 they had parted company with the far right in accepting the reality of the end of the cold war. Both were in direct contact with Soviet scholars and officials and were given opportunities to publish in the Soviet media or to publish exchanges of views with Soviet Japanologists. Their rethinking of the advantages of cooperation with the Soviets, although still within the cautious boundaries of their concerns about the strategic balance in the Asia-Pacific region, helped convince opinion on the right to take the Soviets seriously as negotiating partners. Nakagawa, Sono, and Hōgen are now isolated as a small minority out of the mainstream of Japanese debates.

Japan's third political party, the Kōmeitō, is not often heard on issues concerning socialist countries. Yet its Buddhist orientation toward a harmonious world community sometimes adds a strong idealistic—even utopian—flavor to a debate. As Eastern Europe percolated in the late summer of 1989 with political pluralism, an article appeared in the Kōmeitō journal suggesting that we may be approaching the path of a single free Europe.[25] Gorbachev's July remark about a "European common house" is a big reason for the birth of this new dream, the author explains. Only months later did this view become popular throughout Japan and the world. The terms of debate were changing rapidly.

Huge Soviet-Japanese roundtable discussions have occurred on six occasions, including in October 1988 in Moscow. Over one hundred Japanese dietmen, journalists, academics, businessmen, and representatives of friendship organizations participated. One frequent participant complained that the meetings are a waste of time: the Soviets do not give direct answers to Japanese questions and are long-winded about their own opinions. But in 1988 he was pleasantly surprised by the new atmosphere.[26] Person-to-person contacts helped to transform Japanese images, causing some observers on the right of center to shift toward the center.

In 1987–88 many Japanese on the center and left of the political spectrum doubted that the government and especially the Gaimushō was flexible enough to respond to the new possibilities in Soviet-Japanese relations. While their doubts were somewhat eased by developments in the second half of 1988, they continued to express some concern. Just as Americans perceive the Japanese bureaucracy as slow to address bilateral problems, some Japanese intellectuals do not have confidence that it can seize new international opportunities. Hasegawa Tsuyoshi, who returned to Japan after a period of studying and teaching in the United States, expressed this concern in an article in *Chūō kōron* in January 1989.[27] He wrote that Moscow has a radical plan to change the basic principles that served to manage East-West relations for four decades. It will take time and testing of the Soviet position (along with overcoming the Soviet conservative opposition) to remove the residue of such long-lasting mistrust and create a secure world. Yet we should work to build a new world order. This is a change we must grasp; there may be no second opportunity. Do we have the resolve to meet Gorbachev's challenge? he asked. Here one sees a rare expression of American-style idealism coupled with a note of caution about Japan's readiness to change course.

In various publications one finds the stigma of "pro-Soviet faction" (*shin Sōha*) used to discredit left-of-center and left-wing commentators. Some authors even felt it necessary to preface their relatively mild views with the assurance that they are not in this faction. Then they would object to the monochromatic Japanese discussion on the Soviet Union and call for diverse views to clarify the nation's options. As part of this perspective, the reader could sometimes discern a criticism of the Gaimushō as "anti-Soviet." Such posturing is a remnant of past polarization and a sign of the emergence of a new left of center and center keen on distancing themselves from the old left.

Many in Japan hoped that 1988–89 would begin the building of a new opposition coalition. The union movement reorganized to create Rengo, a broader-based, less ideological workers' association. The opposition parties, excluding the JCP, were searching for common ground. Yet the core of the problem was still that the rebuilding centered on the Japan Socialist Party, which, renaming itself Japan Social Democratic Party, remains socialist and is bereft of a philosophy or a program. Given the state of Japanese public opinion, one would expect a serious opposition contending for power to occupy the center of the political spectrum. Yet it is precisely the center that has a vacuum of leadership and inspiration. Responses to the Gorbachev era from a centrist position have been almost exclusively objective reporting and prognostication without any effort to advance a program for the new era. In April 1990 the DSP and Kōmeitō split with the JSP in recognition of the fact that they were losing political influence as junior partners in the opposition. As the Persian Gulf War was ending in February 1991 it was again these two moderate parties that joined with the LDP to send funds, albeit with some restrictions on their use, to the allies. The center was beginning to reform.

The Left. In the current period Japan lacks an alternative critical worldview. In the Meiji era Western thought and to some degree Christianity for a time provided a framework for criticizing the power structure. For a number of decades to the 1970s Marxism filled that role, but now it cannot since it is seen as a dead ideology supportive of totalitarianism and backwardness. What some Japanese hope to find is a new philosophy for domestic reform and a less passive and more idealistic foreign policy. If so, it may be home grown this time since there are no models in the world that appear to have much appeal.

Occasional strains of idealistic socialism could still be heard in late 1990. Eda Satsuki, a member of the Diet from the Democratic Socialist Alliance, explained that socialism predates Marx, that it represents a humanistic response to capitalist excesses such as the oppression of female labor in Japan, that it prospered in Western Europe, and that at last it is entering the Soviet Union in its original form. It can now play an important role in the coming decade of transition from twentieth-century confrontation to a new century of cooperation.[28]

Taking a position to the left of the Japanese government, the *Asahi shimbun* seeks to broaden the negotiations beyond territorial questions, to reassure Moscow that Tokyo has limited objectives that will not link up with any broader crusade to pare the Soviet Union down to size, and to set limits on the Japanese-American military alliance. In return for the islands, Japan would become a trustworthy partner. Similar ideas were floated on the left of the political spectrum through 1989 and 1990, but no clear political platform emerged.[29]

The Soviet issue was part of the hope on the left that Japan could become more independent of the United States. As Shimotomai Nobuo observed, Japan only has "one-channel diplomacy." By building a Soviet channel it will gain influence, for example, projecting its speaking force on nuclear questions.[30]

"Internationalized" Japanese need consciousness of world history, but they are becoming less and less knowledgeable. In the annual review of historical writings in 1987, Sasayama Haruyuki complained of the widening discrepancy between international opportunities for trust created by the first notable transformation in the world situation that occurred in 1987 and the tightening of secrecy laws in Japan together with the misuse of educational reform to inculcate a narrowly nationalistic view. Japanese youth could become a threat to world peace, warned Sasayama.[31]

From many articles in the far-left journal *Nihon to Sobieto* comes the view that real "internationalization" must be antinuclear and nonaligned. This is the leftist credo of the 1950s still sounded in the late 1980s, but with few listeners.

An article in *Nihon keizai shimbun* suggested in August 1989 that the JSP is really two socialist parties.[32] On the one hand, there is a parliamentary party centering on the Diet and, on the other hand, a party headquarters secretariat in Tokyo divided into nine committees and branch departments. Unlike the LDP, the operating arm of the JSP can function separately from the parliamentary membership and often even claims priority. It is split into factions (*habatsu*), which are mutually distrustful and spy on each other, although not with the intensity of recent periods. Especially on foreign policy, security, and nuclear energy issues, the intraparty clash is severe.

The factions are unruly, even permitting publication of barely veiled direct criticisms of party policy despite the presence of party control efforts. While the Diet members are diverse and often of right-leaning factions, the secretariat's power is held by the leftist factions who enthusiastically involve themselves in the daily activities. Lately, the private sector union support has not gone to the extreme left candidates, further altering the balance of Diet members away from the far left and isolating the secretariat. Factions of pro-Soviet and pro-Chinese complexion are still present. Both the old Katsuma faction on the left and the faction on the right led by Okada, the deputy chairman, are the most closely associated with the Soviet Union, while the faction farthest on the left (the old March meeting) offers strong ideological support. The Nakana faction remains pro-China. Those groupings date from the time of the Sino-Soviet split; a "war" continues to rage inside the JSP.

In 1989 Peter Berton wrote about the JCP's view of Gorbachev's perestroika. He explained that the party's policies are essentially those of its "80-year old Stalinist leader Miyamoto Kenji." The party's relations with Moscow have often not been good over the past three decades. The JSP left wing is more orthodox Marxist than the JCP, while the JCP tries to distinguish itself by its position on particular issues, such as aggressive championing of the antinuclear cause in recent years. Effusive praise for Chernenko at the time of his death (just three months after a meeting with Miyamoto) "as the greatest fighter for peace since Lenin" was followed by virtual silence about Gorbachev's early reforms. In May 1988 General Secretary Fuwa met with Gorbachev just two days before Doi Takako of the JSP arrived. It seemed that the JCP was trying to prevent CPSU ties with the JSP, accusing it of shifting far to the right. When it was rejected, the JCP responded angrily, accusing Moscow of abandoning the working class and failing to appreciate the strategic threat of the U.S.-Japanese alliance. In the summer of 1988 the JCP began to criticize new thinking aggressively, calling it the biggest error since the death of Lenin.[33] Relations in 1989 remained tense.

In 1990 A. I. Senatorov of the CPSU Secretariat accused the JCP of having the most visible difficulty in the world Communist movement of accepting new thinking.[34] He shifts some of the blame to the Soviet leadership's past mistakes, which aroused distrust. Yet he adds that for the JCP it is painful to face the JSP now that the CPSU has widened ties with it as with social democrats in Western Europe. The harsh rhetoric toward the new Soviet policies seen in the JCP newspaper *Akahata* and elsewhere appears, then, to be a sign of desperation to salvage the independence of the JCP before a threat of extinction.

The JCP found Gorbachev a more divisive influence than had been the revived cold war that preceded him. While the Japan-Soviet Society (NisSo Kyōkai) strayed from the party line and worked hard to reinvigorate its activities, the old patriarch of the party Miyamoto Kenji seemed more and more isolated. He wrote in platitudes about his positive outlook for the recovery of socialism and for Gorbachev to bring Lenin's spirit of reform to the Soviet system, and about past underdevelopment of democracy and mistakes of hegemonism, but he could not explain what had happened or identify with Gorbachev's correctives. All that he could do was to offer excuses such as that socialism is only seventy years old while capitalism is three hundred, or that socialism has realized great accomplishments by spreading to the people of the world the values of sexual equality, educational equality, universal health care, and social insurance.[35]

For intellectual circles, the JCP had retained into the 1980s a surprisingly strong moral influence. Now it was rapidly losing influence, which was not easily transferrred to the JSP. Trotskyites and new categories such as Eurocommunists and Bukharinists sought to build a united front on the left, issuing a new bulletin, *Forum '90*. But their approval of socialist pluralism in the world seemed only to fan the fires of fragmentation inside Japan's left wing.

Increasingly from the left of center emerges the argument that the Soviet Union and the United States together form one category and Japan represents a different class of nations. Whereas the two cold war superpowers peered at the world mainly through military sights, Japan looks at it mainly through economic glasses. With the collapse of the Communist world comes also the end of the pax America. Japan must search for its new place, its new burdens, and its international responsibilities in the emerging world order.

Open recanting by sympathizers of socialism was not very common, but the drift toward the center was unmistakable. Among the more flexible and pragmatic sympathizers, Satō Tsuneaki played an influential role. His increasingly pessimistic outlook about the economic prospects of perestroika and of socialism helped to convince others that Gorbachev was incapable of reviving socialism. Among the theoretical economists active in the early postwar socialist heyday, Nonomura Kazuo was exceptional in "confessing" his change of heart in 1989. Earlier in postwar history there had been a succession of famous public conversions from Marxist thinking. By the end of the 1980s hardly anyone noticed, but the process was continuing.

A Split in Academia. Japanese academics were split in their responses in 1988–90 to bilateral negotiations. Those on the far right doubted the chances for success, stressing the need to keep Japanese public opinion resistant to Soviet propaganda. From this perspective, academic inquiry into alternatives often seems more threatening than promising. The right of center concentrated on strategy for gaining the return of the islands, weighing the factors that would determine the outcome such as power relations and events inside each country. The center also was concerned about the territorial disputes but was ready to consider more broadly how Japanese-Soviet relations should evolve. The left of center paid more attention to what Japan might do to improve the negotiating climate, balancing the responsibilities of both parties. Finally, a few on the far left stressed unilateral changes in Japanese policy as a means to spur the Soviet economy, which would somehow become a positive stimulus for realizing the return of territory. Most of these views were expressed during a conference of about seventy scholars at Hokkaidō University during the winter of 1988–89.

When in the final months of 1989 and the first months of 1990 bilateral negotiations were slow to advance, speculation turned to LDP politicians working through informal channels. Was the LDP being targeted by the Kremlin? Did Yakovlev's enigmatic "third way" for achieving a breakthrough call not only for new approaches but also for unofficial channels?[36] The Japanese media grappled with suspicions: for some there was concern that some unsavory deal was being prepared behind closed doors; for others there was the hope that the intransigence of the Gaimushō could be overcome through LDP involvement. At stake was also a shift in the balance between bureaucracy and politics in foreign policy decision making. But shifts perceived in open debates or in behind-the-scenes steps toward negotiations do not alter the reality of a powerful and cautious Gaimushō at the center of the foreign policy process.

THE BILATERAL AGENDA

The Japanese people do not have a compelling or even a principled reason for dramatically improving relations with Moscow. Nor do they, as a rule, act idealistically on the basis of universal beliefs. They are normally pragmatists, eager to win advantage without unduly provoking opposition. Principles can matter, as in the reluctance to push ahead with Soviet ties until the problem of the Northern Territories is resolved. Yet some observers, who do not expect the return of the islands in the near future, predict that hesitation about provoking Washington will be a more serious deterrent for Japanese assistance to Moscow than resentment about the four islands. Others may believe that most serious of all will be the lack of a profit to be made. In any case, without substantial progress on the islands, pragmatism and principle will coincide in opposition to Moscow.

Partial Peace versus Comprehensive Peace. Japan's reentry into the international system remains incomplete. The right blamed the Yalta Treaty and the cold war, provoked by Moscow. The left initially placed most of the blame on the United States, which took advantage of the occupation to leave Japan entangled in the U.S.-Japan mutual security treaty and fully at peace only with America's allies but not with the Soviet Union and China. Each side felt dissatisfied with what seemed to be only a temporary arrangement necessitated (if it really was) by Japan's weakness. The search continues for a comprehensive peace and a world role that will internationalize Japan politically or strategically to complement its existing economic internationalization.

Moscow's Limited Options. Moscow tried over almost the entire postwar era to make a political issue within Japan of Tokyo's refusal to sign a peace treaty with it, of Tokyo's reliance on a security pact making it dependent on the United States rather than on neutrality, and of Tokyo's willingness to station American troops on foreign bases inside Japan. These were hotly contested political questions for more than a decade, but they are not of much concern to the Japanese people any more. Now realizing that it cannot arouse opposition through old tactics, Moscow would like to revive interest in the whole question of the balance of Japan's foreign policy through new methods. It has variously drawn attention to a promised visit by Gorbachev, a Gorbachev speech that demonstrates Moscow's respect and realism, unofficial Soviet proposals on the islands that demonstrate Moscow's flexibility, and other direct and indirect approaches allegedly showing Soviet sincerity. Moscow has looked eagerly for partners—to Nakasone, to influential voices in the LDP, to prominent academics in the mainstream, but not to peripheral figures on the left who might perpetuate its past reputation for scoring propaganda at the expense of realism.

There just does not appear to be any way the Soviet Union can gain a firm spot on the political agenda except to act on the territorial problem. The reformed JSP still wants to reduce dependence on Washington and to find a way in the not-too-distant future to remove American bases and. reduce the Self-Defense Forces; yet despite the obvious overlap in thinking it will not touch the Soviet issue for fear of contamination in the eyes of the public. Few in Japan are predicting a crack in the national consensus on the Northern Territories. That leaves Moscow with no option but to give back the four islands in some negotiated fashion or remain excluded from serious Japanese attention.

Many Japanese are not predicting an agreement on the islands within the foreseeable future. The reasons vary. Moscow was never serious about negotiations, say some on the right. Japan will not compromise, say others on the left. Recently, intermediate views can be heard more often. In 1989–90 one heard that Gorbachev and the reformers would try hard to find a formula, but they are endangered by rampant nationalism that leaves no room for a precedent-setting territorial concession. Another centrist view was that economic circumstances are such that Japanese business is not sufficiently interested in the Soviet economy to put up the stakes necessary to make Moscow feel it has much to gain. With the announcement in the fall of 1989 that Gorbachev will visit Tokyo in 1991, some silver lining appeared through the clouds.

In comparison to the normally fleeting attention of the American public to disparate international concerns, Japan's preoccupation with the Northern Territories issue suggests a less flexible approach to world problems. In the cycles of changing questions that have risen to the fore since 1985, the obsession with one issue never is far from the surface. Yet the range of serious debate about how the issue might be resolved is rather narrow. There is a dearth of spontaneity from below and a carefully managed approach from above. Above all, the decision makers sought unanimity, firmness, and patience. On many issues this could be a formula for delay.

There is reluctance to equate Japan's position to the German position. Raising a doubtful note, Itō Kenichi reminded Japanese that their country is different from Germany, which attacked the Soviet Union.[37] In contrast, it was the Soviets who broke the neutrality treaty and occupied the Northern Territories. Japan has the consciousness of a victim. This places a greater burden on Moscow.

Strategy and Consensus. Japanese officials and experts are largely in agreement on the need for a national consensus to deal with the Soviet Union, and some called for a clear-cut strategy as a means to strengthen the consensus and to increase the likelihood of success in negotiations. Many felt that they already had a tough-minded strategy in place from the beginning of the 1980s and there was no need to tamper with it. Increasingly in 1987–88 others disagreed and sought to forge a new strategy combining the carrot and the stick. This seemed to congeal in the second half of 1988, but as the complexity of negotiations became clearer, various critics suggested that Japan's strategy needed to be further refined. This did not necessarily require a formal blueprint. The Gaimushō prefers an informal consensus, guided from above—a long-term, patient strategy to take advantage of the timing of changing international conditions while keeping the will of the Japanese people firm.

Kimura Hiroshi elaborated such an approach in the fall of 1989. In this strategy the territorial question must be part of an overall political, military, and economic security approach, maintaining the Self Defense Forces and the U.S.-Japan security treaty. Through linkage Japan must use its economic power as its biggest bargaining chip. Ordinarily, Kimura added, Japanese are more interested in the spirit rather than the tactics of negotiations, but tactics are important here. Moscow may be persuaded by its national interests, and Japan has the economic might to make that appeal. Japan must help to prepare the right environment in and out of the Soviet Union for the return of the islands.

Kimura shows concern for saving Soviet face. Japan should take the initiative through back channels, secret diplomacy, unofficial contacts, and so forth to show Moscow what it has to gain. Aware of preliminary contacts of this sort, Kimura was encouraging their expansion.[38]

Yakovlev, the Architect of a New Relationship. When Aleksandr Yakovlev visited Japan in November 1989 at the head of a parliamentary delegation and in preparation for Gorbachev's summit visit, he was welcomed as the Soviet leader's right-hand man and special adviser on Japan. After Yakovlev's earlier visit in November 1984, he had become identified as a strong advocate within the Kremlin for improved relations with Tokyo. According to one interpretation, he had learned that the Japanese political, economic, and cultural system was completely different from the American and Canadian system with which he was very familiar and had decided that Japan was a country of the twenty-first century. Deeply impressed by his visit to the memorial to atomic bomb victims in Hiroshima, he strengthened his support for world peace and his "special feelings" toward the United States, which had dropped the bomb. With this background, it was Yakovlev who drafted the statements about Japan in Gorbachev's Vladivostok speech, recognizing it as one of three great world centers of capitalism and correcting the previous one-sided diplomatic emphasis on the United States. Later he allegedly drafted a plan for exchanging the Soviet return of the Northern Territories for removal of American military bases in Japan and supported the idea of appealing to the antinuclear allergy of Japanese public opinion once the territorial issue is resolved. As a holder of a Ph.D degree in history, Yakovlev understands the Japanese position well and is trying to find a new approach, explains Hamada Kazuo.[39]

The Okhotsk Wall. A month after the October 20 issue of *Ogonyok* carried a story about the prosperous Northern Territories under Japanese control in the year 2009, a Japanese journal asked if this was not a hint that Moscow would return the islands.[40] The journal article concluded with speculation about secret Soviet-Japanese diplomacy involving Yakovlev and Suetsugu Ichirō, the head of the citizens' movement for the return of the islands, during Yakovlev's November visit. It ended optimistically with the impression that Moscow will demand little more than that Tokyo agree not to permit American military bases on the four islands it returns. In other words, the wall can disappear just as suddenly and unexpectedly from the Sea of Okhotsk as it did from Berlin.

Shortly afterward another journal carried an article clarifying the role of Suetsugu.[41] It explained that he has been an adviser of Japanese prime ministers since the Okinawa return and that he has built a pipeline to Soviet scholars, party officials, and government officials. When Yakovlev was still unknown, Suetsugu supposedly had been the first Japanese to meet him, and since that time when Suetsugu visits the Kremlin, Yakovlev always makes time for him. The article concluded that given the rapid turnover of late in Japanese prime ministers and foreign ministers, it is good to have a private citizen "fixer" working as an unofficial channel. The source is careful to add that the fact that Moscow is in a hurry to make a breakthrough by the time of Gorbachev's visit does not mean that all is smooth sailing. Yakovlev's visit was no more than a fact-finding mission to report to Gorbachev, not a real negotiating process to cut a deal, as implied in the earlier sensational article.

In early 1990 Kimura Hiroshi also responded optimistically to the *Ogonyok* article. He suggested that through the decision to return the islands, Japanese-Soviet trade would approach Japanese-Chinese trade rather than remain at one-third of its level.[42]

Dispelling Soviet Apprehension. A member of the editorial board of the *Asahi shimbun* proposed a new strategy for Japan in February 1989.[43] He said that we stand at a big turning point in world history. This year the Soviets have withdrawn from Afghanistan, the Sino-Soviet summit will take place, and the Cambodian problem is being addressed. A new wind is blowing away dead leaves. The cold war structure is beginning to thaw. The source of this is the Gorbachev regime in Moscow. The editorial added that new winds should also blow in Japan-Soviet relations. It is a good sign that tough Soviet attitudes are now softening. Japan needs to change too.

The editorial quickly added that Japan must stay firm to get Gorbachev to resolve the main problem, while at the same time dispelling natural Soviet apprehensions by explaining that a territorial agreement will not be a precedent for tampering with European borders set at Yalta. (In other words, Japan's goal is not to question the Yalta accords.) Also, Japan can erase the vagueness in the security treaty with the United States in a way that will enhance Soviet-American trust. The analysis observes that in history almost never is a territorial dispute resolved by negotiating on it alone. Economic, defense, social, and cultural issues must be addressed in a mix that proves productive. Japan must also expand the information pipeline to the Soviets so it is well understood, as Europe is. Mutual trust will help to produce an agreement.

Persistence and Patience. Kimura Hiroshi explains the psychology behind the national approach to the four islands. Most Japanese have a fixed territorial conception rooted in the continuity of territory from the earliest times to the present. Geography, nationality, language, culture, politics, and administration form a unified environment, the disturbance of which causes psychological distress. To this century Japan did not snatch territory from others nor was it invaded. Although Russians are accustomed to border contractions and expansions with the vicissitudes of war, this thinking is foreign to Japan. For Japanese, Kimura argues, it is not a matter of Soviet weakness to abandon the fruits of its war, because territory is seen not as the spoils of the victor but as the inherent right of a nation. Washington understood this sentiment in returning Okinawa; why cannot Moscow, with its enormous territorial reach, realize this too? If it did, it would win sympathy from the Japanese people and end the use of the territorial tool by those with purposes considered to be "anti-Soviet."[44] Moscow's eyes are narrowly fixed on maintaining the existing order, not on the far-reaching task of stabilizing the international order. It seems to be afraid to break with the past for fear of stirring up countless unsettled issues. Yet the Pandora's box that would supposedly be opened by letting out the four islands may not have many objects ready to stir. After all, the Helsinki accords made European borders inviolable. Kimura does not single out the Baltic states, but just as his book was going into print, a human chain was formed across the three states to remember the fiftieth anniversary of the Hitler-Stalin pact of 1939 that placed their territory in Soviet hands. The Pandora's box was already open before Soviet-Japanese negotiations reached fruition.

Kimura adds that the Japanese people are not guided by military or strategic ambitions in seeking the islands. The main economic benefit to Japan of fishing rights also cannot account for the national scale of the movement for their return. The psychological value is what counts. If the Soviet side is preoccupied with the military and strategic value of the area, it should reexamine its philosophy of what constitutes national security. Japan and the Soviet Union drew directly opposite conclusions from the ending of World War II about the efficacy of military force. There has been a gap in security perceptions; under Gorbachev's new thinking, signs that it is diminishing are at last becoming visible.

Publishing in a Soviet journal, Kimura elaborates on his cautious but not pessimistic expectations that Soviet thinking will continue to evolve and that patiently, through dialogue, the two countries will resolve their dispute.[45] He stresses that Moscow so far has treated Tokyo as a low priority. As a first step, it must be ready to change that view. Until then, Tokyo should not apply pressure but also should not improve relations. It should try to help the Soviet people understand the true state of relations. In his view, the quicker Gorbachev visits, the better. The more complicated the differences, the more intense should be the dialogue.

Full-blooded Relations. On December 18, 1988, Shevardnadze in Tokyo and on May 17, 1989, Gorbachev in Beijing called for "full-blooded" (*polnokrovnye*) relations with Japan. The Soviet foreign minister added the words "good-neighborly and on a large scale" (*dobrososedskie* and *mashtabnye*).[46] While the exact meaning of full-blooded remained obscure, it invokes images of emotion, warmth, kinship, and a single circulatory system pumping sustenance from one country to the other. Japanese who had simply looked to the possibility of signing a peace treaty that would return four islands were reminded that Moscow sought something more: full integration into the world economy.

Concessions through an Academic Channel. In January 1990 Kimura Hiroshi continued the search for an explanation for Yakovlev's tantalizing words in November that the solution to the territorial question can be found in "a third way." This appears to exclude the earlier Soviet position of no return of the islands and the Japanese position of "the *immediate* return of all *four islands in entirety, without compensation.*" Kimura called on Japan to reexamine its position on each of the underlined elements. As long as all four islands are promised at a certain date, Japan need not insist on an immediate return of all simultaneously (for example, the final two might be transferred in 1999), and it should consider compensation for withdrawal of military and civilian personnel and equipment and regional assistance to Soviet development. Minor concessions are justifiable, he added as he continued the role he assumed in late 1988, if not earlier, to serve as a counterpart to Soviet academics who were airing semi-authoritative compromise proposals in Soviet journals and at meetings in Japan.[47]

Kimura's close connections with the Gaimushō gave added credibility to his reasonableness and calls for compromise. Along with Suetsugu and other "pipes" relying on personal informal diplomacy and Nakasone and Abe relying on "genrō" or elder-statesmen diplomacy, he was developing communications channels in addition to the regular ministerial and vice-ministerial diplomatic channels. Relations advanced through these multiple channels working in close association with each other.

The Islands and Japanese Nationalism. Kimura notes the "quiet rise of nationalism in Japan." As a result of this, he asserts, it is unthinkable that Japan would agree to the return of only two islands when that offer was refused in 1956.[48] Some Japanese reject any compromise on the islands, opposing any concessions to Moscow. Dissociating himself from this sort of nationalism, Kimura seems to be alerting Moscow to the consequences of not acting soon and decisively to reach an agreement before the extreme right is able to capitalize on delay by making Soviet relations into a domestic political issue. As long as the momentum is building toward Gorbachev's 1991 visit, the public will trust the Gaimushō to represent Japan's interests. Yet if the momentum falters or if Gorbachev's visit does not lead to a breakthrough, nationalists would seize upon the issue. The fate of right-wing nationalism in the 1990s is closely tied to the Soviet position on the islands.

Future Relations. If Moscow returns the islands, will Japan radically change its view of the Soviet Union? Of course, relations will improve, but few Japanese in 1989 expected a dramatic change in Japanese thinking. It was usually assumed that the Soviet Union will be destined to remain a military superpower. Even with a weak economy it will emphasize high-technology imports and often engage in espionage. This Japanese viewpoint leads to concern for careful controls on exports. There seems to be some anxiety that South Korea and the other NIES will not be equally careful in their trade.

Whatever Japan's difficulties with the United States, it would be far-fetched to expect coziness with the Soviet Union. Empathy with the Soviet people is low. Idealism about Gorbachev was not as high as elsewhere in the West. For the foreseeable future, Moscow can hope for cordiality, not conviviality. Of course, this is much better than the likely outcome if the territorial question is not resolved. If that happened, Moscow could expect resentment, with little or no respect.

For Japanese, Gorbachev's visit presents an opportunity to showcase the ultramodern material world of their society against the backdrop of the backward Soviet economy. Promises of assistance to the Soviets highlight areas where Japan is a world leader, both in technological innovation and in human resources and organizational strengths responsive to desperate Soviet needs. After the spotlight of 1990 often centered on ties with West Germany, the leading Soviet trading partner in Western Europe, it will now suggest a sandwich effect with Japan, which is already the leading trading partner in Asia, serving as the counterpart on the opposite side. Cultural symbolism also is significant, pointing to how deeply embedded distrust is being overcome on the Japanese side, and the "Japanomania" of the Soviet people (in 1989 Japan was found to be the most popular country for the Soviets) is rising to new heights. By assuaging Japanese feelings of being victimized, reevaluating the events of 1945 and the internment policies, Gorbachev could create a psychological climate for a successful summit assuming that the territorial question could be neutralized.

What matters most to the Soviet people is a boost to their ailing economy, with not merely an immediate infusion of urgently needed consumer staples but also the long-term transfer of the technological foundation for building a competitive economy. The fall 1990 Miryukov white paper on the Japanese economy points the way to Soviet expectations. It is not insignificant that simultaneously the papers prepared by Japanese participants from Suetsugu's Council on National Security Problems at the Leningrad meeting of October 1990 presented a rosy picture of what would follow from a new era in bilateral relations. Seeking a positive decision on returning the four islands, they whetted Moscow's appetite the way a lush, tropical oasis would appeal to the desert traveler frighteningly low on provisions. This was no mirage, but it also was no free lunch available simply for the taking.

The balance of power in the Asia-Pacific region had shifted as the United States and Japan fueled spectacular growth in the prosperous regional capitalist economy accompanied by increasing cooperation, while the Soviet Union and China plunged into conflict and economic decline at the same time as other socialist economies in the region were isolated and uncompetitive. Once the Sino-Soviet relationship was being normalized and China opened its door to capitalist economies, regional realignments have followed. Soviet-American cooperation now makes possible new regional ties, but there are also many lingering obstacles. Japanese are aware that some of those obstacles are rooted in their country's ties to China and Southeast Asia and to economic frictions with the United States, but they identify as the first priorities for regionwide cooperation the need to overcome the deep distrust of the Soviet Union among the Japanese people and to resolve the disputes involving the socialist countries of North Korea and Cambodia. Many stages and many types of negotiations, some bilateral and others multilateral, are needed to build a regional community.

Beginning to look beyond the return of the islands, analysts see discussions widening to security issues in Northeast Asia, marked by Soviet promises to reduce military forces in the region substantially. Confidence-building measures would follow, perhaps leading to a conference on security and cooperation in Northeast Asia similar to the one in Europe. Some of the steps would have military significance as the Soviets agreed to a defensive posture and the Japanese promised to maintain their defensive approach toward the SDF, with the United States actively involved in these agreements. Other steps would have symbolic value as Moscow's agreements with Tokyo confirmed its status as a regional political power. Beginning with recognition of its decisive role in Northeast Asia, Japan would then extend its political activism and quest for the trappings of leadership to negotiations centering on other parts of the Asia-Pacific region and beyond. At last in 1990 the way forward could be discerned, unfolding once Japan passed through the gateway of the Gorbachev Tokyo summit. Agreement on the islands was the key to this passage.

THE INTERNATIONAL CONTEXT

A Restraining Superpower. Japan is a predictable country that rarely springs surprises on the world. The Communist bloc, however, is full of unexpected turns in foreign policy. Kimura Hiroshi lists many of them, ranging from the criticism of Stalin in 1956 to the recent improvement in Sino-Soviet relations, and wonders if the return of the Northern Territories will not be added to the list. Soviet diplomacy reveals a strong opportunistic element and many instances of unexpected concessions, recently including territorial ones to China. Either danger or hope could follow. There are circumstances related to security and politics that would lead to a return of the Northern Territories, Kimura concludes.[49] The new Japanese superpower will be more consistent, as it has been pursuing its territorial demand toward Moscow over more than three decades.

One can expect Japan to be a restraining force on the United States. If the Japanese-Soviet conflict continues, either over the territorial issue or over the military balance in the Asia-Pacific region, pressure from Tokyo could slow improvement in Soviet-American relations. If the conflict is ended and Moscow convinces Tokyo of its sincerity in seeking a more peaceful world, Tokyo could eventually pressure Washington to convert more quickly to a post–cold war peacetime economy. Given Tokyo's caution, one would not expect this transition to occur abruptly. It would take clever, long-range thinking in Moscow to figure out how to play the Japan card, not so much against the United States as toward a shift in American thinking.

Internationalism without a clear victory for the extreme right or for a new coalition including the left of center leads to a status quo superpower. This is the pattern visible at the end of the 1980s. On many occasions Tokyo has cautioned its allies about moving too quickly or decisively. Tokyo's reactions toward the Soviet government at the Toronto summit in 1988 and toward the Chinese government at the Paris summit in 1989 were largely supportive of the status quo. It cautioned its allies not to be overeager to embrace ongoing Soviet changes or to condemn the recent Chinese brutality at Tiananmen. At the first stage, it is Moscow that is likely to experience Tokyo's restraining influence.

Japan Is Vulnerable. Former ambassador to the Soviet Union Nakagawa Tōru compares the emerging world attitude toward the Soviet Union to the international response after the Russo-Japanese War.[50] After Russia had advanced into Manchuria, Japan allied with England and, drawing on material and spiritual help from America and England, defeated Russia. When the Russian threat in the Far East soon receded, however, America quickly cooled toward Japan and saw it as the threat in the region. Discriminatory legislation and containment of Japan through the Washington Treaty soon followed. Now the Americans and others see the Soviet Union receding as a threat in military and political competition and the crisis mentality of Japan-bashing intensifying against its economic rival. Again, as in the 1920s, Japanese are exercising patience and self-restraint. Other articles warn of American public opinion switching to the view that the Japanese (economic) threat exceeds the Soviet military threat. In response, they sometimes note, the Japanese are seeing America's economic policies toward Japan as more of a threat than the Soviet military.[51]

Sono Akira referred to the Beijing summit as a joint funeral for Communist dictatorship.[52] Both countries are in a stage of crisis. Normalization that pigeonholes ideology signifies a faint reconciliation. China will not forget Russia's territorial seizures of the past. Antihegemonism is born of a desire for historical, nationalistic revenge. Moscow's appeals to Beijing and to Tokyo are made out of desperation. They are nothing more than a trick to withdraw the Asian countries from the influence of the American security system.

As if to reinforce their point that détente means little in the Asia-Pacific region, the Self-Defense Forces in August 1989 announced a build-up of tanks on Hokkaidō.[53] This action was well-suited to the view in some official circles that tensions with the Soviet Union will increase in a time of so-called détente.

Avoiding Soviet Instability. Might a more dangerous Soviet Union arise if the Gorbachev reforms fail? At first, this question was not often asked. The existing negative image may have preempted it. Moderate voices in 1989 were beginning to ask it, however, especially in response to volatile nationality relations. On August 4, 1989, the *Yomiuri shimbun* expressed the worry that in the worst-case scenario the Soviet Union might become destabilized and Stalinism might return.[54] Its conclusion—one that most Japanese have been hesitant to consider—is for the West to exert influence to help steer Soviet reforms forward. In other words, the capitalist powers should act now to support Gorbachev.

The Japanese preference for social stability and order can be seen in other settings, such as in the weak reaction to the crackdown on Chinese demonstrators in June. It might become more visible in future responses to Soviet internal troubles. Whoever represents both reform and order deserves to succeed.

Yokote Shinji is unusual in looking closely at the Great Russian nationalist reaction to the rising tide of confusion and disorder and to the flood of Western values entering the country. He reveals an in-depth knowledge of its history and of articles concerning Russian nationalism during the Gorbachev era. Yokote concludes that its roots are extending deeper into the society, not only on the political stage but also in social consciousness.[55]

CHAPTER FIFTEEN

An Early Look at the Japanese Superpower

SOVIET SUPERPOWER status is fragile. It has lasted for almost a half a century, based on military superiority on much of the Eurasian land mass along with ideological and political comradeship among Communist parties. The disintegrating Soviet economy can no longer bear the burden of high-technology military advances, and the nation's interparty networks have largely collapsed. Its long-term prospects are bleak, although its current military machine is still formidable. Japanese superpower status is hidden. The "Land of the Rising Sun" has preferred to wield its influence below the horizon, unobtrusively letting its vast financial resources shape regional and global policy. Through the remainder of the 1990s Japan is unlikely to retain this role for at least four reasons: (1) the Soviet collapse creates a vacuum and a heightened emphasis on economic rather than military solutions to global problems; (2) the American financial decline makes Washington more dependent on Japanese resources for coping with world problems; (3) the Asia-Pacific region remains unstable and raises many problems of long-term security and economic integration that cannot be solved without Tokyo's leadership; and (4) the Japanese people and their leaders are reaching a turning point in their thinking as they aspire to a new era that promises a new identity.

HEISEI: A NEW PSYCHOLOGY

The year 1989 opened the new Heisei era; the entire year was renamed in January after the Showa emperor Hirohito died. Japanese are accustomed to thinking of reign periods as separate eras in their history—since 1868, each described as having its own identity and even its own psychology. (Meiji borrowing and modernization and Taishō democracy earned mostly positive images; prewar Shōwa militarism is seen negatively, but postwar Shōwa prosperity and democracy are decidedly positive.) Coincidentally, at almost the same time as Heisei began, Japanese were beginning to look beyond the cold war era to a new relationship with both the United States and the Soviet Union. Without delay, the search began to identify a suitable image for the new era, which, given Emperor Akihito's age (he was born in 1933), was expected to last past the first decade of the next century. High expectations show through the customary caution, indicating that Japanese are predisposed to find a new and different image for their future.

With the advent of the Heisei era, Japan's worldview is on the verge of a major reorientation. Neither regional military strength nor international trade centered on the West will meet the country's global needs. If in the period 1900–45 Japan's first preoccupation was Sino-centered, military dominance on Chinese territory and in the surrounding region, and in the period 1945–88 it had shifted to American-centered, export dominance in the American market and elsewhere in the West, the third era of this century appears to demand a global-centered approach, diversified economic integration around the world with close political cooperation and collective military security through negotiated limits on armaments. A country's exclusion from the increasingly integrated economic order threatens to doom it to perpetual poverty. Even a country as vast and powerful as the Soviet Union appreciates the danger from these trends.

The Soviet Union now seeks to become Japan's partner in this new undertaking. To realize this goal and overcome nine decades of intermittent hostility, the Soviets are anxious to convince the Japanese of the need for a new worldview. This task is eased by the rising pressure from the United States against Japan over the existence of a huge trade imbalance, by the warming ties between Washington and Moscow, and by the normalization of Sino-Soviet relations. Suddenly, at the start of the Heisei era, Japan had good reason to reconsider its low visibility, trade-centered diplomacy of the postwar or cold war era. The cycle of confidence begins in the first year of the new reign period. Moscow seeks to benefit from Japan's reorientation, but it is not clear that Moscow has the political will or expertise to reach this goal. Indeed, dissatisifed Soviet Japanologists were rarely hopeful about their government's capacity to adjust, no less so than in early 1991 when academic reformers felt abandoned by Gorbachev's shift to the right.

Longing for a Different World Order. When Gorbachev shifted back to the side of reform in the spring of 1991, the London summit loomed as a test both for Gorbachev to present a genuine reform program and for the seven capitalist states to forge a response for drawing the Soviet Union into a new world order. Tokyo's dilemma was to keep the pressure on Moscow for territorial concessions while demonstrating its own commitment to Western unity in encouraging Moscow to reform and to become part of a new order. In advance of the summit, Primakov went to Tokyo to try to win Kaifu's support. Meanwhile Kaifu called for a worldwide system to monitor all arms transactions—an initiative to highlight Japan's special peacekeeping role. With Gorbachev encouraging the new Democratic Reform Movement, earlier circumstances not conducive to

Japanese assertiveness about long-term thinking were beginning to change.[1]

As Gorbachev weighed a bold new program of privatization in the early summer of 1991 and simultaneously fended off a challenge by hard-liners including his prime minister Valentin Pavlov, figures of 100 billion or more dollars in requested international assistance became popular headline fare. Grigory Yavlinsky's plan called "the Window of Opportunity" was aimed at convincing the capitalist powers of Soviet seriousness about economic change. Yet the Japanese government remained skeptical that plans and laws on paper would be seriously implemented. It feared that aid would simply be lost and with it Tokyo's leverage. The same opponents of privatization were also diehard defenders of national boundaries and military prowess. Only by sweeping them to the sidelines could a new image of Soviet character be cast. The unification of Soviet reformers that was occuring at this time offered new promise, but, given the high stakes, it was clear that Tokyo would wait for further results. As at the three previous seven-nation summits, Japan led in caution toward Gorbachev.

With the "death of socialism" message still ringing in their ears, Japanese in the latter part of 1989 were aroused by a more resounding call. The issue was not socialism, but capitalism. Much of the vocabulary was transferred from the socialist camp. In place of the old Sino-Soviet split, attention shifted to the impending Japanese-American split. The notion of containment now applied to Washington's policy toward Tokyo. Anti-Soviet rhetoric was paralleled by criticisms of Japan-bashing. The Brezhnev doctrine had its counterpart in the pax Americana. When Prime Minister Kaifu visited Washington in September, some commentators likened it to the old system of alternative residence (*sankin kōtai*) in the Tokugawa era. The regional lords were obliged to journey to Edo (Tokyo) and spend every other year or some other designated time there (along with leaving their families hostage) as a measure of social control. In their domains they enjoyed considerable autonomy, but in interdomain relations they were subject to the will of the shogun in Edo. Moscow and Washington really did not treat their vassal states very differently, some Japanese seemed to be thinking.

The Soviet Disease and the New Age. In the emerging Japanese worldview, the advanced capitalist countries have entered a new age, sometimes called the service-sector revolution, based on advanced technology. The Soviet Union long would not take risks with new technology and, as a result of this conservatism, trails badly. It could not overcome the "technology gap." Accustomed in the 1970s to referring to the "English disease" of economic irresponsibility, wasteful management, slack labor discipline, and slow technological reform, Japanese now focus on a more serious illness. Morimoto Tadao describes the system of storming in the second half of the month as unbelievable to a Japanese.[2] Also in conflict with Japanese principles is the Soviet practice of aging officials who remain in office at all levels and delay the advance of a new generation, leaving able persons demoralized, without career opportunities. Elsewhere we can find the contrasting message that Japan's employment system, with minor modifications, is well-suited to the new age.

Another key point in Japanese reasoning is that in the new information age, even more than in the past, it is essential to be able to compare your country with other countries. Long uninformed about the world's development, the Soviet people did not develop a crisis mentality or burn with reform energy. Implied is a contrast with the earlier desperate efforts of the Japanese to catch up. Initiative from below is accepted and essential for the Japanese. Comparison, in which emphasis is placed on one's own shortcomings, is necessary to elicit a sense of urgency.

In the Lower House election of February 18, 1990, the LDP staked its claim as the party "responding to the call for the twenty-first century."[3] Kaifu used Doi's refusal to renounce her party's old document calling for a "socialist revolution" to associate her with the failed thinking of the past. In turn, the LDP claimed through its economic successes and policies to be in the forefront of the international transition to an era of trade liberalization and economic integration. How quickly the mood about the world had turned optimistic can be appreciated by recalling the response nine months earlier of Uno Sōsuke to Gorbachev's announcement in Beijing of a unilateral troop cut in the Far East. Uno told a Diet committee that this will not change the "basic structure of confrontation between the East and the West."[4] Previously the party that could best handle the confrontation, the LDP, had turned into the party most prepared for integration.

THE END OF THE COLD WAR

The significance of the end of the cold war is enormous for the world and for Japan.[5] This was a sentiment shared by some on the right and by many on the left. The age of confrontation is ending. Ideologically, militarily, and even economically, an enormous historical watershed has been reached.

Yuri Afanasyev's visit to Japan in October 1989 is best remembered for his statement of support for the return of all four islands to Japan. Also during this visit he spoke to a symposium of historians about new currents in socialism. He described the Yalta system as extending from the Berlin Wall to the Japanese Archipelago, adding that a different means apart from this system must be found.[6] This interpretation is in line with Japanese thinking about their victimization at the hands of Moscow and the significance of ending the Yalta system.

When bilateral negotiations were floundering at the end of 1989 as the two sides seemed to be talking past each other, the *Yomiuri shimbun* observed that Moscow wants Tokyo to accept the postwar reality while Tokyo wants Moscow to realize that the Yalta system is dead.[7] To shelve the resolution of the island dispute, for the Japanese, is to leave the postwar order in place. The significance of the four islands is comparable to that of the Berlin Wall.

De-Yaltaization." In November 1989 Nishimura Fumio elucidated the consequences of the "world repartition" being conducted by Gorbachev and Bush, which he called "de-Yaltaization." This result can be traced not only to the Sino-Soviet split dividing the Communist movement and the breakdown of socialism from within, which weakened the Soviet hold over Eastern Europe, but also to the strength of the postwar defense and free trade systems under American leadership and to the reduction of America's relative strength in the face of the economic rise of Europe and Japan. Pluralism developed around the axis of East-West relations based on two military superpowers. As the power of both receded, the basis for the old order shifted. Soviet leaders realized that their country must cross the rubicon to capitalism and democracy to emerge from its stagnation; join world economic organizations and follow the model of the newly industrializing economies in Asia; and live in the common European house. Soon the independence movements engulfed the advanced Baltic areas, while the internal "Northern Territories" problem of Nagorno-Karabakh divided Armenia and Azerbaijan. These circumstances opened the way to Eastern European rejection of communism, to concern about German unification, and also to new interest in peaceful agreement over the Korean question.

According to Nishimura, the Soviet side is now showing understanding of Japan's postwar national feeling about the POW issue, and among Soviet historians are those who advocate returning all four islands in a batch, which shows understanding of Japan's position. More and more important to Moscow are the economic benefits of Japanese ties. There is no doubt that if political relations improve, the opportunity can be grasped for lively development of economic relations too.[8] This would be a further step linking areas as widely separated as East Germany and Japan in the struggle to break out of the unjust and restrictive confines of the postwar Yalta agreement. The Northern Territories symbolize the Yalta order, which, in turn, represents the postwar world division Japan is now eagerly aiming to overturn.

The Collapse of Twentieth-Century Totalitarianism. Amaya Naohiro describes the twentieth century as a tragic age of warring states when first rightist totalitarianism, including Japanese militarism, was destroyed in 1945 and now leftist totalitarianism is collapsing. Altogether on the battlefield, on the execution grounds, and in prisons, tens of millions were killed. In the name of the whole (the public), the individual (the private) was repressed. Failure resulted from believing that somehow bureaucratic control could manage an economy, and that somehow, without criticism of the use of power, corruption could be prevented. Yet Amaya cautiously adds that a decade or two of groping in the dark may be needed before freedom can be expected.[9] The implication is that Japan is ready for this transition, but it will have to be patient.

By the summer of 1990 leading Sovietologists had concluded that the Soviet Union could not avoid the wave of East Europeanization and that Gorbachev himself was transferring power from the Communist party to the parliament and the presidential council, apparently leading to multiple parties. Yet this did not produce high expectations for full-scale convergence. As Hakamada Shigeki wrote, Eastern Europe has a tradition of civil society. The Baltic republics share this, but Russian traditions are different. A mixed result is expected, with dangers of anarchy encouraging a strong hand at the top as part of a distinctive Russian amalgam.[10]

Triangular Superpower Relations. The Japanese media closely followed the American public opinion surveys showing an inverse relationship between the decline in concern over a Soviet military threat and the rise in concern over a Japanese economic threat. For instance, in October 1989 they underlined the *Newsweek* report that the imbalance in favor of the Japanese economic threat had climbed to 52 percent versus 33 percent of respondents. This was also the time when George Bush was proclaiming the end of containment policies, the American media was applauding the administration's decision to help perestroika succeed, and James Baker and Eduard Shevardnadze were invoking the language of mutual interests. According to the *Asahi shimbum*, the United States was converging with the countries of Western Europe in its stance toward Moscow, while the world's second economic great power was pretending to turn a deaf ear to these changes while spinning on top of a pachinko ball and going nowhere.[11] More confident that their course was correct, Japanese also carefully measured their country within a triangular framework.

Is Japan a Winner in the Cold War? The Japanese answer to that question is "no": because their country is politically dependent and still victimized by the USSR, they do not have the psychological fruits of victory. Victory, in Japanese thinking, means just rewards for success in competition. They are successful in postwar competition, but their rewards remain incomplete.

Despite confidence in Japan's competitiveness versus the United States, there is uncertainty about the new era. Many complexities lie ahead—psychologically with the United States now increasingly identifying Japan as an opponent; economically with the Newly Industrializing Economies of Asia as they remain ambivalent about integration with Japan into a regional economy comparable to European economic unity; politically with the "South," poor and desperate enough to destabilize the world; and strategically with the Soviet Union, a declining superpower that may, because of domestic and international problems, have trouble finding a secure place in the world. On the whole, Japanese are rather optimistic about regaining more of their independence and becoming a kind of superpower; yet they are cognizant that a tortuous transition in the 1990s looms ahead before they can achieve the promise of the twenty-first century.

Postwar Thinking Is Incomplete. In September 1990 there was a conjunction of American criticisms of Japan for not supporting the resistance to Iraq sufficiently and Japan's belated rewriting of its "Defense White Paper" to eliminate any reference to a Soviet threat. *Asahi shimbun* asked somewhat noncommittally if Japan has merely become an observer chanting pacifism while leaving the dirty work to the United States, or if America's escalation followed by blame for its allies' insufficient contributions does not actually leave the impression of American isolation.[12] It concluded by asking if other countries can believe in a country that lacks self-confidence.

After six years of transition in thinking, Japan was still far from achieving a confident outlook on its future world role. It still faced the inertia of: (1) isolationism, while speaking of the need to realize internationalism; (2) bureaucratism, slow to respond to new opportunities in the face of departmental divisions and competition as well as distrust of outside participation; (3) factionalism, resulting from rival political factions within the LDP seeking their turn in power; and (4) economism, aiming to continue to gain economic advantage around the world without becoming drawn into the thicket of political responsibility. Without overcoming these problems, Japanese were still groping for a new world role.

The Nightmare of a Return to Pre-Yalta. In Europe one worry in early 1990 was a return to a powerful, united Germany threatening to other countries. Japan is also a defeated power with a strong economy. As the new world order is established, will the two victorious superpowers be no less wary of its potential threat?[13] This concern was being aired in Japanese journals as they tried to understand the psychology of a new era.

RALLYING INTERNATIONAL SUPPORT

In 1988 Tokyo took new initiatives to draw on the support of its two groups of major partners: the West and the East Asian and ASEAN countries. Tokyo sought Washington's direct and public advocacy of the Northern Territories claim at the Moscow superpower summit, and then it again rallied Washington and the other Western powers to its side at the Toronto capitalist industrial power summit. At Toronto, it also played the role of regional spokesman for the interests of Asia-Pacific countries faced with continued Soviet military build-up. Tokyo can be expected to continue to take a lead in expressing a regional position toward Moscow. The old notion of East-West relations was always a misnomer; it might be better to revise our geographic symbols into North (the Soviet Union), West (the United States, its European allies, and Canada), and East (Japan and the region it hopes to represent, or perhaps a separate socialist East for China), assigning North-East relations a separate identity. Tokyo may increasingly take the lead in this pairing.

Japan's internationalization of its concerns also was seen in an August 1988 map mission to redraw world maps that do not clearly show the Northern Territories as Japanese territory.[14] Future educational efforts will undoubtedly be part of the public relations emphasis in the information era. The internationalization of the Northern Territories question begins a new process of the Japanese superpower rallying support for itself.

Beyond Bilateralism. Some Japanese volunteer that the Northern Territories and other problems that divide Japan from the Soviet Union require not a bilateral but a trilateral approach. After all, they add, the United States created the territorial question by its handling of the Yalta agreement and by Dulles's warnings in the 1950s. Furthermore, naval security in the Northwest Pacific is as much an American matter as it is a Japanese one. Occasionally one even hears the suggestion that China is also involved in the general security question; therefore, even a quadrilateral approach is worthy of consideration. Yet few would look favorably on the complexity of bringing China into negotiations until it became absolutely necessary at a late stage.

These ideas about going beyond bilateralism are not shared in official circles. When George Bush asked Prime Minister Uno in mid-1989 whether there is anything he can do on the island dispute, the Japanese response was something to the effect, "It is nice of you to offer, but the problem is basically bilateral." Japanese officials have in the past few years told Americans that they are pleased with the interest and the desire to help, but they have also made it clear that they are in charge this time. Some analysts suggest that as long as there is some hope of Soviet responsiveness, American involvement would be counterproductive—a kind of pressure tactic that would cause Moscow to lose face. Others say that Washington might not handle the matter properly—either because it is too eager for a deal on other matters and could not be counted on, or because American hawks do not relish the prospect of a Soviet-Japanese reconciliation, especially as American paranoia about the Japanese superpower grows. In fact, leading analysts express satisfaction with the way the issue is being handled and with the views of top American leaders, who both stand behind Japan with encouragement and seem to be sincere in desiring progress toward a settlement. It is important to Tokyo that Washington keep its distance and let its Pacific partner manage all but regional security issues with the Soviet Union.

The London Summit. After Boris Yeltsin's popular election as Russian president and his successful visit to Washington in June 1991, Gorbachev sought his cooperation in preparing an economic reform program prior to the seven-nation summit in July, which for the first time would end with the Soviet leader's visit. Despite resistance from others in the Communist leadership, Gorbachev drew on a package aimed at soliciting aid from the summit participants. Japan was placed in a pivotal position, balancing hesitation due to bilateral factors with pressures to work closely with its partners, in finding a formula for support. The response to Gorbachev's renewed reforms became a test even for Japanese-American relations.

The Japanese seek reassurance from Washington that their country is treated in accord with its new superpower status. An absolute necessity is full support for Tokyo's territorial demand for the four islands held by Moscow. To the Japanese public, the issue is becoming increasingly central at summit meetings of Western leaders. So far Washington has understood this concern and has complied. During Kaifu's first meeting with President Bush, Bush reassured him that Washington would not surprise Japan and would stress Japan's interests in its disarmament negotiations with Moscow, adding that the United States completely supports Japan's position on the return of the Northern Territories and is ready to cooperate. Kaifu expressed gratitude for this remark on the Northern Territories question.[15]

Surprises still complicate relations between Japanese and American leaders. For Japan, relations with China are a matter of special sensitivity. The Kissinger "shock" of 1971 when Washington moved secretly to open ties with China left a still relatively weak Japan reeling in disbelief. Revelations in early 1990 that George Bush had sent two of his top foreign policy officials to Beijing twice (once in July at the very time that Americans expressed dismay with the Japanese government for not taking a sufficiently tough stance toward the leadership that had massacred Chinese citizens around Tiananmen) left some influential Japanese feeling betrayed again. Such reactions sow the seeds of Japanese mistrust of Washington's relations with Moscow as well.

Confidence toward the United States. Many Japanese share the belief that the United States is mismanaging its economy and society. While official statements to this effect are rare, in November 1989 negotiations in which both countries were expected to air their criticisms prompted sweeping complaints about American schools, federal deficits, and industrial organization.[16] The Structural Impediments Initiative (SII) soon produced a preliminary agreement and also more clarity about the Japanese point of view.

A Respected Superpower. Japanese are beginning to wonder how they can convert their country's economic might not only into a source of pressure to recover the Northern Territories but also into a building block for the respect and authority customarily granted to a superpower. Of course, its foreign aid program, which is now easily the largest source of civilian economic assistance in the world, can be expected to raise its standing in the Third World. Its cautious response toward China in the summer of 1989, supportive of stability above democracy and continued economic development above pressure for political change, may keep its pursuit of a common regional position with China (and other countries in East Asia and ASEAN) on track despite that socialist country's lurch toward stricter Communist dictatorship. If the atmosphere of confrontation between East and West diminishes in Southeast Asia after the settlement of the Cambodian fighting and in Northeast Asia as the Korean conflict becomes less volatile, Japan can make some gains toward becoming a regional leader. From this region, it seeks what it could not gain by military might and occupation a half century earlier—a coprosperity sphere that enhances Japan's world leadership.

We can expect future international tensions that force Japan to choose between its two partnerships with Asia and the West. As long as the Soviet Union is a potential threat and China is an uncertain supporter of regional stability, Japan can be expected to side with the West on most major issues. Yet to some degree, its values will be in conflict with both sides. Loyalty may take precedence over principle, economic stability may take priority over democracy, consistency may be preferred to idealism. When these preferred values are at the forefront, Japan may find it hard to earn the respect of the United States and some European nations. The way it handles relations with Moscow has become an early test of such differences.

Respect from Moscow is measured partly in priorities. Often in 1988–89 Japanese sources ordered the major countries in terms of their priority to Moscow. Always Japan was well down on the list, below China and below Western European powers.[17] Signs that Japan's turn is coming or that it has lately been rising in priority are taken as evidence that Moscow's reordering—its realism—is advancing, if still incomplete.

One can speculate that there is a connection between receiving respect and realism from Moscow and decreasing deference and dependency on Washington. Japanese are interested not only in the hierarchy of military and economic power, but also in the less tangible hierarchy of political and cultural power. Their success over the past four decades gives them the confidence to aspire to more than economic power. The Soviet Union is the obvious and immediate target that has stood in Japan's way. Whether in supporting Japan against the Soviet Union or as the next or more serious target, the United States will also be tested by this process.

Japan's Diplomatic Cards. As the world was changing abruptly in late 1989, Kamo Takehiko reminded readers that Japan has some cards due to its technological and economic power and asked what proposals Japan should introduce in the new environment in order to play them. He called for abandoning the former localized viewpoint in favor of a global security based on Japan's self-confidence.[18] In other words, Japan must behave as a superpower, taking advantage of the strong hand it has been dealt.

THE SOVIET UNION AS A MICROCOSM FOR A WORLD IN CRISIS

Wada Haruki went to the Soviet Union in the spring of 1987 uncertain about whether perestroika was for real. He verified that it was and returned with a book aimed at showing the Japanese people what he saw. Three years later he updated this analysis with a book demonstrating that perestroika had advanced beyond expectations, but also indicating that it was now at a turning point. Wada recounts the Russian tradition of reforms from above: Peter I's Westernization and modernization on the foundation of serfdom and of a population closed within a traditional culture who saw Peter as a German; Alexander II's balance between reformers on one side, and bureaucrats and aristocrats on the other, leading to great reforms such as the emancipation of the serfs but also to barriers to political democracy and constitutionalism, and finally to assassination by a young member of the Narodniki; Nicholas II's concessions with Stolypin in charge following the 1905 Revolution, leading to individual farming and local administrative autonomy, but also to the tsar's resistance to parliamentary plans, and finally to Stolypin's assassination by a young agent of the secret police; and Stalin's actions within this tradition of revolution from above in seeking industrialization without liberalization.[19] Finally Gorbachev appeared. After four years of reform from above, Gorbachev realized the danger of staying on this course, which was reaching an impasse. Gorbachev at last appreciated that sustained transformation required wide initiative from below. It would be necessary to achieve a linkage with reform from below.

The Soviet atmosphere of 1990 favored a complete rejection of the past. The October Revolution was unnecessary, the Soviet people had decided. An identity crisis in which people stopped believing in anything had been born despite some revival of the Orthodox church. Historians have fallen into a crisis too, unable to offer a new, persuasive historical image to replace the rejected old image.

Wada suggests that Russia has had a dual attitude toward the West, seeing it as teacher and as enemy. This led to the incomplete reforms of Peter, Alexander, and Stalin. But now perestroika is real Westernization, completely linking Russia to human civilization. The essence of this change is democratization, bringing from the West individual autonomy, a civil society, the rule of law, and a separation of powers. But it is insufficient and impossible simply to repeat the path of the West in this post-industrial era and this age of ecological limits on economic growth. Russia is the East as well as the West. It is part of what Wada calls a new "Eurasian house." Ethnically diverse, Russia needs humanistic and democratic principles for peaceful coexistence and mutual aid. Wada argues for a new social democracy but says it will first be necessary to advance to capitalism through parliamentary democracy and a market economy. In our age of world economy, the Japanese model is instructive for growth and efficiency, but on a global scale differences between the rich and poor are widening, and as resources are exhausted a crisis arises in the life system. The Japanese model is not sufficient, Wada indicates. A new model is needed. It points the way to the new model. The Soviet Union is a microcosm of humanity. Perestroika must be linked to a new age of justice and equality on earth, Wada insists.[20]

The nationality question finally became a major Japanese concern in 1990. A book written by five Japanese Sovietologists (four in their forties, among the younger generation in the field) with regional interests offered a well-rounded review of the situation in many parts of the Soviet Union. It discussed the "Lebanonization" of the country, suggesting that growing nationalism could follow either the peaceful Strassburg path of the European Community or the military Sarajevo path which sparked World War I. Gorbachev is trying to reorganize the Soviet Union as a league of sovereign states under a new Soviet constitution that recognizes pluralism on nationality questions. This would lead to a dual character: a kind of British-style commonwealth for Asian regions, with western regions attaching to a greater Europe. The Baltic countries would become completely independent, but a Slavic league would also enter the greater

Europe. The authors acknowledged that this scenario may stumble against the problem of finding a control system in place of Communist party control. Also, they added, the West may be reluctant to incorporate a country still holding onto colonies that have an Islamic and Asian history. Resolving the Northern Territories dispute forms part of the end of the twentieth-century system, the authors noted. The Iraqi invasion of Kuwait heightens the cultural clash between greater Europe and the Islamic world. It also pushes the Gorbachev Soviet Union toward the West and toward a new European-centrism.[21]

ASIA IN THE NEW AGE

Looking ahead to the post–cold war era, some Japanese observers welcome the breakdown in the Yalta system in Asia as well as internationally. To them this system signifies the division of Europe into East and West, Japan's loss of the Northern Territories, and Japanese dependency on the United States to counter the Soviet menace in Asia. Events in Hungary and Poland tore an opening in the Iron Curtain.[22] How that opening might be extended to the post-Yalta system Asia-Pacific region is beginning to interest the analysts.

Asia Is Not Europe. The English word "post" (*posuto*) could be found in many headlines early in 1990. In *Chūō kōron* one group discussed the "post-Malta" world.[23] In *Sekai shūhō* a series of articles centered on "post-Yalta."[24] The future "postsocialism" had become the future "post-postwar."

There were objections to this optimistic outlook about the demise of the old order. Even for some of those who granted that 1989 was an epoch-making turning point in world history, the main line of argument was that Asia and Europe should not be confused: Asian Communist dictatorships remain, and the Northern Territories block progress in Soviet-Japanese relations, which are decisive for resolving Asian tensions. Asia lacks the background for quick resolution of problems as is occurring in Europe. The European balanced state system dates from the mid-seventeenth century and operated as a latent foundation in both West and East Europe. Asia lacks this history and has diverse social systems and standards of living; the conditions are absent for building a common house.[25]

Even after acknowledging the Soviet defeat in the cold war in Europe, some on the far right contended that the threat to Japan would not end. In early 1990 Hōgen Shinsaku argued that Moscow plotted anew for Asia-Pacific hegemony. As is their tradition, Russians would seize an opportunity to attack weaker countries. It would not return the Northern Territories because it regards territory as a means to power, and it profits from the military role of the islands in the region.[26] Katō Eiichi found a different line of argument, contending that Moscow was plotting to drive the United States out of Europe and to seize total control there.[27]

In June 1990 Akino Yutaka argued that the Soviet Union is very weak economically and culturally in the Asia-Pacific region, and before the spring of 1986 it saw the region only as a stage for Soviet-American and Soviet-Chinese confrontation. But later it became fascinated with participation in what may become the world's economic center, finding many plusses in ending the cold war here. If Soviet economic reforms to cast off socialism succeed, the Soviet Union could have a rosy future playing the role of bridge between the two economic spheres of Europe and the Asia-Pacific region. If it fails, it could have a dark future split between its Asian and European parts. If Gorbachev and Yeltsin work together to overcome the crisis of lost identity, Akino is hopeful that a bridge will, indeed, be built.[28]

The Cold War Ends in East Asia. If, as Marc S. Gallicchio contends, Washington and Moscow began the cold war in East Asia, then it should be no surprise that the cold war will end there. Originally the struggle centered on territories abandoned by Japan on the Asian mainland and over islands as well. Stalin sought to occupy Hokkaidō and to play a role in the administration of occupied Japan. "Truman perceived the postwar balance in East Asia as resulting from a 'land grab stampede' in which the Soviets had beaten the United States off the mark."[29] Japan was close to the center of the cold war conflict from the start. In 1990 European restructuring had advanced to concrete steps for German reunification, while East Asia remained tense because of the hostility between North and South Korea, the uncertainty of PRC relations with Taiwan, and the incomplete negotiations between the Soviet Union and Japan. Of all regions, East Asia was the last to shed the cold war structure of conflict between socialism and capitalism.

Is Japan an Asian or a World Power? Faced with the acute needs of Poland and Hungary for economic aid to realize their conversion to a market economy, Gaimushō officials explained why foreign aid should reach beyond Japan's traditional recipients. Despite the continuing needs of Asian countries and the great distance to Eastern Europe, officials argued that Japan is also a member of the West and defends shared values of liberal democracy. With the July 1989 summit of the seven capitalist powers, its commitment to support the joint decisions of these powers has risen. The East-West division of the world economy is gradually receding. Japan's international responsibility is rising.[30]

Occasionally the dream of a greater East Asia is brought clearly into the open. In August 1988 *Asahi shimbun* editorialized about the combination of China's great political power and Japan's great economic power closely linked together in the international arena. Together they can overcome suspicions of Japan in Asia and bring a new era to the region that would contribute to peace and would be welcomed. Improving Sino-Soviet relations removes one obstacle to this sort of nonmilitary regional linkage.[31]

Japanese are more inclined to trust East Asian partners than are Americans, and they are more trusting of Americans than are Americans of Japan. In 1990, 10.9 percent trusted China as opposed to 4.2 percent of Americans in September 1989. And while 50 percent of Japanese trusted the United States (first among all countries), only 15.1 percent of Americans trusted Japanese (eleventh after Canada and a host of European and English-speaking countries). Korea and Singapore were thirteenth and fifteenth on Japan's list, but twenty-third and twenty-fifth on America's.[32]

An Asia-centered outlook spread through the summer and fall of 1990. Under headings such as "The Fate of the Socialist System and the World," international conferences were convened to look ahead to the new world order.[33] The Japanese participants were largely in agreement in supporting international aid to the Soviet Union and Eastern Europe to stabilize the changes in progress and to help speed the abandonment of socialism for a complete market economy. At the same time they recognized the primary responsibility of Western Europe in helping Eastern Europe and expressed the need for Japan to play a greater role in Asia. On the one hand, Japan's political role in Asia would rise. On the other, it faced the complex task of alleviating the lingering suspicions of some Asian countries about Tokyo's long-run intentions. In doing so, Japanese would have to address their own deficiency of universal values, while finding new ways to communicate with their neighbors about the contemporary relevance of a common tradition of Confucian values.

In June Gorbachev's meeting with South Korean President Roh in San Francisco spurred appreciation for South Korea's importance as a political force in the region. Within a few months, Kanemaru had traveled to North Korea and, to the chagrin of the Gaimushō and the South Korean government, agreed that Japan should pay reparations to the North and move quickly toward normalization. American preoccupation with the Iraqi invasion of Kuwait left the Japanese government divided in its response and somewhat isolated because of its military inactivity and its hesitation to become a strong voice for resistance to Iraq. In these circumstances, Japan turned toward its own region.

Encouraged by Shevardnadze's September visit and other signs that Gorbachev's April 1991 visit would defuse the Northern Territories question and the remaining tension with Moscow, Japanese international observers began to look toward building relations of trust in East and Southeast Asia. The end of the age of the bipolar world brought a rise of regionalism. Scholars launched study projects on the East Asian regional heritage. Senior politicians sought to leave a personal mark on diplomatic ties. The media discovered new regional issues. The equivalent of the Berlin Wall was falling in Asia. But with China caught between repression and reform and North Korean leaders fearful of following the East German path, as well as with other lingering tensions from the victims of Japanese wartime aggression, Japan's interest in finding a nearby match for the European Community would not be easily realized.

Nakasone's Visions of the Future. Of all Japanese statesmen, Nakasone was the most eager to speak about the future. From his remarks at the Japan-German Forum on September 21, 1989, one finds the following six approaches to the future.[34] (1) The 1990s should not be a simple transition. They should be a "magnificent springboard launching us into the twenty-first century. There should be a worldwide reconciliation based on new principles and systems for both the West and the East. (2) There is a great danger of instability in the Soviet Union and China. Vast territories and diverse peoples traditionally require strong centralized power. Change can lead in unexpected directions. The Tiananmen incident is a harbinger. Reform that is radical may lead to such explosions. Cautious change is preferable. (3) Even after the Tiananmen incident China retains its basic reform policies. Since Communist dictatorships are incompatible with the competition and individual initiative seen in reform, they will fall as the reforms advance. (4) The West must react cautiously and by maintaining solidarity. So far it has done very well. (5) The European Community after 1992, the United States, and Japan can through their enormous markets and production capability have a great effect on neighboring countries. These effects will become the driving force of history, while the Soviet economy, with its opposite impact on neighbors due to its difficulties, will lose influence. (6) Japan and Germany as defeated powers must be sensitive to world uneasiness. They should strengthen their political roles in the United Nations and work to delete Article 107 of the UN Charter, the enemy clause. They should fight protectionism, especially in their own regions, an integrated Europe, and the Asia-Pacific region, respectively. (7) Friction arises from cultural and historical differences. In an interdependent world it must be settled through increased policy coordination in many fields. The seven-nation Western economic summit needs to expand meetings with the Soviet Union and China. An image of a five-unit world leadership emerges—perhaps even a Security Council in which Britain and France are combined with Germany into one unit, while Japan also is granted membership.

Retaining Past Sources of National Strength. Japanese define their strong points through comparisons, usually with the United States but also with the more striking alter ego of the Soviet Union. Japanese must retain an attitude of striving to catch up, avoiding Soviet arrogance. Japanese must be sensitive to the feelings of other countries, resisting the temptation to dominate to which Moscow yielded. It will not make the mistake of reliance on its military, which leads to neglect of overall modernization of the economy. Japanese must convey to the younger generation the virtues of hard work, avoiding the loss of motivation and social disorder seen among Soviet youth. Finally, Japanese must become internationalized. Soviets were not.

To accomplish these aims, many believe, the first requirement is unity, taking advantage of homogeneity. This requires careful guidance by the national ministries such as the Gaimushō, well-informed about public opinion and attentive to building a consensus. In a more integrated world with fewer communications barriers and more material temptations, Japan will have to work hard to maintain a popular consensus.

This concern for maintaining tradition should not be equated with resistance to all change. There is a consensus that Japanese must become more internationalized. They need to develop a greater sense of responsibility for solving international problems. In this way, they would contribute to a country that now must do its own thinking even if it cannot often insist on its own way in a highly interdependent world. By holding onto traditional values, Japan will prevent total convergence even as it accepts many elements of world convergence natural to our shrinking globe. It is assumed that Japan must be alert to make modest reforms in its social system, but rarely is it proposed that Japanese engage in a major debate about transforming that system apart from the political system that, according to the campaigns of 1989 and 1990, leads to corruption and unfair taxes.

The Psychology of a Superpower. In the summer of 1989 Japanese perceived the Bush administration as supporting the end of Soviet containment and the inclusion of the Soviet Union in "international society," referring to this strategy as the "Bush Doctrine." Gorbachev had already pointed the way by recognizing that each country must follow its own path of development, at last calling into question the Brezhnev Doctrine of limited sovereignty within the socialist community. These and other developments in the middle of the year, even before the dramatic collapse of East European communism at the end of the year, opened the way to new thinking in Japan.

While some Japanese wondered why Tokyo should respond with economic assistance to distant Eastern Europe, official circles answered that Japan is not only an Asian country. As a member of the West it must strive to cooperate in defense of common values. The widened Japanese role in East-West relations indicates a new sense of Japan's international responsibilities. As the wall lowers between East and West, Japanese support for Eastern Europe can have "very great historical significance."[35] Moscow's decline opens the way for Tokyo's further shift from the psychology of a regional power to that of a superpower. Japanese opinion welcomed the shift in psychology.

In the current period Japan lacks an alternative critical worldview. In the Meiji era Western thought and to some degree Christianity for a time provided a framework for criticizing the power structure. For a number of decades to the 1970s Marxism filled that role, but now it cannot since it is seen as a dead ideology supportive of totalitarianism and backwardness. Will the Japanese find a new philosophy for domestic reform and a less passive and more idealistic foreign policy? If so, it may be home grown this time since there are no models in the world that now have much appeal.

The Psychology of a Victor. Accustomed to the determined, but carefully controlled catch-up mentality of the victim, Japanese could not easily adopt the leadership psychology of the victor. Reasoning that the Northern Territories issue would not be fully settled with Gorbachev's visit offered a rationale for retaining the old outlook. For many Japanese, so too did the conflicting pressures of American insistence on drawing Japan deeply into the coalition to oppose Iraq and East and Southeast Asian opposition to the sending of Self-Defense Forces personnel to the Persian Gulf war zone in a noncombative capacity. Both sides were unjustly interfering in the inobtrusive role many Japanese hoped to continue. Many foreign affairs experts eager to use this opportunity to shake off the cold war victim psychology found themselves disappointed both by what they saw as the public's irresponsibility and by a lack of political leadership from the opposition parties, which had never played a constructive role in foreign affairs. Prime Minister Kaifu's indecision and factional in-fighting in the LDP compounded the problem.

Negative Mutual Perceptions. Japanese watch public opinion surveys closely because they think that popular attitudes are important in international relations. They fear that American attitudes toward Japan are becoming more negative, threatening international economic liberalization and perhaps even world stability. The *Times*/CBS poll of January 13–15, 1990, indicated that 67 percent of those polled say they have "generally friendly" feelings toward Japan, down from 74 percent in June 1989 and from 87 percent in 1985. In five years American friendliness toward Japan has dropped by 20 percent, while "generally unfriendly" feelings have risen about as much, from 8 to 19 to 25 percent. As the *New York Times* explained, "the collapse of the Soviet bloc has freed them [Americans] from fears of Communism."[36] This popular mood led to stronger rhetoric on trade issues, which fuels growing resentments in Japan. Japanese worry about the American public as bound to "old thinking" based on U.S. hegemony, as poorly educated about economic matters and thus protectionist, and as racist toward an Asian competitor. The American public may replace the Soviet military as the greatest disruptive force to world stability. If in the past Japan cooperated with the United States to contain the Soviet military, with whom should Japan cooperate to disarm American negativism?

Concern that Japan will remain an outsider is often not far below the surface. One article suggesting that the West fears Japan more than the Soviet Union referred to the latter as a child of the French Revolution, while Japan is a closed country. Japan, as a result, is more distant from the West.[37]

A World in Equilibrium

The Third Way. Yakovlev's enigmatic reference to solving Soviet-Japanese problems through "a third way" caused a sensation in Japan at the end of 1989. Dangled ambiguously before the Japanese people, these words could be interpreted narrowly as a sign of minor Soviet concessions on the four islands or broadly with unknown parameters. It was even possible to speculate about Soviet interest in Japan's third way of development as an alternative to traditional capitalism and socialism. As Japanese were looking ahead to a new era, they were grasping for a new approach to superpower status different from the paths taken by Washington and Moscow. The concept of a third way seemed fitting for this search that had barely begun when Yakovlev visited Tokyo in November 1989.

A New Pax Tokugawa. To find a parallel to expectations about the current transition, one may look to Japan's emergence from a century of warring states into the stability and equilibrium of the Tokugawa era. The twentieth century with its world wars, militarism, and communism is a time of division and misfortune for much of the world. Even the postwar era appears as a time of imbalance and temporary accommodation through containment. Through Soviet cooperation, the current transition can lead us out of this morass. This transition does not spell the end of history, as American Francis Fukuyama argued, but the beginning of a more stable and peaceful era in an integrated world similar to that of Tokugawa Japan. While Americans tend to look back, as one might expect from a country losing its hegemony, Japanese are looking ahead.

On three occasions in the twentieth century, the world order has shifted abruptly. In 1914–18 the old nineteenth-century order gave way, in 1945–49 the postwar order emerged, and now from 1989 a new order for the twenty-first century is appearing. The Soviet Union has played a central role on all three occasions. Through the Bolshevik Revolution it spurred armed revolution, militant nationalism, and the totalitarian state.

Through its international power as a victor in the Second World War, it accelerated these forces. Through Gorbachev's retreat from these pursuits, it is playing a constructive role in the long-delayed shift to a more positive world order. As in the prior turning points, new technology, new approaches to the state, and new concepts of nationalism serve as driving forces toward a different world order.

Convergence Theory Means Aid for Soviet Democracy. Nakayama Hiromasa compares perestroika both to China's socialist reforms and to Japan's postwar reforms. He argues that under socialism the upper structure or politics strongly determines the outcome, while under liberalism the reverse is true. As a result, proceeding with economic reforms before political reforms, as China did, offers little guarantee. Ethnic problems are more serious in the Soviet Union, but the Soviet Communist party has advantages in population, productivity, qualified workers, natural resources. After the brutal Tiananmen crackdown on reform in June 1989, this kind of comparison kept hopes for perestroika alive. Now to leaders, reformers, and the masses, the "Beijing incident" offers a lesson in what to avoid. Nakayama also finds commonalities with Japanese history, such as the reexamination of history, the reversal of orthodox and heterodox, the great transitions in values, democracy, elections, fundamental human rights, and the turn to America. Japan too faced confusion and twists and turns. Moscow's new system of family farms parallels Japan's land reform, although it will not achieve a shift to small farms rapidly. The new Soviet self-management of worker collectives has also not reached the degree of self-interest advocacy of postwar Japan's rough-and-tumble workers' movement. Democratization will take more time in the Soviet case, but this does not mean it cannot be achieved and thus check the system of one-party dictatorship. Nakayama concludes that we in the "West" should do what we can for real Soviet democracy.[38]

As negotiations advanced, Japanese on the far right played on the fear that the Soviets cannot be trusted. They tricked Reagan in the INF talks, they deceived Japan in 1945 by violating the neutrality treaty, and now they are using "smile" diplomacy to lull the West into psychological pacificism. While the Japanese government and media grow silent about Soviet military superiority, Soviet leaders wait for the day to come in the 1990s when it will be advantageous to break the peace. Even if most observers do not carry their distrust so far, the sentiment is deeply rooted in Japan.

Recovering National Pride. There are many stories in Japanese history about revenge or suicide in response to a loss of one's honor. Humiliation may be endured for a time, but sooner or later the situation would be set right. Japanese believe that their country was wrongly humiliated by the Soviet Union in 1945. Whether the San Francisco Peace Treaty of 1951 and the Japan-U.S. security pact exacerbated the wound or only kept it from spreading, no healing was accomplished. The hope is that in 1991 Japan will be whole again.

A new order must guard against similar wounds. This requires a clear set of standards for fairness. International norms must be clearly specified, and the major powers must be careful to observe them. On such matters as rank in seating, Japanese appear literal-minded and sensitive. Diplomats will have to work hard to anticipate every contingency in order to construct a comprehensive system of rules sufficient to satisfy Japan's quest for propriety.

Considerate Relations. The new order should combine elements of democracy and hierarchy. All countries must be given a sense of participation and benefit, as were all 260 domains in the Tokugawa order. At the same time, Japan and other world powers must be treated in a manner commensurate with their rank. A reorganized United Nations in which Japan serves on the Security Council could provide one framework for expressing hierarchy in the midst of democracy.

In addition to legalistic precision, Japanese expect understanding and good faith in international relations. Nations should be considerate of each other and thus develop trust. Cultural interaction is increasing as contacts with other peoples grow rapidly. There is no turning back. Resort to arrogance or nastiness will not help. Citizens of each country must seek understanding of others and exercise restraint to minimize misunderstandings due to different values or misperceptions.

A Cultural Power. Japanese often respond to international criticisms by claiming that they are misunderstood. Their strategy is to help foreigners to know Japanese culture better. This could be applied to the Soviets also as part of a grand plan to convince them to return the islands. Kimura Hiroshi's 1989 book takes that position when he calls for a strategy to make the Soviet people understand what the islands mean to Japan.[39] Given the modest level of world interest, we can expect this strategy to reach out more widely. If the world understands Japanese culture and the importance of winning the goodwill of the Japanese people in matters about which they feel deeply, then Japan will be able to operate more smoothly. Tension reduction is one of the goals. Japanese are proud of their cosmopolitan culture, bridging Asia, Europe, and their own rich native tradition. They can be expected to champion a common human heritage through cultural exchange. If applied to Moscow, this would represent a sharp departure from past aloofness.

As Prime Minister Takeshita stated in a speech in Washington in June 1988, the first problem in Japanese-American relations is a communications gap.[40] Other problems arise from this. The same viewpoint applies more widely. The thrust of Japanese diplomacy may be to find ways to narrow differences in information and outlook. One former ambassador expressed concern that despite much talk about Japan's internationalization, insufficient effort is being made for cultural exchange with developed countries. He added that recognizing the diversity of values and trying to understand one another is necessary for development of an international society.[41]

The Japanese response attaches no importance to ideology. Pragmatism, science, open-mindedness, and tolerance for diversity all matter, but ideology stands in the way. This view recognizes that nations should agree on some principles that unite us, including respect for human rights, but also prefers to concentrate on ways to maintain social order and to achieve economic goals. Japanese recognize that the loss of the Soviet enemy threatens to reduce unity among capitalist countries with the result that problems once overlooked as minor may now be blown out of proportion. They think that they are ready to work hard for unity, but they worry that the West and particularly the United States is less psychologically prepared.

Leadership. There is an expectation that a new generation of leaders is on the threshold of power in the LDP. Chafing under Kaifu's hesitant espousal of the internationalist themes, some LDP leaders in their forties were already beginning to articulate a new foreign policy philosophy. Best known among these quiet internationalists is Ozawa Ichirō, widely seen as a future prime minister. It seems that continued outside pressure from Japan's Western allies and a more active search for principles in the Gaimushō and the scholarly community will be needed to give the edge soon to this type of new leader.

The new leaders will not face an easy task. The political environment continues to favor hesitancy. For instance, in May 1990 at a meeting of the Foreign Affairs Committee of the Lower House, Inoguchi explained that because Japan is an economic power but not a political power it must walk in step with the world, avoiding the dangers of moving ahead or moving too far behind in its relations with other countries, including Moscow. This requires reading in advance the destination of the world and sharing it with the Japanese people so that they join along in democratic diplomacy.[42] Inoguchi's ideas are a prescription for caution, pragmatism, and alertness, but not leadership or principled behavior. Before the Lower House's Foreign Affairs Committee, Inoguchi argued for assistance in economic development west of the Urals rather than in Siberia. He feared that latent military mobilization power would be increased by assistance in Siberia, causing an eventual threat to arise in the region close to Japan.

Regional Elder Statesmen. While I refer to Japan as a rising superpower, in fact if Japanese have their way the term will not be used. Leaders try to avoid such hubris. They seek to be among the managers, to become regional "elder statesmen," to lead through consensus building. The Tokugawa era was managed without strong leaders or powerful domains exercising central control. Similarly, world stability in the foreseeable future can be achieved through limitations on military build-ups or territorial expansion accompanied by checks and balances. Restrictions on military disequilibrium serve as a means to concentrate on new forms of economic, political, and cultural equilibrium.

If military power is regulated and held in reserve, with the expectation that it will not be used, then the weight of economic power rises significantly. This serves Japan well. There is no reason to replace a pax Americana with a pax Nipponica; the world's economic strength may be divided three ways—North America, Europe, and Japan and the NIES. Together they will exercise joint tutelage. There seems also to be some recognition of a third source of power related to culture, which also will grow in importance in an era of integration and cross-influences on public opinion. American hegemony in language and mass culture is pronounced, but Japanese are, by no means, prepared to cede this sphere to the United States. The era of stability must be based on multidimensional integration.

Japan's resistance to hegemonism can be found in the vocabulary proposed for American-Japanese relations. Nakasone talks of an "equal partnership." Others refer to transnational systems as nation-states are restructured beginning in Europe. In one formulation, power politics born in the nineteenth century will give way to common security in the twenty-first century.

Japan's Military. With military cutbacks coming from the two superpowers and the two European blocs, Japan's steadily rising military budget is likely to trail the frontrunners by a somewhat smaller margin and to pull well ahead of the others. Already the increased value of the yen in 1987 lifted Japan into third place in the world. Moreover, as technological innovation plays an increasingly large role in military spending, Japan will have an advantage due to its advanced industrial technology. This unplanned military catchup does not mean that Japanese public opinion has altogether abandoned its antimilitary suspicions of the postwar decades. They are unlikely to resort to war, to be in a hurry to close the military gap, or to reject the balance that continues to leave Japan much weaker than the United States and the Soviet Union with reliance on Washington in case of an unexpected turn in Moscow. Attentive to the long run, Japanese may set their sights on some version of SDI developed cooperatively. Meanwhile, they will proceed cautiously in order not to worry other countries, because the Soviet threat has receded, and because domestic worries about a revival of prewar militarism and state domination of society need not be rekindled. In any case, Japan is comfortable with unobtrusive world power, encouraging the psychology of running second in order to catch up.

Japanese Nationalism. Liberation from the postwar era eases the task of reconciliation with nationalistic elements in Japanese history. The process of finding more positive elements in the history of state building and military prowess is likely to continue. The war of 1904–5 with Russia is relatively unsensitive. Already in 1989 textbooks revived the heroic image of Admiral Togo Heihachirō, commander of the victorious imperial fleet. The most sensitive topics, such as Japan's conduct in the Pacific War, continue to divide Japanese and their Asian neighbors and must still be handled with sensitivity despite the insistence of groups within the LDP that the war itself be less negatively interpreted.

Equilibrium between Europe and Asia. Some Japanese are worried about European exclusivism or a European-American pan-Atlantic bloc in which Washington leans toward its European allies to build on common traditions and to gain a place in the free trade zone under construction. This sort of regionalism would exclude Japan and must be rejected, just as there is no justification for an exclusive Asian regionalism. After all, U.S.-Pacific trade exceeds U.S.-Atlantic trade by 50 percent. Yet the notion of inclusive regionalism does not mean no adjustment in favor of regional integration. Japanese recognize that Europe is becoming more integrated and that Asia is too, despite greater complexity. The U.S. role as the balancer in Asia, serving as the third party to a series of bilateral relations, is ending. By implication, the message is that Japan is becoming the first among Asian powers and only Japanese-American consultation or independent Japanese action will serve the region. The Japan-U.S. security treaty may lose its significance as a deterrent to Moscow, but it can play a role in reassurance to Asia that Japan is not acting unilaterally on military matters. In this relationship, Japan gains a stronger voice.

European unity coupled with increased Asian integration and Japanese influence inevitably curb American unilateralism. The new world structure resembles an equilateral triangle if Japan succeeds in forging a strong link with Europe that balances the close American-European ties. Then new Japanese interest in Eastern Europe together with an improved relationship with the Soviets serve various purposes, one of which is to limit American unilateral exercise of power.

Japanese recognize that a longer transition is needed in Asia before the breakup of the socialist bloc yields to new regional cohesion transcending ideology. Japanese worry that outsiders may behave impatiently, without adequate sensitivity or understanding of the weaker regional foundation for democracy. They could drive countries such as China deeper into isolation. Japan's approach relies on patience and on the long-term effects of economic integration. Its Asian roots presumably enhance its understanding and sensitivity.

Regionalism should not blind observers to what East and West have in common. Japanese assume that these common values are sufficient to build a stable order, but not if American ideology focusing on freedom, democracy, and free trade is brusquely imposed. There is no shortcut to democratization. The unity of the trilateral powers and eventually of the world must accept differences and follow gradual steps that raise confidence. Increased economic interdependence leads the way.

Managing the Soviet Decline. Japan accepts the responsibility of helping to manage the Soviet transition from a one-sided military superpower to a more balanced but also less significant power. Japanese take for granted that the Soviet decline will continue. They do not want it to lead to internal instability or to a coup that would produce a dangerous government. Preventing disintegration is one of Japan's first priorities.

Another priority that remains in the forefront is to reduce the threat of a revitalized Soviet economy still oriented toward military power. Japan is hesitant to help in revitalization until Moscow proceeds further toward military retrenchment. In this connection, Tokyo also worries about expanded Soviet-German ties if the disintegration of Europe is unsettling to Western countries. The Soviet Union should not be quickly or fully integrated into the Western economy until all signs of threat are gone.

Finally, Tokyo is concerned that Moscow and Washington will strike a deal on Europe while Asian problems remain unresolved. Since problems in Europe are more readily solved, the temptation may be to handle them first and conclude that enough has been done. Japan, it is argued, must maintain pressure for answers on East Asian security matters before the major superpower agreements are settled.

U.S.-Japanese Relations. If the Soviet military threat is resolved, the gravest threat to world stability will be American thinking leading to unilateralism, protectionism, or even hegemonism. When it learned about the event many months later, the Gaimushō was upset by the Scowcroft-Eagleburger secret mission to Beijing in July 1990 at a time when Japan was isolated at the Paris economic summit by allied thinking that it was too soft on China. Some Japanese officials felt seriously betrayed by the secrecy and hypocrisy of their ally. The effect was to undermine the America-firsters who had favored following Washington's lead on China and to increase the likelihood of an independent Japanese policy. In this time of uncertainty about the future, centering on America's reliability as a world leader in a new era, this offense was not easily overlooked.

Anticipating the American Response. Japanese wonder if Washington will graciously accept their country as an equal partner. Will Americans appreciate the lessened significance of military power in a world without a serious military rival? Will the American government look with favor on a settlement between Tokyo and Moscow that eliminates the major source of friction and frees them to forge a closer relationship, which may at times leave Washington feeling removed from the center of decision making? Moscow waited too long to abandon its superpower dreams, only searching for deals in an atmosphere of desperation when it had lost most of its leverage. Will Washington be more realistic in accommodating itself to declining power? The Soviet debate brought these questions forward, leaving Japanese wondering as much about their long-time ally as about their putative enemy.

Japanese-Chinese Relations. A time of increased mutual restraint has begun. The Tiananmen massacre served to reduce Japanese feelings of guilt toward China. Clearly, China, not Japan, is now responsible for China's major problems. Emotional attitudes of guilt toward China and retribution toward the Soviet Union are both fading before more calculated thinking. Meanwhile, the Chinese government has exercised more restraint in criticizing Japan since June 1989. Its leaders understand that the Japanese government is in a difficult situation with internal and external pressures to keep sanctions against China, while the government quietly is trying to rebuild relations. Also, China's moral authority has slipped, so that the next criticism of Japan will not have the same impact as before. China may be facing a period of political instability after Deng Xiaoping dies, and also economic instability compounded by high costs for debt repayment from 1991. Japan assumes that it has little leverage, but it wants to be well positioned as conditions are settled.

Japanese caution toward Moscow might be overcome either by a dramatic concession from Gorbachev that would cut short the process of negotiations over the islands and satisfy the Japanese people that their hopes were now realized or by a partial concession from Gorbachev, seen as a very positive sign, along with strong support from Washington for closer ties between Tokyo and Moscow. If Washington is hesitant and might use expanded bilateral ties between its superpower rivals against Japan, then Japan is likely to avoid the risk. Sensitivity to America's quick temper and predisposition to find fault remains strong in Japan. Since Japan does not need Soviet economic ties, it has little to gain by offending the Americans.

Japan does seek to assume its rightful place. While picking and choosing its challenges carefully, it is likely increasingly to say "No." This would happen in Soviet relations only after the problem of the islands was resolved; Tokyo's leverage on Moscow must in no way be diluted before the first priority is settled.

In his first foreign visit as prime minister, Kaifu traveled to Washington in September 1989 and addressed the communications gap. He called for more exchanges of academics, journalists, and others, to improve mutual understanding.[43] At the same time, Japanese continued to watch closely what other nations think and say about them. Even when surveys showed that they are seen, above all, as diligent, efficient, polite, and trustworthy, they could detect some foreign concerns in the responses, for example, that Japanese do not do enough to help by buying American products.

Speedy resolution of the territorial problem with the Soviets and continued progress in the Soviet transition from socialism and integration into the world economy would ease Japan's own transition. In any case, while Soviets are losing confidence that they can keep control of their own country, culture, and destiny, Japanese seem newly confident that even with continuing internationalization they will retain a large measure of control. They are well positioned for the next century.

Epilogue

The timing of the "cherry blossom" summit of April 16–19, 1991 was definitely not ideal. Tokyo's fragile blossoms had already fallen a week earlier, and on the eve of his visit, Mikhail Gorbachev found that his precarious position was weakening further, with a move to oust him as general secretary by Party hardliners and a call for his resignation as Soviet president from Boris Yeltsin. As a result of the Persian Gulf War during the winter, both Soviet-American and Japanese-American relations had been strained, reducing the international trust that could contribute to compromise. In the late winter, many Soviet conservatives and Russian nationalists, on whom Gorbachev was leaning heavily, became aroused by rumors of a crass 28 billion dollar Japanese offer to make a direct exchange of territory for financial aid. Boris Yeltsin, riding high in popularity and looking ahead to the popular vote for president of Russia, also firmly opposed a Soviet deal that did not fully take into account Russia's territorial rights. Gorbachev traveled to Japan virtually empty-handed.

Only a few days after the summit, Soviet domestic events appeared to take another sharp turn—this time from a center-right alliance focused on control toward a center-left alliance centered on reform. Desperate over a free-falling economy and rampant labor unrest, on April 23 Gorbachev made a tactical agreement with Yeltsin along with the leaders of eight other republics. He agreed to share power with the republics through a new union treaty and to shift course from an anti-crisis program emphasizing disciplinary measures to one oriented toward speedier market reform. This new course was welcomed by, among others, those Japanese who had defined the summit as a new beginning in the hope that the Soviet internal logjam would somehow soon be broken. However faint were the hopes for a quick turnabout to the domestic Soviet crisis, only an end to the stalemate between Gorbachev and Yeltsin promised to Tokyo that it would again face a credible negotiating partner.

The summit had occurred after the gradually rising Japanese hopes of late 1990 had been dimmed during a winter of Soviet retreat from reform. Nonetheless, Japanese expectations had begun rising again as a result of the fast pace of preparations in March. The media grasped at every hint of progress, eventually offering what seemed to be a realistic scenario for an upbeat summit. Gorbachev would apologize for the Soviet mistreatment of the Japanese prisoners of war, helping to close a deep wound in the psychology of the Japanese people. He would make at least a vague reference to his country's willingness to adhere to the 1956 joint communiqué, offering hope that two islands would be returned without long delay. An announcement of steps toward demilitarization of the islands and also a realistic proposal for the start of regional arms talks might be expected to impress Japanese that the end of the cold war would transform the Asia-Pacific region. Prime Minister Kaifu and Gorbachev would also fix an accelerated schedule for continued negotiations, including a return summit over the summer, suggesting that new approaches toward the other two islands would soon be on the agenda. In return for Moscow's reasonableness and as a lure to bring the talks to a successful conclusion, Tokyo would set in motion a large-scale economic assistance program. This was the optimistic sketch of what might make an ill-timed summit a modest success for the Japanese people.

There were many Japanese who remained skeptical of this best-case scenario. They warned that even if some vague steps forward seemed to be in sight in the glow of the summit, a breakthrough was unlikely to follow in the foreseeable future, leaving bilateral relations rocky and resulting in a letdown in public opinion once reality had set in.

In fact, obscured by the readiness of both governments to find some common ground for success, what unfolded was practically the worst-case scenario. Gorbachev personally expressed condolences and empathy to the families of the POWs and, as expected, brought with him a long-sought list of many who had died in the labor camps, but he stopped short of making the clearcut apology that had been anticipated. At long last, the issue of the POWs had been formally aired by the Soviet leadership, but not in a manner to impress Japanese that the Soviets were prepared to acknowledge their guilt. More important to the Japanese, Gorbachev agreed to mention the names of all four disputed islands in the final joint stalemate, a step forward cited by the Gaimushō as evidence that the summit had not failed and that the islands were all now on the negotiating table; yet the tense talks dragged into six sessions and the vague outcome conveyed by this list provided little more than a face-saving exit. Critics charged that the result was not a step forward from Moscow's willingness in 1956 to return two islands, but a step backward with little substantive meaning. Not surprisingly, meaningful Japanese economic aid would have to await another turn in bilateral or international relations.

With this summit outcome, neither side could feel satisfied. Having come hat in hand and pleading for the business community to invest heavily, Gorbachev returned home empty-handed apart from the economic payoff he elicited from the South Koreans in a later stopover there. The Soviet population failed to get excited by expanded ties to Japan; aid seemed almost irrelevant when political and economic conditions for their country were deteriorating rapidly. Despite all the Soviet rhetoric about the need to develop trust, the summit failed to create an image of a trustworthy Soviet Union. Japanese officials were wasting no time in renewing the strategy of solidifying international support for their position on the territories.

The outcome was not totally bleak, however. Japan sought Soviet help in dropping its classification as an enemy nation in the United Nations charter, with the possibility of becoming a permanent member of the Security Council. Domestic currents in the USSR remained difficult to predict; the next stage of talks on the islands might bear some fruit. Above all, Japanese appreciated the reality of the Soviet economic deterioration, with the likelihood that the need for Japanese help would become even greater in the near future. An *Asahi shimbun* poll on the day Gorbachev departed showed that the heads of fifty major firms, while rather doubtful about economic gains from the Soviets, expected by the year 2000 that islands (forty percent expected all four islands and twenty percent anticipated two islands) would revert to Japan.

Appreciative of the background circumstances, only a small minority of Japanese faulted their government for refusing to grant Gorbachev the trust and economic support for which he pleaded. Most favored continuing to work hard for a breakthrough, while patiently waiting for the historical clock to keep ticking away.

In the spring of 1991, the state of bilateral relations reinforced doubts among the Japanese. There was still no reason to reassess the long-standing negative image of Russian national character. Optimism about Soviet prospects would have to await a new image of the Soviet people. In contrast to the enthusiasm of Americans in 1987 and of Chinese students in 1989, Gorbachev failed to capture the imagination of the Japanese in 1991. Subdued and perhaps even desperate, Gorbachev represented a divided and declining population.

The Soviet political and economic system had lost all merit in the eyes of the Japanese. The business world made no secret of its conviction that the Soviet industrial system was a mess that would have to be put in order before Japanese would voluntarily invest and then, most likely, with government endorsement. Yet, looking ahead, Japanese business was beginning to identify promising pieces of real estate, to plan long-term projects not very dependent on Soviet labor, and to train Japanese experts prepared to play a leading role in economic ties. Long-range goals were taking shape in the fog of current relations.

The lingering worry after the April summit was that Soviet international behavior would not contribute to stability in the Asia-Pacific region. Accusing Moscow of shifting weapons to Asia in order to avoid having them counted as part of the recently negotiated limits on forces in Europe, Japanese officials voiced doubts that Moscow was prepared to end the cold war in their region. Yet, every hopeful strategy depended heavily on Moscow; Tokyo's primary approach continued to be to work with Gorbachev first in the hope that this would open the door to multilateral approaches to regional security.

The unresolved territorial dispute was but one of many complications in the establishment of a new order in the Asia-Pacific region. Gorbachev's call for a five-nation security conference, also including the United States, China, and India, drew a cool response. Tokyo preferred a step-by-step resolution of bilateral problems. Yet, the proximity of Soviet, American, Chinese, and Japanese vital interests made it likely that regional matters would soon rise to the forefront. The East Asian region's dynamism in a world of intensified economic regionalism was heightening interest in new, multilateral forms of economic cooperation. The Gorbachev era had created new opportunities for the region. It is, above all, Japan's response to these opportunities as well as the final disposition of communism that is likely to shape the outcome.

The passing of the summit narrowed the psychological distance between the Japanese and the Soviets. Relations had now entered onto a new track. Even the vagueness of the results did not obscure the impression that a much anticipated milestone had at last been left behind. The Japanese would, if anything, redouble their efforts to resolve the territorial dispute and, simultaneously, to produce a peace treaty as the start of a new era when the Asia-Pacific region might look forward to cooperation and stability within a new world order.

Notes

Unless otherwise noted, the place of publication is Tokyo. As is customary in Japan, information on publishers is also omitted unless location of the book might prove to be a problem. When authors' names are cited for English-language publications, the order and spelling are given as recorded in the publication. Macrons to show long vowels are often omitted in these sources.

CHAPTER ONE

1. Morimoto Yoshio, *Sobieto to Roshia* (1989), pp. 141–42.
2. Satō Tsuneaki, "Soren, Hangarii no keizai kaikaku," *Gekkan shakaitō* (March 1989): 126–35; Funabashi Yōichi and Hakamada Shigeki, "Gensō to shite no shakaishugi," II, *Asahi jānaru*, May 26, 1989, pp. 80–84; S. Agafonov, "Hasegawa Keitarō: Snachalo eto kazalos' katastrofoi—Iaponskii ekonomist delitsia opytom reformy v svoei strane," *Izvestia*, May 7, 1990, p. 5.
3. Rodger Swearingen, *The Soviet Union and Postwar Japan: Escalating Challenge and Response* (Cambridge, Mass.: Harvard University Press, 1978); Myles L. C. Robertson, *Soviet Policy Towards Japan: An Analysis of Trends in the 1970s and 1980s* (Cambridge: Cambridge University Press, 1988).
4. Igor' Latyshev, "Vo vlasti opasnykh illiuzii," *Pravda*, July 12, 1988, p. 5; Hōgen Shinsaku et al., *TaiSo senryaku* (1986), pp. 185–86; Tamba Minoru, *200% no anzen hoshō o motomeru kuni: Soren senryaku to Nihon no taiō* (1984), pp. 202–3; Hakamada Shigeki, "Kawaru Soren, kawaranu Soren," in *Motto shiritai Soren*, ed. Hakamada Shigeki (1988), p. 16.
5. Morimoto Tadao, *Ajia taiheiyō ni noridasu Soren to Nihon no taiō* (Nihon keizai chōsa kyōgikai, 1989), pp. 20–21; Suzuki Yoshikatsu, "'Hoppō ryōdo mondai' de rakkan wa sōkei," *Sekai shūhō*, January 17, 1989, pp. 21–25.
6. Hakamada Shigeki and Funabashi Yōichi, "Gensō to shite no shakaishugi," I, *Asahi jānaru*, May 19, 1989, pp. 99–104; M. Voslensky and Itō Kenichi, "'Akai kizoku' no o o funda Gorubachofu," *Shokun* (November 1987): 126–30.
7. Nakagawa Yatsuhiro, *Gorubachofu no Nihon senryaku* (1988), p. 1.
8. Kitajima Masamoto, *Edo bakufu no kenryoku kōzō* (1964).
9. Yokote Shinji, "Nihon to no kankei: rekishi to genjō," in *Motto shiritai Soren*, ed. Hakamada, p. 257.
10. Kimura Hiroshi, *Soren o yomu 50 no pointo* (1988), p. 46.
11. Matsumoto Kazuo, *Chūgokujin to Nihonjin: Chūgoku o fukaku rikai suru* (1987), pp. 2–12.
12. Niizeki Kinya, *NisSo kōshō no butaiura* (1989), pp. 12–19 and 85.
13. Tanaka Yozō, *Chūgokujin to Nihonjin: Chūgoku rikai no gokai to sakkaku o tadasu* (1987), pp. 136–60.

14. Kuramochi Shunichi, *Toshindai no Soren: "tengoku de mo jigoku de mo nai" atarimae no kuni* (1983).

15. Yomiuri shimbun shuzaidan, *Gorubachofu no Soren*, (1987), p. 197.

16. "Ishiki imēji nao rakusa: 'sugao no yūkō' NisSo ni hitsuyō," *Yomiuri shimbun*, May 25, 1988, pp. 14–15.

17. Inoki Masamichi, "Soren wa naze reisen ni yabureta ka?" *Seiron* (May 1985): 44–55.

18. Aihara Minoru, *Jōhōka to Soren keizai: peresutoroika no honshitsu* (1988).

19. Kimura Hiroshi, *Soren o yomu 50 no pointo*, pp. 80–83.

20. Kobayashi Michinori, "Kokusaika jidai no hikari to kage," *Jiyū* (March 1988): 42.

21. Yamazaki Takio, "88 nen hageshii kyokutō jōsei: Soren 'kyokutō kairō' no seiha o mezasu," *Jiyū* (March 1988): 48–53.

22. Miyazaki Masahiro, *Naze Soren wa shinyō dekinai ka: Nihon o nerau Gorubachofu no sakujutsu* (1988), p. 17.

23. Satō Atsushi, "Saketai 'detanto' no ni no mai," *Sekai shūhō*, June 21, 1988, pp. 4–5; Tsukihara Shigeaki, "Kurikaesu mai 'detanto boke,'" *Gekkan jiyū minshū* (July 1988): 100–3.

24. Nasu Kiyoshi, *Soren hōkai ga semaru* (1987), pp. 3–4; Maruyama Hiroyuki, "Niu-detanto no gensō," *Shokun* (August 1988): 213.

25. "Gorubachofu to no seiji taiwa: Nakasone zenshushō ni kiku," *Yomiuri shimbun*, August 4, 1988, p. 2.

26. Katori Yasue, "'Hoppō ryōdo' de ichibu zenshin," *Tōkyō shimbun*, December 22, 1988.

27. Ōtsubo Kenichirō, "Kokusai shakai to Nihon no sekinin," *Sekai shūhō*, June 21, 1988, pp. 34–35; "Poll on Internationalization," *The Japan Times*, July 6, 1988, p. 16.

28. Arai Hirokazu, "BeiSo shunō kaidan to kongo no tōzai kankei," *Sekai keizai hyōron* (February 1988): 32–33.

29. Y. M. Zhukov, ed., *The Rise and Fall of the Gunbatsu: A Study in Military History* (Moscow: Progress Publishers, 1975), p. 13.

30. Takubo Tadae, "'PR no tensai' Gorubachofu no majutsu," *Voice* (September 1989): 198.

CHAPTER TWO

1. "Nakasone shi no hosSo kangei," *Asahi shimbun*, June 29, 1988, p. 3.

2. "'Hoppō ryōdo' hajimete teiki," *Yomiuri shimbun*, June 21, 1988, p. 2; "Itchokusen ni heiwa jōyaku e susumu kanōsei mo," *Shūkan tōyō keizai*, February 11, 1989, pp. 56–59.

3. "Kantei kūdōka no naka gaikō de Kaifu fujō naru ka," *Chishiki* (February 1991): 30–31.

4. Hamada Hideo, "Gaimushō ga shibaru Soren muke shokuryō enjo," *AERA*, December 11, 1990, p. 13.

5. Nagata Minoru, "'Ajia taiheiyō no ichiin' to itte mita keredo," *Sekai shūhō*,

January 23, 1990, pp. 26–29; "Abe shi seika wa harashō!?" *Mainichi shimbun*, January 17, 1990, p. 2.

6. "Soren 'nitō henkan' o shisa," *Asahi shimbun*, October 7, 1990, p. 1.

7. Tomohiko Iguchi, "Toshiki Kaifu Comes through with Style, Results," The *Japan Times Weekly International Edition*, September 3–9, 1990, pp. 8–9.

8. "NisSo no teiryū 11, Kanemaru Shin no kuse da," *Mainichi shimbun*, August 18, 1990, p. 1.

9. Suzuki Yoshikatsu, "'Hoppō ryōdo mondai' de rakkan wa sōkei," *Sekai shūhō*, January 17, 1989, pp. 21–25.

10. "TaiSo meguri A Take ryōha ga masatsu," *Asahi shimbun*, October 10, 1990, p. 14.

11. "Soren nado no 6 kōmoku," *Nihon keizai shimbun*, January 15, 1991, p. 5.

12. Kishida Kazuhiro, "Mada Gorubachofu ni odorosareta Nakasone to shimbun," *Shokun* (October 1988): 26–38.

13. "Soren kyōiron ga kūsen," *Asahi shimbun*, April 10, 1989, p. 10.

14. "Japan Reverses Policy on Soviet as a Threat," *The New York Times*, September 19, 1990, p. A13.

15. "Go daitōryo raiNichi nirami jinyō kyōka," *Yomiuri shimbun*, November 26, 1990.

16. "Soren taiNichi seisaku jikken o nigiru shinku tanku," *Foresight* (April 1990): 18.

17. "Soren no yoron bundansaku ni noru na," *Mainichi shimbun*, October 10, 1990, p. 15.

18. Miyauchi Kuniko, "Soren no gunji senryaku wa shinhoshin ni kawatta," *Gaikō forumu* (March 1989): 44–49; Morimoto Tadao, "TaiNichi jōhō shisei tsuyomeru Soren no shini," *Ekonomisuto*, January 31, 1989, pp. 80–82.

19. "Ryōdo henkan no nioi dake ga nokotta," *Shūkan Asahi*, September 21, 1990, pp. 170–72.

20. Mutō Toshiaki, "Soren no jitsujō to peresutoroika no zentō," *Sekai keizai hyōron* (August 1990): 8–21.

21. "Soren wa hoppō ryōdo o henkan suru," *Shūkan bunshun*, November 23, 1989, p. 44; "Yakoburefu shi to hisoka ni atta 'sōri oniwaban' 67 sai no sugao," *Shūkan Yomiuri*, December 3, 1989, pp. 177–81.

22. "Yakoburefu shi to hisoka ni atta 'sōri oniwaban' 67 sai no sugao," p. 178.

23. "Peresutoroika o ou," *Sobieto kenkyū*, no. 1 (1989): 4–141.

24. "Peresutoroika Soren o tazunete," *Gekkan shakaitō* (July 1988): 35–41.

25. "Inoki Seeking Detente with Soviets," *The Japan Times*, August 27, 1989, p. 2.

26. Sono Akira, "'Perestroika' for Japan too?" *The Japan Times*, September 10, 1988, p. 8; Hōgen Shinsaku, "Saredo Soren wa kowashi," *Chishiki* (February 1990): 52–55.

27. Itō Kenichi, "Hoppō ryōdo 'nitō henkan ron' o utagau," *Shokun* (February 1987): 26–42.

28. Sase Masamori and Maruyama Hiroyuki, "INF zenpai jōyaku ga mota-

rashita keiken," *Shokun* (March 1988): 26–33; Kimura Hiroshi, *Soren o yomu 50 no pointo* (1988).

29. Yokokawa Shōichi, *Tobira o hiraite atatakaki hi o: 21 seiki o tempō shi taiSoron ni* (1984).

CHAPTER THREE

1. Nakagawa Yatsuhiro, *Gorubachofu no uso* (1987), pp. 50, 56, 66, 76.

2. Nasu Kiyoshi, *Kuzuredashita Soren teikoku* (1988).

3. Teratani Hiromi, "Soren no 'Tōō shihai' wa owatta ka?" *Sekai shūhō*, July 18, 1989, pp. 18–21.

4. Itō Kenichi, "'Dakkaku jidai' no torai to Nihon no daisenryaku," *Seiron* (July 1988): 32–41.

5. Mitsuoka Akira, "'Jikoku bōei' wa Nihonjin jishin de," *Jiyū* (February 1988): 84–85.

6. Hasegawa Tsuyoshi, "Gorubachofu wa yokuseiron o koerareru ka," *Chūō kōron* (January 1989): 151–62; Hasegawa Tsuyoshi, "The Military Factor in Soviet Foreign Policy," in *The Soviet Union in Transition*, ed. Kinya Niiseki (Boulder: Westview Press, 1987), pp. 147–66.

7. Hakamada Shigeki, *Soren: gokai o toku 25 no shikaku* (1987).

8. Uda Fumio, *Soren: seiji kenryoku no kōzō* (1989).

9. Wada Haruki, *Watakushi no mita peresutoroika: Gorubachofu jidai no Mosukuwa* (1987).

10. Satō Tsuneaki, "ChūsSo o kangaeru," *Mainichi shimbun*, May 16, 1989, p. 6.

11. Shimotomai Nobuo, *Soren gendai seiji* (1987).

12. Taniuchi Yuzuru, *Gendai shakaishugi o kangaeru* (1987).

13. Sobieto kenkyūsho, *Peresutoroika: Gorubachofu kaikaku no sōgōteki kenkyū* (1988).

14. Mochizuki Kiichi, "Soren no taigai keizai seisaku," *Sobieto kenkyū*, no. 2 (1989): 53–54.

15. "Akai kizoku no o o funda Gorubachofu," *Shokun* (November 1987): 126–38.

16. Shimotomai Nobuo, "Shinjidai o mukaeru NisSo," *Tōkyō shimbun*, September 8, 1990, p. 12.

17. Sono Akira, "Ryōdo mondai de no zenshin wa sakkaku da," *Sankei shimbun*, September 14, 1990, p. 10.

18. Saito Motohide, "NisSo kankei kenkyū no genjō to kadai," *Soren kenkyū*, no. 9 (October 1989): 135–49.

19. Shuichi Kojima, "The Changing Japanese Perception of the Soviet Union as Seen in Postwar General-Interest Magazines," *Konan Journal of Social Sciences*, vol. 2 (1988): 22.

20. Kimura Hiroshi, "Nihon no Soren kenkyū," *Soren kenkyū*, no. 5 (October 1987): 93–97; Matsuda Jun, "Sūji de miru Nihon no surabu kenkyū: Soren Tōō kenkyūsha meibo daisanpan 1988 no bunseki," *Surabu kenkyū no teigen—surabu kenkyū suishin no hōhō kentōkai no kiroku* (Sapporo: Hokkaidō University, Slavic Research Center Report Series, no. 26, March 1989).

21. Nobuaki Shiokawa, "Izuchenie istorii SSSR v Iaponii," *Voprosy istorii* (February 1990): 144.

22. Itō Takayuki, *Surabu kenkyū no tame no teigen*, p. 3.

23. Shuichi Kojima, "The Changing Japanese Perception of the Soviet Union," p. 21.

24. *Roshia Soren o shiru jiten* (1989).

25. Imai Yoshio, "Soren kenkyūsha no kokusai kōryū to Soren kenkyūsho e no kitai," *Peresutoroika: Gorubachofu kaikaku no sōgōteki kenkyū* (1987), pp. 98–100.

26. Nakamura Taizo, *Gendai no sobieto sekai* (1983), p. 1; " 'NisSo kyōkai' za razvitie druzhby," *Izvestia*, May 23, 1988.

CHAPTER FOUR

1. Baba Shinichi, Herbert Passin, Sengoku Tamotsu, and Satō Seizaburō, "Nihon chishikijin no shakai ishiki," *Shakai kagaku kiyō* (1978), p. 57.

2. *Peresutoroika wa ima: Rēnin no yume Gorubachofu no genjitsu* (Tōkyō shimbun, 1988); "Shiberia yokuryū no rekishi minaosu," *Tōkyō shimbun*, July 24, 1986, p. 6.

3. Kobayashi Yoshiaki, "Masu media no hōdō to seitō shiji ni kansuru keikaku bunseki," *Hōgaku kenkyū* 61, 1 (January 1988): 189–232.

4. "Sōhō ga kankei kaizen nozomu," *Nishi Nihon shimbun*, March 6, 1988, p. 3.

5. Nakamura Kenichi, "Soren kyōiron kara no dakkyaku," *Sekai* (April 1985): 56–73.

6. "Rēnin riron no atsumari," *Yomiuri shimbun*, March 1, 1989, p. 5.

7. Yuri Vdovin, *Fukuoka kokunai shimpojiumu: kokusaika to komyunikeshion* (Fukuoka: Fukuoka UNESCO Association, 1986), pp. 128–30.

8. Sono Akira, *Sobieto watchingu 40 nen* (1983), pp. 61, 94, 97, 103–16.

9. Sono Akira, "Sayokuteki shimbun no 'mienai dangan,' " *Bungei shunju* (April 1988): 141–42.

10. Sakurai Yoshiko, "Konna ni aru Mosukuwa tokuhain no 'tabū,' " *Shokun* (January 1987): 62–76.

11. Suzuki Takurō, "Asahi shimbun no 'naibu,' " *Shokun* (February 1985): 51.

12. " 'Hoppō ryōdo hi' genjitsu ron ni katamuku jimoto," *Asahi shimbun*, February 7, 1990; "Ryōdo kōshō wa mazu atama o hiyashite," *Tōkyō shimbun*, July 27, 1990, p. 5.

13. Katō Shūichi et al., "Jiānarizumu no fuken o," *Sekai* (February 1991): 27–50.

14. "Shevardnadze Arrives for Talks," *The New York Times*, September 5, 1990, p. A17.

15. Katō Shūichi et al., "Jiānarizumu no fuken o," pp. 27–50.

16. "Nihon yoron nanka nerai," *Yomiuri shimbun*, October 21, 1990, p. 1.

17. "Shashin 400 mai to ichibu kojin kiroku," *Yomiuri shimbun*, October 21, 1990, p. 1.

18. Baba Shinichi et. al., "Nihon chishikijin no shakai ishiki," p. 57.

19. Iwaki Shigeyuki et. al., *Roshia, Soren, Tōō-shi kankei bunken mokuroku (1989)* (Roshiashi kenkyūkai and Tōōshi kenkyūkai, 1990).

20. Shuichi Kojima, "The Changing Japanese Perception," p. 23.

21. Ibid., pp. 43–44.

22. Kurushima Tatsuo and Gunji kenkyū gurūpu, *Sorengun Nihon jōriku: daisanji sekai daisen—Nihon hen* (1979); Nakagawa Yatsuhiro, *Soren wa Nihon o kaku kogeki suru* (1982).

23. Shiokawa Nobuaki, "1930 nendai taisei to peresutoroika"; Shimotomai Nobuo, "Peresutoroika to 'rekishi minaoshi' no bunmyaku"; and Wada Haruki, "Rekishi no naka no peresutoroika," *Roshiashi kenkyū* (1989), pp. 56–69, 70–75, and 76–89.

24. Takada Kazuo, "Kindai Roshiashi kenkyū no 30 nen," *Roshiashi kenkyū*, no. 44, as reported in "Gendai," *Shigaku zasshi* (May 1987): 372.

25. Shimotomai Nobuo, *Soren gendai seiji*.

26. Wada Haruki, *Watakushi no mita peresutoroika: Gorubachofu jidai no Mosukuwa* (1987).

27. Hakamada Shigeki, *Shinsō no shakaishugi* (1987).

28. Kimura Hiroshi, *Soren o yomu 50 no pointo*.

29. "Shuppankai ni Soren būmu," *Nihon keizai shimbun*, August 12, 1988.

30. "'Soren mono' shuppan rasshu," *Nihon keizai shimbun*, October 28, 1990, p. 23.

31. Matsuda Jun, "Sūji de miru Nihon no surabu kenkyū," p. 55.

32. Gilbert Rozman, "China's Soviet-Watchers in the 1980s: A New Era in Scholarship," *World Politics* 37, 4 (July 1985): 437–38.

33. Shiokawa Nobuaki, "Peresutoroika o dō toraeru ka?" *Keizai hyōron* (May 1988): 1.

CHAPTER FIVE

1. Shimizu Hayao, *Nihonjin no Roshia kompurekkusu* (1984), pp. ii–iii; and Shimizu Hayao, *TaiSo kokka senryaku ron* (1981), pp. 135–39.

2. Furumoto Shozo, "NichiRo sengo no ichiban nori," *Mado*, no. 55 (December 1985): 24. Itō Takayuki, "Surabu kenkyū no tame no teigen," p. 2.

3. Kimura Tokio, "Nihon ga miete kuru sekaishi o," *Chishiki*, no. 4 (1988): 45–46.

4. Kimura Akio, *Roshia Soren no Nihonkan* (1984), pp. 23–28.

5. Peter Berton, Paul Langer, and Rodger Swearingen, *Japanese Training and Research in the Russian Field*, Far Eastern and Russian Series, no. 1 (Los Angeles: University of Southern California Press, 1956), pp. 18–19. Other Western scholarship of the 1960s to 1980s by George Alexander Lensen, John Stephan, and Robert A. Scalapino has traced in detail the development of bilateral relations and eventually of the Japanese Communist Party.

6. Togawa Tsuguo, "The Japanese View on Russia Before and After the Meiji Restoration," *The Journal of International Studies* (Sophia University), no. 24 (January 1990): 3–15.

7. Wada Haruki, "Roshia Soren kenkyū," *Roshia Soren o shiru jiten*, p. 680.

8. Togawa Tsuguo, "The Japanese View," p. 4.

9. Egawa Taku, "Roshia bungaku juyō no rekishi," *Kokusai koryū*, no. 48 (1988): 50–54.

10. Berton et al., *Japanese Training and Research in the Russian Field*, p. 28.

11. Niizeki Kinya, "Watakushi no ikikata," *Kōken* (October 1989): 56.

12. Togawa Tsuguo, "The Japanese View," p. 4.

13. Berton et al., *Japanese Training and Research in the Russian Field*, pp. 30–38.

14. Nonomura Kazuo, *Kaisō Mantetsu chōsabu* (1986), pp. 424–25.

15. Masuda Tomijū, "Nihon ni okeru Roshiyashi kenkyū" (Waseda University Politics and Economics Bulletin) *Kyōyo shogaku kenkyū*, no. 8 (1959): 94.

16. Akizuki Toshiyuki, "Edo jidai ni okeru Nihonjin no Roshiakan," *Nihon to Roshia* (1987), pp. 1–12.

17. Sasaki Teruhiro, "Naroduniki N.S. Rusānofu to Meiji matsu Taishō shoki Nihon no seiji ishiki," *Nihon to Roshia*, pp. 82–92.

18. Nakamura Yoshikazu, "Mnenie iaponskogo poeta Isikava Takukobu o Rossii," *Rossiia i Iaponiia* (1986), pp. 70–79.

19. Tetsuya Sakai, "The Soviet Factor in Japanese Foreign Policy, 1923–1937," *Acta Slavica Iaponica*, vol. 6 (1988): 27–40.

20. Alvin D. Coox, *Nomonhan, Japan Against Russia, 1939* (Stanford: Stanford University Press, 1985).

21. Yokote Shinji, "Nihon to no kankei: rekishi to genjō," pp. 261–62.

22. Germaine A. Hoston, *Marxism and the Crisis of Development in Prewar Japan* (Princeton: Princeton University Press, 1986), pp. 4, 19–24, 28.

23. Yokote Shinji, "Nihon to no kankei: rekishi to genjō," p. 263.

24. Itō Kenichi, "Japan and the Soviet Union: Entangled in the Deadlock of the Northern Territories," *The Washington Quarterly* 11, 1 (Winter 1988): 35; Itō Kenichi, "Soren no taiNichi seisaku no henka o yomu," *This Is* (December 1988): 126.

25. "Sousuke Uno Named Prime Minister," *Japan Report* 35, 6 (June 1989): 2.

26. "Wakai omoide Shiberia yokuryū," *Asahi shimbun*, March 6, 1989, p. 13.

27. "Shiberia yokuryū ima kangaeru," *Asahi shimbun*, March 14, 1989, p. 4.

28. Yoshida Tomoko, "44 nen: Soren ni kieta chichi . . . 'fuzai' no hibi wa nao," *Yomiuri shimbun*, evening edition, August 19, 1989, p. 11.

29. "Higeki ni rekishi hyōka o, hakumairi jindoteki tachiba de," *Tōkyō shimbun*, October 4, 1989, p. 3; Aleksei Kirichenko, "Skol'ko eshche zabytykh mogil," *Novoe vremia*, no. 4 (1989): 20; "Soren no meibo ichibu hanmei," *Yomiuri shimbun*, October 10, 1990, p. 1.

30. "'Shiberiya yokuryū' kaimei ni kichō na shiryō," *Asahi shimbun*, January 24, 1991, p. 4.

31. William F. Nimmo, *Behind a Curtain of Silence: Japanese in Soviet Custody, 1945–1956* (Westwood, CT: Greenwood Press, 1988).

32. Nonomura Kazuo, *Sobietogaku nyūmon* (1962), pp. 17–18 and 28.

33. Nobuaki Shiokawa, "Izuchenie istorii SSSR i Iaponii," pp. 135–36.

34. Shuichi Kojima, "The Changing Japanese Perception," p. 26.

35. Alan B. Cole, George O. Totten, and Cecil H. Uyehara, *Socialist Parties in Postwar Japan* (New Haven: Yale University Press, 1966), p. 215.

36. *Kita no rinjin: NisSo kokkyō kaifuku 30 nen* (Sapporo: Hokkaidō shimbun, 1986), p. 94.

37. Peter Berton et. al., *Japanese Training and Research in the Russian Field*, p. 100.

38. Takeyama Michio, *Maboroshi to shinjitsu: watashi no sobieto kenbunki* (1962), pp. 133–54.

39. Tsuyoshi Hasegawa, "Japanese Perceptions of the Soviet Union, 1960–1985," in *The Soviet Union Faces Asia: Perceptions and Policies*, ed. Tsuyoshi Hasegawa (Sapporo: The Slavic Reseach Center, Hokkaidō University, 1987), p. 39.

40. Seki Hiroharu, "Roshiajinron dō yomu ka," in *Sorenjin repōto*, ed. Kimura Hiroshi (1980), p. 171.

41. Egawa Taku, "Roshia bungaku juyō no rekishi," p. 53.

42. Cole, Totten, and Uyehara, *Socialist Parties in Postwar Japan*, p. 215.

43. Shimizu Hayao, *Nihonjin wa naze Soren ga kirai ka*, pp. 15–21.

44. Seki Takehito, "BeiSo gunshuku kōshō to Nihon no anzen hoshō seisaku," *Shokun* (December 1987): 71–84.

45. Rodger Swearingen, *The Soviet Union and Postwar Japan: Escalating Challenge and Response* (Stanford: Hoover Institution Press, 1978), pp. 97–101.

46. Ibid.

47. Robert Scalapino, *The Japanese Communist Movement, 1920–1966* (Berkeley: University of California Press, 1967).

48. Stanislav Levchenko, *On the Wrong Side: My Life in the KGB* (Washington, D.C.: Pergamon-Brasseys, 1988).

49. Itō Kenichi, *Soren wa tsuyoi mono ni wa te o dasanai: Nihon ga kyōsha de aru tame no kokusai senryaku* (1982), pp. 222–31.

50. Shimizu Hayao, *TaiSo kokka senryakuron* (1989), pp. 140–46, 237–39.

51. Sono Akira, *Sobieto watchingu 40 nen* (1983), pp. 61, 84–86, and 94.

52. "Gaikō ni kansuru yoron chōsa," *Yoron chōsa hōkokusho* (October 1988): 36–39.

53. Kimura Hiroshi, "Gorubachofu no Ajia taiheiyō seisaku: henka to keizoku," *Gorubachofu kaikaku no genjō to tempō* (Heiwa anzen hoshō kenkyūsho, 1988), p. 107.

54. Shimizu Hayao, *Nihonjin wa naze Soren ga kirai ka.*

55. Yokote Shinji, "Nihon to no kankei: rekishi to genjō," p. 256.

56. Shimizu Hayao, *Nihonjin no Roshia kompurekkusu.*

57. Yokokawa Shōichi, *Tobira o hiraite atatakaki hi o.*

CHAPTER SIX

1. Nakamura Kenichi, "Soren kyōiron kara no dakkyaku," *Sekai* (April 1985): 56–58.

2. Ibid., pp. 61–64.

3. Shindo Eiichi, "Bōchōshugi' ron no naka no Soren gaikō," *Sekai* (April 1985): 93.

4. Nakamura, "Soren kyōiron kara no dakkyaku," p. 72.

5. Itō Takayuki, "Kyōiku to kenkyū no genjō," in *Surabu kenkyū no tame no teigen*, ed. Itō pp. 7–38.

6. Hōgen Shinsaku, *Nihonjin ni totte Soren wa kiken kokka da* (1983), pp. 14, 92, and 186.

7. Tamba Minoru, *200% no anzen hoshō o motomeru kuni: Soren senryaku to Nihon no taiō* (1984), pp. 12, 70, 73, 202–5.

8. Sase Masamori, "Asahi shimbun no anzen hoshō kan," *Shokun* (June 1986): 64.

9. Shinkai Tetsuo, *Soren mō hitotsu no kowai kao* (1983); *Shūyōsho shakai Soren ni ikiru* (1987).

10. Shimizu Hayao, *Nihonjin no Roshia kompurekkusu* (1984).

11. *Kita no rinjin: NisSo kokkyō kaifuku 30 nen* (Sapporo: Hokkaidō shimbunsha, 1986), pp. 222–29.

12. "Soren taiNichi gaikō ni shin fujin," *Mainichi shimbun*, July 15, 1986, p. 4.

13. "Keizai kaikaku doko made e jitsugen dekiru ka," *Ekonomisuto*, March 3, 1986, pp. 42–49.

14. Hiroshi Kimura, "Soviet Focus on the Pacific," *Problems of Communism* (May–June 1987): 1–16.

15. Nakajima Mineo, "Hoppō ryōdo 'nitō henkan ron' wa tabū ka?" *Shokun* (March 1987): 26–45; Wada Haruki, "'Hoppō ryōdo' mondai ni tsuite kōsatsu," *Sekai* (December 1986): 150–61.

16. Nakajima Mineo, "Whither Foreign Policy?" *The Japan Times*, July 11, 1988, p. 20.

17. Itō Kenichi, "Hoppō ryōdo 'nitō henkan ron' o utagau," *Shokun* (February 1987): 27–29.

18. Sase Masamori, "Nakajima Mineo shi 'Soren taritsu kahen ron' no mujūn," *Shokun* (October 1987): 122–44.

19. Yomiuri shimbun shuzaidan, *Gorubachofu no Soren* (1987), pp. 191–202.

20. Morimoto Tadao, "Hoppō ryōdo henkan ekkusu no shinario: Soren kōkan no hatsugen kara watakushi wa henkan jitsugen no kakushin o eta," *Ushio* (March 1988): 95.

21. Shimotomai Nobuo, "'Atarashii shikō' no kanōsei," *Sekai* (June 1987): 126–32.

22. Kimura Hiroshi, "'Gurasunosuchi' e no chōsenjo," *Shokun* (June 1987): 138–45.

23. Hakamada Shigeki, "Gokai sareru Soren 18 no shikaku," *Chūō kōron* (May 1987): 122–41.

24. Nasu Kiyoshi, *Soren hōkai* (1986) and *Soren hōkai ga semaru* (1987).

25. "TaiSo gaikō: osamui kenkyū taisei," *Asahi shimbun*, January 28, 1986, p. 2.

CHAPTER SEVEN

1. Shimotomai Nobuo, "Gorubachofu taisei keishō ka, tenkan ka," *Sekai* (January 1986): 172–90.

2. Morimoto Tadao, "Hoppō ryōdo henkan ekkusu no shinario," p. 95.

3. Mitsuoka Akira, "'Jikoku bōei' wa Nihonjin jishin de," *Jiyū* (February 1988): 84–85.

4. Sase Masamori, "Detanto taibōron ni hisomu kiken," Seiron (May 1988): 29–30; Sase Masamori and Maruyama Hiroyuki, "INF zenpai jōyaku ga motarashita kiken," Shokun (March 1988): 216–33.

5. Maruyama Hiroyuki, " 'Niu-detanto' no gensō," Shokun (August 1988): 204–15.

6. Kimura Hiroshi, "NisSo kankei kaizen wa atomawashi," Seiron (May 1988): 9–10.

7. Kimura Hiroshi, "Behind Gorbachev's Smile," The Japan Times, December 28, 1987.

8. Igarashi Takeshi, Shimotomai Nobuo, and Kamo Takehiko, " 'Mosukuwa' igo no sekai o yomu," Ekonomisuto, June 21, 1988, pp. 46–55.

9. Morimoto Yoshio, Sobieto to Roshia, p. 79.

10. Akino Yutaka, "INF kyōtei Gorubachofu no shini," Seiron (October 1987): 121.

11. Sase Masamori and Maruyama Hiroyuki, "INF zenpai jōyaku ga motarashita kiken," pp. 216–33.

12. Inoki Masamichi, "BeiSo no 'reisen' o ninshiki seyo," Seiron (October 1987): 29.

13. Mōri Kazuko, "ChūSo detanto wa doko made susumu ka," Jiyū (February 1988): 102.

14. Yamashita Shintarō, "Saikin ni okeru Soren no gaikō to naisei," Kokumin gaikō, no. 121 (1989): 3–25.

15. Morimoto Tadao, "Gorubachofu no omoi tsubuyaki: hoppō ryōdo henkan de gutai an ga deru hi wa tōku nai," Ushio (December 1988): 76–86.

16. Hasegawa Keitarō, "Soren ni futatabi tetsu no kāten ga oriru hi," Asahi jānaru (January 1990): 55–59.

17. Tsuyoshi Hasegawa, "Japanese Perceptions of the Soviet Union: 1960–1985," pp. 37–70.

18. "Tōzai kankei Nihon wa sameta me," Asahi shimbun, December 1987, pp. 1, 3.

19. "NisSo hajimete no gōdō yoron chōsa," Nishi Nihon shimbun, March 6, 1988, pp. 1, 3.

20. "Sōhō ga kankei kaizen nozomu: NisSo hajimete no gōdō yoron chōsa," and "Nihonjin no taiSokan hōten," Nishi Nihon shimbun, March 6, 1988, pp. 1, 3.

21. "NisSo kaizen 9 wari ga nozomu" and "Ishiki imeji nao rakusa," Yomiuri shimbun, May 25, 1988, pp. 1, 15.

22. "Chōsa kekka o mite," and "Shitsumon to kotae," Yomiuri shimbun, May 25, 1988, p. 15.

23. "BeiSo shunō kaidan 68% ga hyōka," Yomiuri shimbun, June 26, 1988, p. 2.

24. Gaikō ni kansuru yoron chōsa (Naikaku soridaijin kanbo kōhōshitsu, 1988), pp. 36–39.

25. Ibid.

26. Ima hoppō ryōdo wa (Sapporo: Hokkaidō shimbun, 1989).

27. " 'Nisso kyokai' za razvitie druzhby," Izvestia, May 23, 1988, p. 5.

28. "Shiberia horyo no rekishi minaosu," Tōkyō shimbun, July 24, 1988, p. 6.

29. "Kyōdō kanri o teian," *Tōkyō shimbun*, July 27, 1988.

30. Sase Masamori, "Soren nankasetsu no shinshō bōdai," *Shokun* (January 1989): 92.

31. "Gorbachev Spurns Nakasone on Matter of Northern Islands," *The Japan Times*, July 23, 1988, p. 2.

32. "Sorengawa no shisei henka o Nakasone zenshushō ga shisa," *Asahi shimbun*, August 3, 1988, p. 2.

33. "Gorubachofu to no seiji taiwa: Nakasone zenshushō ni kiku," *Yomiuri shimbun*, August 4, 1988, p. 2.

34. "TaiNichi seisaku minaoshi mo," *Yomiuri shimbun*, August 6, 1988, p. 3.

35. "Gorabachofu to no seiji taiwa: Nakasone zenshushō ni kiku," *Yomiuri shimbun*, p. 2; "Nakasone zenshushō Mosukuwa kōen: zenbun," *This Is* (September 1988): 230–36.

36. Wada Haruki, " San Furanshisuko kōwa to Chishima rettō," *Sekai* (November 1988): 233–49.

37. Fujimura Shin, "Minami Chishima o torimodosu tame no jōken to wa," *Ekonomisuto*, November 8, 1988, pp. 17–18.

38. Hasegawa Keitarō, "NisSo kankei o hatten saseru ni wa," *Shūkan tōyō keizai*, December 10, 1988, pp. 52–53.

39. Kimura Hiroshi, "Hoppō ryōdo to Gorubachofu," *Voice* (October 1988): 112–22; and Kimura Hiroshi, "Nihon o jūshi shihajimeta Soren," *Seiron*, September 20, 1988.

40. Wada Haruki, "NisSo 'dakyo' de hoppō ryōdo mondai wa ketchaku suru," *Ekonomisuto*, November 15, 1988, pp. 56–61; Wada Haruki, "San Furanshisuko kōwa," pp. 233–49.

41. Kishida Kazuhiro, "Mata Gorubachofu ni odorasareta Nakasone to shimbun," *Shokun* (October 1988): 26–38.

42. Itō Kenichi, "Soren no taiNichi seisaku wa kawatta ka?" *This Is* (December 1988): 119–26.

43. Sase Masamori, "Hoppō ryōdo mondai Soren na nankasetsu no shinshō bōdai," *Shokun* (January 1989): 93.

44. "Saikin no Nakasone ha jijō," *Asahi shimbun*, August 26, 1988, p. 2.

45. "Gaimushō o tobikoshita Nakasone Go shokichō kaidan," *Shūkan shincho* (August 1988): 134–37.

46. Kimura Hiroshi, "Ryōdo mondai de no zenshin wa atta," *Sankei shimbun*, December 27, 1988, p. 5.

47. Morimoto Tadao, "Gorubachofu no omoi tsubuyaki," *Ushio*, no. 123 (1988).

48. Kimura Hiroshi, "Ryōdo mondai de no zenshin wa atta," p. 5.

49. *Ima hoppō ryōdo wa*, pp. 34–55.

50. Ibid., pp. 56–57.

51. Tōgō Kazuhiko, "Soren keizai NisSo kankei no kinkyō," *Kokusai shigen* (April 1989): 11–29.

52. Hakamada Shigeki, "Soren no taiNichi seisaku wa 'shin shikō' no soto," *Kakushin*, p. 30.

53. *Kore ga Kunashiri da* (Sapporo: Hokkaidō shimbunsha, 1989).

54. "Ainu gyomin no taiSo goben jigyō," *Asahi shimbun*, August 31, 1988, p. 3.

55. Togō Takehiro, "Soren no shin shikō gaikō to Uno gaishō Soren hōmon no seika," *Sekai keizai hyōron*, no. 33, July 7, 1989, pp. 16–25; "NisSo heiwa jōyaku koshō," *Nikkan kōgyō shimbun*, January 27, 1989.

56. Tōgō Kazuhiko, "Soren keizai NisSo kankei no kinkyō," pp. 11–29.

57. Kimura Hiroshi, "Kō sureba hoppō ryōdo wa kaeru," *Voice* (May 1989): 116–25.

58. Hiroshi Kimura, "Neterpenie tol'ko vredit," *Novoe vremia*, no. 23 (June 1989): 25.

59. Takubo Tadae, "Uno seiken ni gaikō tetsugaku aru ka?" *Seiron* (September 1989): 15–16, 72.

60. Suzuki Yoshikatsu, "'Hoppō ryōdo mondai' de rakkan wa sōkei" *Sekai shūhō*, January 17, 1989, pp. 20–23; Nakazawa Takayuki, "Shiewarunaze ensetsu ni miru Soren no 'shin shikō' gaikō," *Sekai shūhō*, January 17, 1989.

61. Katori Yasue, "Kongo no NisSo kankei o dō suru ka?" *Ajia jihō* (May 1989): 10–25.

62. Itō Takayuki, "Roshia bunka no yukue," *Kokusai kōryū*, no. 48 (November 1988): 37–38.

63. Ikuta Shinji, "Soren no peresutoroika shin kyokumen ni: jinmin daigiin taikai no senkyo o oete," *Chōken shitsuhō*, no. 80 (Asahi shimbunsha, June 1989): 26.

64. Kitajima Masayuki, "Gorubachofu ryū no shōtai: Nihon wa dō tsukiau ka?" *This Is* (April 1989): 168–78; and Takayanagi Yoshio, "Ashita wa aru no ka peresutoroika," *This Is* (February 1989): 133–41.

65. Togō Takehiro, "Soren shidobu no jinji ido, taiNichi seisaku nado o megutte," *Sekai keizai daiyaru repōto*, no. 322 (November 1988): 2–8.

66. Togō Takehiro, "Soren no shin shikō gaikō to Uno gaishō Soren homon no seika," *Sekai keizai hyōron* (July 1989): 8–25.

67. Katori Yasue, "Kongo no NisSo kankei o dō suru ka?" p. 27.

68. Shimotomai Nobuo, "'Atarashii shikō' no kōki to kiki," *Sekai* (August 1989): 105–18.

69. Yamashita Shintarō, "Saikin ni okeru Soren no gaikō to naisei," *Kokumin gaikō*, no. 121 (August 1989): 13–15.

70. "Seiji kaikaku de peresutoroika wa seikō suru ka?" *Chishiki* (June 1989): 39–45.

71. "Soren peresutoroika no 'omote to ura,'" *Sekai shūhō*, May 16, 1989, pp. 10–40.

72. "Izen anchū mosaku tsuzuku peresutoroika," *Shūkan tōyō keizai*, April 29, 1989, pp. 107–11.

73. Ōkura Yūnosuke, "Saigo wa Sobieto Renpō no kaitai ni tadoritsuku," *Sekai shūhō*, May 16, 1989, pp. 14–17; Haka Yoshiyuki, "Doko ni mo kanjirarenai 'kaikaku' no tegotae," *Sekai shūhō*, May 16, 1989, pp. 22–25.

74. Makino Noboru, "Kyōgyō Seron Nihon wa ikinokoreru ka," *Sankei shimbun*, July 10, 1989.

75. Hakamada Shigeki, "Kawaru Soren, kawaranu Soren," in *Motto shiritai Soren*, ed. Hakamada (1988), pp. 1–25.

CHAPTER EIGHT

1. Katori Yasue, "Kongo no NisSo kankei o dō suru ka," *Ajia jihō* (May 1989): 28.

2. "ChūsSo wakai o megutte," *Sekai keizai daiyaru repōto*, no. 326 (March 1989): 5.

3. "ChūsSo shunō kaidan no seika," *Sekai keizai daiyaru repōto* (*rajio tampa*), no. 329 (June 1989): 17–20.

4. Nakajima Mineo, "Kinchō kanwa e daitenkan suru kokusai seiji kōzō," *Sekai shūhō*, December 20, 1988, p. 13.

5. Saito Yoshikazu, "Keizai kyōryoku no hiyakuteki hatten o nerau," *Sekai shūhō*, December 20, 1988, p. 14.

6. Mōri Kazuko, "'Shin shikō' ga rīdoshita ChūsSo samitto," *Sekai* (July 1989): 168.

7. Nakajima Mineo, "Tsuyomaru shakaishugi koku no sōgō izon," *Sankei shimbun*, December 8, 1988, p. 7; Nakajima Mineo, "Nihon wa taiChū keizai seisai o," *Sekai shūhō*, June 20, 1989, p. 7.

8. Yano Tōru, "Tsumi o nikunde kuni o nikumaza," *Voice* (August 1989): 86–88.

9. Mōri Kazuko, "ChūsSo detanto wa doko made susumu ka," *Jiyū* (February 1988): 102–9.

10. Hasegawa Keitarō, "Sayonara Chūgoku," *Voice* (August 1989): 58–71.

11. Yano Tōru, "Tsumi o nikunde kuni o nikumazu," *Voice* (August 1989): 80–97.

12. Shimotomai Nobuo, "'Atarashii shikō' no kōki to kiki," *Sekai* (August 1989): 116.

13. Uchimura Gōsuke, "Minshuka tonaetsutsu Tenanmon no michi e," *Sankei shimbun*, February 3, 1990.

14. Katsuda Kichitarō, "Chūgoku wa Pōrando no ato ou ka?" *Sankei shimbun*, June 23, 1989; and Nagata Minoru, "Kokusai keizai e no dakikomi," *Nihon keizai shimbun* June 26, 1989, p. 23.

15. Tsuyoshi Hasegawa, "Japanese Perceptions of the Soviet Union: 1960–1985," p. 39.

16. Tanaka Yōzō, *Chūgokujin to Nihonjin* (1987).

17. Hakamada Shigeki, "Roman o ubatta no wa nani ka," *This Is* (August 1989): 38–48.

18. Nakamura Katsunori, "'Tenanmon dai gyakusatsu' osorubeshi kyōsanshugi," *Kakushin* (August 1989): 32–35.

19. "Kyōsanshugi wa shinda ka," *Seiron* (September 1989): 48–69.

20. "Meisō suru komyunizumu," *Sekai shūhō*, August 8–15, 1989, pp. 14–87.

21. Iida Tsuneo, "Kyōsanshugi keikaku keizai e no jishin sonshitsu," *Chūō kōron* (August 1989): 59.

22. Teratani Hiromi, "Soren no 'Tōō shihai' wa owatta ka," *Sekai shūhō*, July 18, 1989, p. 21.

23. Sase Masamori, "Konmei to kinchō no Soren Tōō kankei," *Gekkan jiyū minshu* (May 1989): 64–75; (June 1989): 72–91; and (July 1989): 98–115.

24. Kawato Akio, "Higashi Yōroppa no seiji keizai jōsei," *Sekai keizai daiyaru repōto*, no. 313 (February 1988): 19–23.

25. "Hageshii kankyō no Go daitoryō raiNichi," *Mainichi shimbun*, January 25, 1991, p. 5; "Futōmeikan zō NisSo kankei," *Mainichi shimbun*, January 25, 1991, p. 3; "Taisei nai kaikaku ni genkai," *Sankei shimbun*, January 25, 1991, p. 3.

26. Hōgen Shinsaku, "Shakaishugi wa mohaya jidai sakugō," *Sankei shimbun*, July 27, 1989, p. 7.

27. Ōsaki Heihachirō, "Hashigaki," *Peresutoroika: Gorubachofu kaikaku no sōgōteki kenkyū* (1987), p. 5.

28. Usami Shoichirō, "Sobieto kenkyūsho no setsuritsu," *Mado*, no. 68 (March 1989): 14–15.

29. Fujita Osamu, "Shakaishugi shi ni okeru peresutoroika," *Hōritsu jihō*, 62, 12 (December 1990): 6–13.

30. Satō Tsuneaki, "Soren Hangarii no keizai kaikaku," *Gekkan shakaitō*, March 29, 1989, pp. 126–35; Shimotomai Nobuo, "Seiji kaikaku: shimin shakaiteki shakaishugi wa kanō ka" *Gekkan shakaitō* (March 1989): 75.

31. Nakano Tetsuzō, " 'Atarashii seiji shikō' to kasekika shita shikō," *Gekkan shakaitō* (June 1989): 99–109; (July 1989): 72–84.

32. "Soren kyōiron ni 'chūshaku' " *Asahi shimbun*, April 4, 1990, p. 2; " 'Soren kyōiron' ga kusen," *Asahi shimbun*, April 10, 1990, p. 2.

33. "Yaruta no kabe wa kuzureta no ka," *Sekai* (January 1990): 234–47.

34. "Sobieto no peresutoroika to tōzai kankei," *Sekai keizai daiyaru repōto: rajio tanpa* (March 1988): 14–17; "BeiSo—Mosukuwa shunō kaigi no igi to seika," *Sekai keizai daiyaru repōto: rajio tampa*, no. 318 (July 1988): 2–9.

35. "Hoppō ryōdo mondai to NisSo kankei," *Ajia jihō* (January 1989): 34–78.

36. Akino Yutaka, "Gorubachofu seiken no Ajia-taiheiyō seisaku," *Kokusai mondai* (March 1989): 55–71.

37. "Bōeihi zō, 77% ga hiteiteki," *Asahi shimbun*, June 27, 1988, p. 1.

38. Sugimori Kōji, "Hokkyokuken ni shinro o tore!" *Sansaru* (July 1990): 75–83.

39. Kimura Hiroshi, *Hoppō ryōdo*, pp. 191–96; Kimura Hiroshi, "The Soviet-Japanese Territorial Dispute," *The Harriman Institute Forum* 2, 6 (June 1989): 1–8.

40. Kimura Akio, "Hoppō ryōdo henkan no ishi wa aru ka," *Chishiki* (June 1989): 58–66.

41. Hisane Masaki, "Gorbachev's Visit Won't Be a Cure-all," *The Japan Times*, October 21, 1989, p. 3.

42. "Yakoburefu shi no 11 gatsu raiNichi," *Yomiuri shimbun*, October 22, 1989, p. 3.

43. Nagata Jirō, "Soren jimintō ni shōjun?" *Nikan kōgyō shimbun*, November 18, 1989, p. 3; and "Soren yōjin no hatsugen ni kadai na kitai wa kinmotsu," *Nihon keizai shimbun*, November 16, 1989, p. 4.

44. "Yakoburefu hatsugen no ura o yomu," *Mainichi shimbun*, November 15, 1989, p. 5.

45. "Yakoburefu shi ga mochikaeru mono," *Tōkyō shimbun*, November 16, 1989, p. 4.

46. "Hoppō ryōdo fukume dakyōsaku saguru," *Asahi shimbun*, November 14, 1989, p. 1.

47. "Hoshin tenkan sore to mo bishō senjutsu," *Sankei shimbun*, November 16, 1989, p. 3.

48. "Yontō henkan no hitsuyō ninshiki o Yakoburefu shi hoNichi ni nozomu," *Sankei shimbun*, November 5, 1989, p. 5.

49. Satō Kikuo, "Keizai kyōryoku to no rinkeji ga hitsuyō na hoppō ryōdo seisaku," *Sekai shūhō* November 21, 1989, pp. 62–65.

50. Yunnosuke Ohkura, "A Price for the Northern Isles?" *The Japan Times*, October 23, 1989, p. 8.

51. Ferdinand Protzman, "$1 Billion Plan for Poland and Hungary," *The New York Times*, January 10, 1990, p. A10.

52. "NisSo no hannō saguru," *Asahi shimbun*, April 24, 1990, p. 2.

53. "Sofuto mūdo tadayowase," *Asahi shimbun*, September 7, 1990, p. 3.

54. "'Tenkanki' no ninshiki de wa itchi," *Asahi shimbun*, September 5, 1990, p. 4; "Honkakka suru NisSo kōshō de Soren gaikō ga nokoshita wadai," *Asahi jānaru*, September 21, 1990, pp. 106–7.

55. "No Simplistic Solution to Northern Isles Issue," *Mainichi Daily News*, October 28, 1990, p. 1.

56. Kimura Hiroshi, "Hoppō ryōdo no kachi," *Keizai ōrai* (November 1990): 32–41.

57. Shimotomai Nobuo, "Peresutoroika de Sorenjin no ishiki wa koko made kawatta," *Asahi jānaru*, November 2, 1990, pp. 14–23.

58. Satō Kikuo, "Hoppō ryōdo mondai no kaiketsu wa kanō da," *Sekai shūhō*, October 23, 1990, p. 41.

59. Ibid., pp. 41–45.

60. Inegaki Kiyoshi, "Ugokidashi Nihon kigyō no Soren kyokutō kaihatsu," *Ekonomisuto*, October 23, 1990, p. 212.

61. "NisSo no teiryū 3 and 5," *Mainichi shimbun*, August 9, 1990, p. 1, and August 11, 1990, p. 1; "Hoppō ryōdo zettai jōken de nai," *Asahi shimbun*, August 9, 1990, p. 3; Osuga Mizuo, "Ugokihajimeta hoppō ryōdo mondai," *Sekai* (September 1990): 19–22.

62. "Ryōdo fukume 'heiwa jōyaku' kaiketsu o," *Mainichi shimbun*, October 7, 1990, p. 10.

63. "NichiBei no taiSo 'kokando' ni sa," and "Shakai no henka ni yureru Soren," *Asahi shimbun*, October 22, 1990, pp. 16–17.

64. Shimamori Michiko, "Nanimo shinai koken," *Hokkaidō shimbun*, November 2, 1990, p. 1.

65. Shimotomai Nobuo, "NisSo kankei o dō hirogeru ka, *Sekai* (February 1991): 150–58.

66. Wada Haruki, "'Hoppō ryōdo' futatsu no sentaku," *Sekai* (February 1991): 170–77.

67. Sasaki Tōru, "Sōgo rieki o zenmen ni," *Asahi shimbun*, October 31, 1989 (evening), p. 7.

68. Ozaki Hisashi, "Tōō wa 'seiōka' shinai," *Voice* (December 1989): 96–103.

69. Kurakawa Masato, *Makka na kuni no makka na uso* (1989).

70. Yamauchi Masayuki, Sakuma Kunio, and Nakai Kazuo, *Bunretsu suru Soren* (1990).

71. Saeki Seiichi, "Wareware wa shima kara tachinokanai," *Shūkan tōyō keizai*, October 27, 1990, pp. 28–38.

72. "'Nitō henkan' o teishō," *Asahi shimbun*, April 24, 1990, p. 1; "NisSo no hannō saguru," *Asahi shimbun*, April 24, 1990, p. 2.

73. "Majority Favor Step-by-Step Approach to Territory," *SUPAR Report*, no. 10 (January 1991): 92.

74. "Yazov Says Moscow to Keep Northern Islands," *SUPAR Report*, no. 10 (January 1991): 92.

75. "Baruto no ryūketsu o kurikaesu na," *Asahi shimbun*, January 20, 1991, p. 5.

76. Satō Tsuneaki and Morimoto Tadao, "Nokosareta te wa Mosukuwa kuyu," *Chishiki* (February 1991): 32–46.

77. "Hoppō ryōdo 2 senoku doru de teuchi," *Mainichi shimbun*, February 1, 1991, p. 2.

78. Kimura Hiroshi and Kimisaka Fuyuko, "Hoppō ryōdo to Nihonjin 4, *Sankei shimbun*, February 21, 1991, p. 18; and "Hoppō ryōdo to Nihonjin 5," *Sankei shimbun*, February 28, 1991, p. 20.

79. "Hoppō ryōdo kiseki 11," *Asahi shimbun*, March 1, 1990, p. 7.

80. Suzuki Keisuke and Matsumoto Akio, "Shūshi ikkan 'hoppō ryōdo' o shuchōshita zaikai," *Will* (March 1991): 137–44.

81. Georgyi Kunāze, "Gorubachofu ni wa mo genmetsushita," *Sekai shūhō*, February 26, 1991, pp. 6–7.

82. "Hoppō ryōdo henkan (nitō ijō) 43% yōnin," *Yomiuri shimbun*, February 22, 1991, p. 1.

83. Hasegawa Tsuyoshi, "Gorubachofu to Sorengun: peresutoroika no naka no terumidōra hando," *Chūō kōron* (March 1991): 110–23.

84. Ōguma Hidehari, "Eritsin shi no tairitsu ga ōkiku eikyō," *Tōkyō shimbun*, March 1991, p. 2.

85. Kimura Hiroshi et al., "NisSo kankei to hoppō ryodō mondai," *Gekkan shakaitō* (March 1991): 53–59.

CHAPTER NINE

1. Arai Hirokazu, "BeiSo shunō kaidan to kongo no tōzai kankei," *Sekai keizai hyōron* (February 1988): 35.

2. Itō Kenichi, "Roshia = Soren no taigai kōdō patān no keizokusei," in *The Soviet Union in Transition*, ed. Kinya Niiseki, pp. 197–206.

3. Ibid., pp. 212–16.

4. Ibid., p. 219.

5. Shiba Ryōtarō, *Roshia ni tsuite* (1986).

6. Togawa Tsuguo, "Taikai inshōki," *Roshiashi kenkyū*, no. 41 (1985): 55–56.

7. Shiba, *Roshia ni tsuite*, p. 244.

8. Hōgen Shinsaku, *Nihonjin ni totte Soren wa kiken kokka da* (1983), pp. 39, 72, 170.

9. Shiba, *Roshia ni tsuite*, p. 25.

10. Ibid., p. 41.

11. Ibid., *Roshia ni tsuite*, pp. 242–43; Shimizu Hayao, *Nihonjin wa naze Roshia ga kirai ka*, pp. 15–21.

12. Morimoto Yoshio, *Sobieto to Roshia*, pp. 60, 68–71, 140–41.

13. Kimura Hiroshi, *Soren to Roshiajin* (1980), pp. 22, 26–43.

14. Ibid., pp. 68, 75, 88–90, 228.

15. Morimoto Yoshio, *Sobieto to Roshia*, pp. 16–23.

16. Kimura Akio, *Soren: sono kyozō to jitsuzō* (1977), pp. 231–50.

17. Nakamura Yoshikazu "Roshiajin," *Roshia Soren o shiru jiten*, p. 678.

18. Morimoto Tadao, *Soren o shiranai de kanemōke dekiru ka* (1989), pp. 25–26, 42, 84.

19. Morimoto Yoshio, *Sobieto to Roshia*, pp. 44–50.

20. Katsuda Kichitarō et al., *Soren hōkai ron* (1990), pp. 45, 49, 52, 70, 84.

21. Ibid., pp. 44–50, 74–79, 168–71.

22. Borisu Eritsin and Hakamada Shigeki, *Soren, Tōō o yomu* (1990), pp. 125–26, 130, 142, 156.

23. Morimoto Yoshio, *Sobieto to Roshia*, pp. 158–56, 205–6.

24. Niizeki Kinya, "Watakushi no ikikata," *Kōken* 27, 10 (October 1989): 52.

25. Yamauchi Masayuki, "Homeinii to Gorubachofu," *Kikan Asuteion*, no. 14 (1989): 48–63.

26. Igeta Sadayoshi, "20 seiki kakkoku bunka ga konzai," *Yomiuri shimbun*, December 1, 1989 (evening), p. 15.

CHAPTER TEN

1. *Sobietoshi no kenkyū* (1956), p. 246.

2. "Tōō," *Shigaku zasshi* (May 1968): 315–21.

3. "Gendai: Roshiashi," *Shigaku zasshi* (May 1963): 375–76.

4. "Gendai: Roshiashi," *Shigaku zasshi* (May 1965): 391.

5. "Chūsei: Tōō," *Shigaku zasshi* (May 1974): 275–76; "Chūsei," *Shigaku zasshi* (May 1983): 297; "Chūsei," *Shigaku zasshi* (May 1985): 316.

6. Nobuaki Shiokawa, "Izuchenie istorii SSSR v Iaponii," *Voprosy istorii* (February 1990): 136.

7. "Gendai: Roshiashi," *Shigaku zasshi* (May 1969): 353; and "Gendai: Roshiashi," *Shigaku zasshi* (May 1970): 350.

8. *Roshiashi kenkyū* (1988), pp. 58–60.

9. Nobuaki Shiokawa, "Some Aspects of Japanese Studies on Russian and Soviet History," *Acta Slavica Iaponica*, no. 3 (1985), pp. 36–50.

10. Nobuaki Shiokawa, "Izuchenie istorii SSSR v Iaponii," pp. 136–38, 144.

11. Kimura Hiroshi, "Nihon no Soren kenkyū," pp. 95–96.

12. Kikuchi Masanori, *Roshiya kakumei no shinwa* (1986).

13. Wada Haruki, "Kikuchi Masanori 'Roshia Kakumei' (Chūkō shinsho) ni tsuite," *Roshiashi kenkyū*, no. 16 (December 1987): 53–79.

14. I. A. D'iakonova, "Pervaia rossiiskaia revoliutsiia v osveshchenii sovremennoi iaponskoi istoriografii," *Istoriia SSSR* (March–April 1989): 179–91.

15. I. A. D'iakonova, "Kh. Nakayama. Tsarskaia Rossiia: inostrannyi kapital," *Istoriia SSSR*, no. 2 (1990): 213–15.

16. Kojima Noburo, *NichiRo sensō*, vols. 1–5 (1990). Examples of jointly authored books include Peter Juviler and Hiroshi Kimura, eds., *Gorbachev's Reforms: U.S. and Japanese Assessments* (New York: Aldine de Gruyter, 1988), and Tsuyoshi Hasegawa and Alex Pravda, eds, *Perestroika: Soviet Domestic and Foreign Policies* (London: Sage Publications, The Royal Institute of International Affairs, 1990). The improving Hokkaidō journal, *Acta Slavica Iaponica*, edited by Kimura Hiroshi, is published largely in English and Russian.

17. Shiokawa Nobuaki, "Kenryoku to kyōdōtai no setten: Taniuchi Yuzuru 'Sutārin seiji taisei no seiritsu' (zenyonbu) o megutte," *Kokka gakkai zasshi* 52, 3–4 (March 1989): 207–29.

18. "Gendai: Roshiashi," *Shigaku zasshi* (May 1974): 311.

19. Naoko Hirooka, Hiroshi Okuda, and Kenji Uchida, "Sutārin seiji taisei no seiritsu," *Acta Slavica Iaponica*, vol. 6 (1988): 100–8.

20. Ibid., pp. 107–8.

21. Shiokawa Nobuaki, "Kenryoku to kyōdōtai no setten," pp. 207–29.

22. Shiokawa Nobuaki, "Shimotomai Nobuo, 'Sobieto seiji to rōdō kumiai—Neppuki seijishi jōsetsu,'" *Keizaigaku zasshi* 49, 1 (April 1983): 81–85; "Neppuki rōdō kumiai no shomondai: Shimotomai shi no kinchō o megutte," *Roshiashi kenkyū*, no. 37 (May 1983): 53–75; Shimotomai Nobuo, "Shiokawa Nobuaki shi e no henshin," *Roshiashi kenkyū*, no. 38 (November 1983): 64–83.

23. Inoki Masamichi, "Renin," *Keizai ōrai* (November 1989): 20–21.

24. Taniuchi Yuzuru, *Gendai shakaishugi o kangaeru: Roshia kakumei kara 21 seiki e* (1988).

25. Shiokawa Nobuaki, "1930 nendai taisei to peresutoroika," *Roshiashi kenkyū*, no. 47 (April 1989): 56–69.

26. Nobuo Shimotomai, "New Interpretation of the NEP and the Stalinist System under Glasnost,'" in *Facing Up to the Past: Soviet Historiography under Perestroika*, ed. Takayuki Ito (Sapporo: Slavic Research Center, Hokkaidō University, 1989), p. 194.

27. "Chūsei: Roshiashi," *Shigaku zasshi* (May 1965): 370; "Chūsei: Roshiashi," *Shigaku zasshi* (May 1966): 356–58; and "Seiyōshi: Gendai," *Shigaku zasshi* (May 1968): 370.

28. "Chūsei: Roshia Tōō shi," *Shigaku zasshi* (May 1968): 315–16; "Tōō," *Shigaku zasshi* (May 1968): 315–16.

29. Katsuda Kichitaro, "An Analysis of the Modernization of Russia: A Study of Revolution and Intelligentsia from the Viewpoint of Comparative History," *Review: A Quarterly Journal for the Study of Communism and Communist Countries*, no. 29 (April 1971): 1–87.

30. Kikuchi Masanori, *Shakaishugi wa doko e iku ka* (1985), pp. 7–36, 49, 180–84.

31. Wada Haruki, "Rekishi no naka no peresutoroika," *Roshiashi kenkyū*, no. 47 (April 1989): 76–87.

32. Satō Tsuneaki, "Gonengo no peresutoroika," *Keizai ōrai* (February 1988): 38–41; Satō Tsuneaki, "Soren, Hangarii no keizai kaikaku," *Gekkan shakaitō* (March 1989): 126–35.

33. Iwata Kenji, *Soren no naiseirikigaku to gaikō* (1989).

34. Nakayama Hiromasa, *Peresutoroika no naka ni sunde* (1989), pp. 13 and 51–59.

35. Kojima Atsushi, "Gorubachofu no Soren: denwa to peresutoroika," *This Is* (July 1989): 158–63.

36. Kanamori Hisao, "1989 nendo NisSo keizai senmonka kaigi hōkokukai," 1, *Soren Tōō keizai sokuhō*, pp. 1–7; Kanamori Hisao, "Soren keizai wa kashō hyōka sarete iru," *Chūō kōron* (July 1989): 148–57.

37. Ogawa Kazuo, "Minzoku rihan de kyōsanshugi no chōshō," *This Is* (November 1989): 144–53.

38. Mori Akira, "Miete kita keizai kiki no kōzo: Mosukuwa de jitsu seikatsu ni furete," *Chōken shitsuhō*, no. 82 (October 1989): 1–21.

39. Hasegawa Keitarō, "Sore de mo Gorubachofu wa ikinokoru," *Voice* (December 1989): 62–75.

40. "Hasegawa Keitarō: Snachala eto kazalos' katastrofoi—Iaponskii ekonomist delitsia opytom reformy v svoei strane," *Izvestia*, May 7, 1990, p. 5.

41. Satō Tsuneaki, "Shiren ni tatsu Gorubachofu kaikaku," *Kōmei*, no. 330 (July 1987): 138–49; Satō Tsuneaki, "ChūsSo o kangaeru," *Mainichi shimbun*, May 16, 1989.

42. Saga Tōru, *Soren no shiren* (1989), p. 9.

43. Ibid., pp. 377–89.

44. Kanamori Hisao, "Soren keizai wa kashō hyōka sarete iru," *Chūō kōron* (July 1989): 149–57.

45. Morimoto Tadao, *Ajia taiheiyō ni noridasu Soren to Nihon no taiō* (Nihon keizai chōsa kyōgikai, 1989), pp. 1–29.

46. "Soren keizai wa saisei dekiru ka," *Nihon keizai shimbun*, August 12, 1990, p. 24.

47. Shirai Hisaya, "Kiken suiiki ni haitta Soren keizai," *Asahi jānaru*, April 7, 1989, p. 88.

48. "Saikin no Soren keizai kaikaku no dōkō to waga kuni no sangyō: chōsa kenkyū hōkokusho" (Kikai shinkō kyōkai keizai kenkyūsho, 1988), pp. 1–103.

49. S. Tsutsumi, "Istoki stabil'nogo rosta," *Problemy Dal'nego Vostoka*, no. 2, 1990, pp. 53–57.

50. Hachiya Minami, "Ministerstva v Iaponii," *EKO* (August 1989): 56.

51. Kaneda Tatsuo, "Gorubachofu no nōgyō kaikaku," *Soren, Tōō 5 kakkoku no shokuryō, nōgyō mondai oyobi tōmen no nōeijō no kadai* (Kokusai nōringyō kyōryoku kyōkai, 1988), pp. 1–22.

52. Kaneda Tatsuo, *Nōgyō peresutoroika to Soren no yukue* (1990), pp. 207–8.

53. Mochizuki Kiichi, "Soren no taigai keizai seisaku," *Sobieto kenkyū*, no. 2 (1989): 53–54.

54. "Soren keizai kaikaku no genjō to mondaiten," *Gorubachofu kaikaku no hamon* (Sapporo: Hokkaidō University, Slavic Research Center, 1988), pp. 49–53. Mochizuki Kiichi, "Dappi o hakaru Soren keizai: sono senzairyoku no kaimei," *Soren kenkyū*, no. 6 (April 1988): 93–108.

55. Sawa Hidetake, "Doko e iku Soren nōgyō," *Sekai to Nihon* (1989), pp. 10–52.

56. "Itchokusen ni heiwa jōyaku e susumu kanōsei mo,' " *Shūkan tōyō keizai*, February 11, 1989, pp. 50–58.

57. Morimoto Tadao, *Soren o shiranai de kanemōke dekiru ka*, pp. 96–99, 102–9, 132–34.

58. Kanamori Hisao, "Future Prospects of Economic Relations Between Soviet Far East and East Asia as Well as South East Asian Nations," ms., 1989.

59. "Henkakuki no Soren to NisSo kankei," *Mainichi shimbun*, October 1, 1990, p. 3.

60. "NisSo no teiryū, 18," *Mainichi shimbun*, August 27, 1990, p. 1.

61. "Soren no Nihon keizai hōkokusho," *Asahi shimbun*, September 8, 1990, p. 14.

CHAPTER ELEVEN

1. Hayashi Kentarō, "Kyōsanshugi wa shinda ka: shamin ni mo ashita wa nai," *Seiron* (September 1989): 49–54.

2. Shibata Yoshimatsu, "Kurūpusukaya," *Roshia Soren o shiru jiten* (1989), p. 174.

3. Hōgen Shinsaku, *Nihonjin ni totte Soren wa kiken kokka da*, pp. 72–73.

4. Ibid., pp. 52–56, 59–62.

5. Nasu Kiyoshi, *Soren no hōkai*, pp. 28, 38, 56.

6. Suzuki Toshiko, *Dare mo kakanakatta Soren* (1979).

7. *Soren Roshia o shiru jiten.*

8. Shiokawa Nobuaki, "Peresutoroika o dō haeru ka," parts 1–3, *Keizai hyōron* (May 1988): 2–16; (June 1988): 2–17; (July 1988): 22–39.

9. Shimizu Hayao, *Nihonjin wa naze Soren ga kirai ka.*

10. Hakamada Shigeki, "ChūSSo 'sōgō gokai' no shinri kōzō," in *Gendai Chūgoku to Soren*, ed. Yamagiwa Akira and Mōri Kazuko (1987), pp. 140–70.

11. Hakamada Shigeki, "Gorubachofu no 'katsuseika' rosen to kaikakuha no shakai ninshiki," *Soren kenkyū*, no. 4 (1987): 5–28.

12. Hakamada Shigeki, "Gokai sareru Soren no 18 no shikaku," *Chūō kōron* (May 1987): 122–41.

13. Uda Fumio, *Soren seiji kenryoku no kōzō*, p. 322.

14. Shimotomai Nobuo, "Peresutoroika to 'rekishi minaoshi' no bunmyaku," *Roshiashi kenkyū*, no. 47 (April 1989): 70–75.

15. Shimotomai Nobuo, "Seiji kaikaku: shimin shakaiteki shakaishugi wa kanō ka," *Heiwa keizai* (May 1989): 42–50.

16. Hakamada Shigeki, "Kawaru Soren, kawaranu Soren," in *Motto shiritai Soren*, ed. Hakamada, p. 17, 23.

17. Saga Tōru, "Soren: sono kawaru mono kawarazaru mono," *Kokusai*

koryū, no. 48 (1988): 58–59; Saga Tōru, *Soren shakai wa kawaru ka: peresutoroika to taishū* (1988).

18. Hakamada Shigeki and Funabashi Yōichi, "Gensō to shite no shakaishugi," 1, *Asahi jānaru*, May 19, 1989, pp. 99–104.

19. Hakamada Shigeki, "Mosukuwa de mita hapuningu," *Bungei shunjū* (March 1988): 138–51.

20. Hakamada Shigeki, *Shinsō no shakaishugi*, pp. 276–79.

21. Hakamada Shigeki, "Tankō suto to Kanto no jinkakushugi," *Sankei shimbun*, August 19, 1989.

22. Hakamada Shigeki, "Minzoku mondai de yureru Soren," *Keizai kurabu kōen* (March 1989): 67–69.

23. Hakamada Shigeki, "ChūSSo 'sōgo gokai' no shinri kōzō," pp. 140–70, and *Soren: gokai o toku 25 no shikaku* (1987).

24. Hakamada Shigeki, "Kawaru Soren, kawaranu Soren," pp. 11–13.

25. Ibid.

26. Hakamada Shigeki, "Gokai sareru Soren no 18 no shikaku," *Chūō kōron* (May 1987): 122–41.

27. Hakamada Shigeki, *Shinsō no shakaishugi*, pp. 259–66.

28. Shiokawa Nobuaki, "Peresutoroika o dō haeru ka."

29. "Soren Tōō shokoku no kazoku kōzō to kinō ni kansuru kenkyū," *NIRA OUTPUT* (May 1989): 3–8, 77–137.

30. Morimoto Yoshio, *Sobieto to Roshia*, pp. 26–27.

31. Kikuchi Masanori, *Shakaishugi wa doko e iku ka* (1985), pp. 29–30.

32. Aoki Makoto, "Tōsei Sobieto hanzai jijō: jika keizai o gyūjiru mafuia no taitō," *Sekai shūhō*, October 17, 1989, pp. 18–21.

33. Hirooka Masahisa, "Gorubachofu kaikaku to shūkyō," *Mainichi shimbun*, December 16, 1989 (evening), p. 6.

34. Morimoto Tadao, "TaiNichi jōhō shisei tsuyomeru Soren no shini," *Ekonomisuto*, January 31, 1989, pp. 80–85.

35. Hasegawa Keitarō, "Sore demo Gorubachofu wa ikinokoru," *Voice* (December 1989): 62–70.

36. Hakamada Shigeki, "Soren Tōō ga mita minshuka undo," *Chūō kōron* (August 1989): 97–105.

37. Clyde Haberman, "Pope Warns on Rekindling of Rivalries in East," *The New York Times*, January 14, 1990 (international), p. 13.

CHAPTER TWELVE

1. Shimotomai Nobuo, "Tagenka kakumei no naka no Soren, part I: seiji kaikaku kara 'kakumei' e," *Sekai* (July 1989): 154.

2. Sawa Hidetake, "Gorubachofu no kake: mite kita peresutoroika," *Kakushin* (December 1988): 53.

3. Sase Masamori, "Soren no ittōsei hitei wa honmono ka," *Sankei shimbun*, August 5, 1989, p. 7.

4. Kimura Akio, "Kieta Kuremulin daini shoki to shokikyoku: zetsudai na kenryoku o motta Gorubachofu," *Sekai shūhō*, December 20, 1988, p. 23.

5. Ōkura Yūnosuke, "Seiji kaikaku de peresutoroika wa seikō suru ka," *Chishiki* (June 1989): 39, 45–46.

6. Ōkura Yūnosuke, "Shūsei shihonshugiteki teikoku to shite no hanto o shishu: 'minshuka' no tame dokusaisha ni naru Gorubachofu," *Sekai shūhō*, January 3, 1989, pp. 40–42.

7. Yoshinari Taishi, "Gurasunosuchi: genkai wa miete iru kōkai seisaku," *Sekai shūhō*, August 8–15, 1989, pp. 28–29.

8. Kimura Hiroshi, "Peresutoroika to bōmei Roshia chishikijin," *Sankei shimbun*, August 4, 1989, p. 6.

9. Kimura Hiroshi, "Bunkakai: Sorujenitsin kaikin de kuru tokoro made kita gurasunosuchi," *Sekai shūhō*, May 16, 1989, pp. 18–21.

10. Ōkura Yūnosuke, "Minzoku funsō: Saigo wa Sobieto Renpō no hōkai ni tadoritsuku," *Sekai shūhō*, May 16, 1989, p. 14.

11. Hakamada Shigeki, "Shakaishugikoku no yukue: Soren, daikaikaku ni umi no kurushimi," *Yomiuri shimbun*, evening edition, February 14, 1990, p. 13.

12. Kimura Hiroshi, "Seisaku no dakyō koso chūmoku subeki," *Sankei shimbun*, January 30, 1990, p. 7.

13. Nishimura Fumio, "Kokunai seiji: minshuka yōkyu ga funshutsu shita jinmin daigiin senkyo," *Sekai shūhō*, May 16, 1989, pp. 11–12.

14. Suzuki Hironobu, "Gorubachofu no senkyo kaikaku to sono shūhen," in *Gendai sekai no seiji jōkyō: rekishi to genjō bunseki*, ed. Katsube Hajime (1989), pp. 238–42.

15. Shimotomai Nobuo, "Gaikō no tāgetto wa higashi Ajia ni utsutta: 'gunji henchō' kara keizai jūshi no shisei senmei ni," *Ekonomisuto*, December 27, 1988, p. 13.

16. Shimotomai Nobuo, "Tagenka kakumei no naka no Soren, Part I: Seiji kaikaku kara 'kakumei' e," p. 153.

17. Ibid., pp. 154–62.

18. Ibid., pp. 163–64.

19. Shimotomai Nobuo, "Tagenka kakumei no naka no Soren, Part II: 'Atarashii shikō' no kōki to kiki," *Sekai* (August 1989): 118.

20. Shimotomai Nobuo, "Peresutoroika de Sorenjin no ishiki wa koko made kawatta," *Asahi jānaru*, November 2, 1990, p. 20.

21. Katori Yasue, "Kongo no NisSo kankei o dō suru ka," *Ajia jihō* (May 1989): 22–23.

22. Togō Takehiro, "Soren no shin shikō gaikō to Uno gaishō Soren hōmon no seika," *Sekai keizai daiyaru repōto*, no. 407 (July 1989): 1–12.

23. Morimoto Yoshio, "Gorubachofu gaikō to Ajia taiheiyō chiiki," in *Gendai sekai no seiji jōkyō*, ed. Katsube Hajime, pp. 208–9.

24. Akino Yutaka, "Gorubachofu seiken no Ajia taiheiyō seisaku," *Kokusai mondai* (March 1989): 57–61.

25. Akino Yutaka, "Senkyūhyakuhachijūshichinen ni okeru Soren gaikōjō no arata na yosō," in "Gorubachofu kaikaku no hamon: Soren naigai jōsei no takakuteki bunseki," Research Report Series no. 23 (Slavic Research Center, Hokkaidō University, March 30, 1988), p. 46.

26. Shimotomai Nobuo, "Tagenka kakumei no naka no Soren, Part II: 'Atarashii shikō' no kōki to kiki," *Sekai* (August 1989): 112–13.

27. Nakano Tetsuzo, "'Atarashii seiji shikō, Part I," *Gekkan shakaitō* (June 1989): 100–6.

28. Nakano Tetsuzo, "Atarashii seiji shikō to kasekika shita shikō, Part II," *Gekkan shakaitō* (July 1989): 72–79.

29. Takubo Tadae, "Opinion: Gorubachofu kokuren enzetsu ni hisomu torikku," *Sekai shūhō*, December 20, 1988, p. 5.

30. Sase Masamori, "Aienuefu zenpai jōyaku ga motarashita kiken" *Shokun* (January 1989): 218–20.

31. Nakagawa Yatsuhiro, "Gunshuku: gunji yūi tassei e no puropaganda," *Sekai shūhō*, May 16, 1989, pp. 26–27.

32. Ibid., pp. 26, 29.

33. Takubo Tadae, "Opinion: Gorubachefu kokuren enzetsu ni hisomu torikku," p. 5.

34. Shigeta Hiroshi, "Sobieto no peresutoroika to tōzai kankei," *Sekai keizai daiyaru repōto*, no. 314 (March 25, 1988): 14.

35. Hyodo Nagao, "BeiSo Mosukuwa shunō kaigi no igi to seika," *Sekai keizai daiyaru repōto*, no. 318 (July 1988): 3–4, 9.

36. Maruyama Hiroyuki, "Soren gun no peresutoroika: daironsō 'kaku no ken ka haiteku no ken ka,'" *Asahi jānaru*, March 24, 1989, p. 42.

37. Nagai Yōnosuke, "Shakaishugi kokka no seikimatsu," *Bungei shunjū* (August 1989): 167–69.

38. Takizawa Ichirō, "Soren gun ni okeru tōsoshiki to tōgun," *Bōeihō kenkyū*, no. 12 (October 1988): 29.

39. Hasegawa Tsuyoshi, "Gorubachofu kaikaku no hamon: Soren naigai jōsei no takakuteki bunseki," p. 38.

40. Hakamada Shigeki, "Soren no taiNichi seisaku wa 'shin shikō' no soto," *Kakushin* (February 1989): 32.

41. Togō Takehiro, "Soren shidōbu no jinji idō: taiNichi seisaku nado o megutte," *Sekai keizai daiyaru repōto*, no. 322 (November 1988): 2–8.

42. Katori Yasue, "NisSo taiwa chakujitsu ni zenshin," *Yomiuri shimbun*, December 22, 1988, p. 8.

43. Hakamada Shigeki, "NisSo taiwa chakujitsu ni zenshin," *Yomiuri shimbun*, December 22, 1988, p. 8.

44. Katō Masahiko, "Kiro ni tatsu peresutoroika," *Heiwa keizai* (May 1989): 3–5.

CHAPTER THIRTEEN

1. Itō Kenichi, "Hoppō ryōdo 'nitō henkan ron' o utagau," *Shokun* (February 1987): 26–42.

2. Otemachi Saburō, "Gakeggachi ni tatsu Gorubachofu," *This Is* (February 1990): 81–83.

3. *Kita no rinjin*.

4. Hakamada Shigeki, *Motto shiritai Soren*, pp. i-ii.

5. "90 nendai no shinro o hake 5 tōshu ga seisaku tou," *Asahi shimbun*, February 3, 1990, pp. 16–17.

6. "Soren yori ojiri Nihon keizai," *Yomiuri shimbun*, April 19, 1989, p. 4.

7. Saga Tōru, *Soren no shiren* (1989), pp. 3–4, 382.

8. Watanabe Taizō, "Sengo saidai no tenkanki o mukaeta kokusai jōsei," *Kokumin gaikō*, no. 189 (June 1989): 12–25.

9. Nakazawa Takayuki, "Shiewarunaze enzetsu ni miru Soren no 'shin shikō gaikō,'" *Sekai shūhō*, January 17, 1989, pp. 24–27.

10. Niizeki Kinya, *Berurin saigo no hi: aru gaikōkan no kiroku* (1988), pp. 105–11, 198–99; and Niizeki Kinya, *NisSo kōshō no butaiura* (1989), pp. 12, 16, 19, 55, 227–28.

11. Suetsugu Ichirō, *'Sengo' e no chōsen* (1981), pp. 59–62, 67–68.

12. Ibid., pp. 67–68.

13. Eguchi Keiichi, "Kyōkasho kentei wa jitsu ni shiiteki," *Asahi shimbun*, October 26, 1989, p. 5.

14. "Shiberiya yokuryū: 40 nenme no junrei," *Asahi shimbun*, October 9, 1989, p. 30; October 11, 1989, p. 30; October 16, 1989, p. 30.

15. Gilbert Rozman, "Moscow's Japan-Watchers in the First Years of the Gorbachev Era: The Struggle for Realism and Respect in Foreign Affairs," *The Pacific Review* 1, 3 (1988): 269–70.

16. "Yakoburefu shi hamon nokoshi riNichi," *Asahi shimbun*, November 19, 1989, p. 2.

17. Hamada Kazuyuki, "A Yakoburefu ga Soren no taiNichi senryaku o kaete iku!" *Asahi jānaru*, November 17, 1989, p. 95.

18. Hakamada Shigeki, "Gokai sareru Soren 18 no shikaku," pp. 122–41.

19. Kimura Hiroshi, "Gorubachofu seiken no shihonshugi kan," *Soren kenkyū*, no. 9 (October 1989): 94–113.

20. Shimotomai Nobuo, "Gaikō no tāgetto wa higashi Ajia e utsutta: 'gunji henchō' kara keizai jūshi no shisei senmei ni," p. 13.

21. "Nihon kokumin no kanjō wa kizuite iru," *Tōkyō shimbun*, November 17, 1989, p. 3.

22. "Yakoburefu shi no kaiken yōshi, "*Asahi shimbun*, November 16, 1989, p. 4.

23. Nakagawa Takayuki, "Peresutoroika wa seikō suru ka," *Sekai shūhō*, November 26, 1989, pp. 8–9.

24. Noda Nobuo, "Ima koso 'reijū e no michi' yomu toki," *Sankei shimbun*, November 16, 1989, p. 7.

25. "Roshiago ninki futatabi," *Nihon keizai shimbun*, November 26, 1989, p. 35.

26. Wada Haruki, "Soren Tōō shokoku to ningen," *Jurisuto*, no. 944 (November 1, 1989): 86–87.

27. "Kaikaku no yukue takai kanshin," *Yomiuri shimbun*, December 28, 1989, p. 9.

28. "'Tōzai kyōchō no jidai' o jikkan," *Asahi shimbun*, December 27, 1989, p. 13.

29. "NisSo kankei, tenkan no kizashi," *Yomiuri shimbun*, June 20, 1990, p. 15.

30. "Soviet, Japanese Expectations Regarding Gorbachev Visit Differ, Survey Indicates," *The Japan Times Weekly International Edition*, December 3–9, 1990, p. 3.

31. NHK yoron chōsa shiryōshu, *Nihonjin no kokusai ishiki* (1989), pp. 1086–99; "Waga kuni no heiwa to anzen ni kansuru yoron chōsa," *Yoron chōsa hōkokusho* (Naikaku sōridaijin kanbo kōhōshitsu, January 1989); "Zenkoku chōsa no yoron genkyō," *Yoron chōsa nenkan* (1988).

32. Masaru Tamamoto, "Internationalization of Japan: Conservative Views on Japan as a Normal Country," ms., Center for International Studies, Princeton University, October 1989, p. 1.

33. Shimizu Hayao, *TaiSo kokka senryakuron*, pp. 141–47.

34. Utsunomiya Tokuma, "NiChūBeiSo no wakai o mezashita Ishibashi gaikō," *Gunshuku mondai shiryō* (July 1988): 2–10.

35. Niizeki Kinya, "Watakushi no ikikata," *Kōken* (October 1989): 58.

36. Shimotomai Nobuo, "Kagehisometa 'teki' ishiki," *Asahi shimbun*, October 22, 1990, p. 15.

37. "Peresutoroika de Sorenjin no ishiki wa koko made kawatta," *Asahi jānaru*, November 2, 1990, pp. 14–23; and "Shakai no henka ni yureru Soren," *Asahi shimbun*, October 22, 1990, p. 17.

38. "Volunteer Stage Exhibition to Remember Auschwitz Victims," *The Japan Times*, August 20, 1989.

39. Kenichi Ito, "Japan and the Soviet Union: Entangled in the Deadlock of the Northern Territories," *The Washington Quarterly* 11, 1 (Winter 1988): 35.

Chapter Fourteen

1. Morimoto Tadao, "Soren o shiranai de kanemōke dekiru ka," pp. 96–99, 102–9.

2. Inoki Masamichi, "Soren no zento wa futōmei de aru," *Sankei shimbun*, July 18, 1990, p. 6.

3. Aihara Minoru, *Jōhōka to Soren keizai: peresutoroika no honshitsu* (1989), pp. 17–22.

4. Itō Kenichi, "'Dakkaku jidai' no tōrai to Nihon no daisenryaku," pp. 33–41.

5. Itō Kenichi, *Nihon no daisenryaku* (1990), pp. 17–24, 226.

6. Ibid., pp. 272–73.

7. Hōgen Shinsaku, Iwade Toshio, and Watanabe Keitarō, *TaiSo senryaku*, (1986).

8. Tamba Minoru, *200% no anzen hoshō o motomeru kuni*, pp. 5–7, 204.

9. Miyamoto Katsutoge, "Peresutoroika to NisSo keizai kankei," *Kokubō* (February 1989): 9–17; Matsui Hiroaki, "Sorengun to gurasunosuchi," *Kokubō* (February 1989): 37–46.

10. Takizawa Ichirō, "Sorengun ni okeru tō soshiki to tō gun kankei no genjō," *Bōeihō kenkyū*, no. 12, (October 1988): 29–39.

11. "Foreign Minister Nakayama Addresses U.N. General Assembly," *Japan Report* 35, 10 (October 1989): 1–2.

12. Nishimura Fumio, "Gorubachofu to Busshu no sekai saibunkatsu," *Shūkan daiyamondo*, November 4, 1989, pp. 41–51.

13. Ogawa Kazuo, "NisSo keizai kankei wa shinten suru ka," *Sekai shūhō*, October 10, 1989, pp. 26–29.

14. "'Kan Nihonkai en' e moeru Niigata," *Sekai shūhō*, November 11, 1990, pp. 52–53.

15. "Jidai okure de misumatchi," *Nihon keizai shimbun*, September 1, 1989.

16. "Soviet Political Problems Not Seen as JV Obstacle," *BLOC* (August/September 1990): 4.

17. Morimoto Tadao, *Soren o shiranai de kanemōke dekiru ka*, pp. 178–80, 199–200, 209–10, 228–46.

18. "Roshiago ninki futatabi," *Nihon keizai shimbun*, November 26, 1989, p. 35.

19. Sase Masamori, "Fūjikome senryaku wa seikō shita," *Seiron* (May 1988).

20. Sase Masamori, "Detanto taibōron ni hisomu kiken," *Seiron* (May 1988): 29–30.

21. Kimura Hiroshi, *Hoppō ryōdo*, pp. 199–204, 212–15.

22. Sono Akira, "Soren no sekai senryaku wa iki ga nagai," *Sankei shimbun*, November 30, 1989, p. 7.

23. Nakagawa Yatsuhiro, "Hoppō ryōdo mondai ni 'daisan no michi' wa nai," *Shokun*, October 1990, pp. 185–99.

24. Saeki Kiichi, "TaiSo gaikō de ryūisubeki santen," *Seiron*, (August 1989): 11–12.

25. Kido Shigeru, "Tanan na 'hitotsu no jiyū no Ōshu' e no michi," *Kōmei*, September 9, 1989, pp. 115–21.

26. Seki Yoshihiko, "Soren kakumei no direnma," *Kaikakusha* (January 1989): 40–51.

27. Hasegawa Tsuyoshi, "Gorubachofu wa yokushiron o koerareru ka," *Chūō kōron* (January 1989): 151–62.

28. Eda Satsuki, "Shakaishugi wa, ima shakaiminshushugi to shite ketsujitsu suru," *Saishin Sorenron, kokusairon shiriizu*, vol. 1 (1990): 30–34.

29. Wada Jun, "Ryōdo kōshō wa takakuteki ni," *Asahi shimbun*, February 19, 1989, p. 4.

30. Shimotomai Nobuo, "'Shūnō kaidan' senmonka zadankai," *Yomiuri shimbun*, June 3, 1988, p. 4.

31. Sasayama Haruyuki, "Sosetsu," *Shigaku zasshi* (May 1988): 1–2.

32. "Za shakaitō, " *Nihon keizai shimbun*, August 25, 1989, p. 2.

33. Peter Berton, "The Japanese Communist Party's View of Gorbachev's Perestroika," *Acta Slavica Iaponica*, vol. 7 (1989): 121–44.

34. A. I. Senatorov, "O trudnostiakh vospriiatiia novogo myshleniia," *Rabochii klass i sovremennyi mir*, no. 3 (May–June 1990): 72–82.

35. Miyamoto Kenji, "Peresutoroika to Nihon kyōsantō no tachiba," *Sekai seiji* (April 1988): 3–9.

36. "Soren, jimintō ni shōjun?" *Nikkan kōgyō shimbun*, November 18, 1989, p. 3.

37. "Henkaku o sayu shinkeizai shisutemu," *Yomiuri shimbun*, October 12, 1990, p. 15.

38. Kimura Hiroshi, *Hoppō ryōdo*, pp. 220–51.

39. Hamada Kazuyuki, "A Yakoburefu ga Soren no taiNichi senryaku o kaete iku," *Asahi jānaru*, November 17, 1989, pp. 94–95.

40. "Soren wa hoppō ryōdo o henkan suru," *Shūkan bunshun*, November 23, 1989, pp. 40–44.

41. "Yakoburefu shi to hisoka ni atta 'sōri oniwaban' 67 sai no sugao," *Shūkan Yomiuri*, December 3, 1989, pp. 177–81.

42. Kimura Hiroshi, "Ayumiyoru Soren no taiNichi seisaku," *Voice* (January 1990): 191–94.

43. Wada Jun, "Ryōdo kōshō wa takakutelsi ni," *Asahi shimbun*, February 19, 1989, p. 4.

44. Kimura Hiroshi, *Hoppō ryōdo*, part 1.

45. Kimura Hiroshi, "Neterpenie tol'ko vredit," *Novoe vremia*, no. 23 (1989): 25.

46. "Hoppō ryōdo kōshō dō ashigakari," *Asahi shimbun*, December 19, 1988, p. 2.

47. Hiroshi Kimura, "Japan-Soviet Relations: A Time to Compromise," *The Japan Times Weekly Overseas Edition*, January 20, 1990, p. 8.

48. Ibid.

49. Kimura Hiroshi, *Hoppō ryōdo*, pp. 196–99.

50. Nakagawa Tōru, "Posuto reisen jidai no Nihon gaikō," *Seiron* (September 1989): 8–9.

51. Takubo Tadae, "Uno seiken ni gaikō to tetsugaku wa aru ka," *Seiron* (September 1989): 15–16.

52. Sono Akira, "ChūsSo seijōka to Chūgoku no kaigenrei," *Seiron* (September 1989): 4–5.

53. "SDF Draws Its Front Line of Defense on Hokkaido," *The Japan Times*, August 19, 1989, p. 3.

54. "Ittō shihai' ni mo idomu Soren kaikaku," *Yomiuri shimbun*, August 4, 1989, p. 3.

55. Yokote Shinji, "Gorubachofu ka no dai Roshiashugi," *Kaigai jijō* (June 1989): 89–104.

CHAPTER FIFTEEN

1. David E. Sanger, "Japan Will Offer Arms Control Plan," and Frances X. Clines, "Gorbachev Welcomes New Opposition Movement," *The New York Times*, July 3, 1991, pp. A4, A7.

2. Morimoto Tadao, *Soren o shiranai de kanemōke dekiru ka*, pp. 48–53, 58, 89.

3. Steven R. Weisman, "In the Left Corner, Fire; in the Right Corner, Ice," *The New York Times*, February 14, 1990, p. A4.

4. "Troop Cuts Won't Change Confrontation," *SUPAR Report*, no. 7 (Manoa: University of Hawaii, July 1989), p. 50.

5. Kamo Takehiko, Shimotomai Nobuo, and Takahashi Noboru, "Yaruta no kabe wa kuzureta no ka," *Sekai* (January 1990): 234–47.

6. Yuri Afanashiefu, "Nihon ni yontō o henkan seyo," *Bungei shunjū* (December 1989): 192; Hakamada Shigeki, "Yūri Afanashiefu," *Bungei shunjū* (December 1989): 190–99.

7. "Heikōsen no NisSo taiwa ga kataru mono," *Yomiuri shimbun*, December 21, 1989, p. 3.

8. Nishimura Fumio, "Gorubachofu to Busshu no sekai saibunkatsu," *Shūkan daiyamondo*, November 4, 1989, pp. 41–51.

9. Amaya Naohiro, "Kyōsanshugi no hōkai," *Tōkyō shimbun*, December 28, 1989, p. 7.

10. Hakamada Shigeki, *Sobieto 70 nenme no hanran* (1990), pp. 345–49.

11. Sasaki Tōru, " 'Sōgo rieki' o zenmen ni," *Asahi shimbun*, evening edition, October 31, 1989, p. 4.

12. Funabashi Yōichi, "Keizai chikyūgi: Wangan kiki taiō to jieitai," *Asahi shimbun*, September 19, 1990, p. 11.

13. " 'Posuto-Yaruta' o yomu," *Sekai shūhō*, January 23, 1990, p. 19.

14. "Map Mission," *The Japan Times Weekly International Edition*, August 27, 1988.

15. "NichiBei shunō kaidan yōshi," *Yomiuri shimbun*, September 2, 1989, p. 2.

16. Steven R. Weisman, "Japan, Weary of Barbs on Trade, Tells Americans Why They Trail," *The New York Times*, November 20, 1989, p. 1.

17. Nagai Yōnosuke, "Shakaishugi kokka no seiki matsu," *Bungei shunjū* (August 1989): 160–73.

18. "BeiSo shunō kaidan senmonka zadankai," *Yomiuri shimbun* (evening), November 1, 1989, p. 3.

19. Wada Haruki, *Peresutoroika seika to kiki* (1990), pp. 7–11.

20. Ibid., pp. 238–46.

21. Yamauchi Masayuki, Sakuma Kumio, Nakai Kazuo, Kitayama Seiichi, and Hirooka Masahiko, *Bunretsu suru Soren: naze minzoku hanran ya okotta ka* (1990), pp. 236–49.

22. Sase Masamori, " 'Yaruta taisei' no chikaku hendo," *Seiron* (September 1989): 28–47.

23. "Posuto-Maruta' no sekai o tempō suru," *Chūō kōron* (February 1990): 166–89.

24. " 'Posuto-Yaruta' o yomu, Part 3" *Sekai shūhō*, January 23, 1990, pp. 16–21.

25. Ibid., pp. 16–18.

26. Hōgen Shinsaku, "Saredo Soren wa kowashi," *Chishiki* (February 1990): 52–54.

27. Katō Eiichi, "Tōō minshuka wa Toroi no mokuba," *Chishiki* (February 1990): 81–83.

28. Akino Yutaka, "Soren to taiheiyō," *Mainichi shimbun*, June 20, 1990, p. 10.

29. Marc S. Gallicchio, *The Cold War Begins in Asia: American East Asian Policy and the Fall of the Japanese Empire* (New York: Columbia University Press, 1988), pp. 87–88, 116, 143–44.

30. "Pōrando, Hangarii no dōkō to ryōkoku enjo kaigi no naiyō," *Sekai keizai daiyaru repōto*, no. 332 (September 1989): 2–8.

31. "TaiChū sotchi wa kanwa ni mukatta ga," *Asahi shimbun*, August 19 1989, p. 5.

32. "Henkaki no ugoki, mini ni mo," *Yomiuri shimbun*, June 20, 1990, p. 14.

33. "Henkaku o sayu shin keizai shisutemu," *Yomiuri shimbun*, October 12, 1990, p. 15.

34. Yasuhiro Nakasone, "Hopes and Uncertainties for the 90s—Restructuring of International Political and Economic Relations," *International Institute for Global Peace Lecture Series*, 3, September 21, 1989, pp. 1–8.

35. Togō Takehiro and Nirasawa Yoshio, "Pōrando, Hangarii no dōkō to ryōkoku enjo kaigi no naiyō," *Sekai keizai hyōron* (October 1989): 17–23.

36. Michael Oreskes, "Poll Detects Erosion of Positive Attitudes toward Japan among Americans," *The New York Times*, February 6, 1990, p. B7.

37. Shimizu Kunio, "Soren ga samitto ni sanka suru hi," *Seiron* (September 1989): 133.

38. Nakayama Hiromasa, *Peresutoroika no naka ni sunde*, pp. 239–43.

39. Kimura Hiyoshi, *Hoppō ryōdo*, pp. 263–65.

40. Yoshihiro Nakajima, "Japan Must Work Toward Bridging East-West Culture Gap," *The Japan Time Weekly International Edition*, July 30–August 5, 1990, p. 9.

41. "Gaikō 4 gensoku o happyō e," *Asahi shimbun*, June 15, 1988, p. 1.

42. *Gaimuiin kaigiroku*, no. 5 (108th Diet, shūgiin), p. 6.

43. "NichiBei shunō kaidan yōshi," p. 2.

Index